Africa in World Politics

SECOND EDITION

AFRICA IN WORLD POLITICS

Post–Cold War Challenges

edited by

JOHN W. HARBESON

City University of New York

and

DONALD ROTHCHILD

University of California–Davis

WESTVIEW PRESS
Boulder • San Francisco • Oxford

Published in 1995 in the United States of America by Westview Press, Inc., 5500 Central Avenue, Boulder, Colorado 80301-2877, and in the United Kingdom by Westview Press, 12 Hid's Copse Road, Cumner Hill, Oxford OX2 9JJ

Library of Congress Cataloging-in-Publication Data
Africa in world politics : post–cold war challenges / edited by John
     W. Harbeson and Donald Rothchild. — 2nd ed.
       p.   cm.
     Includes bibliographical references and index.
     ISBN 0-8133-2102-6. — ISBN 0-8133-2103-4 (pbk.)
       1. Africa—Politics and government—1960-   —Congresses. 2. World
politics—1985–1995—Congresses. I. Harbeson, John W. (John
Willis), 1938–   . II. Rothchild, Donald S.
DT30.5.A3544   1995
960.3′2—dc20   94-35035
                                                                                                        CIP

Printed and bound in the United States of America

   The paper used in this publication meets the requirements
          of the American National Standard for Permanence of Paper
          for Printed Library Materials Z39.48-1984.

10   9   8   7   6   5   4   3   2

Contents

List of Tables   VII
Acknowledgments   IX

PART ONE   INTRODUCTION

1   Africa in World Politics: Amid Renewal, Deepening Crisis,
     John W. Harbeson   3

PART TWO   PARAMETERS OF AFRICAN PERIPHERALIZATION

2   The Heritage of Colonialism, *Crawford Young*   23

3   Africa and the World Political Economy: Still Caught Between
     a Rock and a Hard Place, *Thomas M. Callaghy*   41

4   Africa and Other Civilizations: Conquest and Counterconquest,
     Ali A. Mazrui   69

5   Dependent by Default: Africa's Relations with the European Union,
     John Ravenhill   95

PART THREE   REGIONAL THEATERS OF AFRICAN INTERNATIONAL RELATIONS

6   Post–Cold War Politics in the Horn of Africa: The Quest for
     Political Identity Intensified, *John W. Harbeson*   127

7   South Africa and Southern Africa After Apartheid, *Jeffrey Herbst*   147

8   Francophone Africa in the Context of Franco-African Relations,
    Guy Martin   163

9   The Lagos Three: Economic Regionalism in Sub-Saharan Africa,
    Carol Lancaster   189

PART FOUR   MAJOR ISSUES

10 The United States and Conflict Management in Africa,
    Donald Rothchild   209

11 Inter-African Negotiation, *I. William Zartman*   234

12 Promoting Democracy in Africa: U.S. and International
    Policies in Transition, *Larry Diamond*   250

13 Political and Military Security, *Herman J. Cohen*   278

14 Reconciling Sovereignty with Responsibility: A Basis for
    International Humanitarian Action, *Francis M. Deng*   295

About the Book and Editors   311
About the Contributors   313
Index   317

Tables

5.1   Sub-Saharan Africa's Share of European Union Imports   97
5.2   Sub-Saharan Africa's Share of European Union Exports   97
5.3   European Union's Share in Sub-Saharan Imports and Exports   98
5.4   European Union's Share in Africa's Total Net ODA Receipts   99
5.5   Major Aid Donors to Africa in 1991   100
5.6   Sub-Saharan Africa's Share in Net Disbursements of ODA
        by European Union Countries   100
5.7   South African Customs Union's Share in European Union's
        Imports and Exports   115

7.1   Share of Gross Regional Product, by Country   149
7.2   Share of Regional Product Outside South Africa in 1990,
        by Country   150
7.3   South Africa's Regional Trade   151
7.4   South African Defense Investment   155

9.1   The Lagos Three: Member States and Organizations   194

12.1 Official Development Assistance to Sub-Saharan Africa, 1981–1990   256

Acknowledgments

We appreciate very much the encouragement and support of Westview Press editor Barbara Ellington in the planning and development of this edition, particularly given the difficulties inherent in international editorial collaboration. We appreciate also the comments and suggestions we received on the first edition, and we hope we have put them to good use in the second edition. We thank Mary Jo Lawrence and Joan Sherman for expert assistance in the editorial stages of preparing this edition. As with the first edition, our hope is that collectively the editors and authors have helped to fill a critical niche in the fields of African studies and international relations. Errors of fact and interpretation that remain are, of course, our responsibility.

PART ONE

Introduction

1

Africa in World Politics: Amid Renewal, Deepening Crisis

JOHN W. HARBESON

THE DAWNING of the post–Cold War era in Africa has inspired both new visions of political and economic renewal unmatched since the first years of independence and a growing awareness that the paths to the realization of these visions may be more tortuous than ever before. Campaigns for democratization in much of the continent have energized African peoples perhaps as profoundly as did the nationalist movements a generation ago, when it became apparent that the achievement of political independence was within their reach. Similarly, the popular belief and determination in the 1990s that democratization holds the key to economic development and social progress, elusive for most Africans in most countries since independence, is reminiscent of the nationalist credo that political independence would bring deliverance from decades of colonial socioeconomic oppression.

Less than a decade after most of Africa gained independence from colonial rule, the nationalist vision had begun to fade. African peoples sought the causes for this in the political alignments and economic structure of the Cold War international economy into which independence had delivered them as much or more than in the domestic policies and behavior of their own new leaders. Similarly, in the mid-1990s, when movements for democratization are still in their infancy, warning signals have appeared, suggesting that political and economic renewal may dissipate in the face of new and unforeseen obstacles. And once again, both African peoples and students of development may look for causes not only in the domestic sphere but also in the evolving contours of the international political and economic order, this time those of the post–Cold War era.

In this introductory chapter, I will outline briefly the fresh visions and the emerging realities of this second moment of African political and economic renewal that are explored in the chapters that follow, drawing comparisons where possible to the first moment of vision, hope, and expectation in the 1960s. The

3

chapter begins with a consideration of the post–Cold War international political and economic context as it bears upon Africa. Next, the prospects, patterns, and problems of political renewal in Africa within that international context are outlined. Finally, some of the emerging issues are considered—issues that must be addressed if the second moment of African renewal is to produce better and more durable outcomes than the first.

Fresh Visions, Emerging Realities

The international contexts of the moments of African political and economic renewal in the 1960s and the 1990s both resemble and differ from each other. One common thread has been that they have occurred against a backdrop of the enduring peripheral status of African countries in the international order. That international order, although everchanging, continues to influence greatly what African countries can employ as working definitions of progress and to establish the parameters within which progress so defined is possible. A second common element has been the influence of international politics in shaping the timing, directions, and parameters of both moments. A third thread, common to each moment of anticipated renaissance, has been the widespread hope and expectation that the driving vision will be sufficiently compelling to mobilize African energies and successfully lessen the region's peripheral and dependent status within the international order.

At the same time, the major difference between the two moments of political and economic renewal lies in the degree of clarity with which the major international powers and the African countries have articulated their interests in and pursued their engagement with each other. It is a mark of the scale, scope, and complexity of global transformation in the post–Cold War era that the dilemmas and uncertainties of the African-major power relationships appear far more extensive for both sides than was the case in the comparable era of the 1960s. As a consequence, African countries and the major powers alike have defined their interests with respect to each other in a much more inchoate form than in the past.

The First Moment

In the 1960s, the two superpowers and their alliance partners, preoccupied with the balance of power between them, were quite unambiguous in their strategic understandings concerning Africa's importance. Although Africa was generally considered peripheral in the Cold War geographically, militarily, politically, and economically, the competing blocs recognized that the continent had at least an incremental potential to add to or subtract from the strength and security of the Cold War alliances. Each bloc recognized that, to that end, it lay within its interests to support those economic and political developments in African countries that might favor its respective alliance.

The Cold War not only led the two alliances to seek strategic and ideological allies, it also explained, at least in part, the nature of their strategies of involvement in Africa's developmental processes. On the one hand, the Soviet Union and its allies found justification for their activities on the continent in their strong opposition to capitalist practices and in their commitment to fostering a socialist path to development in Africa. Within that framework, they encouraged African countries to adopt working concepts of development compatible with their own ultimate ends.[1] On the other hand, as the subtitle of W. W. Rostow's influential work, *The Stages of Economic Growth: A Non-Communist Manifesto,* revealed, there was a linkage, more consciously for some exponents of this approach than for others, between Cold War bipolarity and strategies for promoting development. Modernization theory projected an evolution from traditional societies that would involve the incorporation of Western values, including market economies, individualism, pluralism, secularism, and political democracy.[2] Whether intended or not, this theory of modernization lent a philosophical and historical rationale to the continued engagement of the United States and other Western countries in the affairs of postcolonial Africa.

Born into the Cold War world, African countries and their leaders were equally clear that their own interests lay in nonalignment: They allowed countries of the two Cold War blocs to compete in offering them aid and investment without committing themselves to either side. At the same time, they had visions of syncretic self-reliance, derived from the contradictions they experienced while subjected to Western colonial policies and those they perceived in scientific socialism as practiced by the Soviet Union and its allies. Through self-reliance, they sought to escape the shortcomings of the rival doctrines, while incorporating each doctrine's pertinent strengths and integrating them with elements of their own precolonial heritages. Through policies drawn from this syncretic vision, African leaders sought to bypass complex transitional stages envisaged by both Western and Soviet models and to expedite progress toward developmental goals compatible with a restored and strengthened sense of cultural identity.

Nonetheless, even those new African states that were more sympathetic to the Soviet models of development in effect retained and emphasized their identification with many of the norms and institutions of the post–World War II international order as defined by the Western powers. Although they were inclined to reject some institutions and values implicit in the constitutions bequeathed them by the departing colonial powers (bills of rights, bicameral legislatures, multiparty systems, federalism, and limitations on executive power), they accepted with modifications many of the defining features of the contemporary state: political parties, armies, police, bureaucracies, cooperatives, and universities. More fundamentally, they subscribed to the state system upon which Western conceptions of the international political economy rested: the norms of sovereignty, international law and protocols, membership in the United Nations, and the principles enshrined in the U.N. Charter. Indeed, acceptance of and participation in the Western-led state system became a significant and continuing source of political legitimacy for new African states, counterbalancing strong challenges to that legitimacy that were to be visited upon them in the decades just ahead.[3]

Between the Moments

Despite sharp military engagements between or within African countries in which the two superpowers found themselves involved—notably, the war over the Ogaden region and the Angolan civil war—patterns of major power engagement in Africa began to change in the 1970s.[4] This change came about as a consequence of U.S.-Soviet détente, important shifts in the structure of the global economy, the performance of developing countries, and the reflections by non-African and African political actors upon these happenings.

Bipolar alliances began to loosen, prompting both African and non-African powers to begin altering their foreign policy agendas. In such areas as economic development, cultural exchange, and communications, the major and middle powers articulated new interests that were less closely linked to Cold War imperatives. A disillusionment with Africa's lack of progress also led to a willingness on the part of the great powers to develop new aid and development strategies more closely attuned to regional realities. The United States, for example, placed unprecedented emphasis upon "development from below," including land reform, appropriate technology, participatory development, and broadened access to education and health care at the grassroots level.[5] Other Western countries did likewise. Finally, during this period, the World Bank, under the leadership of Robert McNamara, began to play a larger and more influential role in defining the directions of foreign assistance, a leadership position that was to grow still more powerful in the years ahead.

Corresponding changes took place in global economic relations. The erosion of the U.S. economic hegemony, signaled in part by Richard Nixon's decision to permit the value of the U.S. dollar to float against other currencies, marked an end to the unchallenged U.S. dominance in the global economic arena upon which the post–World War II Bretton Woods Agreements had been built. The growing economic ascendancy of Germany, Japan, and the newly industrialized countries of East Asia, together with the United States, produced a new, increasingly multipolar international economic order. The processes of restructuring the international economic order to conform to these new economic realities prompted corresponding changes in the way the superpowers defined their interests vis-à-vis developing countries in Africa and other areas. Feeling increasingly overextended economically and militarily and constrained by growing pressures to attend to domestic concerns, the major powers began to substitute disengagement and mutual cooperation for direct, costly involvement and competition in regional rivalries.[6]

African countries responded to the changing priorities and patterns of international relations that détente created by increasing pressure on the industrialized countries for greater external economic assistance. While responding positively to the donors' new emphasis on economic development in north-south relations, African countries and an expanding community of scholars challenged the structural foundations of that assistance.[7] Ethiopia, Mozambique, and Zimbabwe, for example, turned to more aggressive forms of self-reliant socialism and articulated Marxist-Leninist perspectives concerning the inherent contradictions of capitalism. They called increasingly for a new economic order in which less developed countries would be able to escape the same domination·in the global arena that Marx and Lenin had found to be oppressing the proletariats in industrial countries. In so doing, they were, in part, taking advantage of somewhat more loosely asserted alliance politics during détente, but in much larger part, they were reacting to their countries' more and more desperate economic circumstances. They attributed their economic dilemmas as much or more to an international economy damaged by oil-price shocks, inflation, and structural instability brought on by the decline of U.S. economic hegemony as to the failure of their own policy experiments.

The second, contemporary moment of African renewal grew from foundations established during the 1970s: (1) the major powers' renewed efforts to define and institutionalize the terms of their increasing economic interdependence and rules of the game for the global economy as a whole, together with the relative de-emphasis on military preparedness in favor of economic development; (2) the implicit connection African countries drew between the failure of their own policy experiments and alleged structural failings of the global economy that the industrial powers were seeking to redefine and shore up; and (3) the World Bank's newly asserted leadership in defining multilateral approaches to promote development in the less developed countries of Africa and other areas.[8]

The Contemporary Moment of African Renewal

The initial years of the 1980s were marked by mixed signals from the major powers both toward each other and toward the less developed countries. The Reagan administration ushered in a renewal of Cold War tensions, boosting expenditures on sophisticated war matériel and giving increasing support to African and other anti-Communist insurgencies. In the last years of the Brezhnev era, the Soviet Union sustained its ideological agenda in Africa by supporting its beleaguered Afro-Marxist allies. This it did even as it kept alive embryonic, improved diplomatic communications with the West in order to help contain the regional conflicts in which it was engaged with the United States and other Western countries.

At the same time, however, fatigue in helping to combat Africa's continuing economic malaise and alarm at the possible effects that debt cancellation by larger countries of the less developed world would have on the global international economy spurred the beginnings of a new campaign for African economic renewal. In bilateral terms, major industrial powers reduced aid and investment flows to African countries and diversified their holdings more broadly through-

out the less developed nations.[9] Meanwhile, encouraged by conservative governments throughout most of the industrialized world, the International Monetary
Fund (IMF) and the World Bank defined a new and far more assertive strategy
for lifting less developed countries out of their economic malaise and jump-
starting an economic renaissance in Africa and elsewhere.[10]

In retrospect, however, it is clear that in the twilight years of the Cold War, the
logics of bipolar political and military competition, for the superpowers and for
their alliance partners, yielded to those of an increasingly interdependent, multipolar, and global economic order. For Africa, that meant a new form of external
hegemony: As superpower competition in Africa and at Africa's expense gradually faded, the major industrial powers, more and more preoccupied with their
domestic economies, collectively pressured African countries to concentrate on
their own economies as well. They pressed upon Africa reform prescriptions
rooted in classical liberal theories of political economy, to which the Soviet
Union no longer offered objections—a harbinger of the post–Cold War abandonment of statist policies derived from Marxism-Leninism.

Under Mikhail Gorbachev, the Soviet Union began to edge away from its ideological moorings toward cautious experimentation with a reliance upon market
economic forces and a somewhat reduced isolation from the free-world economy. Meanwhile, in the West, the objective of reclaiming leadership in an increasingly competitive global economy gained a greater ascendancy over the
Reagan administration's goal of military primacy vis-à-vis the Soviet Union, particularly later in the Bush administration. Among the important consequences
were improved diplomatic cooperation between the superpowers in attempting
to moderate, if not mediate, Cold War-fueled conflicts in the Horn of Africa and
in southern Africa. In at least one case, Ethiopia, the Soviet Union counseled mediation of regional disputes in order to facilitate the reallocation of resources
from military preparedness toward economic development.[11] It advised Ethiopia
to do so along essentially the same lines as prescribed by the World Bank, the
International Monetary Fund, and Western industrial powers since 1981—something the Soviet Union itself had begun to explore. This increased diplomatic cooperation with the United States and the new interest in Western economic models as solutions to African problems presaged Soviet military and economic
disengagement from Africa prior to the USSR's collapse at the conclusion of the
Cold War. That policy has generally been sustained by its successor states, principally Russia.

Meanwhile, European industrial powers had already begun to back away from
special economic relationships with their former colonies, and—along with the
United States, Canada, and Japan—they began to concentrate on managing their
own complex and competitive economic interdependence. Western industrial
powers began to disengage from aid, trade, and investment commitments in Africa while continuing the quest for new rules of the game to structure their own
growing engagement with each other. Even France—long the most aggressive of
the Western countries in maintaining economic, cultural, political, and military

ties with the francophone countries of Africa—began to signal clearly its intention to cut back on aid commitments to its African partners. Conversely, African
countries increasingly found themselves in direct competition with other regions
for entry into Europe's lucrative markets, notwithstanding their ties with Europe
under the Lomé Convention.[12] The opening up of new markets in Eastern Europe and in the states of the former Soviet Union following the end of the Cold
War further challenged the capacity of African countries to compete in global
markets and attract flows of development aid and private investment.

Since the early 1980s, the world's major industrial powers have relied more and
more heavily on multilateral economic diplomacy with sub-Saharan Africa, even
as they have tended toward bilateral delinkage. Through the International Monetary Fund and the World Bank, industrial nations and other more affluent powers have collectively imposed an economic discipline rooted in classical liberalism: the liberation of the market from the shackles of governmental planning and
direction. The ideological support has come from conservative governments in
nearly all the major industrial countries, and the threatened effect on their banking sectors of large-scale debt cancellations by less developed countries outside
Africa provided an economic impetus.

One feature that distinguishes the contemporary moment of African renewal
from that of the 1960s is the far greater, even dominant, role played by industrialized countries in defining the goals of that renaissance vis-à-vis African countries
themselves. This comes as a result of two mutually reinforcing trends: the greater
preoccupation of industrial economies with their own competitive interdependence and the continuing weakness of African economies in international markets. African countries have, therefore, been in a very weak position in dealing
with the industrial countries' démarche in defining goals and policies for an African economic renaissance in concert with each other and through the IMF and
the World Bank.

The World Bank-IMF prescriptions, resolutely and uniformly prescribed since
the early 1980s, are well known: (1) more open, market-driven economies that are
less encumbered by state regulation in order to promote international competitiveness as a part of domestic economic growth; (2) the devaluation of artificially
inflated currencies to bring imports into line with exports and to increase export
earnings as a percentage of the gross national product (GNP); and (3) the removal of urban consumer subsidies as a step toward increasing production incentives to rural producers, long disadvantaged by the relatively greater political
capacity of urban elites to tailor public policies to their own interests. A fourth,
less rigorously enforced World Bank-IMF injunction was to bring political decisionmaking closer to the grass roots, not only by shifting costs of key social infrastructure (such as schools and health care) to users but also by suggesting that
local communities of consumers needed to decide collectively what they should
pay for in these areas. An understated objective of the structural adjustment
along these lines promoted by the World Bank and the IMF was to reach informal sectors operating beyond the control of governments that seemed to stultify

enterprise. The premise was that participants in informal sectors would not resist legitimate government regulation and taxation, thereby enabling governments to function more effectively and efficiently.

Considerable debate has ensued on the merits, effectiveness, and outcomes of structural adjustment. Meanwhile, the scope of multilateral conditionality evolved considerably during the 1980s and early 1990s because, as originally conceived, this conditionality rested upon a fundamentally incorrect and unrealistic premise: that the structural adjustment of African economies could proceed autonomously without regard to input from the peoples it was supposed to benefit and without concern for their socioeconomic requirements and priorities and their domestic politics. Strong opposition to structural adjustment festered in some African circles on the grounds that such adjustment was based on naive assumptions about the existence in reality of markets as conceived in liberal economic theory. More fundamentally, opponents struck at the implicit assumption that the pursuit of economic self-interest was divorced from social and cultural motivations and purposes that drove the exchange of goods and services in African markets. Directly—but also through the United Nations, where their political influence was greater—African governments gradually persuaded the World Bank, if perhaps never quite the IMF, that the cultivation of human and environmental resources as well as capital accumulation and productivity must be part and parcel of the restructuring of African economies.[13] Those in Africa and beyond who criticized structural adjustment persuaded its champions at least to inquire into its possibly distributional effects. In short, gradually and with great difficulty, African governments and peoples gained some influence in terms of their own socioeconomic renewal by forcing a modification of the assumption of autonomous economic reconstruction.

The end of the Cold War shattered a final dimension of the tacit assumption of self-contained economic reconstruction: that it could advance without corresponding political reform. Inspired and instructed by the end of authoritarian regimes throughout Latin America, save only Cuba, and by the simultaneous revolutions in favor of capitalism and democracy throughout Eastern Europe, peoples across sub-Saharan Africa came to see multiparty democracy as their salvation from more than a quarter century of corrupt, authoritarian, and economically ineffective regimes.[14] To an extent that is difficult to gauge, popular movements for democratization in Africa also drew ammunition from World Bank-IMF structural adjustment programs that proclaimed the state to be the enemy of their economic progress. African peoples, however, had long since drawn the same conclusion when their governments, greatly weakened by failed policies and ineffective governance, lost control of significant portions of their economies and even of their own personnel to the informal sectors.

Thus, in the first years of the 1990s, in one country after another, popular pressure forced governments to allow competition from opposition parties, to accede to national conventions of elected private citizens called to redefine policies and political structures, and to sometimes grudgingly recognize that the violation of internationally charted human rights cannot be condoned.

The industrialized countries, however, have not surrendered the initiative to African countries. To varying degrees, they have added political conditionality to structural adjustment conditionality as a requirement for continued development aid. Consequently, by the early 1990s, a majority of the countries of sub-Saharan Africa not only continued to follow multilateral prescriptions for economic structural adjustment but simultaneously also began to take steps toward multiparty democracy, principally at the insistence of bilateral donors acting in concert. To ongoing demands for a greater respect for internationally recognized human rights, the donors added an insistence on free and fair multiparty elections, strengthened legislatures, more transparent and accountable public administration, independent judiciaries capable of enforcing the rule of law, and recognition of the important role of civil society. Civil society is understood to mean nongovernmental organizations (NGOs)—including the media—dedicated to upholding democratic institutions and deepening the roots of democratic political culture.[15]

The implementation of political conditionality has differed from that of structural adjustment in significant ways. First, support for the work of host country NGOs has long been an important feature, especially of bilateral assistance provided by the United States and other donors. However, political conditionality has produced something closer to a de facto alliance between bilateral donors and the leaders of African civil society: those NGOs centered on the advancement of human rights protection, political competitiveness through multiparty elections, and corruption-free governance. A notable example has been Kenya, where major donors suspended quick-disbursing aid until the Moi administration ended abuses in all three areas, in particular by allowing multiparty elections for the first time in a quarter century. In this case, the donors acted to strengthen the hand of the churches, almost the only centers of political power within society at large that were not controlled by the Moi government. An even clearer example has been South Africa, where donors have directly funded NGOs as a strategy for helping force white minority governments to accept majority rule established by universal suffrage.

Second, political conditionality has been less directly tied to African participation in international relations. Structural adjustment has forced export-led economic development not only to encourage African entrepreneurial initiative but also to make African markets more attractive to Western investors. In this respect, industrial countries have sent mixed messages to Africa: They encourage integration with the global economy they dominate through multilateral channels while they discourage integration in bilateral relationships by disengagement and by retaining barriers to African participation.[16] Political conditionality, by contrast, has a less direct relationship to the national self-interest of the major players in global political and economic relations. Based, in part, on historical evidence that democracies do not fight each other, the major premise of the new political conditionality is that democratization promotes international political security. By exercising a form of collective hegemony, donors have attempted to promote their own security interests by projecting them globally, on the assumption that the interests of all other powers will coalesce with their own.

Several points, however, are worth noting.

1. Unlike export-led economic reform under structural adjustment, the favorable foreign policy outcomes expected from democratization are indirect, underspecified, and problematic. The implicit foreign policy assumption is that democratization promotes domestic security and that countries featuring domestic security are less likely to be aggressive in their foreign relations. The problem, however, is that *transitions* to democracy may not necessarily be accompanied by more domestic political security. Indeed, there may, in fact, be less security in these situations.

2. Because programs for political conditionality have no specific foreign policy components—although, alternatively, foreign policy is wholly derivative from domestic policy—the imposition of political conditionality has entailed no specific injunction to political leaders to build, strengthen, and institutionalize democratic, stable, and secure institutions in international relations.

3. Even if democracies tend not to fight one another, they have, of course, found themselves at war with nondemocracies since Athens and Sparta. It follows that the presumed security benefits of democratization come into play only when all or most countries, at least within a given region, have become democracies.

4. The rationale for political conditionality is not directly centered on an African assessment of African interests. Rather, it is derivative from a global policy that is historically and presently centered on the experience of powerful countries whose domestic turmoil can challenge international security far more directly than is the case for most countries in Africa—with the possible exception of South Africa.

5. Political conditionality may do more to consolidate domestic security than to create it. Within the African context, the countries whose domestic turbulence has most directly threatened regional security and exercised the greatest claims on major power military resources are countries where democratization measures cannot easily be undertaken until after those conflicts are resolved: Somalia, Angola, Sudan, and, arguably, Mozambique and Djibouti. The Bosnian conflict suggests strongly that the same is true outside Africa.

6. Most important of all, by assuming that democratization on a global basis will produce international peace and security because democracies do not fight each other, one risks overlooking, at potential peril, some empiri-

cally grounded principles of realist and neorealist international relations theory.[17] One of the reasons why realist theory, in particular, faltered was that its key conceptions of power and nationalism were too incorrigibly vague and all-encompassing to be operationalized for empirical hypothesis testing. But at the same time, realist theory's critique of the Wilsonian vision of a world made peaceful and simple by the universalization of democracy has remained intact: Ideology is an important component of national interest and of power, but it is not synonymous with either term.

The lesson for contemporary campaigns to create a world of democracies is clear and direct: Democratization and economic reform may be important parts of any country's national interest, but they cannot be imposed in such a fashion as to deny the existence of other important elements of national interest. The corollaries are that bilateral and multilateral donors must recognize (1) that governments are responsible for defining and upholding their countries' national interests *as a whole*, (2) that the legitimacy of those governments comes from doing so clearly and effectively and from *appearing* to do so, and (3) that the governments derive their legitimacy primarily from domestic rather than international sources.

There may be a subtle but significant difference between the priorities of individual donors and those of the multilateral lending institutions. The World Bank and the IMF have apparently placed somewhat greater emphasis upon improved governance rather than democratization, although the bilateral donors generally appear to give the two components equal billing. The implicit issue seems to be how important democratization is to improved governance or, more specifically, to what extent democratization is essential to sustaining administrations capable of implementing structural adjustment.

To date, progress in political liberalization, as in economic liberalization, has been uneven, mixed, and not without relapses. On the positive side, 1994 is expected to be a year of stunning progress: the beginning of majority government in South Africa, multiparty elections in Malawi after two decades of Kamuzu Banda's authoritarian rule, multiparty elections signifying the rebuilding of Uganda, an end to one-party rule in Tanzania, and constituency assembly elections in Ethiopia. Moreover, the island republics of Mauritius and the Seychelles have made the transition to multiparty democracy with little or no external pressure. On the other hand, several countries remain inaccessible to both economic and political reform campaigns because they are failed states or states in fundamental disarray: Somalia, Sudan, Angola, Rwanda, and perhaps Mozambique and Djibouti. The leaders of other states—such as Zimbabwe—insist more democratization is inappropriate at this stage in their development. And in Burundi, one promising democratic transition has suffered a relapse.

Underlying these uncertain achievements lurk profound and somewhat uncharted issues concerning the intertwining of parallel processes of economic and political liberalization. Thoroughness in exploring the issues and in evolving

strategies to address them may well be the key to the outcomes of this second
moment of African renewal.

The Post–Cold War Era in Africa

With the beginning of the post–Cold War era of the 1990s, Africa became, if anything, even more peripheral to the international political and economic order. Its
relevance to the national interests of the major powers is now less clear to their
policymakers than it once was. But the demands of the major world powers that
Africa conform its ways to their post–Cold War liberal ideological consensus are,
if anything, more insistent and uncompromising than were those of the Cold
War blocs. At the same time, that very ideological consensus among the major
players in the post–Cold War international order has not helped African countries to remove the long-standing barriers to effective African participation.[18] Arguably, these barriers have become even greater because the diminished major
power military and political interest in the continent is now added to the existing
barriers to full economic participation. The major powers feel much less obli-
gated to undergird African political orders now that the mortal political and military competition between the two blocs has ceased.

African political leaders' strategies for distinguishing and defending their
countries' national interests with respect to those of the great powers are much
more inchoate and uncertain in the new era than before. In an era of major power
ideological consensus and multilateral cooperation, nonalignment is not as effective in binding African nations together as it once was, at least symbolically.
Furthermore, no bases and formulations for replacements have emerged or won
comparably broad adherence. On the contrary, the addition of political conditionality to economic conditionality has made it more difficult than ever for African countries to develop viable strategies for participating in the global economy
and political order.

Moreover, the world's industrial powers have defined their ideological consensus in a way that discriminates against African governments. They have carved
out significant roles for governments in managing their countries' participation
in what was to be a market-driven post–World War II international economy.[19]
Broadly speaking, they have recognized that governments would be required, at
least intermittently and temporarily, to cushion the impact of the international
market competition on their domestic economies in order to protect their countries' domestic and external national interests. By contrast, in the design and application of structural adjustment guidelines, bilateral donors have allowed or
encouraged the World Bank and the IMF to impose a far purer working doctrine
of liberal political economy on African countries than they have been prepared to
impose on themselves. They have made no allowance in principle—and, at best,
only a grudging allowance in practice—for the existence of the national interests
that governments must uphold. Nonetheless, they have, in fact, relied heavily on

African governments to implement both political and economic conditionalities without acknowledging, let alone addressing, the issues of political theory thereby raised.

While seeming (and presumably intending) to increase the legitimacy of African governments through democratization and to strengthen their economies through structural adjustment, these policies taken together may actually be having the opposite effects in both concept and implementation. In concept, they appear to legitimize processes of economic and political liberalization while failing to legitimize—or at least failing to strengthen—revamped political institutions created by those processes and by which they must be governed. In practice, therefore, multidonor campaigns for simultaneous economic and political liberalization risk becoming counterproductive, self-defeating, and accessories to the troubled political and economic circumstances of African countries in the early 1990s, which will be summarized shortly. The reasons and the underlying issues are complicated, and the solutions continue to be elusive.

In the broadest terms, the working presumption of the simultaneous political and economic liberalization campaigns has been that, because they may point toward philosophically compatible goals, the processes of transition toward their realization are mutually reinforcing. As Thomas Callaghy has observed, there are many theoretical and historical reasons to believe otherwise.[20] Either process can be captured by the other: Even more easily than established democratic institutions, fledgling ones in the process of development can be captured by groups achieving dominance in a market economy. Their legitimacy can also be undermined by the seeming subservience of democratically elected leaders to unelected external bodies prescribing needed but unpopular economic reform policies. Conversely, the rigor and integrity of externally mandated economic reforms can be compromised to the extent that elected leaders, undergirded by popular support, decline to accept such international dictates.

Moreover, the foundations of strong economies in the world's most established multiparty democracies historically have been laid by nondemocratic regimes (the newly industrialized countries of South Korea, Hong Kong, Singapore, and Taiwan) or by regimes in which one party was clearly dominant (Germany, the United States, and Japan). Similarly, earlier weaknesses in the economies of France and Italy might arguably be attributed to the absence of such regimes. In short, there may be only shallow theoretical and limited historical support for the proposition, urged by donors on African countries, that economic and political liberalization can and must proceed simultaneously in the early stages.

These connections between the simultaneous pursuit of economic and political liberalization come to a focus in the African state. As presently conceived, simultaneous campaigns for political and economic liberalization may become counterproductive because by misconceiving the nature and importance of the state, they may undermine both the state and the transitions as a whole. Samuel Huntington made a similar point with respect to theoretical assumptions of development policy in the 1960s.[21] But both the problem in practice and the theoretical issues involved are significantly different in the 1990s.

Conceptions of processes of political and economic liberalization in the 1990s bear a family resemblance to those growing loosely out of modernization theory during the first moment of African renewal in the 1960s. In both eras, transitions toward political democracy and market economies were envisaged. However, the presumption in the 1960s was that there was some clarity about where the beginning and ending points of those transitions lay. They were broadly presumed to be founded on surviving African traditions and were thought to lead toward "modern" societies encompassing secular and pragmatic political cultures, mixed but essentially market-based economies, and democratic political systems. To the extent that African countries departed from these prescriptions, they emphasized recovering African political identity, greater state participation in the organization of economy and society, and single-party democracies. Donor policies emphasized institution building within the parameters of this dialogue between themselves and African governments regarding the ends of development. The problem, as Huntington pointed out, lay in the presumed inevitability of those transitions, not in the ideas about where they began or ended. Huntington's criticism of modernization theory's reductionism—that is, the reduction of political institution-building processes to those of the economy and society—was overcome in practice by donor institution-building initiatives.

By contrast, the teleological expectations in the 1990s are more inchoate, and the political reductionism occurs at a different level. The teleological expectations are more unformed not only in terms of external relations, as explained earlier, but also and perhaps more importantly in domestic terms. The externally prescribed, parallel political and economic transitions are billed as necessary rather than inevitable, and retrogression is characterized as unacceptable rather than implausible. Donors present the starting points not as evolutionary modifications of and departures from African cultural realities but as aberrant African structural and policy departures from preordained classical liberal theories of political economy. They thus preclude analyses of African variants of common political and economic problems to which governmental policies have been addressed. Instead, they center only on the alleged theoretical validity of those policies. Similarly, they present the end point of these transitions as confessions of adherence to those theories, as witnessed by indicated structural and policy changes; any creative, realistic African variants on those theories, tacitly accepted in the 1960s, are now excluded.

In short, current donors' conceptions of political and economic transitions appear to preclude both a recognition of African cultural realities and a dialogue on how the ends of those transitions might accommodate evolving African cultural norms and identity, even within the broad outlines of classical theories of political economy. They are inchoate because, in their preoccupation with theoretical orthodoxy to the exclusion of African realities and ideals, they also preclude dialogue on and analysis of intermediate stages, benchmarks, and objec-

tives: in what ways they might or might not represent progress toward ultimate
objectives, what accommodations to the specific circumstances and concerns of a
given country might or might not be possible, how the elements of political and
economic transitions can reinforce rather than undermine one another, what viable intermediate goals can be attained, and how fast it is reasonable and realistic
to expect given changes to occur.

External donor approaches to African political and economic transitions thus
imply a crisis of the African state that is far more profound than that during the
analogous initiatives of the 1960s. They incorporate a different kind of reductionism than Huntington witnessed: no longer the reduction of political processes to
those of the economy and society but rather the reduction of the idea of the state
to the structure of government as it currently exists. A further comparison of the
two moments of African renewal clarifies this point.

In the 1960s, the afterglow of nationalist movements and the projections by
new leaders, in most cases, of African socialist ideals implied a conceptualization
of the state, featuring culturally legitimized rules of the game by which peoples
agreed to be governed and to conduct their economic and social affairs. Donors
assisted African countries by helping to build institutions to structure these processes. In the 1990s, however, these implied conceptualizations of the states have
long since lost their credibility, and to a significant degree, political, social, and
economic institutions have atrophied. They are casualties of well-documented
errant policies and seemingly intractable international and domestic economic
realities. Donor prescriptions for political and economic transitions have, as just
explained, in effect precluded dialogue on how they might relate to African realities and ideals. Thus, current donor campaigns for the democratization of African governmental structures overlook the first and most important purpose of
such democratization: to facilitate African peoples' negotiations on the reconstruction of their states, taking into account the totality of their economic, social,
cultural, and political circumstances—that is, to constitute the basic rules of the
game that those democratic governmental structures are to exemplify.

Even where donors include constitutional change in their programs for supporting political transitions, the emphasis on what rules of the game might suit-
ably encompass the African cultural, economic, and political realities that inspired popular campaigns for national conventions has yielded to more legalistic
debates by government-appointed commissions, focused more on how to implement received Western constitutional wisdom. In thereby becoming more amenable to management and manipulation by the governments of the day, the real
constitutional debates are in danger of becoming merged with, rather than de-
tached from, day-to-day politics.

The risks entailed include deepening political conflict caused by conflating
fundamental and less fundamental issues, more civil violence, and a further
weakening of African states. In these circumstances, the relevance of democratization and economic reform to long-term national interests becomes more ab-
stract than real as the pursuit of the national interest itself yields to the more

immediate survival concerns of individuals and groups. In other words, for donors to prescribe political and economic transitions without reference to African
realities is to commit in domestic contexts the Wilsonian fallacy in international
relations: to lose sight of the fact that ideological convictions are part of but not
synonymous with power and the pursuit of national interests.

The foregoing reflections help to explain the uncertain progress of the still-
embryonic African transitions to political democracy and market economies.
The preliminary evidence suggests that the processes of political and economic
liberalization have secured beachheads in many African countries, but as yet,
they have by no means fully established their legitimacy and utility in the eyes of
the African peoples and leaders whom they are intended to benefit. Why is this
so?

It is instructive to realize that perhaps the most successful and likely irreversible transitions may have occurred in the smallest countries, for example, the island republics of Mauritius and the Seychelles. Larger and more heterogeneous
countries whose artificial origins remain as lingering political realities have, not
surprisingly, presented more serious impediments to political and economic liberalization. Here, the underlying and related realities are that resurgent ethnic
consciousness has further weakened the capacity of governments to survive and
that endemic—and in some cases, increasing—economic distress has rendered
more difficult and less realistic the possibility of overcoming the corruption that
has already greatly corroded the governments' legitimacy. The effects on the
decay of public order are clear.

The adverse effects on the ability of governments to democratize and manage
economic reforms are evident in some of the "older" transitions: the overthrow
of democratic governments in Burundi and Nigeria, the loss of momentum in
Zambia, the possible sacrifice of political reform to the implementation of economic conditionality in Kenya, and a serious struggle over the reconstruction of
the Ethiopian state that debates on a new constitution have been unable to influence, moderate, or focus to date. It remains to be seen whether "younger" transitions, such as those in Uganda, Tanzania, Malawi, Namibia, and Eritrea, will ex-
hibit similar pathologies.

Political and Economic Realities

For African countries as for major powers—and largely because of the influence
of those major powers—domestic political and economic realities govern participation in and, thereby, the international political and economic patterns of the
post–Cold War world. This is, in itself, one of the defining and differentiating
features of the post–Cold War era to date. The major powers have benefited
from greater international consensus, using it as the basis on which to regenerate
their domestic economies and restructure their international economic relationships. But the foregoing analysis has suggested that that same major power

ideological consensus has been applied to prescribing African political and economic reforms in ways that may make it more difficult for African countries to realize the same benefits. They therefore risk losing ground both domestically and internationally.

The fundamental challenge for African nations in the evolving post–Cold War era is to define, build consensus on, and energetically implement new strategies for rebuilding their domestic orders in the midst of new international realities that make meeting this challenge more difficult. They must address several fundamental realities: a decreasing bilateral investment in their development, combined with broader and more insistent demands concerning how that goal is to be accomplished; a greater unity among the major powers in projecting their demands, in conjunction with diminished African domestic resources available to construct collective international responses of their own; and major power prescriptions for African economic and political reform that seem to ground African participation in the post–Cold War international economic and political order on the same foundations of domestic recovery as they themselves use. These prescriptions, however, have been formulated in ways that seem destined to weaken further African domestic political and economic orders rather than stimulate their renaissance.

In sum, the underlying challenges to African states in the emerging post–Cold War era are to reclaim as their own the vision of their renewal that has thus far largely been preempted by the major powers. Through their own energies, they must seek to realize their African identity domestically and ultimately project that identity upon the world stage.

Notes

1. Marina Ottaway, "The Soviet Union and Africa," in John W. Harbeson and Donald Rothchild, eds., *Africa in World Politics,* 1st ed. (Boulder: Westview Press, 1991).

2. W. W. Rostow, *The Stages of Economic Growth: A Non-Communist Manifesto* (Cambridge: Cambridge University Press, 1960).

3. Robert H. Jackson and Carl G. Rosberg, "Why Africa's Weak States Persist: The Empirical and the Juridical in Statehood," *World Politics* 35, no. 1 (1982), pp. 1–25.

4. Marita Kaw, "Choosing Sides: Testing a Political Proximity Model," *American Political Science Review* 34, no. 2 (1990), p. 460.

5. Although there has been no overall analysis of this remarkable period in regard to U.S. foreign assistance, its theoretical foundations are articulated in Coralie Bryant and Louise White, *Managing Development in the Third World* (Boulder: Westview Press, 1982); Hollis Chenery et al., *Redistribution with Growth* (New York: Oxford University Press, 1974); David Korten and Rudi Klauss, *People-Centered Development* (West Hartford, Conn.: Kumarian Press, 1984); and Milton Esman and Norman Uphoff, *Local Organizations: Intermediaries in Rural Development* (Ithaca: Cornell University Press, 1984).

6. Donald Rothchild, "Regional Peacemaking in Africa: The Role of the Great Powers as Facilitators," in John W. Harbeson and Donald Rothchild, eds., *Africa in World Politics,* 1st ed. (Boulder: Westview Press, 1991), pp. 284–307.

7. See, for example, Samir Amin, *Accumulation on a World Scale: A Critique of the Theory of Underdevelopment,* vols. 1 and 2 (New York: Monthly Review Press, 1974), and his *Unequal Development: Essays on the Social Transformation of Peripheral Capitalism* (New York: Monthly Review Press, 1980).

8. The World Bank's new approach was signaled by the publication of its *Accelerated Development in Sub-Saharan Africa: An Agenda for Action* (Washington, D.C.: World Bank, 1981).

9. John Ravenhill, "Africa and Europe: The Dilution of a Special Relationship," in John W. Harbeson and Donald Rothchild, eds., *Africa in World Politics,* 1st ed. (Boulder: Westview Press, 1991), pp. 179–202.

10. World Bank, *Accelerated Development.*

11. *Considerations on the Economic Policy of Ethiopia for the Next Few Years,* report prepared by a team of Soviet consulting advisers attached to the National Planning Commission of Socialist Ethiopia (n.p., September, 1984).

12. Shada Islam, "Lome IV: Frayed Tempers," *West Africa* (April 16–22, 1990), p. 567.

13. The change was evident by the time the World Bank published its *Sub-Saharan Africa: From Crisis to Sustainable Growth* (Washington, D.C.: World Bank, 1989).

14. See a review of this new agenda in Larry Diamond, "The Globalization of Democracy," in Robert Slater, Barry M. Schutz, and Steven R. Dorr, eds., *Global Transformation and the Third World* (Boulder: Lynne Rienner Publishers, 1993), pp. 31–71.

15. For a discussion of the meaning of civil society and its relevance to political reform in Africa, see John W. Harbeson, Donald Rothchild, and Naomi Chazan, eds., *Civil Society and the State in Africa* (Boulder: Lynne Rienner Publishers, 1994).

16. This point is made in a seminal essay by Thomas Callaghy, "Vision and Politics in the Transformation of the Global Political Economy: Lessons from the Second and Third World," in Robert Slater, Barry M. Schutz, and Steven R. Dorr, eds., *Global Transformation and the Third World* (Boulder: Lynne Rienner Publishers, 1993), pp. 161–259.

17. Among the many sources on realist and neorealist theories of international relations are Robert Keohane, *Neo-Realism and Its Critics* (New York: Columbia University Press, 1986), and Kenneth Waltz, *The Theory of International Politics* (Reading, Mass.: Addison-Wesley, 1979). Other sources are cited in the notes to my chapter on the Horn of Africa in this volume (Chapter 6).

18. Callaghy, "Vision and Politics."

19. Ibid.

20. Ibid.

21. Samuel Huntington, "Political Development and Political Decay," *World Politics* 17 (1965), pp. 386–430.

PART TWO

Parameters of African Peripheralization

2

The Heritage
of Colonialism

CRAWFORD YOUNG

AFRICA, IN THE RHETORICAL metaphor of imperial jingoism, was a ripe melon awaiting carving in the late nineteenth century. Those who scrambled fastest won the largest slices and the right to consume at their leisure the sweet, succulent flesh. Stragglers snatched only small servings or tasteless portions; Italians, for example, found only desserts on their plate. In this mad moment of imperial atavism—in Schumpeterian terms, the objectless disposition to limitless frontier expansion—no one imagined that a system of states was being created. Colonial rule, assumed by its initiators to be perpetual, later proved to be a mere interlude in the broader sweep of African history; however, the steel grid of territorial partition that colonialism imposed appears permanent.

Colonial heritage is the necessary point of departure for analysis of African international relations. The state system—which is, transnational vectors notwithstanding, the fundamental structural basis of the international realm—inherits the colonial partition. A few African states have a meaningful precolonial identity (Morocco, Tunisia, Egypt, Ethiopia, Burundi, Rwanda, Madagascar, Swaziland, Lesotho, and Botswana), but most are products of the competitive subordination of Africa—mostly between 1875 and 1900—by seven European powers (Great Britain, France, Germany, Belgium, Portugal, Italy, and Spain).

African Colonial Heritage Compared

The colonial system totally transformed the historical political geography of Africa in a few years' time, and the depth and intensity of alien penetration of subordinated societies continues to cast its shadow.[1] The comprehensive linkages with the metropolitan economies in many instances were difficult to disentangle. In the majority of cases in which decolonization was negotiated, the colonizer retained some capacity to shape the choice of postcolonial successors and often—especially in the French case—enjoyed extensive networks of access and influence after independence was attained. The cultural and linguistic impact was pervasive, especially in sub-Saharan Africa. Embedded in the institutions of the new states was the deep imprint of the mentalities and routines of their colonial predecessors. Overall, colonial legacy cast its shadow over the emergent African state system to a degree unique among the major world regions.

In Latin America, although colonial administrative subdivisions shaped the state system, Spain and Portugal swiftly ceased to be major regional players after Creole elites won independence in the nineteenth century. Great Britain and, later, the United States were the major external forces impinging upon the region. In Asia, the first target and long the crown jewel of the colonial enterprise, imperial conquest tended to follow the contours of an older state system; not all Asian states have a historical pedigree (the Philippines, Pakistan, Papua New Guinea), but a majority do. The circumstances surrounding Asian independence, the discontinuities imposed by the Japanese wartime occupation of Southeast Asia, and the larger sale of most Asian states and the greater autonomy of their economies all meant that the demise of the colonial order there was far more sharp and definitive than was the case in Africa.

Perhaps the closest parallel to Africa in terms of durable and troubled colonial impact on regional international relations if found in the Middle East. The partition of the Ottoman domains in the Levant between Great Britain and France and the imperial calculus employed in territorial definitions and structures of domination left in their wake a series of cancerous conflicts. Thrones had to be found for Great Britain's Hashemite allies; the duplicity of incompatible wartime promises to Arabs and Zionists bore the seeds of inextricable conflict over whether the Palestine mandate awarded to Great Britain by the League of Nations would develop as a Jewish homeland or an Arab state; Great Britain invented Jordan as a territory for its wartime ally Prince Abdullah; Lebanese borders were drawn so as to maximize the zone of dominance for Maronite Christians; Sunni Arab nationalism in Syria was countered by heavy recruitment of minority Alawites for the colonial militia; and Kurdish state demands were denied so that oil-rich zones could be attached to the British-Iraqi mandate.[2] The unending turbulence in this region provides daily confirmation of the colonial roots of many intractable contemporary conflicts. But even here, colonial penetration of Middle Eastern Arab societies and economies was much less than was the case in Africa, and the erstwhile colonial connections weigh less heavily.

In the African instance, the shadow of the colonial past falls upon the contemporary state system in several critical features. The sheer number of sovereign units and the weakness and vulnerability of many due to their small scale are the most obvious. The continuing importance of former economic and political colonial linkages, most of all for the twenty states formerly under French rule, significantly shapes regional politics—both as an active channel of influence and as a negative point of reference. Most of the festering regional crises that torment the continent—Western Sahara, Eritrea, Sudan, southern Africa—are rooted in one way or another in ill-considered decolonization strategies driven by metropolitan interests. In this chapter, I will consider these components of the colonial heritage in turn.

Fragmentation of Africa

The African continent in 1993 (and its offshore islands) contained no fewer than fifty-three sovereign units (using U.N. membership as the criterion)—nearly one-third of the world total.[3] Although this large number has some advantages in guaranteeing a voice in international forums where the doctrine of sovereign equality assures equal voting rights for states large and small, this is little compensation for the disabilities of being tiny. Sheer economic weakness is one disadvantage; in 1988 in all of Africa, only South Africa had a gross national product exceeding that of Hong Kong.[4] Most African states had a GNP less than the Harvard University endowment or the profits of a major multinational corporation. The limits of choice imposed by a narrow national market and circumscribed agricultural and mineral resource bases rendered most states highly vulnerable to the vagaries of commodity markets and the workings of the global economic system. Although some minuscule mercantile states elsewhere have achieved prosperity—Singapore is an obvious example—and tiny sovereignties perched on vast oil pools may accumulate enormous wealth—Bahrain, Qatar, and United Arab Emirates are illustrations—the rapid Iraqi military seizure of Kuwait in 1990 (which was rolled back only by a vast U.S.-led military intervention) amply demonstrated the vulnerability of the small state, however rich. Of the microstates among Africa's fifty-three polities, only Mauritius has prospered.

The full scope of the fragmentation of independent Africa was not apparent until the virtual eve of independence. Most of the vast sub-Saharan domains under French domination were joined in two large administrative federations, Afrique Occidentale Française (AOF) and Afrique Equatoriale Française (AEF). Political life, however, germinated first at the territorial level; the crucial 1956 *Loi-cadre* (framework law) located the vital institutions of African political autonomy at this echelon. Although some nationalist leaders dreamed of achieving independence within the broader unit, especially in the AOF, the wealthier territories (Ivory Coast, Gabon) were opposed to this. In the final compressed surge to independence, the interaction of divisions among nationalist leaders and movements, combined with French interests, resulted in twelve states of modest size rather than two large ones.[5] In the 1950s, Great Britain did promote federations of its colonial possessions as a formula for self-government in the West Indies, the United Arab Emirates, and Malaysia, as well as in east and central Africa, but with indifferent success. In east and central Africa, the fatal flaw was linking the project of broader political units to the entrenchment of special privilege for the European settler communities. Thus contaminated, the federation idea was bound to fail.[6] In instances in which large territories had been governed as single entities—Nigeria, Sudan, Zaire—independence as one polity was possible, although all three countries have, at times, been beset by separatist pressures.

Once sovereignty gave life to colonial territories as independent nations, the African state system has proven to be singularly refractory to broader movements of unification. The 1964 unification of Tanganyika and Zanzibar to form Tanzania remains the sole case of political amalgamation. This occurred only in extraordinary circumstances—the bizarre overthrow of the first independent Zanzibar government by a small armed band led by Ugandan herder John Okello, who returned to obscurity as swiftly as he emerged to leadership. This unexpected act set in motion events that made amalgamation of these two unequal units suddenly feasible; to this day, however, the integration of Zanzibar with mainland Tanzania remains incomplete.

Dream of African Unity

The dream of a broader African unity persists, first nurtured by intellectuals of the diaspora and expressed through a series of pan-African conferences beginning in 1900, then embraced by the radical wing of African nationalism in the 1950s, above all by Kwame Nkrumah of Ghana. The Organization of African Unity (OAU) was created in 1963 to embody this dream, but even its charter demonstrated its contradictions. The OAU was structured as a cartel of states whose territorial integrity was a foundational principle. Rather than transcending the state system, the OAU consolidated it.

The urgency of regional and ultimately continental unification is repeatedly endorsed in solemn documents, including the 1980 Lagos Plan of Action and the 1989 African alternative framework to structural adjustment programs of the Economic Commission for Africa.[7] Innumerable regional integration schemes have been launched, of which the most important are the Union du Maghreb Arabe, the Economic Community of West African States, the Southern African Development Coordination Council, and the various customs and monetary unions of the francophonic west African states.[8] But the goal of effective integration remains elusive; the impact of the colonial partition remains an enduring obstacle.

The colonial origins of most African states weighed heavily upon the consciousness of postindependence rulers. Initially, the fundamental illegitimacy of the boundaries was a central tenet of pan-African nationalism; the 1945 Manchester Pan-African Congress excoriated "the artificial divisions and territorial boundaries created by the Imperialist Powers." As late as 1958, the Accra All-African Peoples' Conference denounced "artificial frontiers drawn by the imperialist Powers to divide the peoples of Africa" and called for "the abolition or adjustment of such frontiers at an early date."[9] But once African normative doctrine was enunciated by the states rather than by nationalist movements, the tone changed, and the sanctity of colonial partition frontiers was asserted. The consensus of the first assembly of African independent states—also in Accra in 1958—was expressed by Nkrumah, the leading apostle of African unification: "Our conference came to the conclusion that in the interests of that Peace which is so essential, we should respect the independence, sovereignty and territorial integrity of one another."[10]

The OAU Charter makes reference to territorial integrity no less than three times; at the Cairo OAU summit in 1964, the assembled heads of state made the commitment even more emphatic by a solemn pledge to actively uphold existing borders, a level of responsibility that goes significantly further than the mere passive recognition of the inviolability of frontiers.[11] Although a certain number of boundary disputes have arisen in independent Africa, the principle of the sanctity of colonial partition boundaries—the juridical concept of *uti possidetis*—remains a cornerstone of a solidifying African regional international law.[12] Most of the disputes have been resolved by negotiation, applying the colonial treaties as the point of juridical reference.[13] The enduring fear of the fragility of the African state system paradoxically endows the artificial colonially imposed boundaries with astonishing durability. The one apparent exception—the independence of Eritrea from Ethiopia in 1993—can be said to prove the point. Eritrean nationalists grounded their claim to self-determination in the argument that Eritrea, as a former Italian colonial territory, should have had the opportunity for independence like all other former colonies, rather than being forcibly joined (in the Eritrean view) to Ethiopia by the international community.

The colonial system profoundly reordered economic as well as political space. During their seventy-five years of uncurbed sovereignty, colonial powers viewed their African domains as veritable *chasses gardées* (private preserves). Metropolitan capital enjoyed privileged access; to varying degrees, other capital was viewed with reserve or even hostility (especially by the Portuguese until the final colonial years). The security logic of the colonial state joined the metropolitan conviction that the occupant was entitled to exclusive economic benefits in return for the "sacrifice" of supplying governance services to foster trade and investment linkages, which tied African territories to metropolitan economies as subordinated appendages. Territorial infrastructures, particularly the communications systems, were shaped by the vision of imperial integration; road nets ran from the centers of production to the ports and colonial capitals. Although over time a shrinkage of the once-exclusive economic ties with the erstwhile colonizers has occurred, these bonds were so pervasive that they have been difficult to disentangle. It is no accident that regional economic integration schemes joining states once under different colonial jurisdictions have had only limited success; the most resilient mechanism of regional economic cooperation has been the Communauté Financière Africaine "CFA" franc zone, a product of the economic space defined by the former French empire in sub-Saharan Africa.

Influence of Former Colonizers

The colonial occupation of Africa, which occurred relatively late in the global
history of imperial expansion, was comparatively dense and thorough. The mul-
tiplex apparatus of domination, which was constructed to assure the "effective
occupation" stipulated by the 1884–1885 Berlin Conference as a condition for the
security of the proprietary title and to extract from the impoverished subjects the
labor service and fiscal tribute to make alien hegemony self-financing, as metropolitan finance ministries required, was unlikely to dissolve instantly once the
occupying country's flag was lowered on independence day. Over time, the many
linkages—both manifest and submerged—binding the decolonized state to the
former metropole have slowly eroded. They were a central dimension in the international relations of new states, especially in the early years of independence.
Even more than three decades later, especially in the case of France, colonial connections still play a significant role.

Several factors influence the importance of ties with former colonizers. In
those cases in which independence was won through armed liberation struggles
rather than bargaining, the power transfer brought initial rupture (Algeria,
Guinea-Bissau, Mozambique, Angola). In some other cases (Guinea, Zaire), the
circumstances of independence brought immediate crisis and discontinuity in
relationships; even though relations were ultimately restored, the degree of intimacy between the two countries could never be the same. Generally, the smaller erstwhile colonial powers played a less visible role than did the two major imperial occupants, Great Britain and France.

Italy was largely eliminated by being on the losing side in World War II. Although it regained a ten-year trust territory mission in Somalia in 1950, Rome
was never permitted to return to Libya and Eritrea and quickly ceased to be a
factor in either territory. Spain was the last country to enter the colonial scramble, and it had only a superficial hold on its territories in northwest Africa
(former Spanish Morocco, Ifni, Western Sahara, Equatorial Guinea). Its minor
interests were swallowed up in postcolonial turmoil in its erstwhile domains (the
Moroccan annexation of Western Sahara, the Macias Nguema capricious tyranny
in Equatorial Guinea from its independence in 1968 until 1979). Emblematic of
Spain's elimination from Africa was the affiliation of Equatorial Guinea with
French-tied CFA franc zone after Macias Nguema was overthrown in 1979.[14]

Belgium retained an important and uninterrupted role in its small former colonies of Rwanda and Burundi, but its economic interests in these states were not
large. In Zaire, where the financial stake was considerable, relationships were
punctuated with repeated crises.[15] The sudden and aborted power transfer left
inextricably contentious disputes over the succession to the extensive colonial
state holdings in a wide array of colonial corporations. These disputes were seemingly resolved several times, only to reemerge in new forms of contention.[16]

In the Portuguese case, an imperial mythology of the global Lusotropical
multiracial community was a keystone of the corporatist authoritarianism of the

Salazar-Caetano *Estado Novo*. However, the utter discrediting of this regime by its ruinous and unending colonial wars in Africa from 1961 to 1974 brought it repudiation. More broadly, in the postcolonial era, a common element for the minor participants in the African partition was an abandonment of earlier notions that overseas proprietary domains validated national claims to standing and respect in the international arena.

Particularly intriguing has been the relative effacement over time of Great Britain on the African scene. Great Britain has long seen itself as a great power, although the resources to support such a claim silently ebbed away because of imperial overreach, according to one influential analysis.[17] In the 1950s, as the era of decolonization opened for Africa, conventional wisdom held that Great Britain was the most likely of the colonizers to maintain a permanent role in its vast colonial estates because of the flexible framework for evolution supplied by the British Commonwealth. This illusion proved to be based upon false inferences deduced from the older constellation of self-governing dominions, which had remained closely bound in imperial security relationships with London. Many thought the Commonwealth could preserve a British-ordered global ensemble beyond the formal grant of sovereignty in Asia and Africa. The illusion of permanence in which British imperialism so long basked dissipated slowly.[18] The doctrine enunciated at the 1926 Imperial Conference still dominated official thinking as the African hour of self-government approached. This document perceived the future as incorporating "autonomous communities within the British Empire, equal in status, in no way subordinate one to another in any aspect of their domestic or external affairs, though united by a common allegiance to the Crown and freely associated as members of the British Commonwealth of Nations"[19] As one of its commentators then wrote, "The British Empire is a strange complex. It is a heterogeneous collection of separate entities, and yet it is a political unit. It is wholly unprecedented; it has no written constitution; it is of quite recent growth; and its development has been amazingly rapid."[20]

These lyrical notions of a global commonwealth's operating in a loose way as a political unit in world affairs so that Great Britain's claim to major power status might survive the decolonization of the empire eroded slowly. India's independence in 1947 was a crucial turning point; the true jewel in the imperial crown, its metamorphosis from the pivot of empire security to a self-assertive "neutralist" Asian power should have ended the illusion that an enlarged commonwealth could remain in any sense a "political unit." Yet when African members of the Commonwealth began joining Ghanaian independence in 1957, some of the older mystique still persisted.

For most former British territories, joining the Commonwealth formed part of the *rite de passage* of independence; only Egypt and Sudan declined to enter its ranks.[21] Paradoxically, as Commonwealth membership became numerically dominated by Asian, African, and Caribbean states, it ceased to serve as a loose-knit, worldwide, British-inspired combine, and its meetings became occasions for heated attacks on British policy in Rhodesia and South Africa. Instead of the

't for the subtle nurture of British global influence imagined
...le Commonwealth thus seemed a funnel for unwelcome pres-
..ritish diplomacy. Even imperial nostalgia could not stave off recog-
.. of these facts; <u>waning British interest removed the Commonwealth's ener-</u>
<u>..izing center.</u> In the words of a recent study, "The Commonwealth has survived
only in [a] very attenuated form . . . [it is] still a useful argumentative forum for
its governments, offering a place for small states to be heard, extending benefits
(albeit on a modest scale) to its members, and providing opportunities for discussion of problems of common interest."[22] This adjustment in the British im-
ages of the Commonwealth goes hand in hand with the gradual reduction of
London's self-perception—from global hegemon to middle-sized European
power.

The diminishing mystique of the Commonwealth as the vessel for a global
British role helps to explain the relative effacement of Great Britain on the African scene. In the first years of African independence, British disposition for intervention was still visible. In the army mutinies that swept Uganda, Kenya, and
Tanganyika in 1964, British troops intervened to check the mutineers, at the request of the embattled regimes. In Nigeria, Great Britain initially had a defense
agreement; however, this was annulled in 1962 due to Nigerian nationalist pressure. In a number of cases, national armies remained under British command for
a few years after independence; in 1964, the British commander of the Nigerian
army refused the solicitation of some Nigerian leaders to intervene after scandal-
ridden national elections brought the country to the brink of disintegration. Security assistance and economic aid in modest quantities continue, and in a few
cases—most notably Kenya—influence remains significant. But since 1970, the
relatively subdued role of Britain, if set against the expectations of 1960, is what
stands out.

The French Connection

The case of France, which has played a pervasive role in the seventeen sub-
Saharan states formerly under its rule, is completely different from that of Great
Britain. The political, cultural, economic, and military connection Paris has
maintained with the erstwhile *bloc africain de l'empire* has been frequently tutelary, often intrusive, and sometimes overtly interventionist. The intimacy and
durability of these linkages are as surprising as the eclipse of the United Kingdom. When African independence loomed on the horizon, France still suffered
from its World War II humiliation and bitter internal divisions. The country was
weakened by the chronic instability of the Fourth Republic, with one-third of its
electorate aligned with the antiregime Stalinist French Communist party and its
army locked in unending and unwinnable colonial wars—first in Indochina,
then in Algeria. *France Against Itself* was the title of the most influential portrait

of the epoch;[23] few anticipated the recapture of its European status and sub-Saharan role as regional hegemon under the Fifth Republic.

In grasping the pervasive African role of the resurrected postcolonial France, one needs first to draw a sharp distinction between the Maghreb and sub-Saharan Africa, which is sometimes overlooked in the fascination with the French connection. In reality, French influence was shattered in what had been the most important parts of the former empire—North Africa and Indochina. In terms of the size of the economic stake, AOF and especially AEF were far behind the core regions of the imperial era. Psychologically, the heart of overseas France was Algeria, whose northern portions were considered to be full French departments. The savagery of the eight-year war for Algerian independence, especially the self-destructive fury of its final phases, compelled the exodus of most of the one million French settlers and the abandonment of much of their stranglehold on the Algerian economy.[24] The independent Algerian state pursued a consistently radical anti-imperial foreign policy, rendered financially possible by its relatively ample oil and natural gas revenues. Although Tunisia and Morocco were less assertive in international politics and leaned to Western positions in their nonalignment, neither accepted the degree of French tutelage that was common in sub-Saharan Africa.

Several factors explain the comprehensive nature of the French relationship with sub-Saharan states formerly under its domination.[25] The terminal colonial effort in this zone to construct an elusive "federalism" as permanent institutional bonding, although failing in its manifest goal of defining political status short of independence, had important consequences. The representation accorded emergent African leaders in the Fourth and (briefly) the Fifth Republics in French institutions drew much of the sub-Saharan independence generation into the heart of French political processes. In the Algerian instance, Paris representation was dominated by settler interests and a small number of collaborating Algerians; Tunisia and Morocco, which had a different international legal status, were not given parliamentary seats.

Although electoral manipulation occurred in sub-Saharan Africa as well, nonetheless those Africans chosen were far more representative of emergent political forces. As early as the 1946 constitutional deliberations, Leopold Senghor of Senegal played an influential role. By the late Fourth Republic, African leaders held ministerial positions (Felix Houphouet-Boigny of the Ivory Coast, Modibo Keita of Mali). Until literally the eve of independence, the "federal" formula the Fifth Republic Constitution sought to institutionalize had the assent of most of the current political class, with the exception of the more radical intelligentsia—especially the students. The referendum approving the Fifth Republic Constitution in 1958 drew large, usually overwhelming majorities in all sub-Saharan territories except Guinea, reflecting the strong wishes of the African leadership for its approval. Jarring as his words now sound, Houphouet-Boigny spoke for a political generation in his often-quoted 1956 statement: "To the mystique of independence we oppose the reality of fraternity." The degree of incorporation of the sub-Saharan African political elite into the French political world has no parallel, and it left a lasting imprint on the texture of postcolonial relationships. Successive French presidents from Charles de Gaulle to François Mitterrand brought to office long-standing intimate ties with many sub-Saharan political leaders.

The original Fifth Republic concept of sub-Saharan territorial autonomy with an array of core sovereign functions (defense, money, and justice, for example) vested in the France-centered French community swiftly vanished.[26] In its place emerged an array of devices giving institutional expression to intimacy. Some form of defense accords was negotiated with fourteen sub-Saharan ex-colonies;[27] French troops were permanently garrisoned in Djibouti, the Central African Republic, Gabon, the Ivory Coast, and Senegal; and a reserve intervention force earmarked for swift African deployment was held in readiness in France. Except for Guinea, Mali, Mauritania, and Madagascar, all these ex-colonies remained within a French currency zone (and Guinea and Mali eventually sought reentry).

By the 1970s, Franco-African summit conferences became a regular and lavish part of the diplomatic landscape; often these attracted more heads of state than the OAU summits. *Francophonie* as a cultural instrument finds expression in the French educational systems and linguistic policies; the nurture of the French language enjoys a priority in French diplomacy that is unique among former colonizers. In the Maghreb, *francophonie* competes with the active policies of affirmation of the Arab language and culture; in sub-Saharan Africa (excepting Madagascar and Mauritania), retention of French as the primary state vehicle has been internalized as a political value by most of the state class.[28] Even a populist leader such as Alphonse Massemba-Debat of Congo-Brazzaville exclaimed in the late 1960s that the Congolese and the French were "Siamese twins," separable only by surgery.[29] Senghor, who was the most intellectually brilliant member of the independence political generation, summed up the pervasive relationship as *francité* (Frenchness, Francehood).[30] Such a neologism has plausible resonance in the Franco-African case, but its analogues would be preposterous in characterizing any other postcolonial ties.

A singular form of tutelary, or dependent, linkages results from this broad-front set of connections, not all of which are well captured in the visible aspect of politics or in the asymmetrical core-periphery economic flows to which "dependency theory" draws attention. The francophonic African community counts upon the senior French partner to defend its interests within the European Community and among the international financial institutions, both public and private. Priority access to French aid is assumed, including periodic budgetary bailouts for the more impoverished states.[31] French willingness to occasionally intervene militarily to protect clients is of crucial importance; between 1963 and 1983, Guy Martin tallies twenty instances of such intervention.[32] As then-President Valéry Giscard d'Estaing stated, "We have intervened in Africa whenever an unacceptable situation had to be remedied."[33] Perhaps even more critical to the nurture of tutelary standing are French security services of a more clandestine nature. French intelligence services provide invaluable protection to rulers by their capacity to monitor and penetrate opposition groups and to foil potential conspiracies by providing early warning to incumbents. These security operations have always enjoyed high-level attention in Paris through such presidential advisers as éminence grise Jacques Foccart; President Mitterrand had entrusted these functions to his son, Jean-Christophe Mitterrand.

In the early 1990s, there are some signs that the silken threads binding francophonic Africa to France may begin to fray. France made no move to prevent the overthrow of Hissene Habré by armed insurgents enjoying Libyan support in Chad at the end of 1990, although French troops in Chad could easily have prevented the takeover. Nor did France lift a finger to avert the collapse of the Moussa Traore regime in Mali in April 1991.[34] Supporting the CFA franc zone is more expensive and less profitable than it once was. Pessimism has spread concerning Africa's infirm economic and political condition.[35] Protection of friendly incumbents appears to have lost some of its attractions, as in early 1990, France moved away from its long-held view that single-party rule, with its corollary of life presidency, was the most "realistic" political formula for Africa.[36] But the closely woven fabric of the French connection is too sturdy to quickly unravel.

Struggle to Eliminate Colonial Influence

The importance of the colonial past in shaping contemporary African international relations is thus beyond dispute. At the same time, the colonial system serves—paradoxically—as a negative point of reference for the African concert of nations. The legitimacy of the first generation of African regimes was rooted in the regimes' achievement—by conquest or negotiation—of independence. The two transcendent unifying principles of the pan-African movement from its inception have been opposition to both colonialism and racism, evils that were joined on the African continent. The independent states that assembled to create the OAU in 1963 were divided on many questions of ideology and interpretation of nonalignment; all could rally behind the combat to complete the liberation of Africa from colonial occupation and regimes of white racial domination. The elemental notion of African solidarity arose out of the shared experience of racial oppression, a point made explicit by W.E.B. Dubois many years ago.

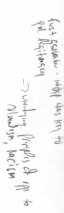

> There is slowly arising not only a curiously strong brotherhood of Negro blood throughout the world, but the common cause of the darker races against the intolerable assumption and insults of Europeans has already found expression. Most men in this world are coloured. A belief in humanity means a belief in coloured men. The future world will in all reasonable possibility be what coloured men make of it.[37]

Nearly five decades later, Julius Nyerere translated these thoughts into African nationalist language: "Africans all over the continent, without a word being spoken, either from one individual to another, or from one African country to another, looked at the European, looked at one another, and knew that in relation to the European they were one."[38]

Indeed, at the moment of the OAU's creation, many of the most arduous independence struggles still lay ahead, such as those in the Portuguese territories, Zimbabwe, and Namibia and the mortal combat with apartheid in South Africa. The OAU has a mediocre record in coping with conflicts within Africa (Somalia, Liberia, Eritrea, Western Sahara, the Nigerian civil war, the Zaire rebellions, and Chad-Libya, for example). However, its anticolonial role has been important in providing a continental focus for African liberation diplomacy.

Within their own territorial domain, independent states faced a compulsion to demarcate themselves from their colonial past, to render visible the new status. The superficial symbolic accoutrements of independence—flags and postage stamps—might serve for a time. Africanization of the state apparatus might help as well, although over time, the perception could arise that the real benefits of this change accrued above all to state personnel.

The imperative of demarcation eventually spread to the economic realm. In the 1970s, a wave of seizures of foreign assets with potent colonial connotations swept through Africa: Idi Amin's "economic war" against the Asian community in 1972, Mobutu Sese Seko's "Zairianization" and "radicalization" compaigns of 1973 and 1974, Tanzania's socialization measures after the 1967 Arusha Declaration, the 1972 and 1976 Nigerian "indigenization decrees," the copper mine nationalizations in Zambia and Zaire, and parallel measures in many other countries. Measures of expropriation of foreign assets almost exclusively affected holdings associated with the colonial past. This partly reflected a distinction often made between postindependence investments, which involved contractual commitments (presumably) freely made by the African state, and those made under alien sovereignty, which lacked moral standing (and doubtless had been well amortized). More important, moves to indigenize the economy reflected pressures to move beyond purely political independence, which would be denatured if all the structures of economic subordination remained intact. By the 1980s, this surge of economic demarcation had run its course; the deepening economic crisis and heightened vulnerability to external pressures made such measures unfeasible. In addition, the measures were frequently discredited by the chaotic improvisation of their implementation and consequent dislocations (Zaire, Uganda) or by the perception that only narrow mercantile classes had benefitted (Nigeria).[39]

The compulsion for demarcation from the colonial past was driven by psychological as well as political and economic factors. Particularly in sub-Saharan Africa, the colonial era brought a broad-front assault upon African culture that was far more comprehensive than similar experiences in the Middle East and Asia. The "colonial situation," to borrow Georges Balandier's evocative concept,[40] was saturated with racism. African culture was, for the most part, regarded as having little value, and its religious aspect—outside the zones in which Islam was well

Need to reassert African culture, etc. - language, religion, etc.

implanted—was subject to uprooting through intensive Christian evangelical efforts, which were often state-supported. European languages supplanted indigenous ones for most state purposes; for the colonial subject, social mobility required mastering the idiom of the colonizer. In innumerable ways, colonial subjugation in Africa brought not only political oppression and economic exploitation but also profound psychological humiliation. In the nationalist response to colonialism, psychological themes are prevalent to a degree unique in Third World anti-imperialist thought. Frantz Fanon, the Martinique psychiatrist who supplied so powerful a voice to the Algerian revolution, was only the most eloquent such spokesman.[41] Such doctrines as *négritude* and "African personality" were central components in nationalist thought, asserting the authenticity and value of African culture. This dimension of African nationalism gave a special emotional edge to the postcolonial quest for demarcation, as well as to the fervor of African state reaction to racism and colonialism.

Colonial heritage as a negative point of reference also influenced the contours of Cold War intrusion into Africa. The United States and the Soviet Union both represented themselves as alternatives to the African nations' exclusive reliance upon the erstwhile colonizers for succor and support. Particularly in the early phases of independence, visible Soviet linkages served as a badge of demarcation. The extravagant fears of all colonizers—and of the West generally—regarding "Communist penetration" of Africa enhanced the value of Soviet relations, even if Soviet economic assistance was minimal. For those states that wanted (or felt compelled to undertake) a more comprehensive break with the Western colonial system, for a brief moment in the early 1960s and again in the late 1970s, the Soviet bloc appeared to offer an alternative—a hope that quickly proved illusory.

Colonial Roots of Regional Crises

A final legacy of the colonial system is the series of regional crises it has left in its wake, particularly in southern Africa and the Horn. In southern Africa, the roots of conflict can be ultimately traced to the catastrophic British mistake of transferring power to an exclusively white regime in South Africa in 1910. Imperial security calculus at the time focused exclusively upon the relationships between the English and Afrikaner communities. Virtually the only concession to African interests was the retention of colonial sovereignty over the Basutoland, Bechuanaland, and Swaziland protectorates. The terms of the Act of Union ultimately led to apartheid in South Africa. The year before the doctrine of "paramountcy of native interests" was proclaimed for Kenya in 1924, Great Britain granted full internal self-government to the white settlers in Southern Rhodesia (now Zimbabwe), an error that resulted in a costly liberation war before independence based upon equal rights for all Zimbabweans was won in 1980. When the hour of decolonization sounded elsewhere in Africa, South Africa, Rhodesia, and the Portuguese were in a position to construct a solid redoubt of white domination, which

White-dom South

left the oppressed no other choices than the passive acceptance of permanent exploitation or armed uprising. The ensuing militarization of society on all sides had far-reaching consequences: Some of these were positive, such as the 1974 army coup that ended corporatist autocracy in Portugal; others were much more negative, such as the entrenchment of competing insurgent movements in Angola. When independence came to Angola and Mozambique after the 1974 Portuguese coup, the white redoubt shrank, but it escalated its efforts to new and more destructive levels by arming, supplying, and guiding insurgent forces—the União Nacional para a Independência Total de Angola and the Resistência Nacional Mozambiquano. The ultimate cost is incalculable: the literal destruction of civil society in Mozambique and endless civil war with heavy external involvement in Angola with a colossal wastage of its precious oil revenues, which are entirely absorbed in military operations.[42] Only the full dismantling of apartheid—deracialization of the South African polity to undo the false decolonization of 1910—can bring this infernal cycle of violence to an end.

In the case of the Horn, the spiral of decomposition affecting both Ethiopia and Sudan reflects choices made at the moment of decolonization when external strategic interests overrode regional considerations. The decision made by the United Nations General Assembly in 1952 to turn Eritrea over to Ethiopia was powerfully influenced by U.S. desires to enjoy an air and communications base at Asmara and to nurture a developing military cooperation with Ethiopia. Eritrean preferences were divided at the time, and significant sentiment in favor of union existed among the highland populations. However, there was overwhelming insistence on distinctive autonomous institutions for Eritrea (elected assembly; its own government, language rights, and flag); the reluctant and apprehensive acquiescence of coastal Muslims to the federation, as a fait accompli imposed from without, was absolutely conditioned upon this autonomy. Once the veil of sovereignty enveloped Eritrea, Ethiopia moved to progressively dismantle the autonomous institutions, finally moving to full annexation in 1962 with no protest from the United Nations or the United States, which was the chief sponsor of the settlement. The result was a thirty-year war for independence, finally achieved in 1993—but not before inflicting untold devastation on Eritrea and bankrupting Ethiopia.[43]

In the case of Sudan, as Sudanese nationalism—Arab-centered and concentrated in the north—forced the pace of change in the 1950s, British state interests were, above all, anti-Egyptian, particularly after the Free Officers seized power in Cairo in 1952. The prime British objective in the decolonization negotiations was to ensure that Sudan became independent, separate from its "condominium" partner Egypt. The ransom of this goal was deference to the northern Sudanese desire for a unitary state under their control. The deepening fears of southern Sudanese regarding their subordination to a state that defined itself as Arab and Muslim—identities they did not share—and their marginalization by the northern elite were ignored. As in Eritrea, the reaction was swift; by 1960, a hydra-headed revolt was in evidence in a number of southern zones. Southern insurrection was brought to a momentary halt in 1972 by a creative political settlement; however, by 1983, its terms had been flagrantly violated, and guerrilla war broke out again—this time at a higher level of violence and associated with widespread famine-induced starvation, which took 250,000 lives in 1988. Beyond the guerrilla forces and the national army, diverse groups of armed bands have proliferated, and the banalization of violence permeates daily existence. The indictment of decolonization policy and of earlier colonial policies that encouraged regional division in Sudan cannot cover all of the miscalculations, insensitivities, and repression that have followed 1956 independence in Sudan. Colonial legacy nonetheless is an inseparable element in any pattern of explanation.[44]

The Western Sahara is yet another festering sore in which an aborted decolonization opened the wound. In this instance, although Spain belatedly abandoned its short-lived (1958–1973) experiment to fully incorporate the colony as an "overseas province," the brief effort begun in 1973 to encourage institutions of autonomy was soon caught between the independence demands of the Frente Popular para la Liberación de Saguia el Hamra y Rio de Oro and Moroccan annexation claims. With Franco on his deathbed and with grave fears about instability that might lie ahead, Spain simply abandoned the territory when faced with the threat of the October 1975 Moroccan *marche verte*.[45]

Thus, in various ways, the colonial heritage intrudes into postindependence African international relations. Perhaps more than three decades after the great surge to independence in 1960, the colonial shadow will begin to fade. Important new trends that may tug colonial legacy further into the background will have a critical impact in the 1990s. The end of the Cold War will certainly have a profound influence. The depth of the economic crisis and a widening consensus that regional integration that bridges the old colonial divisions is indispensable to overcoming them may lead to innovations in the state system that will begin to transcend the colonial partition. The ending of apartheid in South Africa could bring peace to a tormented region and permit movement beyond the bitter residues of the colonial situation. For the first thirty-plus years of African independence, however, colonial heritage has powerfully shaped the African international system.

Notes

1. For a more extended argument on the pathology of the African colonial state, see Crawford Young, "The African Colonial State and Its Political Legacy," in Donald Rothchild and Naomi Chazan, eds., *The Precarious Balance: State and Society in Africa* (Boulder: Westview Press, 1988), pp. 25–66.

2. Great Britain was awarded a mandate over the former Ottoman provinces, which became Iraq, by the League of Nations; Iraq achieved nominal independence in 1930 but remained within a British sphere of influence until the late 1950s. In the extensive literature on these themes, I have found especially useful Charles Issawi, *An Economic History of the Middle East and North Africa* (New York: Columbia University Press, 1972); Peter Sluglett, *Britain in Iraq 1914–1932* (London: Ithaca Press, 1976); William Roger Louis, *The*

British Empire in the Middle East 1945–1951: Arab Nationalism, the United States, and Post-war Imperialism (Oxford: Clarendon Press, 1984); George Antonius, *The Arab Awakening* (New York: Capricorn Books, 1965); and Mary C. Wilson, *King Abdulla, Britain and the Making of Jordan* (Cambridge: Cambridge University Press, 1987).

3. This total does not include Western Sahara, which is recognized as a member state by the Organization of African Unity but not by the United Nations. Eritrea and South Africa have been added in the 1990s.

4. World Bank, *World Development Report 1990* (New York: Oxford University Press, 1990), pp. 178–179.

5. The most careful political history of this process of fragmentation is Joseph-Roger de Benoist, *La Balkanisation de l'Afrique Occidentale Française* (Dakar: Nouvelles Éditions Africaines, 1979). His study clearly demonstrates that the balkanization was less a product of Machiavellian French design than the outcome of a complicated interplay of African political competition and French improvised response. Resentment of the distant bureaucratic despotism of the AOF French administrative headquarters was common in the outlying territories. Those nationalist leaders who, at various times, fought to preserve the unit—Leopold Senghor, Sekou Toure, Modibo Keita—were constrained both by their own rivalries and by the absence of a strong popular attachment to the AOF as a geographical entity.

6. Among the works on this subject, see Arthur Hazlewood, ed., *African Integration and Disintegration* (London: Oxford University Press, 1967); Joseph S. Nye, *Pan-Africanism and East African Integration* (Cambridge: Cambridge University Press, 1965); Patrick Keatley, *The Politics of Partnership* (Harmondsworth: Penguin Books, 1964); Philip Mason, *Year of Decision: Rhodesia and Nyasaland in 1960* (London: Oxford University Press, 1960); and Donald S. Rothchild, *Toward Unity in Africa: A Study of Federalism in British Africa* (Washington, D.C.: Public Affairs Press, 1960).

7. Robert S. Brown and Robert J. Cummings, *The Lagos Plan of Action vs. the Berg Report* (Lawrenceville, Va: Brunswick Publishing, 1984, and United Nations Economic Commission for Africa, *African Alternative Framework to Structural Adjustment Programmes for Socio-Economic Recovery and Transformation* (AAF-SAP), E/ECA/CM> 15/6/ rev. 3, 1989.

8. See, among others, Ahmed Aghrout and Keith Sutton, "Regional Economic Union in the Maghreb, *Journal of Modern African Studies* 28, no. 1 (1990), pp.115–139, and Elaine A. Friedland, "S.A.D.C.C. and the West: Cooperation or Conflict?" *Journal of Modern African Studies* 23, no. 2 (1985), pp. 287–314.

9. Saadia Touval, *The Boundary Politics of Independent Africa* (Cambridge, Mass.: Harvard University Press, 1972), pp. 22–23, 56–57.

10. Ibid., p. 54.

11. Onyeonoro S. Kamanu, "Secession and the Right of Self-Determination: An O.A.U. Dilemma," *Journal of Modern African Studies* 12, no. 3 (1974), pp. 371–373.

12. *Uti possidetis* is derived from a Roman private law concept, which holds that pending litigation, the existing state of possession of immovable property is retained. Translated into international law, the phrase means that irrespective of the legitimacy of the original acquisition of territory, the existing disposition of the territory remains in effect until altered by a freely negotiated treaty. For a passionate attack on this doctrine by a Moroccan jurist, see "L'uti possidetis' ou le non-sens du 'principe de base' d l'OUA pour le réglement des differends territoriaux," *Mois en Afrique* 217–218 (February-March 1984), pp. 3–30.

13. For major studies on African boundary issues, see, in addition to the previously cited Touval work (Note 9), Carl Gosta Widstrand, ed., *African Boundary Problems* (Uppsala: Scandinavian Institute of African Studies, 1969); A.I. Asiwaju, *Partitioned Africans: Ethnic Relations Across Africa's International Boundaries 1884–1984* (London: C. Hurst, 1984); Yves Person, "L'Afrique Noire et ses frontieres," *Revue Française d'Etudes Politiques Africaines* 80 (August 1972), pp. 18–42; and Ian Brownlie, *African Boundaries: A Legal and Diplomatic Encyclopedia* (Berkeley: University of California Press, 1979).

14. On the limited nature of Spanish rule, see Ibrahim Sundiata, *Equatorial Guinea* (Boulder: Westview Press, 1989), and Tony Hodges, *Western Sahara: The Roots of a Desert War* (Westport, Conn.: Lawrence Hill, 1983).

15. For thorough detail, see Gauthier de Villers, "Belgique-Zaire: Le grand affrontement," *Cahiers du CEDAF* 1–2 (1990).

16. For detail on the *contentieux*, see Crawford Young and Thomas Turner, *The Rise and Decline of the Zairian State* (Madison: University of Wisconsin Press, 1985), pp. 276–325.

17. Paul Kennedy, *The Rise and Fall of the Great Powers: Economic Change and Military Conflict from 1500 to 2000* (New York: Vintage Books, 1987).

18. The phrase is drawn from the intriguing study by Francis G. Hutchins, *The Illusion of Permanence: British Imperialism in India* (Princeton: Princeton University Press, 1967).

19. Cited in Cecil J.B. Hurst et al., *Great Britain and the Dominions* (Chicago: University of Chicago Press, 1928), p. 9.

20. Ibid., p. 3.

21. South Africa, which had been a member since its accession to "dominion" status in 1910, quit in 1961 in the face of increasing attack from the swelling ranks of African members.

22. Dennis Austin, *The Commonwealth and Britain* (London: Routledge and Kegan Paul, 1988), pp. 62, 64.

23. Herbert Luthy, *France Against Itself* (New York: Meridian Books, 1959).

24. For a graphic account of the holocaust during the final year of the Algerian war, with mutinous army and a murderous settler force—the Organization de l'Armée Secrète—see Paul Henissart, *Wolves in the City: The Death of French Algeria* (New York: Simon and Schuster, 1970).

25. Useful studies on this topic include Edward Corbett, *The French Presence in Black Africa* (Washington, D.C.: Black Orpheus Press, 1972); Guy Martin, "Bases of France's African Policy," *Journal of Modern African Studies* 23, no. 2 (1985), pp. 189–208; George Chaffard, *Les carnets secrets de la décolonisation* (Paris: Calmann-Levy, 1965); Pierre Pean, *Affaires africaines* (Paris: Fayard, 1983); and Charles-Robert Ageron, *Les chemins de la décolonisation de l'empire français 1936–1956* (Paris: Editions du CNRS, 1986).

26. For a painstaking account by a highly informed French observer, see Joseph-Roger de Benoist, *Afrique Occidentale Française de 1944 à 1960* (Dakar: Nouvelles Editions Africaines, 1982).

27. Martin, "Bases of France's African Policy," p. 204.

28. One encounters some exceptions among the intelligentsia; one example was the late Cheikh Anta Diop of Senegal, a cultural nationalist of great influence who strongly urged promotion of the most widely spoken Senegalese language, Wolof. But overall, the commitment to French as the cultural medium is far more entrenched in the former French sub-Saharan territories than anywhere else in Africa.

29. Corbett, *The French Presence*, p. 66.

30. Leopold Sedar Senghor, *Ce que je crois: Négritude, francité et civilisation de l'universel* (Paris: B. Crasset, 1988).

31. In theory, financial injections to meet budgetary crises—most commonly, payments to civil servants—have long ceased; in practice, they continue to occur. For fascinating details on the process and its political importance, see Raymond Webb, "State Politics in the Central African Republic," Ph.D. diss., University of Wisconsin–Madison, 1990.

32. Martin, "Bases of France's African Policy," p. 194.

33. Ibid.

34. See the special issue of *Africa Report* devoted to "France and Africa: The End of an Era" 36, no. 1 (December-January 1991).

35. Symptomatic was the appearance in 1990 of an array of major reportage on the African situation in leading French newspapers, bearing such titles as "The Shipwreck of Africa," "The Failure of Africa," and "What to Do About Africa?" More generally, there seems to be reason to expect, as Ravenhill argues, that the gradual pattern of economic disengagement from Africa by former colonizers will continue and perhaps accelerate in the 1990s.

36. See *Africa Confidential* 31, no. 5 (March 9, 1990) for details.

37. Quoted in Victor Bakpetu Thompson, *Africa and Unity: The Evolution of Pan-Africanism* (London: Longman 1969), p. 36.

38. Lecture by Julius Nyerere at Wellesley College, Wellesley, Mass., April 1961; from my notes.

39. For details, see Crawford Young, *Ideology and Development in Africa* (New Haven: Yale University Press, 1982).

40. Georges Balandier, "The Colonial Situation," in Pierre van den Berghe, ed., *Africa: Social Problems of Change and Conflict* (San Francisco: Chandler Publishing, 1965), pp. 36–57.

41. See, for example, Frantz Fanon, *Black Skin, White Masks* (New York: Grove Press, 1967). On this theme, see also O. Mannoni, *Prospero and Caliban: The Psychology of Colonization* (London: Methuen, 1956), and A. Mennoni, *Portrait du colonisé, precede du portrait du colonisateur* (Paris: Buchet-Chastel, 1957).

42. For some calculations on the magnitude of the damage done by South African destabilization in the region, see Joseph Hanlon, *Beggar Your Neighbors: Apartheid Power in Southern Africa* (Bloomington: Indiana University Press, 1986).

43. On the Eritrean case, see Berekhet Habte Selassie, *Conflict and Intervention in the Horn of Africa* (New York: Monthly Review Press, 1980); I. M. Lewis, ed., *Nationalism and Self-Determination in the Horn of Africa* (London: Ithaca Press, 1983); Richard Sherman, *Eritrea: The Unfinished Revolution* (New York: Praeger, 1980); John Markakis, "The Nationalist Revolution in Eritrea," *Journal of Modern African Studies* 26, no. 4 (1987), pp. 643–668; and Mesfin Araya, "The Eritrean Question: An Alternative Explanation," *Journal of Modern African Studies* 28, no. 1 (1990), pp. 79–100.

44. For two excellent scholarly monographs reflecting southern and northern Sudanese perspectives, see Dunstan M. Wai, *The Africa-Arab Conflict in the Sudan* (New York: African Publishing House, 1978), and Mohammed Omar Beshir, *The Southern Sudan: Background to Conflict* (London: William Blackwood and Sons, 1968).

45. Half a million Moroccans signed on to participate in this proposed citizen invasion and annexation of the western Sahara; 145,000 actually began the move to the frontier. For details, see Hodges, *Western Sahara.*

3

Africa and the World Political Economy: Still Caught Between a Rock and a Hard Place

THOMAS M. CALLAGHY

There is tremendous suffering, not only physically but also psychologically that while people in other societies are making progress, Africa is going backwards. Therefore we must ensure that as we pursue democracy, we also pursue the goals of development. And what Africa needs in that regard is not [structural] adjustment, it is fundamental restructuring and transformation of African economies. . . .

The donor countries that are encouraging Africans to take the democratic path are also the countries that are encouraging Africans to adopt economic policies that alienate the people, that make development extremely difficult because of their misunderstanding of the nature and causes of Africa's economic crisis.

—Adebayo Adediji[1]
Former executive secretary
U.N. Economic Commission for Africa

Marginalization and Dependence

IN THE MIDDLE OF THE NINETEENTH CENTURY, Africa went through a wrenching adjustment from one set of terrible realities to another. With the end of the slave trade, African societies had to find other ways to interact with the world economy and with powerful foreign states, all in the context of seriously disrupted economies and considerable political flux. In this period just before the imposition of direct colonial domination, Africa found itself both marginalized from the world economy and highly dependent on it. Referring to this era, a leading historian of

Africa has pointed to "the paradox of Africa's simultaneous involvement and marginalization in the world economy"; "Africa was becoming less significant to the world economy at the same time [that] it involved itself more closely in international commercial relationships." This paradox operated in the opposite direction as well: The world's "increasing involvement in the African economy . . . [was] at odds with the decreasing economic importance of Africa" for the world economy.[2] At the end of the twentieth century, this paradox is still valid; in fact, it is more applicable now than it was in the middle of the last century. As we shall see, this paradox and the dilemmas that arise from it are captured by Adebayo Adediji's words.

Increased Marginalization: "Post Neocolonialism"

The increased marginalization of Africa is twofold—economic and politico-strategic—and both aspects are tightly linked in their consequences. The first and primarily economic aspect is that Africa is no longer very important to the major actors in the world economy (multinational corporations, international banks, the economies of the major Western countries or those of the newly industrializing countries such as Korea, Taiwan, Brazil, and Mexico) and to that economy's changing international division of labor. The second aspect of Africa's marginalization is that, with the end of the Cold War, African countries have little politico-strategic importance for the major world powers.

Africa generates a declining share of world output. The main commodities it produces are becoming less and less important or are being more effectively produced by other Third World countries. Trade is declining, nobody wants to lend, and few want to invest except in narrowly defined mineral enclave sectors.

Africa's per capita income levels and growth rates have declined since the first oil crisis in 1973, while its percentage of worldwide official development assistance rose from 17 percent in 1970 to about 38 percent in 1991.[3] Since 1970, its nominal gross domestic product (GDP) has risen more slowly than that of other developing countries, and real GDP growth rates have dropped dramatically since 1965.

Other developing countries performed better in spite of the poor world economic climate, especially in the 1980s. Cross-regional comparisons are quite revealing. For the period 1982–1992, average GDP growth for Africa was 2.0 percent; for South Asia, the most comparable region, it was 5.2 percent, and the East Asian rate was 8.0. The rate for all developing countries was 2.7 percent. The GDP per capita rates are even more revealing: Africa's was 1.1 percent, South Asia's was 2.9 percent, and East Asia's was 6.4 percent. The World Bank's baseline projections for 1992–2002 are more optimistic. The GDP growth rates are predicted at 3.7 percent for Africa, 5.3 percent for South Asia, and 7.3 percent for East Asia; the GDP per capita estimates are 0.6 percent for Africa, 3.4 percent for South Asia, and 5.9 percent for East Asia. The bank's estimates for Africa have often proved to be overly optimistic, and the assumptions of the current baseline forecast are startling. The forecast for Africa assumes less unfavorable external conditions, including a break in declining commodity prices, more liberalized world trade regimes, and no real decline in industrial country growth; a decline in civil strife; improvement in economic policies and implementation; a higher percentage of foreign investment in overall capital flows; a continuation of current foreign assistance flows; and no major adverse weather conditions! It does, however, assume a 50 percent increase in the number of poor, rising from 200 to 300 million people, making Africa the only region in the world with an overall increase in poverty. At current rates of per capita GDP growth, it will be forty years before Africa gets back to mid-1970s' levels.

In addition, African export levels have stayed relatively flat or have actually declined since 1970, while those of other developing countries have risen significantly. For example, the continent's share of developing country agricultural primary product and food exports declined from 17 percent to 8 percent between 1970 and 1990, with South and East Asian exports growing rapidly. If the 1970 share had been maintained, export earnings in the early 1990s would have been significantly higher. Average annual growth rates for all exports have fared poorly.

Africa's marginalization becomes even more obvious when its performance is compared with that of other low-income countries. This is particularly true in regard to South Asia, with which Africa has the most in common. (South Asia is composed of Bangladesh, Bhutan, Burma, India, Maldives, Nepal, Pakistan, and Sri Lanka.) The difference in per capita GDP growth between the two regions is striking—Africa's has declined dramatically, while that of South Asia has risen slowly but steadily. Africa's population growth rate continues to climb, while that of South Asia has begun to decline.

The most startling differences between the two regions relate to the level and quality of investment. Africa's investment as a percentage of GDP declined in the 1980s, South Asia's continued to increase despite the difficult economic conditions of the decade. South Asia followed better economic policies and, above all, provided a much more propitious socioeconomic and politico-administrative context for investment. This is most vividly manifested in the comparative rates of return on investment: Africa's fell from 30.7 percent in the 1960s to just 2.5 percent in the 1980s, and South Asia's increased slowly but steadily, if only marginally, from 21.3 percent to 22.4 percent in the same period.

A similar picture emerges from the comparative figures for the growth of production for both agriculture and industry. In 1965, manufacturing accounted for 9 percent of economic activity in Africa, and by the late 1980s, this figure had risen to only 11 percent—much of which was extremely inefficient by world standards. As a result, major actors in the world economy showed little interest in lending or investing in Africa by the 1980s. From 1983 to 1985, for example, net nonconcessional capital flows to Africa dropped from more than $8 billion to less than $1 billion.

Given this dismal economic performance, both substantively and comparatively, it is not surprising that world business leaders take an increasingly jaundiced view of Africa. As one business executive expressed it to me, "Who cares about Africa; it is not important to us; leave it to the IMF and the World Bank."[4] Some observers have referred to this phenomenon as *post-neocolonialism*. For the most dynamic actors in a rapidly changing world economy, even a neocolonial Africa is not of much interest, especially after the amazing changes wrought in Eastern Europe and elsewhere beginning in 1989. According to this viewpoint, the African crisis really should be left to the international financial institutions as a salvage operation, and if that effort works, fine; if not, so be it—the world economy will hardly notice.

Thus, whatever one thinks about the role of foreign merchant, monopoly, and finance capital, it is important to remember that Africa increasingly imposes enormous difficulties for these actors, such as political arbitrariness and administrative, infrastructural, and economic inefficiency. Foreign capital has considerable ability to select the type of state with which it cooperates; it is therefore doubtful that Africa will play any significant role in current shifts in the patterns of production within the international division of labor. For most external businesspeople, Africa has become a voracious sinkhole that swallows their money with little or no longer-run return. Two arresting facts further underscore Africa's marginalization: (1) The amount of external financing done in 1991 through bonds was $2.4 billion for East Asia and $1.9 billion for South Asia, while it was zero for Africa, and (2) flight capital at the end of 1990 as a percentage of GDP was 14.9 for South Asia, 18.9 for East Asia, 27.8 for developing Europe, and 27.8 for Central Asia, while it was 80.3 for Africa.

Some observers have hoped that a post-apartheid South Africa will help lead the region to sustained growth. Such a hope now appears quite unrealistic. The new South African government will face enormous difficulties for quite some time, although foreign investment is more likely to go there than elsewhere in Africa.

From this perspective, the laments of international organizations and development economists about the intractable underdevelopment of Africa is not just a conspiratorial attempt to conceal the pillage of Africa but rather a reflection of the fact (although they would not put it this way) that Africa, from the point of view of major private economic actors, is an underexploited continent with weak states and weak markets.

Disinvestment, in fact, has emerged as a new trend. During the 1980s, for example, 43 of 139 British firms with industrial investments in Africa withdrew their holdings—mostly from Zimbabwe, Nigeria, and Kenya—despite ongoing economic reforms. Ironically, the retrenchment has been due, in part, to the economic reforms themselves, for they removed overvalued exchange rates and import tariff protection. The British firms were unwilling to inject new capital to make their investments efficient by world standards of competitiveness. Although Japan is now the major donor to Africa, it is not likely to be a major investor. During the 1980s, for instance, the number of Japanese commercial companies operating in Kenya declined from 15 to 2. U.S. investment in Kenya has also dropped. A number of African countries—including Ghana and Kenya—are attempting to attract new investment by creating export processing zones, but they have had little success so far.

The second aspect of Africa's marginalization is politico-strategic, but it entails negative economic consequences as well. Africa has become of much less interest to the major world powers with the dramatic changes in the international arena, especially with the end of the Cold War. As one senior African diplomat put it, "Eastern Europe is the most sexy beautiful girl, and we are an old tattered lady. People are tired of Africa. So many countries, so many wars."[5] The rise of warlords in regional and civil wars similar to those in nineteenth-century Africa has challenged the very notion of the nation-state borrowed at the time of independence in the 1960s. The independence of Eritrea and the potential breakup of places such as Zaire open the Pandora's box of redrawing the old colonial boundaries that were sacrosanct for thirty years.

Debates about Africa used to pit internationalists concerned with rivalry between the big powers against regionalists concerned with African issues.[6] Ironically, the internationalists have now largely ceded the field to the regionalists. The latter used to call for the major powers not to turn Africa into an international battlefield but rather to let Africans solve their own problems—to leave Africa alone. Now that the internationalists have declared the game over, the regionalists are desperately searching for a rationale to keep external interest—and resources— focused on Africa. External intervention on the scale recently seen in Somalia is not likely to be repeated; malign neglect, as applied to the greater Liberian, Angolan, and Sudanese civil wars, is likely to be the more common reaction.

At the same time, however, the dramatic changes of 1989, Africa's politico-strategic marginalization, and the search for a new foreign policy rationale by Western industrial democracies have meant that economic conditionality has now been joined by forms of political conditionality, under the assumption that economic and political liberalization must go hand in hand.[7]

Increased Involvement: The New Neocolonialism

Yet in other ways, Africa has become more tightly linked to the world economy. This increased involvement has two aspects: (1) an extreme dependence on external public actors, particularly the IMF and the World Bank, in the determination of African economic policy, and (2) the liberal or neoclassical thrust of this economic policy conditionality, which pushes the continent toward a more intense reliance on and integration with the world economy. Both these aspects are linked directly to Africa's debt crisis.

In 1974, total African debt was about $14.8 billion; by 1992, it had reached an estimated $183.4 billion, or about 109 percent of Africa's total GNP. South Asia's percentage was only 36.3, and East Asia's was 27.9. Much of the recent rise has come from international financial institutions (IFIs), especially the IMF and the World Bank; this increase results largely from the borrowing associated with externally sponsored economic reform programs, usually referred to as structural adjustment. In 1980, IFI debt equaled 19 percent of the total; by 1992, it accounted for 28 percent. This debt cannot be rescheduled, and significant arrears are accumulating, with the result that some countries have been cut off from IMF and World Bank assistance. Much of the rest of Africa's debt is bilateral or government-guaranteed, medium- and long-term debt through private sources and thus is rescheduled by Western governments through the Paris Club, not by the private banks as done in Latin America. A key norm of the debt regime is that countries cannot obtain Paris Club rescheduling relief without being in the good graces of the IMF and the World Bank.

Despite its small aggregate size by world standards, however, the enormous buildup of African debt puts terrible strains on fragile economies. By the end of the 1980s, the debt was the equivalent of 350 percent of exports. Africa's debt-service ratio (debt service owed as a percentage of export earnings) averaged a little less than 30 percent by the mid-1980s. By 1992, it still averaged more than 25 percent, with some African countries showing much higher rates; Uganda's, for example, was 80 percent. The debt-service ratios would be significantly lower, however, if African export growth had kept pace with the performance of other less developed countries. In fact, only about half of the debt service owed is paid in any given year, which tends to dampen foreign direct investment.

Given such debt, African countries have benefited from concessions such as longer terms and grace periods, lower interest rates, and the rescheduling of previously rescheduled debt. Since 1988, Africa and especially the continent's low-income countries have received some debt cancellation, including that from the United States, which strongly opposed it at first. Between 1989 and 1991, about $10 billion in concessional debt was written off by Western countries. Given the speed with which debt to the major international financial institutions is accumulating, however, this relief is quite modest. Despite strong pressure from the IMF, the World Bank, various United Nations agencies, and private organizations such as Oxfam, most of the major donor countries are still resisting significant debt cancellation.

As in other areas of the Third World, this difficult external debt burden and the resulting desperate need for foreign exchange have made African countries very dependent on a variety of external actors, all of whom have used their leverage to "encourage" economic liberalization. This process, which some have referred to as the *new neocolonialism,* means intense dependence on the International Monetary Fund, the World Bank, and major Western countries for the design of economic reform packages and the resources needed to implement them. This leverage has been converted into economic policy conditionality: specific economic policy changes in return for borrowed resources. The primary thrust of these economic reform efforts is to integrate African economies more fully into the world economy by resurrecting the primary-product export economies that existed at the time of independence and making them work correctly this time by creating a more "liberal" political economy.

One good indicator of this increased international involvement is the number of African countries that have ongoing relationships with the IMF and the World Bank. Between 1970 and 1978, African countries accounted for 3 percent of the total assistance from IMF-approved economic reform programs. Their share of the total number of IMF programs for this period was 17 percent; by the end of 1979, it had risen to 55 percent. In 1978, only two African countries had agreements with the IMF; in March 1990, twenty-eight countries had agreements with the IMF (60 percent of the agreements). Despite the large number of new members from Eastern Europe and the former Soviet Union, African countries still accounted for 38 percent of the agreements in September 1993. Most of these countries also had simultaneous agreements with the World Bank. Lastly, African countries have the highest number of repeat programs of any region of the world.

In sum, Africa's current dismal situation is not caused predominantly by its relationship to the world economy or to dominant countries or actors in the international state system. Clearly, however, what happens to Africa will be the *combined* result of the effects of world market forces, the international state system, African socioeconomic structures, and the nature and performance of African state structures. The continent has always been relatively marginal to the world economy. It is now becoming even more so and at an accelerating rate. In many respects, Africa is lost between state and market: It wanders between an ineffective state and weak markets, both domestic and international, and the latter are increasingly indifferent. Many African officials fail to realize just how unimportant their continent is becoming to the world economy; they still fear this reality and seek to run from it. Many of them are still looking for a shortcut, a quick fix, despite the fact that world events since 1980 show that one does not exist. If African countries are to survive, changes must be made. If not, changes in the world political economy will continue to pass Africa by, with very serious long-term consequences for the people of the continent.[8]

In the context of Africa's increased marginalization, dependence, and poverty, I will look at the experience of economic reform in the 1980s and early 1990s, the factors that facilitated and impeded it, the near collapse of an "implicit bargain" between African governments and external actors about resource flows, and the nature and extent of policy learning over the decade. With the frustratingly modest results of these efforts in mind, I will then examine the debate that raged between African and Western officials at the end of the 1980s and the early 1990s over what steps should be taken. The beginning of the 1990s brought the threat of an even more intrusive form of conditionality. I will assess this new political conditionality, which is supposed to improve African governance and thereby increase the chances of successful economic reform. I will conclude by discussing some prospects for the future, particularly the growing differentiation between African countries and two key factors that will affect it—levels of state capacity and the nature and openness of the world economy.

The Political Economy of Attempted
Economic Reform in the 1980s

By the early 1980s, the key question was not whether Africa had a serious economic crisis but rather what could be done about it. Avoiding the problem and
policy drift were common reactions, despite external warnings and pressure. To a
large extent, the African response was to rail against the prescriptions of external
actors. For governments that did decide—out of conviction or because of a desperate need for foreign exchange and debt rescheduling—to attack the problem,
the dilemmas were enormous, the risks great, and the uncertainties pervasive.
Throughout the 1980s, economic reform did take place in Africa in large and
small ways. Many countries went through the motions (or at least appeared to do
so), resulting in a series of small reforms. However, in only a few cases did large
reform—that is, multisector reform sustained over time—occur.

Ghana, in fact, is the only clear-cut example, and it illustrates the enormous
difficulties involved in the process. Kwesi Botchwey, Ghana's longtime finance
minister, portrayed them vividly:

> We were faced with two options, which we debated very fiercely before we finally
> chose this path. I know because I participated very actively in these debates. Two
> choices: We had to maneuver our way around the naiveties of leftism, which has a
> sort of disdain for any talk of financial discipline, which seek refuge in some vague
> concept of structuralism in which everything doable is possible. . . . Moreover, [we
> had to find a way between] this naivete and the crudities and rigidities and dogma
> of monetarism, which behaves as if once you set the monetary incentives everybody
> will do the right thing and the market will be perfect.[9]

As the Rawlings regime in Ghana discovered, neither position is fully correct:
Everything is not possible, and policy incentives do not ensure that markets will
work well. In addition, a revenue imperative exists no matter which path is chosen: Resources have to come from somewhere. In 1982–1983, the Rawlings government engaged in a series of radical mobilization efforts, such as using students to harvest and transport food and repair roads, and it turned to the Soviets
and East Europeans for assistance. Although the radical mobilization efforts had
some success, the government realized that those efforts could not be sustained
over time, and the Soviets and East Europeans politely but firmly suggested that
Ghana should turn to the Western countries, the IMF, and the World Bank for
assistance. A quite rare conjuncture of factors has allowed the economic reform
efforts in Ghana to be sustained, and Ghana's success at large reform—itself still
fragile—is a rarity on the continent.[10]

How, then, do we explain the varied abilities of African governments, caught as
they are between strong and often contradictory internal and external pressures,
to engage in sustained economic reform? The degree to which an African government can adjust appears to be determined by its ability to insulate itself from the
political logics, characteristics, and effects of the statist syndrome that has dominated Africa since independence. The ability to insulate is affected primarily by

the following variables: (1) the manner in which the economic crisis is perceived by African rulers—particularly whether it is caused by external or internal factors and whether it is temporary or systemic; (2) the degree to which decisionmaking is influenced by technocratic rather that political considerations—patron-client politics and rent seeking, for example; (3) the degree of the government's autonomy from powerful sociopolitical forces and groups, particularly relating to distributional demands; (4) the administrative capabilities of the state apparatus and the overall level of economic development; and (5) the nature, dependence on, and extent of external influence, support, and resource flows, including the market forces of the world economy.

This argument maintains a balance between voluntarist perspectives that stress political will—so common to external actors—on the one hand, and pessimistic ones that stress structural constraints—so common to academic and African analyses—on the other. Adequate levels of understanding, commitment, and statecraft skill (plus luck—a variable we greatly underestimate) are necessary but not sufficient; state capacity, sociopolitical insulation, and adequate external resources are also necessary but not sufficient. Some combination of both sets of factors is required. Given this argument and the nature of African postcolonial political economies, it is not surprising that there have been few examples of sustained neoorthodox economic reform in Africa.

Economic Reform and the Implicit Bargain

Africans and external actors alike have asked how serious attempts at economic reform can be prevented from collapsing, as one such program did in dramatic fashion in Zambia in 1987 (which I will discuss). How can others that are limping along become more effective and sustainable? How can the enormous burdens of such efforts be softened or ameliorated? In a very real sense, these are classic issues of statecraft, at both the national and international levels.

Africans have long maintained that substantial resource flows and debt relief are required for sustained reform. One of the lessons of Ghana is that this is certainly a necessary but not a sufficient condition. By the late 1980s, external actors began to realize that greater resources flows and debt relief were going to be required for Africa. This realization began to sink in as the enormous obstacles to reform and the possibility of widespread failure became increasingly apparent. Whether the resource flows and debt relief will come is another matter. The special new lending facilities of the IMF and the World Bank, such as the Structural Adjustment Facility and the Enhanced Structural Adjustment Facility, are steps in that direction, but substantial support for them will be needed from all donor countries.

A larger problem exists, however, and is directly linked to Africa's increasing marginalization from the world economy. An implicit bargain has existed between the international financial institutions and the major Western countries, on the one hand, and the Africans, on the other. The provisions of the bargain are that if African countries successfully reformed their economies in a neoorthodox direction with the help and direction of the IMF and the World Bank, then new international private bank lending and direct foreign investment would be available to underpin and sustain the reform efforts.

By 1992, this implicit bargain had largely collapsed. It was not really the fault of the IMF and the World Bank, both of which have worked to increase voluntary lending and direct foreign investment, or of reforming African governments. Rather, it was due to Africa's thirty-year history of dismal economic performance, a track record that banks and investors do not forget easily, and to structural shifts in the world economy and state system that have made other areas of the world more attractive to investors. Proponents of neoorthodox reform in Africa have argued that the track record of poor performance can be overcome if Africa provides relatively predictable opportunities for profit. But even if the African end of the bargain were to be fulfilled (which is not likely), the bargain would hold only if other areas of the world did not provide better opportunities.

In a speech in March 1990, Michel Camdessus, the managing director of the IMF, provided a good description of the implicit bargain—what he called "the unwritten contract"—and, seemingly without intending to do so, of the precarious nature of it. The speech is worth quoting at length:

> In other words, we must all strive to come back to what I would call the core idea of the unwritten contract of international cooperation: that countries adopt good policies, and that these [are] supported by adequate internal and external financing. . . . Every country has responsibility for its own destiny, and the main source of its future prosperity lies in its own efforts. Foreign investment and other assistance can only supplement the actions of the country itself. . . .
>
> In view of the rapid growth in Africa's debt-servicing burden, strenuous efforts to reduce the debt overhang must continue. For the future, African countries will need to be prudent about their borrowing, both as regards its scale and terms, and be careful to use new resources wisely and efficiently, so that they contribute to growth and external viability.
>
> The availability of the traditional types of finance will be limited. But I am sure that the Fund itself will be able to continue to play successfully its role as a catalyst of international financing, if African countries come forward with economic programs that are strong enough, and credible enough, to convince Africans themselves to invest in Africa. If this occurs—and it is possible—then the banks can be expected to overcome their hesitations, to support their long-term customers, and to direct their new lending to those countries that are creating growth and good business opportunities. They will lend on a very selective basis, and within limits, although these limits may expand for countries that succeed in their adjustment efforts.
>
> Other forms of private lending can become more important. For example, there may be wider scope for direct and portfolio investment in many African countries. But this will happen only for those countries that consistently show a good economic performance, and that attract and welcome financing from abroad. This includes, not least, their own flight capital. By persevering with sound policies, any

African country can gradually increase the confidence of its own population and of foreign investors in its long-term potential. . . .

You all know that the Fund also has heavy ongoing responsibilities in the global debt strategy, and new challenges in helping Eastern European countries to reform. Despite these demands on our resources, we shall be able to continue to support all African countries that are prepared to persevere with far-reaching reforms and that back up these reforms with firm financial discipline.[11]

Note the degree to which this description of the terms of the "unwritten contract" is hedged by repeated and careful qualifications. These are a reflection of the degree of Africa's marginalization, the larger changes in the international division of labor and state system, and the enormity of the economic and political obstacles to restructuring African political economies after thirty years of decline. The message is that it is, indeed, a self-help international system and that resources will flow only to those who help themselves.

In the 1980s, Africa's share of global foreign investment was 4.5 percent; by 1990, it was only 0.7 percent. Over the last several years, net foreign direct investment for the whole region has been only about $500 million a year, or less than 1 percent of total global investment, and three-quarters of this was in the mineral sectors. In other words, only about $125 million net investment existed in the nonmineral sectors.

Even assuming that resources continue to flow at least at current levels from the IMF, the World Bank, and Western governments—if not from international private banks and investors—conditionality is likely to continue. The exceptions make this point. Between 1985 and early 1987, the Kaunda government in Zambia halfheartedly attempted to implement a very unpopular IMF-World Bank economic reform package. After deadly riots, strikes, and protests, Kenneth Kaunda terminated the program in May 1987, announcing that Zambia would formulate and implement its own reform package without external resources and the conditionality that comes with them. If Zambia after 1987 is an example of what African economic reform would look like without conditionality, Africa is in serious trouble. The tough decisions were simply not made, the economy continued to decline, and external actors essentially cut off resource flows. Economic conditionality is, then, an international fact of life and a key element of the implicit bargain. But conditionality went wild in the 1980s. By the end of the decade, overly minute and crosscutting conditionality stimulated game playing by both African and external officials that tended to undermine both the efficacy of reform and the scarce resources that existed to support it.

In addition, the capacity of African states to absorb new resources effectively can be easily overloaded. Although more resources are definitely needed to increase the chances of sustained economic reform, only so much can be absorbed, both technically and politically. Inefficient programs and renewed rent seeking are real possibilities, as the post-Kaunda democratic government of Frederick Chiluba in Zambia demonstrated in 1993. One of the ways of coping with this problem has been to use expatriates, and a striking new expatriation has quietly taken place in many African countries. In mid-1990, the head of the World Bank noted "the extraordinary fact that there are more expatriate advisors in Africa today than at the end of the colonial period. This fact is even more extraordinary, given the evidence that some $7 per head or $4 billion a year is spent on technical assistance."[12] Although this renewed expatriation has increased the technical capacity of African governments, it has also become a very sensitive political issue. In Ghana, for example, the country's largest union—the Industrial and Commercial Workers Union—demanded that the Rawlings government make public all its agreements with the IMF and the World Bank and disclose the cost of maintaining all foreign advisers. By 1993, the World Bank had made a concerted effort to cope with this problem.

Learning: The Fear of Failure

By the mid-1980s, some international officials began to realize that many efforts at economic reform in Africa would fail unless changes were made in the way in which the programs were designed and implemented. This often quite palpable fear of failure became an impetus to international learning. One senior World Bank official addressed this problem bluntly and honestly in 1987:

> The alternative—a series of failed programs in Africa—is not worth thinking about, and not only because of the human suffering. . . . The basic idea of moving to a market economy, shifting policies out of grandiosity to step-by-step solid progress, will be discredited. If they fail in a series of countries . . . then it is a failure of our approach to the economy, a failure of our institutions, a failure of our political will, and there's no way that we'll be able to say that it is just the failure of Africa! So we have a very, very big stake in this.[13]

This realization prompted some reassessment of the economic reform process, and by the end of the decade, important learning was taking place—slowly and unevenly—by both external actors and some African officials.

External officials began to realize that stop-and-go cycles of reform were a fact of life and that they needed to learn to adjust to them. Both sides became more attuned to the need for the politics of fine tuning—the more careful calibration of policy measures, instruments, pace, timing, and sequencing, especially for the sensitive issues of food, health, fuel, and wages—in order to modulate the socioeconomic and political impacts of adjustment measures and thereby increase the chances of sustained reform. Some external officials now believe, for example, that Zambia's 1985–1987 effort at reform might not have failed if these lessons had been learned earlier.

Structural adjustment is an enormously difficult and politically sensitive task in Africa, especially since the benefits are often uncertain and come quite far down the road. Reform is often complicated by other factors, such as drought, famine, civil and regional wars, destabilization, and AIDS. The hardest part to accept is that even successful neoorthodox reform will not eliminate Africa's marginality to the world economy in the short and medium runs. It might, however, begin to lessen and prevent the continent (or parts of it at least) from becoming totally unimportant to the world economy.

Although some policy lessons are being learned, Africa's problems are larger still. Even if proper policies are implemented and resources are found to support them, it is not certain that they would result in a high number of sustained, large reform efforts. A link clearly exists between debt and structural adjustment in Africa, but it is not predominantly a causal one. The need for structural adjustment long predated the debt crisis—despite the views of Adebayo Adediji with which this chapter started; the debt crisis merely brought the structural adjustment crisis to a head. Thus, even if the debt crisis were somehow miraculously solved tomorrow—through a total write-off, for example—the structural adjustment crisis would remain. The case of Nigeria has shown that massive amounts of new resources from oil can intensify rather than ameliorate economic decline.

For Africa, the task of confronting this decline is enormous, much more so than for any other region of the world. External actors have learned that Africa is a special case; it has not responded as neoclassical theory predicted it should. In 1989, the World Bank noted that:

> The supply response to adjustment lending in low-income countries, especially in SSA [sub-Saharan Africa] has been slow because of the legacy of deep-seated structural problems. Inadequate infrastructure, poorly developed markets, rudimentary industrial sectors, and severe institutional and managerial weaknesses in the public and the private sectors have proved unexpectedly serious as constraints to better performance—especially in the poorer countries of SSA. Greater recognition thus needs to be given to the time and attention needed for structural changes, especially institutional reforms and their effects.[14]

Note the revealing use of *unexpectedly:* It indicates a changed perception—that Africa is a particularly difficult case.

It is not just a case of reordering policies but rather one of constructing a whole new context—what the World Bank is now calling an "enabling environment." By the early 1980s, liberal neoorthodoxy had become, as had radical structuralism before it, explicitly linked to economic development concerns. Its two central tenets are export-led growth and a minimalist state. The new orthodoxy views the state itself as a key obstacle to development, whereas for the structuralists, the main obstacles are to be found in socioeconomic patterns, both internal and external.

For Africa, *both* sides are, in a sense, right: As the structuralists maintain, there are enormous economic and social structure obstacles to development, and as the adherents of neoorthodoxy maintain, the state is also an impediment. Moreover, both sets of obstacles inhibit import-substitution industrialization and export-oriented economic activity, public and private. The structuralists are correct that socioeconomic obstacles prevent neoclassical monoeconomics—the presumption that economic processes work the same everywhere—from being fully operative in Africa, as the World Bank has "unexpectedly" discovered, and the proponents of neoorthodoxy are correct that the nature of the state in Africa makes import-substitution industrialization ineffective and wasteful, something that many African structuralists still have not admitted.

Structuralists do have a theory of reform; it is just a weak one, however, because its instrument of reform—the state—is itself terribly ineffective in Africa. Yet in the course of attempted reform, the external proponents of neoclassical change have confronted an orthodox paradox—in order to implement such reform, they, too, have to use what they perceive to be the major obstacle to reform, the African state, as the primary instrument of that reform. Everybody knows what kind of state he or she would like to have, but nobody knows how to obtain it. Other than getting the state out of the economy, the neoclassical strategists do not have a theory of state reform, and they are finding that getting the state out of the economy is much more difficult that they expected—politically, administratively, and technically. In addition, the adherents of neoorthodoxy are learning that their own proclaimed instrument of reform, the market, is also terribly weak in Africa. Over time, it becomes increasingly clear that nobody understands the functioning of African economies; even the basic data set for the formal economy is extremely limited and unreliable, and systematic data on the informal economy are almost nonexistent.

After over thirty years of independence, most of Africa is neither effectively socialist nor capitalist; it is not even competently statist. Socialist and statist efforts have yielded few results, and modern capitalism hardly exists. Current liberalization efforts may not have a major impact in many places, and the rest of the world increasingly passes the continent by. In many ways, then, African countries are still lost between state and market, and although—as Ghana demonstrates—successful large reform is not impossible, it takes an extraordinary confluence of forces to bring it about and to sustain it.

The Debate: Into the 1990s

Despite the learning that occurred, by the end of the 1980s—with obstacles to reform apparent on all sides—the key question remained: What should Africa do to cope with its devastating economic crisis? The answer of the external actors, led by the World Bank, was to persevere with the neoorthodox thrust of reforms, with modifications to make them work in a more effective manner. Many Africans remained unconvinced. This fundamental disagreement had simmered quietly throughout the 1980s behind what appeared to many as an increasing consensus around a modified neoorthodox position.

This disagreement burst forth with surprising vigor in what could be called "the bloody spring of 1989." A major battle ensued between the World Bank and the U.N.'s Economic Commission for Africa (ECA), headed by Adediji, as the former tried to defend structural adjustment and the latter tried to attack it and present its own alternative strategy. The battle was fought around two reports: the World Bank's *Africa's Adjustment and Growth in the 1980s* and the ECA's *African Alternative Framework to Structural Adjustment Programmes.*[15] Both sides made inappropriate claims. The record of structural adjustment was not nearly as strong as the World Bank tried to make it appear; expectations were clearly out of line with hard African and international realities. On the African side, the ECA's "alternative framework" was a warmed-over version of earlier statist and "self-reliant" policies, which were vague and often contradictory and could not be implemented under the best of conditions, all linked to quite staggering demands for external resource flows. Many Africans were still running from the world economy while looking for an easy shortcut to development.

What was taken as consensus by powerful external actors was really a quiet waiting game generated by the desperate need of African countries for external resources and the hope of a major bailout through substantial debt relief, higher export prices, greatly increased bilateral and multilateral aid, commercial bank lending, or direct foreign investment. When most of these things failed to materialize, a sense of betrayal set in for many African officials.

For their part, the World Bank and other external actors had helped to generate this crisis by being unduly optimistic about the expected results of the reform efforts in order to sell them. As part of an attempt to sustain positive expectations, the bank fell victim to what I have elsewhere called the "fault of analytic hurry"—wanting to see things as real before they were.[16] The backlash from failed expectations should not have been a surprise. The time frame was too narrow, the data were unreliable, reform measures were not fully or consistently implemented, and designating strong versus weak reformers (other than for a clear-cut case such as Ghana) was arbitrary and misleading. In addition, expectations about positive outcomes have always been out of line with what could really be expected. Even if all reform measures were fully implemented in a sustained manner, the results would not be spectacular; they would be modest at best. And though modest results would be a major accomplishment, they would unfortunately not be perceived that way by most Africans.

By late 1989, the visceral emotions of the bloody spring had been substantially tamed but without resolving many of the underlying disagreements. One of the main pacifying factors was the November 1989 release by the World Bank of its long-awaited "long-term perspective study," *Sub-Saharan Africa: From Crisis to Sustainable Growth.*[17] The report demonstrated a realization on the part of the bank that it was necessary to go beyond policy change toward the construction of a more propitious context for reform. It incorporated many of the lessons derived from the experiences of the 1980s, above all the desperate need for institutional change and for a slower, more sequenced transition that recognized the sociopolitical obstacles to change. Its major themes were that Africa requires an enabling environment, more technical and administrative capacity (both state and private), and better governance.

Because the report appeared to take seriously numerous lessons of the 1980s, it was initially welcomed by many African officials. It had, after all, been drafted following quite extensive consultation with Africans from many diverse backgrounds—from government officials and entrepreneurs in both formal and informal economies to the heads of African private volunteer organizations. The welcome was reinforced by the fact that the report also appeared to represent an ambivalent and fragile shift away from the more vehement antistatist aspects of neoorthodoxy and toward a more balanced view of the relationship between state and market. It seemed to represent a tacit admission that earlier versions of neoorthodoxy had, to use Tony Killick's nice phrase, been "a reaction too far."[18]

The report sought a second-generation development strategy in which the state listens carefully to the market even if it does not precisely follow the market. Although not put in these terms, this strategy would attempt a move away from the predatory and inefficient mercantilism of the first thirty years of independence and toward a more productive and efficient, though limited, version of what some have called "benign mercantilism," that is, toward a more balanced tension between state and market.

In reality, this effort would take African political economies back to their position at the time of independence and make them work correctly this time. From the African point of view, this second-generation strategy is clearly a second-best one. The primary point remains, however, that the Africans have no viable counterfactual to this modified version of neoorthodoxy. As I have indicated, recent African efforts to provide such a counterfactual strategy are still riddled with incredible levels of state voluntarism, of the kind mentioned by Kwesi Botchwey. The current African state does not have the capabilities for the more interventionist versions of benign mercantilism represented by Korea and Taiwan. Africans can and should work in that direction, but the transition will be slow and uneven. As Goran Hyden has stressed, there really are "no shortcuts," especially to developing productive linkages to the world economy.[19] At best, current meager efforts at reform will only stem, not reverse, Africa's decline. Creative tinkering with the neoorthodox strategy both by African governments and by the IMF and the World Bank could begin to move the continent in beneficial directions; the long-term perspective study may represent a step down that road. Ultimately, though, it is not just a question of finding the precarious balance between state and market or state and society but rather searching for the precarious trialectic between state, market, and the international arena.

Nevertheless, by 1993, the debate had flared up again. The IMF and the World Bank now had to defend themselves on a wider variety of fronts, most urgently at the annual fund-bank meetings in September. Africa was a major topic of discussion because, compared to other regions, economic reform was not doing well. The IMF and the World Bank now concede that reform has been modest and that it is taking longer that they expected. They admit that in 1980–1990, half of the IMF programs broke down, as did two-thirds of the World Bank structural adjustment loans. By their own reckoning, only 1 of 26 countries with reform efforts did well in 1990–1991; in 14 others, results were only fair, and in 11 others, they were poor to very poor.

Earlier in 1993, Oxfam had issued a stinging attack on structural adjustment, entitled *Africa Make or Break: Action for Recovery,*[20] which was complemented by attacks from the Environmental Defense Fund, Development Gap, Christian Aid, and others. Oxfam declared bluntly that IMF reform in Africa had failed and that if the fund did not undergo major reform, it should withdraw from Africa. At the same time, some Western legislators also complained of the marginal reform results in Africa funded by the taxes of their citizens, and academics and Asian governments insisted that there were statist lessons to be learned from East Asian experience. In October 1993, Japan held a major conference on Africa in Tokyo, at which it pushed these views while making no new pledges of assistance. The Japanese were quite dissatisfied with a recently released World Bank report, entitled *The East Asian Miracle: Economic Growth and Public Policy,*[21] which was meant to reassess neoclassical economic views in light of Asian experience; they believed the report greatly underplayed the importance of certain types of statist policies that they think other countries, including African ones, could copy.

Although African institutions and voices did not actively participate in the debates swirling around the fund-bank meetings, it is clear that representative African views have not changed much since 1989. Structural adjustment is still largely seen as an externally imposed evil, and many Africans believe that the world should accept an African alternative *and* pay for it. This alternative perspective is evident in the statement that opened this chapter by Adebayo Adedeji, the prime mover behind the ECA's 1989 *African Alternative Framework*. In an interview in late 1993, he asserted that "structural adjustment probably contributed to [our] total economic collapse." He noted that "when we took over at independence, we did within 20 years what the colonial authorities could not so in one century. We have lost all those gains because of structural adjustment programs. . . . People should not just brush aside the African alternative. The Africans know what is good for them. The *only problem* is that because they think they need foreign exchange they are just being pushed around because they are in debt."

But what is this alternative? Has it evolved since the late 1980s, become more coherent, more viable? The answer is no. Adedeji contended: "We *want* to transform our economies, we *want* to do all those things that have made the miracle in Southeast Asia possible. The difference between us and Southeast Asian countries is that because they don't have debt, they are lucky, they did not have leaders who have borrowed so heavily as to put their nations in debt, they are not under the throes of the international financial institutions. So they can ask them to go home, and they do what they believe is in their interest. And what they are doing are the things contained in our African alternative." Besides offering a very inaccurate reading of the East Asian experience, Adedeji seems to think that if Africa's debt problems went away, African governments could do what the East Asian ones have done. This view sees debt as the cause of Africa's economic crisis rather than the reflection of much deeper problems. This contrasts vividly with a comment Adediji made earlier in the interview about his own country, Nigeria—one of the few African countries without a severe resource problem. Nigeria did not have to have a debt problem: The debt it has could have been dealt with adequately. Yet as Dr. Adediji noted, "The economy is in tatters. Nobody now thinks seriously about the economy. Things have fallen apart. The greatest tragedy of the Babangida administration is the state of paralysis into which the Nigerian economy has degenerated."[22]

Africa's problems go far beyond debt, and a viable African alternative to IMF and World Bank reform does not exist, especially given the weak state capabilities of African countries. The hard truth is that a desire for transformation does not an alternative make. An East Asian option is not possible under current conditions, although some elements of it may be applicable in the future. At present, the fund-bank strategy is a second-best option, but a modified version of it is probably the most viable alternative: As Ghana's Kwesi Botchwey is fond of saying, "Structural adjustment is very painful, but structural maladjustment is much worse."[23] This is a reflection of how hemmed in Africa really is.

I would argue that the debate was reignited in 1993 because many of the nice-sounding "lessons" of *From Crisis to Sustainable Growth,* which were meant to placate a variety of African and non-African critics, have been very difficult to implement—or the IMF and the World Bank have simply not tried to do so seriously. This is largely because structural adjustment requires very difficult trade-offs that most critics refuse to face squarely. Structural adjustment cannot be all things to all people; if it could, there would be no crisis. The lesson of the early 1990s appears to be that there are real limits to the IFI learning of the 1980s, discussed in the previous section. By late 1993, the World Bank had clearly pulled back from any move toward benign mercantilism, and hence, the battles are likely to continue. In early 1994, the World Bank released yet another report on Africa, entitled *Adjustment in Africa: Reforms, Results, and the Road Ahead*; despite many nuanced judgments, it is yet another pullback toward more orthodox views.

Governance and Democracy: The New Political Conditionality

Hence, the trialectic between state, market, and the international arena has proved to be very difficult to achieve. In part, this is because the international arena has a habit of presenting new and unexpected challenges for African rulers. Although *From Crisis to Sustainable Growth* was initially well received by many Africans, it contained a quiet time bomb—the issue of governance, which brought considerable new tension and uncertainty to relations between Africa and external actors in the first half of the 1990s. The World Bank's emphasis on governance emerged from what it had learned about the primary importance of creating a more facilitative sociopolitical context for structural adjustment in Africa. Due to the dramatic changes in the world in 1989–1990—especially in Eastern Europe and the former Soviet Union but also in Central America and South Africa—and the search for a new foreign policy thrust to replace containment (what the Clinton administration called "enlargement" of the world's free community of market democracies), governance was being transformed by the major Western industrial democracies into political conditionality focusing on the promotion of democracy. The convergence of these two policy thrusts—one largely technocratic from the World Bank, the other distinctly political from the major powers—has posed a real dilemma for African leaders.

Warnings about governance and political liberalization came from the highest levels of the international financial institutions and the most important Western industrial democracies. In April 1990, for example, Barber Conable, president of the World Bank, put the case in very blunt terms:

> The development of many Sub-Saharan African countries has been quite unnecessarily constrained by their political systems. Africans can and must tackle this issue. . . . Indisputably, three decades after independence too many African countries have failed to produce political and economic systems in which development can flourish. . . . People need freedom to realize individual and collective potential. . . . Open political participation has been restricted and even condemned, and those brave enough to speak their minds have too frequently taken grave political risks. I fear that many of Africa's leaders have been more concerned about retaining power than about the long-term development interests of their people. The cost to millions of Africans . . . has been unforgivably high.[24]

Making bilateral and IFI assistance conditional on domestic political changes greatly increases African dependence on external actors. Many African leaders fear this conditionality, including a few who are committed to economic reform. Guinea's finance minister, Soriba Kaba, for example, complained about the proliferation of conditions that African regimes have to face, "especially relating to governance and performance." As he noted, "The application of these criteria, without agreed parameters and precise definitions, may be used as a pretext to reduce the volume of resource flows to our continent."[25] Some leaders resist energetically, such as Zaire's Mobutu Sese Seko; others, such as Kenya's Daniel arap Moi and Cameroon's Paul Biya, stall while playing charades with both internal and external critics.

But is political conditionality a good idea, especially in terms of the prospects for major economic change? A serious contradiction between economic and political conditionality may, indeed, exist, one that Western governments either do not see or choose to ignore. The primary assumptions appear to be that economic structural adjustment and political liberalization are mutually reinforcing processes and that since authoritarian politics in large part caused the economic malaise, democratic politics can help change it. These may be incorrect assumptions, however; evidence from the Second and Third Worlds over the last decade certainly does not support optimism about the mutually reinforcing character of economic reform and political liberalization. This is not to say that authoritarian regimes can guarantee economic reform or even produce it very often, nor does it mean that economic reform under democratic conditions is impossible. It is just very difficult.[26]

The presumption of the mutually reinforcing character of political and economic reform in Africa relies on an extension of neoclassical economic logic: Economic liberalization creates sustained growth, growth produces winners as well as losers, and winners will organize to defend their newfound welfare and to create sociopolitical coalitions to support continued economic reform. This logic, however, does not appear to hold for Africa even under authoritarian conditions, much less under democratic ones.

As I have argued, given the evidence from Africa so far, successful economic reform requires a quite rare conjuncture of factors, such as those that have existed in Ghana since 1983. Central to that argument is the fact that successful reform comes from insulating the policy process from the rent-seeking and distributional pressures that so dominated the first thirty years of independence in Africa. Ghana under Jerry Rawlings demonstrates that successful and sustained economic reform is possible without the presence of an existing societal support coalition.

The winners of economic reform in Africa are few, appear only slowly over time, and are difficult to organize politically. The neoclassical political logic of reform is too mechanistic for the African context; there are real transaction costs to organizing winners, not just infrastructural ones. Cocoa farmers, for example, have other interests, political loyalties, and histories of organization that make direct political organization in support of a given set of economic policies difficult. Moreover, other organizational bases of political solidarity exist—ethnic, regional, religious, linguistic, and patron-client—that make mobilization around policy-specific economic interests hard to achieve. Even where farmers or other groups of Africans might so organize, they would not likely support the full range of economic measures, and the viability of reform would thereby be threatened.

In addition, no strong evidence exists to prove that African politics has shifted from distributional to productionist logics and forms of behavior. Neoorthodox economic reform in Africa is very unpopular because its political, social, and distributional effects are negative, as Ghana shows, even in the medium run. Economic learning by political leaders and societal groups is possible, but it is usually a fragile creature, requiring special circumstances to survive, and can be easily upset.

Some have argued that Africa does not have a democratic legacy, but this is not true. The democratic period right after independence, though brief, was vivid, and the reasons for its demise have not disappeared. The periodic reemergence of democratic regimes in Ghana and Nigeria since the late 1960s indicates that old patterns of political organization reappear with quite amazing vigor under conditions of free political association. Renewed democratic politics on a diminished and still-shrinking production base might be even more difficult to sustain than in the 1960s: Political liberalization is not likely to guarantee the appearance of new political alignments that favor sustained economic reform.

In fact, the progress of democratization in Africa has been very uneven, especially in its relationship to economic reform. At one end of the spectrum, Jerry Rawlings in Ghana kept his options open by resisting pressure to liberalize politically until he was ready, then he launched a rapid and controlled liberalization process. Catching the opposition off guard, he won a presidential election, and the opposition boycotted subsequent parliamentary elections. The result was a sort of one-party democracy, allowing Rawlings to continue the impressive economic reform effort. At the other end of the spectrum, the military government of General Ibrahim Babangida in Nigeria botched a long, complex, and manipulated liberalization process by abrogating presidential elections in June 1993. The resulting crisis led to General Babangida's resignation, an interim civilian government, and then yet another coup d'état in November 1993. After eight years of effort, Nigeria had neither democracy nor effective economic reform.

External actors used political conditionality in Kenya only to find it undermined by both the maneuvering of the Moi government and the inability of the opposition to come up with a single presidential candidate and slate of legislators. In Zambia, where a full transition did take place in late 1992, the new government of Frederick Chiluba was confronted with political factionalism, renewed corruption, ethnic and regional tension, and uneven economic performance despite good intentions and external help.

The case of Zambia is particularly interesting. The normal, practical realities of statecraft confronted President Chiluba with considerable difficulties. The demise of the long-running authoritarian government of Kenneth Kaunda was facilitated by the existence of only one major opposition group, the Movement for Multi-party Democracy (MMD), and a single presidential candidate. But once Chiluba took to power, it became clear that MMD was more a loose opposition coalition than a coherent party. Factionalism and corruption emerged quickly as a stringent economic reform program was instituted, with little room for a social safety net despite strong pressure from church and other "civil society" groups. In addition, Chiluba found it difficult to cut military spending as he had promised for fear of armed opposition. The combination of ethnic and regional tensions, which merged new discontents with long-suppressed conflicts, was aggravated by personal tensions and led to an increasing reliance on loyalty rather than competence in political appointments. Eventually, this brought a state of emergency and other authoritarian control measures.

These everyday political realities fed political cycles of uncertainty that were not propitious for economic reform. When linked to the lack of any tangible payoff for the electorate and the reality and perception of ruling group corruption, political logics took precedence over economic ones. Finally, all these problems were intensified by a mass expectation that democracy would end authoritarian abuse, including corruption, and bring better economic times. As one primary school teacher put it, "We thought Chiluba was our man, that he was the champion of workers, because he was the head of the ZCTU [Zambian Congress of Trade Unions]. He tells us we must sacrifice so the economy can recover, but is he sacrificing?"[27]

These tensions led to a split in MMD in August 1993, with the creation of a strong new opposition group, the National Party. Speaking about its economic program, one high party official said, "Our policy will be to continue to implement the structural adjustment program, *but* we will focus on people, prices, and production. First of all, we won't just talk about it, we will put a social safety net into practice."[28] It is not at all clear that such views are compatible with effective economic reform, however compatible they may be with democratic politics. Structural adjustment involves hard trade-offs, ones with severe political consequences.

The renewed factionalism and corruption in Zambia point to deeper problems for the relationship between democracy and economic reform in Africa. As my colleague Achille Mbembe pointed out, current political liberalization might not represent a transition to a new form of politics as much as yet another intense renegotiation of powerful older political rules and logics.[29] Central to this is the deeply embedded belief that everything is always renegotiable, reversible, and open-ended—that nothing is ever completely fixed or decided. This has long been a problem for policymaking in Africa because African countries have patrimonial administrative states. But it is particularly severe in terms of attempts at economic reform under democratic conditions. Intensified renegotiation of old and deeply rooted political norms—not political or economic transformation—appears to be under way in those parts of Africa with some form of political liberalization.

Is this version of the "thesis of the perverse effect"[30]—that political liberalization might have a negative impact on the chances for sustained economic reform—likely to hold across the board for Africa? No, it is not. It is important to assess particular countries, but a probabilistic, not a deterministic, perverse effect is likely to operate. If not handled properly, political conditionality might impede rather than facilitate the productive relinking of Africa to the world economy. The widespread emergence of what Richard L. Sklar has called "developmental democracies" is not likely to be seen anytime soon in Africa.[31]

Finally, the actions of Western governments in individual African countries and in other areas of the world will be important. The major powers' decision, for example, in November 1993 to renew assistance flows to the Moi government in Kenya and the refusal to cut off arms sales to the Nigerian military after the coup d'état by General Sani Abacha makes Africans cynical about Western intentions. Likewise, many Africans see external support for Boris Yeltsin's accumulation of executive power in Russia and his manipulation of constitutional and electoral practices, largely in hopes of getting more coherent economic reform, as highly hypocritical—using one standard for strategically important Russia and another for marginal and dependent Africa.

Prospects for the Future

Given the enormous constraints discussed here, with or without political conditionality, what are the prospects that African countries will engage successfully in economic reform and establish more effective linkages to the world economy? The answer appears to be that simultaneous marginalization and dependence are likely to continue and probably increase for most countries. A few—with hard work, propitious facilitating circumstances, and luck—may begin to lessen their marginalization from the world economy and their dependence on the IMF and the World Bank. Differentiation among African states, already long evident, may well increase. A few will stay in the Third World and do relatively better economically, but most will continue to descend into the Fourth and Fifth Worlds—fulfilling the ECA's own nightmare scenario.[32] The countries that are likely to do better are those that are already move advantaged, partly because of better performance since the early 1960s—Kenya, Ivory Coast, Cameroon, Nigeria, Zimbabwe, and possibly Senegal. Even these cases are fragile, however, as has become evident since the late 1980s, largely for political reasons. A very small number of countries in serious decline, such as Ghana, may be able to reverse course, but their prospects are even more fragile.

A quiet debate about Africa under these circumstances is under way among Western officials and businesspeople about what to do with Africa: Do you provide some resources to all countries across the board to create a sort of international social safety net for declining countries, who then become de facto wards of the world community? Or, as one Western official put it to me, do you "pick a few and work with them"?[33] Under the first option, it is not at all clear how effective an international safety net would be. Under the second option, countries would be chosen that have some eventual prospect for better and sustained economic performance and possibly some strategic importance—Nigeria and Zimbabwe, for example; resources would then be concentrated in these countries. Obviously, it is a tough world, and it will probably become more so as the last decade of the century unfolds.

Continued assistance from the major powers at 1980s' levels is in doubt. In the early 1980s, external assistance was growing at about 5 percent a year; by the end of the decade, it was beginning to stagnate. In 1993, France, Germany, and Sweden announced some cuts in assistance to Africa, and the United States planned cuts in assistance and missions as part of the Clinton administration's ongoing restructuring of the Agency for International Development (AID). The agency's new director, J. Brian Atwood, observed that "we were just spread too thin. We were an agency on the road to mediocrity or worse."[34] Limits to Western assistance were reflected in the 1993 debate over whether and how to renew the IMF's Enhanced Structural Adjustment Facility (ESAF), which has provided resources to low-income countries at lower rates and longer terms. Reflecting the economic and political difficulties of the industrial democracies and the increasing tensions among them over sharing the burden for assistance, Britain threatened not to provide any resources for ESAF, and Germany said it could give only modest support. Britain called for the sale of some of the IMF's gold reserves to support the ESAF, a move flatly rejected by the other countries, and it continued to push its "Trinidad terms" proposal for more generous debt relief, again to little avail. In addition, the French government, with its strong franc policy due to European Community and domestic politics, found itself under intense pressure to devalue the greatly overvalued CFA franc, which would negatively affect economic reform in francophone Africa.[35]

The trajectory of individual countries will be affected by both internal and external factors. On the internal side, the degree of effective "stateness"—the technical and administrative capabilities to formulate *and* implement rational economic policies—will be crucial. On average, Africa has the lowest level of state capabilities and overall development of any region in the world. But as the IMF and the World Bank have begun to realize, it takes a relatively capable state to implement successful neoorthodox economic reform consistently over time. High degrees of stateness are central to better position a country in the international political economy; above all, a country needs the ability to bargain with all types of actors—private business groups, states, and the international financial institutions. Whether increased stateness will emerge in many places, however, is very questionable. Certainly, political dynamics will play a central role in achieving a productive, balanced tension between state and market and between state and society. Some African leaders have begun to understand this. They know that, at bottom, it is a self-help world and that one should not wait for external miracles. As President Chiluba of Zambia put it recently: "One of the greatest refrains in Africa's vocabulary has been [that] the poor state of our economies and politics are a creation of forces external to the African continent. Yes, Africa was dominated and there is a legacy of that domination, especially the dependency syndrome. However, a new generation of Africans is saying to all of us leaders, and indeed to all Africans at large, that it is high time we internalized our criticism. No one else is going to solve our problems."[36] But Chiluba's experience since coming to power in late 1992 only underscores how difficult it will be for Africa's "new generation," especially under democratic conditions.

Although it is largely a self-help world, external factors affecting country trajectories are also very important. They revolve around two central issues: (1) the degree of openness of the world political economy, and (2) the degree to which the implicit bargain discussed earlier is fulfilled. John Gerard Ruggie has characterized the current international political economy as one of "embedded liberalism," in which the relative international economic openness of the postwar era is maintained by the major Western countries intervening in their own domestic arenas to buffer the costs of adjusting to shifts in the world economy. A precarious openness, based on liberal economic norms, is maintained despite increasing tensions. Others, such as Robert Gilpin, see the world moving toward an increasingly conflictual and closed international political economy, which might be characterized as "malign mercantilism." Still other analysts—Kenneth Oye and Susan Strange, for example—do not dispute the assessment that the international political economy is moving in a more mercantilist direction, but they do dispute its effect on openness. According to them, the world has always been more mercantilist than liberal theorists have maintained, and they feel that considerable openness can be sustained as liberal economic norms continue to recede in practice, if not in rhetoric. They stress the importance of bilateral bargaining and a regionalization of the world economy as crucial to maintaining openness in the world economy. Again, the role of the state is absolutely essential.[37]

Africa's prospects under a shift from embedded liberalism to malign mercantilism would not be very bright. Despite its marginalization and dependence, the continent desperately needs openness in the world economy: In fact, the neo-orthodox adjustment strategy is predicated on it. Whether some form of benign mercantilism would benefit Africa is very open to question.

Prospects for fulfillment of the implicit bargain may not be much brighter, however. As private actors in the world economy increasingly pass Africa by, Western countries—even with declining interest—and the international financial institutions will continue to play central roles. If African countries are to have any chance of making economic progress, these actors must help to fulfill this bargain, primarily through increased aid levels and substantial debt relief. Given the domestic politics of Western industrial democracies, debt relief might be the easier route to take, for it is more politically malleable. Since resources are scarce, aid and debt relief should be given only to those actually undertaking these difficult changes, and such assistance should not be tied automatically to political conditionality. It is not clear, however, how many reformist rulers the external actors can actually support at the level required for sustained economic change. Since such reform is difficult, stop-and-go cycles are a fact of life, and external actors must learn to adjust to them. Some lessons have been learned, and creative proposals have been put forward for Zambia since it ended its externally sponsored reform effort in May 1987. But the progress has been halting. The primary obstacle is how to cope with a huge debt overhang and substantial arrears to the IMF and the World Bank without setting precedents with worldwide implications.

Finally, external actors should avoid the "faults of analytic and policy hurry" and not create undue expectations about what can be achieved in Africa over the medium run. Given the enormous obstacles confronting African countries, overly optimistic expectations can be very dangerous. Slow, steady, consistent progress is far preferable, and there are no shortcuts. The lessons of the development administration movement of the late 1960s and 1970s should not be forgotten: Productive change in state capabilities and contextual variables comes about very slowly and unevenly. Neither international nor African policymakers can unduly hasten or control social processes such as institution and capacity building. Given that change is incremental, uneven, often contradictory, and dependent on the outcome of unpredictable socioeconomic and political struggles, policymakers—both international and African—must try to bring about important changes, but they must retain a sense of the historical complexity involved. If they do not, unwarranted expectations can get in the way of making slow but steady progress over difficult obstacles. Today's policy fads can easily become tomorrow's failed initiatives.[38]

Despite the 1993 pullback toward a more narrow orthodoxy, external actors need to work closely with Africans to find ways to effectively implement the lessons learned from the experience with structural adjustment in the 1980s— lessons apparent in the World Bank's long-term perspective study. If not, adjustment with a human face, capacity building, and governance will just become the latest in passing international fancies. *Policy dialogue,* another of the current buzzwords, is used mostly by external actors to suggest that intensified consultation with a reforming government will lead to more effective adjustment because it will then "own" the reforms. Policy dialogue is based, however, on the tacit assumptions that greater discussion leads to greater agreement and that the parties who need to be convinced are the African actors. In truth, though, more consultation does not necessarily increase agreement, and policy dialogue can therefore only be effective if both sides are willing to learn and give ground.

One sector that has been most subject to the "faults of analytic and policy hurry" is the informal economy. Undue expectations about the salvation potential of the informal economy and the ability of policymakers to relink it effectively to the formal economy, including the world economy, should be avoided. The informal economy *is* one of the bright spots on the African scene: Entrepreneurial groups might emerge from it and possibly provide the basis of the coalitional support needed to sustain economic reform, reorder the state, and link African countries to the world economy more productively. But this will not happen overnight, easily, or evenly.[39] Africa is caught between a rock and a hard place in regard to the world political economy, and all actors will have to work very hard to alter that fact. But try they must, for not trying could have even worse consequences for Africa's long-suffering peoples.

Notes

1. Quoted in Margaret A. Novicki, "Interview with Adebayo Adediji: Democracy and Development," *Africa Report* 38, no. 6 (November-December 1993), p. 60. For both descriptive and statistical purposes, *Africa* as used in this chapter refers to sub-Saharan Africa minus South Africa.

2. Ralph Austen, *African Economic History* (London: James Currey, 1987), pp. 102, 109.

3. The economic and financial data in this chapter come from: the 1989–1993 editions of World Bank, *World Development Report* (Washington, D.C.: World Bank, 1989–1993); the 1991–1993 editions of World Bank, *Global Economic Prospects and the Developing Countries* (Washington, D.C.: World Bank, 1991–1993); World Bank, *Sub-Saharan Africa: From Crisis to Sustainable Growth* (Washington, D.C.: World Bank, 1989); World Bank, *Africa's Adjustment and Growth in the 1980s* (Washington, D.C.: World Bank, 1989); *IMF Survey* 22, no. 19 (October 11, 1993); other IMF and World Bank documents; *Financial Times* (London) surveys "Africa: A Continent at Stake," September 1, 1993, and "IMF: World

Economy and Finance," September 24, 1993; Department of Public Information, "African Debt Crisis: A Continuing Impediment to Development" (New York: United Nations, 1993); and various issues of *Africa Recovery* (New York: United Nations) and the *Financial Times* (London).

4. Author's confidential interview with the business executive, New York, April 26, 1990.

5. B. A. Kiplagat, quoted in "Africa Fears Its Needs Will Become Secondary," *New York Times*, December 26, 1989; also see Marguerite Michaels, "Retreat from Africa," *Foreign Affairs* 72, no. 1 (1993), pp. 93–108.

6. See Gerald Bender, James S. Coleman, and Richard L. Sklar, eds., *African Crisis Areas and U.S. Foreign Policy* (Berkeley: University of California Press, 1985).

7. See Thomas M. Callaghy, "Vision and Politics in the Transformation of the Global Political Economy: Lessons from the Second and Third Worlds," in Robert O. Slater, Barry Schutz, and Steven R. Dorr, eds., *Global Transformation and the Third World* (Boulder: Lynne Rienner Publishers, 1993), pp. 161–257.

8. See Thomas M. Callaghy and John Ravenhill, eds., *Hemmed In: Responses to Africa's Economic Decline* (New York: Columbia University Press, 1993).

9. Quoted in "Ghana: High Stakes Gamble," *Africa News* 31, no. 2 (January 23, 1989), p. 10.

10. For a more detailed analysis of the Ghana case, see Thomas M. Callaghy, "Lost Between State and Market: The Politics of Economic Adjustment in Ghana, Zambia, and Nigeria," in Joan M. Nelson, ed., *Economic Crisis and Policy Choice* (Princeton: Princeton University Press, 1990), pp. 257–319; Donald Rothchild, ed., *Ghana: The Political Economy of Recovery* (Boulder: Lynne Rienner Publishers, 1991); and Jeffrey Herbst, *The Politics of Reform in Ghana, 1982–1991* (Berkeley: University of California Press, 1993).

11. Excerpts from the speech are reprinted in *IMF Survey* 19, no. 7 (1990), pp. 108–111, emphases added.

12. Barber B. Conable, "Address as Prepared for Delivery to the Bretton Woods Conference on Africa's Finance and Development Crisis," Washington, D.C., April 25, 1990, World Bank mimeograph, p. 3.

13. Quoted in Margaret A. Novicki, "Interview with Edward V.K. Jaycox," *Africa Report* 32, no. 6 (November-December 1987), p. 32.

14. World Bank, *Adjustment Lending* (Washington, D.C., World Bank, 1988), p. 3, emphases added.

15. World Bank, *Sub-Saharan Africa*; United Nations Economic Commission for Africa (ECA), *African Alternative Framework to Structural Adjustment Programmes for Socioeconomic Recovery and Transformation* (Addis Ababa: ECA, 1989).

16. Thomas M. Callaghy, "State and the Development of Capitalism in Africa," in Donald Rothchild and Naomi Chazan, eds., *The Precarious Balance: State and Society in Africa* (Boulder: Westview Press, 1988), p. 92.

17. World Bank, *Sub-Saharan Africa*.

18. Tony Killick, *A Reaction Too Far* (Boulder: Westview Press, 1990).

19. Goran Hyden, *No Shortcuts to Progress* (Berkeley: University of California Press, 1983).

20. Oxfam, *Africa Make or Break: Action for Recovery* (London: Oxfam, 1993).

21. World Bank, *The East Asian Miracle: Economic Growth and Public Policy* (Washington, D.C.: World Bank, 1993).

22. All quoted in Novicki, "Interview with Adebayo Adediji," pp. 59–60.

23. Quoted in Edward Balls, "Structural Maladjustment and the CFA Franc," *Financial Times* (London), November 15, 1993.

24. Conable, "Address," pp. 2–3.

25. Quoted in "The IMF and the World Bank: Arguing About Africa," *Africa Confidential* 34, no. 20 (October 8, 1993), p. 3.

26. For an expanded version of this argument, see Thomas M. Callaghy, "Political Passions and Economic Interests: Economic Reform and Political Structure," in Thomas M. Callaghy and John Ravenhill, eds., *Hemmed In: Responses to Africa's Economic Decline* (New York: Columbia University Press, 1993), pp. 463–519.

27. Quoted in Melinda Ham, "Zambia: An Outspoken Opposition," *Africa Report* 38, no. 6 (November-December 1993), p. 33.

28. Ibid.

29. Achille Mbembe, "Des figures du sujet en postcolonie," paper, University of Pennsylvania, October 1993.

30. On the "thesis of the perverse effect," see Albert O. Hirschman, "Reactionary Rhetoric," *Atlantic Monthly* 263, no. 5 (May 1989), pp. 63–70.

31. See Richard L. Sklar, "Democracy in Africa," in Patrick Chabal, ed., *Political Domination in Africa* (Cambridge: Cambridge University Press, 1986), pp. 17–29.

32. On the "nightmare scenario," see ECA, "ECA and Africa's Development: 1983–2008," Addis Ababa, April 1983, and "Beyond Recovery: ECA—Revised Perspective of Africa's Development," Addis Ababa, March 1988.

33. Author's confidential interview with the Western official, Washington, D.C., May 4, 1990.

34. Quoted in "U.S. Agency for Development Plans to Cut Aid to 35 Nations," *New York Times,* November 20, 1993.

35. See Nicolas van de Walle, "The Decline of the Franc Zone: Monetary Politics in Francophone Africa," *African Affairs,* no. 90 (July 1991), pp. 383–405, and two papers presented at the 1993 meeting of the African Studies Association, Boston, December 4–7, 1993: Nicolas van de Walle, "Economic Ideas and Structural Adjustment in Francophone Africa," and David Stasavage, "The Politics of Monetary Union in the Franc Zone."

36. Quoted in "'No One Else Will Solve Our Problems,' Chiluba Tells OAU," *Africa News* 36, no. 7 (August 3–16, 1993), p. 6.

37. See John Gerard Ruggie, "International Regimes, Transactions and Change," *International Organization* 36, no. 2 (Spring 1982), pp. 379–415; Robert Gilpin, *The Political Economy of International Relations* (Princeton: Princeton University Press, 1987); Kenneth A. Oye, *Economic Discrimination and Political Exchange: World Political Economy in the 1930s and the 1980s* (Princeton: Princeton University Press, 1992); and Susan Strange, "Protectionism and World Politics," *International Organization* 36, no. 2 (Spring 1982), pp. 417–455, and *States and Markets* (New York: Blackwell, 1988).

38. For a look at changing scholarly views on Africa, see David E. Apter and Carl G. Rosberg, "Changing African Perspectives," in Apter and Rosberg, eds., *Political Development and the New Realism in Sub-Saharan Africa* (Charlottesville: University Press of Virginia, 1994), pp. 1–57, and Thomas M. Callaghy, "State, Choice, and Context: Comparative Reflections on Reform and Intractability," in the same volume, pp. 184–219.

39. On the informal economy, see Janet MacGaffey, *Entrepreneurs and Parasites: The Struggle for Indigenous Capitalism in Zaire* (Cambridge: Cambridge University Press, 1987).

4

Africa and Other Civilizations: Conquest and Counterconquest

ALI A. MAZRUI

Introduction: Cultural Receptivity

ONE OF THE MOST INTRIGUING aspects of the historical sociology of Africa in recent times has been its remarkable cultural receptivity. For example, Christianity has spread faster in a single century in Africa than it did in several countries in Asia. Similarly, European languages have acquired political legitimacy in Africa more completely than they have ever done in formerly colonized Asian countries like India, Indonesia, and Vietnam. Indeed, though nobody talks about "English-speaking Asian countries" or "francophone Asia," African countries are routinely categorized in terms of which particular European language they have adopted as their official medium (lusophone, English-speaking, and francophone African states).

North Africa and much of the Nile Valley were not only converted to the Muslim religion, millions of the inhabitants were also linguistically transformed into Arabs. Elsewhere in Africa, the Muslim faith has continued to make new converts in spite of the competitive impact of Euro-Christian colonial rule following the Berlin conference of 1884–1885.

Linguistic nationalism favoring indigenous languages in postcolonial Africa has been relatively weak, and only a handful of African countries allocate much money toward developing African languages for modern needs. However, most African governments south of the Sahara give high priority to the teaching of European languages in African schools.

No African country has officially allocated a national holiday in honor of the gods of indigenous religions. But all African countries have a national holiday celebrating either Christian festivals (especially Christmas) or Muslim festivals (e.g., Idd el Fitr) or perhaps even both categories of imported festivals. The Semitic religions (Christianity and Islam) are nationally honored in much of Africa; the indigenous religions are, at best, ethnic occasions, certainly not national ones.

Toward Conquering the Conquerors

Africa's readiness to welcome new cultures is both a strength and a weakness. There is an African preparedness to learn from others, but there is also a looming danger in Africa's dependency and intellectual imitation. But what has so often been overlooked is the third dimension of this equation. Africa's cultural receptivity can over the years make others dependent on Africa, for there is a cyclic dynamic at play. Those who have culturally conquered Africa have, over time, become culturally dependent upon Africa: The biter has sometimes been bitten; the conqueror has sometimes been counterconquered. Africa has sometimes counterpenetrated the citadels of its own conquerors. This chapter is about this boomerang effect in acculturation and assimilation.

This process of Africa's counterpenetration has at times been facilitated by Africa's political fragmentation in the egalitarian age. The majority of the members of the nonaligned movement, for example, are from Africa, and almost half the members of the Organization of the Islamic Conference are also members of the Organization of African Unity. Furthermore, much of the agenda of the Commonwealth since the 1960s has been set by its African members—as they have used the "Britannic" fraternity to help liberate southern Africa and dismantle apartheid. Although African countries comprise only a third of the fifty members of the Commonwealth (including Namibia), they have been by far the most influential regional group in shaping its agenda and decisions. Now, African influence has been enhanced by the election of the first African secretary-general of the Commonwealth, Chief Eleazar Emeka Anyaoku of Nigeria. South Africa's readmission under majority rule will bring the whole story full circle.

In the United Nations, countries from Africa also represented almost one-third of the total global membership until the Soviet Union and Yugoslavia collapsed. For a period of time, Africa's fragmentation in an egalitarian age had augmented its voting power in the U.N. General Assembly. Africa's percentage of the total membership has declined in the 1990s.

However, there are limits to the egalitarianism of the age in terms of power. The United States almost single-handedly prevented the election of the first African secretary-general of the United Nations, Ambassador Salim Ahmed Salim of Tanzania, and, in concert with Great Britain, it also succeeded in hounding out of power the first African director-general of UNESCO, Moukhtar M'Bow. Even in this relatively egalitarian age in human history, real power continues to be decisive—when there is enough at stake to invoke it.

Nevertheless, even Africa's weakness has—on other occasions—been a source of power. As I indicated, the continent's territorial fragmentation has translated into voting influence even in UNESCO, in spite of what happened to M'Bow.

And the U.N. General Assembly continues to take into account the liberation concerns of the African group.

Similarly, cultural receptivity—though often excessive and a cause of Africa's intellectual dependency—has sometimes become the basis of Africa's counterinfluence on those who have conquered it. This report about Africa's counterpenetration is illustrative rather than exhaustive. I shall examine Africa's relationship with two interrelated civilizations—Arab and Islamic—and then study the French connection as an illustration of Africa's potential in counterinfluencing the Western world. I will then look at Africa's interaction with India, with special reference to the legacies of Mahatma Gandhi and Jawaharlal Nehru. I shall conclude with Africa's conquest of Africa—the full circle of autocolonization.

The Arab factor in Africa's experience illustrates the politics of *identity*; just as the Islamic factor illustrates the politics of *religion*. With the French connection, we enter the politics of *language,* and the Afro-Indian interaction involves the politics of *liberation*. Finally, I will examine the future politics of *self-conquest*. Let us now turn to the five case studies (Afro-Arab, Afro-Islamic, Afro-French, Afro-Indian, and Afro-African) in greater detail.

Africa Conquers the Arabs

In the seventh century A.D., parts of Africa were captured by the Arabs in the name of Islam. Three factors speeded up the Arabization of north Africa and the lower Nile Valley. One factor was, indeed, Africa's cultural receptivity—a remarkable degree of assimilability. The second factor that facilitated Arabization was the Arab lineage system and how it defined the offspring of mixed marriages. The third factor behind Arabization was the spread of the Arabic language and its role in defining what constitutes an Arab.

At first glance, the story is a clear case of how the Arabs took over large chunks of Africa, but on closer scrutiny, the Afro-Arab saga is a story of both conquest and counterconquest. It is comparable to the story of the role played by the British in colonizing North America: Much later, imperial Britain was being protected and led by its former colonies, the United States of America.

But there is one important difference in the case of reciprocal conquest between the Arabs and the Africans—the actual creation of new Arabs is still continuing. Let us examine this remarkable process of "Arab formation" in Africa across the centuries more closely.

The Arab conquest of north Africa in the seventh and eighth centuries initiated two processes: Arabization (through language) and Islamization (through religion). The spread of Arabic as a native language created new Semites (the Arabs of north Africa). Meanwhile, the diffusion of Islam created new monotheists but not necessarily new Semites: The Copts of Egypt are linguistically Arabized, but they are not, of course, Muslims. On the other hand, the Wolof and Hausa are preponderantly Islamized, but they are not Arabs.

The process by which the majority of north Africans became Arabized was partly biological and cultural. The biological process involved intermarriage and was considerably facilitated by the upward lineage system of the Arabs. Basically, if the father of a child is an Arab, the child is an Arab—regardless of the ethnic or racial origins of the mother. This lineage system could be described as *ascending miscegenation,* since the offspring ascends to the more privileged parent.

This is in sharp contrast to the lineage system of a country such as the United States, where the child of a white father and a black mother actually descends to the less privileged race in that society. Indeed, in a system of descending miscegenation like that of the United States, it does not matter whether it is the father or the mother who is black. An offspring of such a racial mixture descends to black underprivilege. The U.S. system therefore does not co-opt "impurities" upward across the racial barrier to high status; it pushes "impurities" downward into the pool of disadvantage.

It is precisely because the Arabs have the opposite lineage system (ascending miscegenation) that north Africa was so rapidly transformed into part of the Arab world (and not merely the Muslim world). The Arab lineage system permitted considerable racial co-optation. "Impurities" were admitted to higher echelons as new full members—provided their fathers were Arabs. And so, colors in the Arab world range from the whites of Syria and Iraq to the browns of Yemen, from blonde-haired Lebanese to the black Arabs of Sudan.

Within Africa, the valley of the White Nile is a particularly fascinating story of evolving Arabization. The Egyptians, of course, were not Arabs when the Muslim conquest occurred in the seventh century A.D. The process of Islamization in the sense of an actual change of religion took place fairly rapidly after the Arab conquerors had consolidated their hold on the country. The Arabization of Egypt, however, turned out to occur significantly more slowly than its Islamization. The Egyptians changed their religious garment from Christianity to Islam more quickly than they changed their linguistic garment from ancient Egyptian and ancient Greek to Arabic. And even when Arabic became the mother tongue of the majority of Egyptians, it took centuries before Egyptians began to call themselves Arabs.

But this is all relative. When one considers the pace of Arabization in the first millennium of Islam, it was still significantly faster than average in the history of human acculturation. The number of people in the Middle East who called themselves Arabs expanded dramatically in a relatively short period. This was partly because of the exuberance of the new religion, partly because of the rising prestige of the Arabic language, and partly due to the rewards of belonging to a conquering civilization. Religious, political, and psychological factors transformed Arabism into an expansionist culture that absorbed the conquered into the body politic of the conquerors. In the beginning, there was an "island" or a peninsula called Arabia. But in time, there were far more Arabs outside Arabia than within. At the end of it all, there was an "Arab world."

Along the valley of the White Nile, northern Sudan was also gradually Islamized—and more recently, it has been increasingly Arabized. Again, a people who were not originally Arabs have come to see themselves more and more as Arabs.

The question that arises is whether there is a manifest destiny of the White Nile—pushing it toward further Arabization. It began with the Egyptians and their gradual acquisition of an Arab identity. The northern Sudanese have been in the process of similar Arabization. Are the southern Sudanese the next target of the conquering wave of Arabization over the next one hundred to two hundred years? Will the twin forces of biological mixture (intermarriage between northerners and southerners) and cultural assimilation transform the Dinkas and Nuers of today into the black Arabs of tomorrow?

It is not inconceivable, provided the country, as a whole, holds together. As intermarriage increases, northern Sudanese will become more black in color, and as acculturation increases in the south, southerners will become more Arab. Biological Africanization of the north and cultural Arabization of the south will reinforce each other and help to forge a more integrated Sudan.

Southern Sudanese are the only sub-Saharan Africans who are being Arabized faster than they are being Islamized: They are acquiring the Arabic language faster than they are acquiring Islam. This is in sharp contrast to the experience of such sub-Saharan peoples as the Wolof, the Yoruba, the Hausa, or even the Somali—among all of whom the religion of Islam has been more triumphant than the language of the Arabs. This rapid Arabization of the southern Sudanese linguistically has two possible outcomes in the future. The southern Sudanese could become Sudan's equivalent of the Copts of Egypt—a Christian minority whose mother tongue would then be Arabic. Or the Arabization of the southern Sudanese could be followed by their religious Islamization—in time, making southern and northern Sudanese truly intermingled and eventually indistinguishable.

Meanwhile, the Swahili language has been creeping northward toward Juba from east Africa as surely as Arabic has been creeping southward from the Mediterranean. As a result, the Swahilization of Tanzania, Kenya, Uganda, and eastern Zaire has been gathering momentum. With Arabic coming up the Nile toward Juba and Kiswahili down the same valley, southern Sudanese will find themselves caught between the forces of Arabization and the forces of Swahilization. Historically, these two cultures (Arab and Swahili) can so easily reinforce each other, and because of this pattern of trends, the manifest destiny of the valley of the White Nile appears to be a slow but definite assimilation into the Arab fold over the next century or two.

But racial ambivalence will maintain a linkage with Africanity. Indeed, the southern Sudanese are bound to be the most negritudist of all Sudanese—even if they do become Arabized. There is a precedent of black nationalism even among northern Sudanese, and it is not often realized how much "negritude" sentiment there is among important sectors of northern Sudanese opinion. Muhammad al-Mahdi al-Majdhub has been described as "probably the first Sudanese poet to tap the possibility of writing poetry in the Arabic language with a consciousness of a profound belonging to a 'Negro' tradition."[1] The poet al-Mahdi has, indeed, affirmed: "In the Negroes I am firmly rooted though the Arabs may boastfully claim my origin. . . . My tradition is: beads, feathers, and a palm-tree which I embrace, and the forest is singing around us."[2]

Muhammad Miftah al-Fayturi is another Arab negritudist. Information about his ancestry is somewhat contradictory. His father was probably Libyan, and his mother was Egyptian but of southern Sudanese ancestry. In his words:

> Do not be a coward
> Do not be a coward
> say it in the face
> of the human race:
> My father is of a Negro father,
> My mother is a Negro woman,
> and I am black.[3]

In some notes about al-Fayturi's early poetic experiences, there is his anguished cry: "I have unriddled the mystery, the mystery of my tragedy: I am short, black and ugly."

Then there are the Arab negritudists who sometimes revel in the fact that they are racially mixed. They can also be defiant and angrily defensive about their mixture. Salah A. Ibrahim, in his piece on "The Anger of the Al-Hababy Sandstorm," declared: "Liar is he who proclaims:/'I am the unmixed. . . .' Yes, a liar!"[4] In the Sudan of the future, there may be even less room for such "lies" than there is at present. After all, Arabization is, almost by definition, a process of creating mixture—and its relentless force along the White Nile is heading southward toward Juba and beyond.

How has the boomerang effect worked in relation to the Arabization of Africa? In what sense has there been an Africanization of the Arab world? In what way has the whole process been cyclic?

It is worth reminding ourselves that the majority of the Arab people are in Africa. Over 60 percent of the population of the Arab world is now west of the Red Sea, on African soil. The largest Arab country in population is Egypt—which in 1989 and 1993, became the presiding country in the Organization of African Unity, while its president was, at the same time, seeking a resolution of the Palestinian-Israeli impasse during both years.

The headquarters of the Arab League is in Africa. From 1979 to 1989, it was located in Tunis, having previously been located in Cairo; in 1990, it was decided to return the league headquarters to Cairo. If the headquarters of the Arab League symbolizes the capital of the entire Arab world, then the capital of the Arabs in the second half of the twentieth century has been located on the African continent.

When the Palestine Liberation Organization and its warriors were expelled from Lebanon by the Israeli military invasion of 1982, the headquarters of the Palestinian movement also moved to Africa. Major decisions about the Palestinians, including the declaration of the Palestinian state, are now made on African soil—from Tunis. Partly because of this evolving Afro-Palestinian solidarity,

Yassir Arafat was in Lusaka in 1990 to embrace Nelson Mandela when the latter made his first trip outside South Africa in thirty years.

The largest city in the Arab world—Cairo—is located on its African side, and the population of this city exceeds the population of Saudi Arabia as a whole. Cairo also has become the cultural capital of the Arab world. The greatest singers and musicians of the Arab world—including the incredible Umm Kulthum, affectionately known as "the Star at Sunrise"—used to mesmerize the Middle East from the studios of the Voice of the Arabs Broadcasting System in Cairo. Israelis even invented yet another anti-Arab joke in this regard—"O yes, the Arabs have at last found unity—every Thursday night when they all tune in to listen to the voice of Umm Kulthum." Her funeral was second only to President Gamal Abdel Nasser's burial in 1970 in terms of the size of the crowds and the passions and public grief displayed.

The most famous Arab musical composer of the twentieth century has also come from the African side of the Arab world. Al-Ustadh Muhammad Abdul Wahab was, in his younger days, primarily a singer and instrumentalist. His musical compositions were initially modest, though they suited his vocal power. After deeper study of Western classical music—with special reference to Beethoven—Muhammad Abdul Wahab took Egyptian music to new levels of cross-cultural complexity and developed new styles of Arab orchestral and even symphonic music.

Culture has its technological and professional infrastructure, as well, and Egypt is by far the most important film-making country in both Africa and the Arab world. Egyptian shows feature prominently on cinema screens and television programs on both sides of the Red Sea.

Other skills of the Arab people also disproportionately emanate from the African side. Boutros Boutros-Ghali, when he was Egypt's minister of state for foreign affairs, estimated that as many as two million Egyptians were sometimes scattered across the region providing technical assistance to other Arab countries.[5] Boutros-Ghali later became secretary-general of the United Nations.

All this is quite apart from the importance of Egypt in the Arab military equation in at least four of the Arab-Israeli wars. Until the 1973 war, the Arab armies were no match for the Israelis, and even in 1973, Arab triumphs occurred mainly at the beginning of the conflict. What is clear, however, is that the nearest thing to a credible Arab military force in these conflicts came from the African side of the Arab region. This is why the United States invested so heavily in the Camp David Accords and the neutralization of Egypt as a "confrontation state" against Israel.

In the year 639 A.D., the Arabs had crossed into Africa and conquered Egypt. By the second half of the twentieth century, Egypt had become the most important pillar of the military defense of the Arab world. Thus, history has once again played its cyclic boomerang game in the interaction between Africa and its conquerors. And as a result, the ancestral home of the Arabs in Asia is now heavily dependent, culturally and militarily, on the African side of the Arab nation.

In His infinite wisdom, Allah has thus far permitted the ancestral home of Islam—Saudi Arabia—to retain a preponderance of oil reserves and petro power.

Perhaps only the petro factor has prevented the African side of the Arab nation from attaining complete preponderance. Arabized Africa now leads the way demographically, culturally, technologically, militarily, and artistically. Allah has permitted the birthplace of the prophet Muhammad to lead the way in petro power for the time being.

Africa: The First Islamic Continent?

Why are Islam and Christianity continuing to spread so fast in sub-Saharan Africa? Why has *religious* receptivity in Africa been so remarkable?

The spread of Christianity during Africa's colonial period was particularly spectacular. The Christian gospel spread faster in a single century in Africa than it did in several centuries in places like India and China. (Indeed, Christianity in southern India is almost two thousand years old—going back to the days of the disciples of Jesus, yet to the present day, the Christian population in the whole of India is little more than 20 million in a country with a total population of 850 million.[6]) There is a chance that Africa will become to Islam what Europe has been to Christianity—the first continent to have a preponderance of believers. Europe was the first continent with a majority of Christians. Is Africa becoming the first continent to have a majority of Muslims?

Since independence, two issues have been central to religious speculation in Africa: Islamic expansion and Islamic revivalism. Expansion involves the spread of religion and its scale of new conversions. Revivalism concerns the rebirth of faith among those who are already converted. Expansion is a matter of geography and populations in search of new worlds to conquer. Revivalism is a matter of history and nostalgia in search of ancient worlds to reenact. The spread of Islam in postcolonial Africa is basically a peaceful process of persuasion and consent. The revival of Islam is often an angry process of rediscovered "fundamentalism."

In Arab Africa, there is little expansion taking place, although some Egyptian Muslim militants regard the Coptic Church as a historical anachronism that ought to end. For north Africa as a whole, Islamic revivalism is the main issue. It probably cost President Anwar Sadat his life in 1981 and has sometimes threatened the ruling regimes of Tunisia, Algeria, and Morocco (whether or not Iran or Libya has been implicated).

Outside Arab Africa, the central issue concerning Islam is not merely its revival; it is also the speed of its expansion. Thus, we come back to the issue of receptivity. It is not often realized that there are more Muslims in Nigeria than in any Arab country, including Egypt, and Muslims in Ethiopia are not a small minority—they are nearly half the population. Islam elsewhere in Africa has spread—however unevenly—all the way down to the Cape of Good Hope. In South Africa, Islam is three hundred years old, having first arrived not directly from Arabia but from Southeast Asia with Malay immigrants.

The largest countries in Africa in terms of population are Nigeria, Egypt, Ethiopia, and Zaire, and these four countries together account for some 150 million Muslims. (The Islamic part of Zaire lies mainly to the east.) Thus, virtually half the population of the African continent is now Muslim.

But religion in Africa does not, of course, exist in isolation, and the world of religious experience in Africa is rich in diversity. It is even affected by the rivalry between the written word and the oral tradition. Although the written word and literacy are often regarded as allies of modernization, the written word can also, in fact, be an adversary to modernization. This is particularly true in situations where a holy book or sacred text commands so much loyalty that it hinders the process of secularization. The primordial power of the Qur'an on Muslim believers has tended to make modernization in the Muslim world more difficult—for better or for worse.

Religions in the oral tradition, on the other hand, tend to be more receptive to new religious influences. African traditional religions are particularly ecumenical: The same African individual may, for example, combine either Islam or Christianity with his or her ethnic religion. This is what so-called syncretism is all about. However, although an African may be both a Muslim and a follower of a traditional creed, he or she is unlikely to be both a Muslim and a Christian. One religion of sacred text (e.g., Islam) can be combined with a religion of oral message (e.g., the Yoruba religion), but it is rare that two religions of sacred text (e.g., Sunni Islam and Roman Catholicism) can be adhered to by the same individual: Religions of sacred text tend to be mutually exclusive—Shiite Muslims are unlikely to be simultaneously Methodists or Greek Orthodox.

Of the three principal religious legacies of Africa (indigenous, Islamic, and Christian), the most tolerant on record must be the indigenous tradition. One might even argue that Africa did not have religious wars before Christianity and Islam arrived, for indigenous religions were neither universalist (seeking to convert the whole of the human race) nor competitive (in bitter rivalry against other creeds). Christianity and Islam, on the other hand, were both universalist and competitive, perhaps especially in black Africa. In that arena south of the Sahara, these two religions have often been in competition for the soul of the continent. And rivalry has sometimes resulted in conflict.

Indigenous African religions, by contrast, are basically communal rather than universalist. Like Hinduism and modern Judaism—and unlike Christianity and Islam—indigenous African traditions have not sought to convert the whole of humanity. The Yoruba do not seek to convert the Ibo to the Yoruba religion—or vice versa—and neither the Yoruba nor the Ibo compete with each other for the souls of a third group, such as the Hausa. Because they are not proselytizing religions, indigenous African creeds have not fought with each other. Over the centuries, Africans have waged many kinds of wars with each other, but they were rarely religious ones before the universalist creeds arrived.

But what has this to do with cultural receptivity in contemporary Africa? The indigenous toleration today has often mitigated the competitiveness of the imported Semitic religions (Christianity and Islam). Let us illustrate this point with

Senegal, which is over 80 percent Muslim. The founding president of this pre-dominantly Islamic society, Leopold Sedar Senghor, presided over the fortunes of postcolonial Senegal for two decades (1960–1980) in a basic political partnership with the Muslim leaders of the country, the Marabouts.

Contrast this phenomenon with the history of the United States as a predomi-nantly Protestant society. In spite of a constitution that has ostensibly separated church and state since the eighteenth century, it was not until 1960 that American voters were ready to elect a Roman Catholic as president. When will the United States elect a Jew to that highest office? Although U.S. Jews have occupied some of the highest offices of the land (and have been represented on the Supreme Court), it seems unlikely that there will be a Jewish president of the United States in the twentieth century.

Muslims in the United States may now equal the Jews in numbers (but not in influence and power). Although the constitution still insists on separating church and state, the idea of a Muslim President of the United States currently remains a mind-boggling proposition.

And yet, newly independent Senegal could, in 1960, calmly accept a Roman Catholic to preside over the fortunes of a basically Muslim country. Senghor was not just a fellow Muslim but from a different denomination (as John Kennedy was a fellow Christian to most Americans) but from a different sect. Senghor be-longed to an entirely different faith from most Senegalese. Nonetheless, he was president of a stable Muslim country for some twenty years.

His successor as president (partly sponsored by him) was Abdou Diouf—at last, the Muslim society had a Muslim ruler. But the tradition of ecumenical tolerance continued in Senegal. The first lady of the country, Madame Elizabeth Diouf, was Roman Catholic, and several of the ministers of the new president were Christian.

Senegalese religious tolerance has continued in other spheres since that time. What might be regarded as provocative in other Islamic countries in the world has been tolerated in Senegal. Christian festivals like the first communion—with much feasting, merry-making, and singing—have, at times, been publicly celebrated in Dakar, right in the middle of the Islamic fast of Ramadhan. The feast has coexisted with the fast, and the Christian merry-makers have been left undisturbed.

To summarize the argument thus far, predominantly Muslim countries south of the Sahara have sometimes been above average in religious tolerance. The ca-pacity to accommodate other faiths may, to some extent, be part of the historical Islamic tradition in multireligious empires. But far more religiously tolerant than either Islam or Christianity have been indigenous African traditions, especially since they do not aspire to universalism and are not inherently competitive. In black Africa, this indigenous tolerance has, as indicated, often moderated the competitive propensities of Christianity and Islam.

During his first term as president of Uganda, Milton Obote (a Protestant) used to boast that his extended family in Lango consisted of Muslims, Catholics, and

Protestants "at peace with each other." Obote's successor, Idi Amin Dada (a Muslim), had a similarly multireligious extended family and even once declared that he planned to have at least one of his sons trained for the Christian priesthood. Amin may have reconsidered the matter when, upon losing office, he found political refuge in Saudi Arabia as a guest of the custodians of the Islamic holy cities of Mecca and Medina. Religious ecumenicalism and cultural receptivity continue to moderate the sensibilities of contemporary Africa.

When we place Islam in the context of the African continent as a whole, the cultural cyclic boomerang effect is once again discernible. The most influential Islamic university in the world, Al-Azhar University, is on the African continent, in Cairo. Al-Azhar is credited with presenting some of the most important *fatwa* under the *Shari'a* (legal opinions under Islamic law) in the last six hundred years. Al-Azhar was founded by the Fatimids in A.D. 970, making it one of the oldest and most durable universities in the world. The basic program of studies through the ages has focused on Islamic law, theology, and the Arabic language. Other subjects have more recently been added, especially since the nineteenth century. Women were first admitted in 1962. The university, which has continued to attract Muslim students from as far afield as China and Indonesia, is widely regarded as the chief center of Islamic learning in the world.

Islamic modernism has also been led from the African side of the Muslim world. Muhammad Abduh (1849–1905) is still widely acclaimed as the chief architect of the modernization and reform of Islam. Born in the Nile delta, he was later influenced by the great pan-Islamic revolutionary, Jamal al Din al-Afghani, who had settled in Cairo before being expelled for political activity in 1879. Abduh himself also suffered exile more than once. He lived to become the leading jurist of the Arab world, a professor at Al-Azhar University, and eventually *mufti* of Egypt (chief Islamic chancellor). His doctrinal reforms included freedom of will in Islam, the harmony of reason with revelation, the primacy of ethics over ritual and dogma in religion, and the legitimacy of interest on loans under Islamic law.

A much more recent disciple of Abduh and al-Afghani was the Sudanese scholar Mahmoud Muhammad Taha. Taha's own version of Islamic modernism in Sudan earned him a punishment more severe than any that Abduh and al-Afghani suffered in nineteenth-century Egypt: Under the presidency of Jaafar el-Nimeiry in Sudan, Taha was executed as an old man in January 1985 on charges of apostasy and heresy.[7]

Although this history of Islamic modernism includes personal tragedy as well as intellectual originality, there is no doubt about Africa's role in the reformation of Islam. In fact, it has often been the very vanguard of Islamic innovation and doctrinal review. Africa's remarkable presence in the global Islamic equation includes the scale of Africa's membership in the Organization of the Islamic Conference (OIC). Almost half the members of this global Islamic organization are also members of the Organization of African Unity, and Africa has produced some of the leaders of the OIC. The late Ahmed Sekou Toure of Guinea (Conakry) was chairman of the organization when he attempted to mediate between Iraq and Iran in the earlier phases of their war.

In distribution, Islam is, indeed, an Afro-Asian religion. Almost all Muslim countries are either in Africa or in Asia. In 1988, the Muslim population of the world was estimated at 984 million people; early in the twenty-first century, the Muslim population of the globe may encompass a quarter of the human race.

The fastest rate of increase in the Muslim population of the world is currently occurring in Africa. This is partly because the continent is undergoing the fastest rate of Islamic conversion of any major region on earth. Moreover, natural fertility rates in Africa are higher than anywhere else, and Muslims in Africa are reproducing at a faster rate than most other Africans. As one study has demonstrated: "The single most remarkable demographic aspect of Islamic societies is the nearly universal high level of fertility—the average of childbearing in Islamic nations is 6 children per woman. . . . Fertility rates are highest for those Islamic nations in sub-Saharan Africa—an average of 6.6 births per woman. Furthermore, African Islamic nations south of the Sahara have higher fertility on average than do other developing nations in that region."[8]

There is evidence that Muslim women not only marry significantly earlier than other women in developing countries but also that they aspire to have more children. The Kenya Fertility Survey of 1977 (part of the World Fertility Survey) helped to demonstrate that among currently married Muslim women in that country, the average desired family size was 8.4 children. "This was the highest of any religious grouping, with Catholic women preferring 7.1 children and Protestant women an average of 7.0 children."[9]

Though Asia still has many more millions of Muslims than Africa, the demographic indicators show that the African continent is narrowing the gap dramatically. Before the end of this century, Africa may become the only continent of the world with an absolute Muslim majority: The second largest continent geographically may become the first in terms of Muslim preponderance. A part of Asia once conquered Africa in the name of Islam, and Africa is now repaying the debt by overshadowing Asia in the fortunes of Islam. The cultural boomerang effect has once again been at work,[10] bringing the process full circle.

History is playing out a remarkable prophetic destiny. The first great muezzin of Islam was a black man—the great Bilal, of Ethiopian extraction. Bilal called Muslim believers to prayer in seventh-century Arabia. Symbolically, his call to prayer has echoed down through the centuries. In the twentieth century, has Bilal been heard particularly clearly in his ancestral continent of Africa? Perhaps the cultural boomerang effect has now taken the form of echoes of an African muezzin reverberating back across the centuries.

But what of the echoes from that other great civilization in Africa's destiny, the Western heritage? Our case study here concerns the French version of the idea of "Eurafrica."

Eurafrica: The French Connection

France invented the concept of Eurafrica, asserting an organic relationship between Europe and Africa that was deep enough to transform the two continents into a single integrated international subsystem. How does this concept relate to the French language?

The majority of French-speaking people in the world are in the Western world, mainly in France itself. However, the majority of French-speaking states are in Africa. Over twenty members of the Organization of African Unity are French-speaking: Algeria, Benin, Burundi, Chad, Cameroon, Central African Republic, Comoros, Congo, Côte d'Ivoire, Djibouti, Burkina Faso, Gabon, Guinea, Malagasy, Mali, Mauritania, Morocco, Niger, Rwanda, Senegal, Réunion, Togo, Tunisia, and Zaire.

Without Africa, the French language would be almost a provincial language. Zaire is the largest French-speaking country after France in population and is destined to be the largest early in the twenty-first century. If Zaire succeeds in stabilizing itself and in assuming effective control over its resources, it may become France's rival in influence and power in French-speaking Africa as a whole.

When we look at the global scene, the French language is shrinking in usage in the Northern Hemisphere. On the other hand, French is spreading and gaining in influence in the Southern Hemisphere, especially in Africa. Let us take each of these propositions in turn. Why is French declining in Europe and the north?

The most important challenge to the French language in the Northern Hemisphere has been caused by the vast expansion of U.S. influence in the twentieth century. The dominant language has, of course, been English. Although the spread of the English language in Africa has been mainly due to the impact of imperial Britain, the spread of the English language in Europe and its expanding role in international affairs has been largely due to the new U.S. hegemony in the Northern Hemisphere. The triumph of the English language globally has ranged from an increasing usage in diplomacy to its preeminent role as the supreme language of aviation and air control.

A related reason for the shrinkage of French in the Northern Hemisphere concerns the computer revolution. The amount of information circulating in English is so much greater than that transmitted in French that English is gaining even further ascendancy. The old adage that "nothing succeeds like success" has now been computerized. The global influence of U.S. computer firms such as IBM has reinforced this Anglo computer revolution.

At the other end of social concerns is the decline of the cultural influence of the upper classes in Europe. Royal houses in continental Europe as a whole once preferred to use the French language extensively. In the aftermath of the Russian Revolution in 1917 and the subsequent development of social egalitarianism across Europe, however, linguistic snobbery declined, and linguistic pragmatism became the norm. Aristocratic linguistic snobbery had once favored French;

egalitarian linguistic pragmatism in continental Europe would later favor the English language.

The fourth factor behind the decline of French in the Northern Hemisphere was Britain's entry into the European Economic Community. This made English more decisively one of the official languages of the community. The new language became increasingly influential in the written and oral affairs of the European Union. Smaller members of the union have more frequently turned to English rather than French in the post-Gaullist era of European affairs.

The fifth factor behind the decline of French in the Northern Hemisphere is linked to the decline in the power of the French-speaking Walloons in Belgium. The days of French preeminence in Belgium were coming to an end in the 1980s, although francophone Brussels still remained the capital of the country. Belgium moved toward a neofederal structure, rooted in the principle of linguistic parity between French and Flemish.

It is arguable that the French language has made some gains in North America due to a greater recognition of bilingualism in the federation of Canada. But there has also been a decline of linguistic nationalism in Quebec as compared to the old militancy of the 1960s.

The decline of the role of German in Europe has also tended to favor English rather than French. When the Scandinavian countries regarded German as virtually their first foreign language, there was a tendency to invest in the French language as well for a sense of balance. But when Scandinavians turned more decisively to the English language as their first foreign tongue, it was not just German that suffered; it was also French. Since English was, in any case, of wider international utility than German, its adoption by Scandinavians as the premier foreign language reduced the need to "balance" it with French.

Of course, Scandinavians are greater linguists than average. Their schools are still sensitized to the importance of French and German as well as English. But linguistic priorities have, indeed, changed in the Nordic syllabi and curricula—and in class enrollments. The English language has definitely been the main beneficiary of the decline of German, and the French language has sustained a decline in educational emphasis.

Japan, itself a part of the Northern Hemisphere, has also experienced shifts in emphasis that have demoted German and French—and raised the role of English in educational and linguistic priorities. Between the Meiji Restoration in 1868 and Japan's defeat in World War II in 1945, the main Western role models in Japan were, indeed, Germany and France. This Franco-German orientation affected Japan's curricula and syllabi, and it profoundly influenced the nation's legal system and civil code.

It was the U.S. occupation of Japan after World War II that decisively shifted Japan from a Franco-German role model to the Anglo-Saxon alternative. The continuing special relationship of the United States with Japan after the occupation consolidated Japan's cultural reorientation. Under General Douglas MacArthur, the Americans imposed upon Japan a national constitution basically drawn from continental European experience, and much of the rest of the West-ernization of Japan has been a case of cultural Americanization—from Japan's introduction to baseball to its enthusiasm for American pop stars. The very econ-omy of Japan has interlocked itself with the U.S. economy. The confirmation of the English language as Japan's first Western language in the postwar era has been part of this American phase of Japan's transformation. The decline of French and German languages in Japanese priorities was an inevitable consequence of the Americanization of Japan.

A particularly surprising development was the decision of the Socialist party of Japan to adopt a campaign anthem written in the English language in the election campaign for the Lower House in 1989–1990.

If these are the main factors that have resulted in the decline of the French language in the Northern Hemisphere, which factors have contributed to its ex-pansion in the south?

What must be emphasized in the first instance is that the southern expansion is occurring mainly in Africa. On the whole, the distribution of the French lan-guage is bicontinental—large numbers of French-speaking individuals in Europe and large numbers of French-speaking states in Africa. Europe and Africa are, by far, the primary constituencies of the French language.

Of course, there are smaller francophone constituencies in Quebec, Lebanon, Syria, Indochina, and elsewhere, but these are peripheries of the francophone world. The main theater of action is in Europe and Africa.

Factors that have favored expansion in Africa include the type of states that French and Belgian imperialism created during the colonial period. These were often multiethnic countries that needed a lingua franca. Colonial policy had cho-sen the French language as the lingua franca, and the entire educational system and domestic political process consolidated that linguistic choice.

A related factor was the assimilationist policy of France as an imperial power, which created an elite mesmerized by French culture and civilization. A surpris-ing number of people still retained dual citizenship with France even after inde-pendence, and if President Jean-Bedel Bokassa is typical, some African heads of state may secretly still be citizens of France. Furthermore, annual holidays in France continue to be part of the elite culture of francophone west and north Africa.

With some subsidies and technical assistance, the French language is also fea-tured more and more in classrooms in anglophone Africa. Before independence, British educational policymakers were more committed to the promotion of in-digenous African languages than to the promotion of the rival French legacy in British colonies. French offers of language teachers for schools in British colonies were not welcome.

The difference Africa's independence has made is partly due to a greater readi-ness on the part of anglophone governments to accept France's offers of teachers of the French language. Many an African university in the Commonwealth has been the beneficiary of technical assistance and cultural subsidies from the local

French embassy or directly from France. France's policy in Africa is consolidated partly through an aggressive cultural diplomacy. Considerable amounts of money are spent on French-style syllabi and curricula in African schools and on the provision of French teachers, advisers, and reading materials. A residual French economic and administrative presence in most former French colonies has deepened Africa's orientation toward Paris.

In addition, every French president since Charles de Gaulle has attempted to cultivate special personal relations with at least some of the African leaders. There is little doubt that French-speaking African presidents have greater and more personalized access to the French president than their anglophone counterparts have had to either the British prime minister or the British head of state, the queen, in spite of Commonwealth conferences.

Here again is a case of reciprocal conquest. There is little doubt that the French language and culture have conquered large parts of Africa, and many decisions about the future of Africa are being made by people deeply imbued with French values and perspectives. Moreover, French is expanding its constituency in Africa, at least outside Algeria. It is true that the postcolonial policy of re-Arabization in Algeria is designed to increase the role of Arabic in schools and public affairs at the expense of the preeminent colonial role of the French language. The rise of Islamic militancy in Algeria may also pose new problems to aspects of French culture. It is also true the Mobutu Sese Seko's policy of promoting regional languages in Zaire (Lingala, Kikongo, Tchiluba, and Kiswahili) is partly at the expense of French in Zairean curricula. But such setbacks for French in Africa are the exception rather than the rule. On the whole, French is still on the ascendancy in Africa, though the pace of expansion has drastically declined.

However, when all is said and done, France's aspiration to remain a global power requires a cultural constituency as well as an economic one. It seems likely that the 1990s will continue to signify a change in France's economic priorities in favor of the new pan-European opportunities and against the older investments in Africa. But it seems equally certain that a more open Europe after the end of the Cold War favors the English language at the expense of French even within France itself. The collapse of the Soviet empire has been a further gain for the English language. As custodian of the fortunes of French civilization, France could not afford to abandon the cultural constituency of Africa entirely in favor of a more open Europe. France may need Africa more culturally but less economically. As France's cultural constituency in Europe has been declining, its cultural constituency in Africa becomes more valuable than ever. A remarkable interdependence has emerged—still imperfect and uneven but real enough to make Africa indispensable for the recognition of France as a truly global power and for the acceptance of the French language as a credible world language.

Eurafrica as a concept gets its maximum significance in the destiny of the French language. But is there also a concept of Afrindia worth exploring? And how does this relate to the legacies of Gandhi and Nehru?

Afrindia: Between Gandhi and Nehru

Quite early in his life, Mahatma Gandhi saw nonviolent resistance as a method that would be well suited to the African as well as the Indian. In 1924, Gandhi said that if the black people "caught the spirit of the Indian movement their progress must be rapid."[11] In 1936, he went even further. And to understand his claim, one should perhaps link it to something that was later said by his disciple, Jawaharlal Nehru: "Reading through history I think the agony of the African continent . . . has not been equalled anywhere."[12]

To the extent, then, that blacks had more to be angry about than other individuals, they would need greater self-discipline than others to be passive in their resistance. But by the same token, to the extent that blacks in the last three centuries had suffered more than any others, passive but purposeful self-sacrifice for the cause should come easier to them. And to the extent that blacks had more for which to forgive the rest of the world, that forgiveness, when it came, should be all the more weighty. Perhaps after adding up these considerations, Gandhi came to the conclusion by 1936 that it was "maybe through the Negroes that the unadulterated message of non-violence will be delivered to the world."[13]

And so it was that in America, the torch came to be passed to Martin Luther King Jr. And in South Africa, where Gandhi first experimented with his methods, it passed to Albert Luthuli and later Desmond Tutu. In Northern Rhodesia (Zambia after independence), Kenneth Kaunda became a vigorous Gandhian: "I reject absolutely violence in any of its forms as a solution to our problems."[14]

In the Gold Coast (Ghana before independence), Nkrumah had translated *Satyagraha* (soul force) into a program of "positive action," a program that he himself defined as "non-cooperation based on the principle of absolute non-violence, as used by Gandhi in India."[15] In 1949, *The Morning Telegraph* of Accra went as far as to call Nkrumah the "Gandhi of Ghana."[16]

African conceptions of dignity now seemed very different from what was implied by that old ceremonial affirmation of young Kikuyu initiates that Jomo Kenyatta once told us about, the glorification of the spear as "the symbol of our courageous and fighting spirit." But these new conceptions of dignity could now also be differentiated from the submissive virtues of early missionary teachings.

Yet one question remained to be answered: Could passive resistance survive the attainment of independence? Would Gandhism retain political relevance once its immediate objective of liberation from colonialism was achieved?

It is perhaps not entirely accidental that the two most important Indian contributions to African political thought were the doctrines of nonviolence and of nonalignment. In a sense, they were almost twin doctrines. Gandhi contributed passive resistance to one school of African thought; Nehru contributed nonalignment to almost all African countries. We should note how Uganda's President Obote put it in his tribute to Nehru on his death: "Nehru will be remembered as a founder of nonalignment. . . . The new nations of the world owe him a debt of gratitude in this respect."[17] However, Gandhi and Nehru both taught Africa and learned from it.

But how related are the two doctrines in their assumptions? For India itself, Gandhi's nonviolence was a method of seeking freedom, but Nehru's nonalignment came to be a method of seeking peace. And yet nonalignment was, in some ways, a translation into foreign policy of some of the moral assumptions that underlay passive resistance in the domestic struggle for India's independence.

Nehru's armed ejection of Portuguese colonialism from Goa in 1961 had a significant impact on Africa. In the U.N., Foreign Minister Khrishna Menon described colonialism as "permanent aggression." Particularly "permanent" was the colonialism of those who regarded their colonies as part of the metropole—as Portugal had pretended to do. In such a situation when colonialism threatened to be more durable even than "permanent," the military solution was a necessary option.

Nehru's use of armed force against the Portuguese set a grand precedent for an Africa still shackled by Portuguese imperialism in Angola, Mozambique, and Guinea-Bissau. Had Gandhi's *Satyagraha* been replaced in 1961 by Nehru's *Satya-Goa*? Was there a Hegelian negation of the negation? Was Nehru's negation of nonviolence a legitimation of the violence of liberation?

If Gandhi had taught Africa civil disobedience, had Nehru now taught Africa armed liberation? Had the armed ejection of Portugal from the Indian subcontinent strengthened Africa's resolve to eject Portugal from Angola, Mozambique, and Guinea-Bissau?

The impact of India upon twentieth-century Africa goes beyond even such towering figures as Mahatma Gandhi and Jawaharlal Nehru. But there is no doubt about the special significance for Africa of Gandhi's strategies of civil disobedience and Nehru's principles of nonalignment and armed liberation. Gandhi's *satyagraha* inspired African political figures as diverse as Nobel laureate Albert Luthuli of South Africa and Ivorian president Felix Houphouet-Boigny. Nehru's ideas about what used to be called "positive neutralism" helped to shape African approaches to foreign policy in the entire postcolonial era.

Africa's Reverse Impact on Gandhi and Nehru

What has seldom been adequately examined is the reverse flow of influence *from* Africa *into* both Gandhi's vision of *satyagraha* and Nehru's concept of nonalignment. Experience in the southern part of Africa must be counted as part of the genesis of Gandhi's political philosophy. And the 1956 Suez war in the northern part of Africa was probably a major influence on Nehru's vision of nonalignment.

South Africa was the cradle and threatened to be the grave of passive resistance as a strategy of Africa's liberation. Gandhi first confronted the problem of politicized evil in the context of racism in South Africa. Racial humiliation in that part of the continent helped to radicalize him and therefore helped to prepare him for his more decisive historical role in British India later in the century.

Gandhi's political philosophy developed from both the world of ideas and the world of experience. Moreover, in the realm of ideas, he relied heavily on both Western liberalism and Indian thought. But what helped to radicalize Gandhi's own interpretation of those ideas was the power of experience. And within that crucible of experience, we have to include Gandhi's exposure to sustained segregation in South Africa—a deeper form of racism than even the racist horrors of British India at that time.

Under the stimulus of activated evil and the need to combat it, Gandhi reinterpreted in radical ways important concepts in Indian thought. For example, he reinterpreted *Ahimsa,* transforming it from nonresistance to passive resistance. This provoked the criticism of such Western students of Indian philosophy as Albert Schweitzer, who was also deeply fascinated by Africa. Schweitzer objected to Gandhi's reformulation of *Ahimsa* on the following grounds:

> Gandhi places Ahimsa at the services of world-affirmation and life-affirmation, directly to activity within the world, and in this way it ceases to be what in essence it is. Passive resistance is a non-violent use of force. The idea is that, by circumstances brought about without violence, pressure is brought to bear on the opponent and he is forced to yield. Being an attack that is more difficult to parry than an active attack, passive resistance may be the more successful method. But there is also a danger that this concealed application of force may cause more bitterness than an open use of violence. In any case the difference between passive and active resistance is only quite relative.[18]

Schweitzer and Gandhi were both profound humanitarians, and both retained a fascination with Africa. But though Schweitzer ultimately sought to serve humanity by curing the physical body of disease, Gandhi sought to serve humanity by curing the social condition of injustice. Schweitzer approached his physiological mission through medical work in Gabon. Gandhi approached his sociological mission through passive resistance, first in South Africa and later, of course, in British India.

If Gandhi's *satyagraha* was a response to the moral confrontation between good and evil, Nehru's nonalignment was a response to the militarized confrontation between capitalism and socialism. If Gandhi's political philosophy was originally a response to racial intolerance, Nehru's nonalignment was originally a response to ideological intolerance. The regime in South Africa became the symbol of racial bigotry for Gandhi. The Cold War between East and West became the essence of ideological bigotry for Nehru.

South Africa's role in inspiring Gandhi is well documented, but North Africa's role as an inspiration for Nehru's nonalignment has been less explored. Two wars in North Africa in the 1950s were particularly important in Afro-Asian interaction. The Algerian war from 1954 to 1962 took African resistance beyond the passive level into the militarized, active domain. African Gandhism was in crisis.

Had *satyagraha* been rejected as no longer relevant for the struggle against colonialism?

The second great war in North Africa in the 1950s was the Suez conflict of 1956. If the Algerian war marked a possible end to *satyagraha* as a strategy for African liberation movements, the Suez war marked a possible birth of nonalignment as a policy of the postcolonial era. Gamal Abdel Nasser of Egypt was economically punished by the United States, Britain, and the World Bank for purchasing arms from the Communist bloc, and Washington, London, and the bank reneged on their commitment to help Egypt build the Aswan High Dam. Nasser's nationalization of the Suez Canal was an assertion of self-reliance, for revenue from the canal was going to help Egypt construct the great dam. Egypt's sovereign right to purchase arms from either East or West was not for sale. In retrospect, Nasser's nationalization of the Suez Canal Company was a kind of unilateral declaration of nonalignment, made before the nonaligned movement itself was as yet formally constituted.

Before the actual outbreak of the Suez hostilities, the diplomatic division at the level of the big powers was, indeed, East versus West. Socialist governments were also neatly aligned in support of Nasser, and the capitalist world was alarmed by his nationalization of the canal. However, when Britain, France, and Israel actually invaded Egypt, the Western world was divided, and the United States was strongly opposed to the military action taken by its own closest allies.

However, the Soviet Union went further than merely condemning the aggression by Britain, France, and Israel against Egypt. When the Western powers withdrew their canal pilots in an attempt to sabotage Egypt's efforts to operate the canal after nationalization, the Soviets lent Egypt their pilots until Nasser could train his own. And in the wake of the West's reneging on the commitment to build the Aswan High Dam, the Soviet Union stepped into the breach and became the builder of the dam. What became apparent in the entire experience was the value of trying to balance traditional Egyptian dependence on the West with a readiness to find areas of cooperation with the East. The central principle of nonalignment was being conceptualized at Suez.

Jawaharlal Nehru helped to mobilize Third World opinion on the side of Gamal Abdel Nasser during the whole crisis. Although there was not yet a nonalignment movement in world politics, the Suez conflict was part of the labor pains of its birth, and Jawaharlal Nehru was the leading midwife in attendance.

It is these factors that made the Suez crisis part of the genesis of Pandit Nehru's diplomatic thought and vision, just as racism in South Africa remains part of the genesis of Mahatma Gandhi's principle of *satyagraha*.

Suez was the most dramatic test of a Third World country under invasion, in this case by two members of NATO, France and Britain. Never before had a Third World country been the subject of aggression by *two* members of NATO, with the leader of NATO—the U.S.—protesting against its allies. Nehru both taught important lessons from Suez and learned from it.

What all this eventually meant was that after Mahatma Gandhi had inspired many Africans to pursue the path of passive resistance, Nehru's liberation of Goa in 1961–1962 converted still more Africans south of the Sahara to the possibilities of military action. Gandhi was the prophet of nonviolence; Nehru became the symbol of armed struggle. Were the two Indians contradicting each other in the corridors of history? Or were passive resistance and armed struggle two sides of the same coin of liberation?

The answer probably lies in the unfolding struggle in the Republic of South Africa in the concluding years of the twentieth century. Both civil disobedience and armed struggle may still occur in South Africa—and the two forms of struggle appear to be at once complementary and contradictory. I have noted that, in a sense, South Africa was the cradle of Gandhi's *satyagraha*. Has *satyagraha* received a new moral validation in the process of dismantling apartheid?

The answer rests in the womb of history. Only two things about South Africa are almost totally predictable. With the fires of struggle out, a new *black-ruled* republic has joined the community of nations. Almost equally predictable is the foreign policy that the new Republic of South Africa will adopt: It will be one of nonalignment. When the republic joins the nonaligned movement, the heritage of Gandhi and the legacy of Nehru will at last be fused on the very continent where they were once separately born. Morally, Afrindia is about to be vindicated. South Africa is, indeed, the last testing ground. If India was the brightest jewel of the British crown, Africa is now the richest source of all jewels.

Significantly, four black men influenced by Gandhi have won the Nobel Peace Prize: Ralph Bunche (1950), Albert Luthuli (1960), Martin Luther King, Jr. (1964), and Desmond Tutu (1984). By a strange twist of fate, Mahatma Gandhi himself never won the Nobel Prize. His black disciples did.

Africa's capacity to turn weakness into a form of influence has found a new arena of fulfillment. Fragmentation and excessive cultural receptivity are weaknesses, and weakness is not an adequate currency in the marketplace of power. But quite often, the power of the weak is, in human terms, less dangerous than the weakness of the powerful, given their arrogance and so on. And yet, when all is said and done, the ultimate conquest is Africa's conquest of itself. The ultimate colonization is self-colonization under the banner of *Pax Africana*. It is to this ultimate full circle that we must now turn.

Toward an African Conquest of Itself

Is the process of Africa's decolonization reversible? As we approach the twenty-first century, a serious question has arisen: Is Africa creating conditions that will sooner or later result in some kind of recolonization? And, if so, who will be the new colonizer?

A thousand people a day died in the Angolan civil war during the fall of 1993. Somalia is torn between chaos and *clanocracy* (rule on the basis of clans), and Burundi has a long history of brutal *ethnocracy* (rule by a particular ethnic group). The 1993 compromise between the Tutsi and the Hutu in Burundi soon collapsed in a bloody coup and its aftermath. And at the end of 1993, Liberia and Mozambique stood poised on a cliffhanger, close to anarchy.

In the nineteenth century, imperialism justified itself by claiming to end tribal wars—hence, *Pax Britannica.* But in some parts of Africa, the real tribal wars have come *after* colonial rule rather than before. *Pax Britannica* created future conflicts instead of ending old tribal feuds, and the specter of recolonization remains.

The issue has arisen as to whether colonization and decolonization are unilinear. We had previously assumed a neat sequence. There was a precolonial period covering millennia of African history. Then there was about a century of European colonial history, with immense economic, political, and cultural consequences, followed by the postcolonial period, ostensibly extending into infinity. But international intervention in Somalia has raised the question of whether our complacency about neat periodization is, indeed, justified. Is there really a neat unilinear sequence of precolonial, colonial, and postcolonial period conditions?

Is *recolonization* feasible? Indeed, could colonization itself be part of yet another cycle rather than a unilinear experience? Could colonialism have different incarnations—a kind of transmigration of the imperial soul? The imperial soul had previously resided in separate European powers: Britain, France, Portugal, Belgium, and so on. Has the imperial soul transmigrated to the United States? Is the soul trying to decide whether to settle in the bosom of the United States or to become part of the United Nations? Is this a period of cosmic imperial indecision between the United States and the United Nations as voices of "the world community"?

The next phase of colonialism may be through *collective* rather than individual powers. It may, indeed, be the transmigration of the soul of the United Nations Trusteeship Council to some new U.N. decisionmaking machinery. Will Africa play a role both as guardian and as ward?

A new form of U.N. trusteeship started in 1960 when things fell apart in the former Belgian Congo as the imperial power withdrew: On that occasion, the U.N. intervened to oppose Katanga's secession from the Congo. Officially, the United Nations ceased to be a trusteeship power in Africa as recently as 1990 when Namibia became independent. In Somalia in the 1990s, the U.N. has thus far ignored the self-proclaimed separatist Republic of Somaliland, which has declared its independence from the rest of Somalia. But if the problem of stability and anarchy in Somalia turns out to be insurmountable, the sanctity of Somalia's borders may one day be reexamined. Separatist Somaliland may yet survive to enjoy a legitimate U.N. seat—if not this time around, then after the next collapse of the Somali political patchwork. External recolonization under the banner of humanitarianism is entirely conceivable. Countries like Somalia and Liberia, where central control has collapsed, may invite an inevitable intervention—but by whom in the future?

Although colonialism may be resurfacing, it is likely to look rather different this time around. A future trusteeship system will be more genuinely international and less Western than that under the old guise. Administering powers for the trusteeship territories could come from Africa and Asia, as well as from the rest of the membership of the U.N. For example, might Ethiopia one day be called upon to run Somalia on behalf of the U.N.? This would assume the survival and transformation of Ethiopia, as well as the disappearance of the historical animosities between the Somali and the ruling elites of Ethiopia. But if Ethiopians and Eritreans can forgive each other, why not the Ethiopians and the Somali?

Ethiopia was once a black imperial power, annexing neighboring communities. The future may hold a more benign imperial role for it, though this may take a century to evolve. The recolonization of the future will not be based on "the white man's burden" or the "lion of Judah." It may, instead, be based on a shared human burden: Ethiopia may become an administering power on behalf of the U.N., helping to nurture the sovereignties of its smaller neighbors, Somalia and Djibouti being the more likely to need that kind of help in the decades to come.[19]

However, regional hegemonic power can lose influence as well as gain it. Just as there is subcolonization of one African country by another, there can be subdecolonization as the weaker country reasserts itself. This is part of what has happened between Egypt and Sudan in the 1990s. Sudan under the Bashir Islamic regime started asserting more independence from Egypt than ever before since the Mahdiyya movement under Seyyid Muhammad el Mahdi in the nineteenth century.

Relations between Somalia and Egypt in the era after Mohamed Siad Barre may also be a case of subdecolonization, the reassertion of the weaker country (Somalia) against the influence of its more powerful brother (Egypt). Secretary-General Boutros-Ghali's problems with Muhammad Farah Aideed were perhaps part of the same story of subdecolonization. Boutros-Ghali was seen more as an Egyptian than as the chief executive of the world body.

If subcolonization of one African country by another is possible, and subdecolonization has also been demonstrated, what about subrecolonization? Will Egypt reestablish its "big brother's" relationship with Sudan and Somalia? Will there be another full circle? As the Arabs would affirm: *Allahu Yaalam* (only God knows).

In west Africa, the situation is especially complex. Nigeria is a giant with nearly 90 million people. Its real rival in the region was never Ghana under Kwame Nkrumah or Libya under Muammar Qaddafi or distant South Africa. The real rival to postcolonial Nigeria has always been France. By all measurements of size, resources, and population in west Africa, Nigeria should rapidly have become what India is in South Asia or what South Africa has been in southern Africa—a hegemonic power. But Nigeria was marginalized not only by civil war in 1967–1970 but also by its own chronic incompetence and by the massive French presence in west Africa, mainly in its own former colonies but also in Nigeria itself.

In the twenty-first century, France will be withdrawing from west Africa as it becomes increasingly involved in the affairs of Eastern and Western Europe. France's west African sphere of influence will be filled by Nigeria—a more natural hegemonic power in the area. Under those circumstances, Nigeria's own boundaries are eventually likely to expand to incorporate the Republic of Niger (the Hausa link), the Republic of Benin (the Yoruba link), and conceivably Cameroon (part of which nearly became Nigerian in a referendum in 1959).

The case of post-apartheid South Africa also raises questions about a regional hegemonic power. On the positive and optimistic side, this will make it possible to achieve regional integration in southern Africa: Regional unification is easier where one country is more equal than others and can provide the leadership.

On the negative side, post-apartheid South Africa may be a kind of subimperial power, and questions of subcolonization, subdecolonization, and subrecolonization may become part of the future historical agenda of southern Africa. Another full circle appears.

Another African giant is Zaire. It is already the largest French-speaking country in the world after France; in the course of the twenty-first century, it will become, as I indicated, absolutely the largest French-speaking in the world. In mineral resources, it is already the richest French-speaking country. If Zaire attains stability, it may become the magnet for the whole of French-speaking Africa. Will its boundaries remain the same? Congo (Brazzaville) may work out a federal relationship with Zaire in the course of the next century; it would help the transition if Zaire reverted to its own older name of Congo (Kinshasa). A confederal relationship of Zaire, Burundi, and Rwanda is also conceivable in the next century, for all three were once ruled by Belgium and have been deepening their relationships as a result of that experience.

If I have presented some frightening possibilities, it is because some African countries may need to be temporarily controlled by others. The umbrella of *Pax Africana* is needed—an African peace enforced by Africans themselves. Africa may have to conquer itself.

A thousand lives a day were lost in the Angolan civil war in 1993. Had South Africa already been black-ruled, it could have intervened; benevolent subcolonization could have been attempted for the greater good. It would have been comparable to India's intervention in East Pakistan in 1971 when the Pakistani army was on the rampage against its own Bengali citizens: India intervened and created Bangladesh. But India had a vested interest in dividing Pakistan, whereas a post-apartheid South Africa could intervene in a civil war in Angola for humanitarian and pan-African reasons and still preserve the territorial integrity of its smaller neighbors.

New possibilities are on the horizon. We may yet learn to distinguish between benevolent intervention and malignant invasion in the years ahead. Africa could conquer itself without colonizing itself. .

Conclusion

I have sought to demonstrate in this chapter the paradox of counterpenetration and the cyclic boomerang effect in Africa's interaction with other civilizations. Africa's cultural receptivity to its Arab conquerors has now tilted the demographic balance and changed the Arab cultural equation. The majority of Arabs are now in Africa, and the African side of the Arab world has become the most innovative in art and science.

Africa's receptivity to Islam may make Africa the first truly Islamic continent. What Europe was to Christianity, Africa may become to Islam—the first continent to have a preponderance of believers. African Islam since the nineteenth century has also been the vanguard of Islamic reformation and modernism, especially since the Egyptian thinker, Muhammad Abduh. The fatal martyrdom of Mahmoud Mohamed Taha in Numeiry's Sudan in 1985 is part of the story of daring innovation within the African constituency of the Islamic *ummah* (community).

Africa's cultural receptivity to the French language and culture has already made Africa the second most important home of French civilization after France itself. The majority of French-speaking countries are already in Africa. And Zaire stands a chance of one day becoming a rival to France in leading the French-speaking part of the world: It is in the process of closing the population gap and the resource gap with France. Meanwhile, Africa's response to Gandhian ideas, reinforced by Christian pacifism, has already given the continent more Nobel Peace Prizes than India. Gandhi himself had once predicted that the torch of *Satyagraha* would eventually be borne by the black world. Black winners of the Nobel Prize in the second half of the twentieth century have included two South Africans (Albert Luthuli and Desmond Tutu) and two African-Americans (Ralph Bunche and Martin Luther King, Jr.). Mahatma Gandhi himself was never awarded the Nobel Prize.

Africa's response to Nehru's ideas of nonalignment have now resulted in a majority of the nonaligned countries being from Africa. Africa was, in fact, the first continent to become almost completely nonaligned. If nonalignment once penetrated Africa, Africa has now truly penetrated the nonaligned movement.

But in the future, Africa's cultural receptivity has to be more systematically moderated by cultural selectivity. Counterpenetrating one's conquerors may be one worthy trend. But at least as important for Africa is a reduced danger of being excessively penetrated by others.

Perhaps the sequence of cultural penetration will be reversed one day. Instead of Africans being Arabized so completely that the majority of Arabs are in Africa, some other Asians will be Africanized so completely that they are indistinguishable from native Africans. Instead of Zaire being the largest French-speaking nation after France, some European nation may become the second heartland of Yoruba civilization after west Africa.

Meanwhile, Africa must conquer itself if it is to avoid further colonization by others. Africa needs to establish a *Pax Africana*—an African peace promoted and maintained by Africans themselves. One day, each African will look in the mirror and behold the fusion of the guardian and the ward.

Notes

1. See Muhammad Abdul-Hai, *Conflict and Identity: The Cultural Poetics of Contemporary Sudanese Poetry*, African Seminar Series no. 26 (Khartoum: Institute of African and Asian Studies, University of Khartoum, 1976), pp. 26–27.

2. *Nar al Majadhib* (Khartoum, 1969), pp. 195, 287. See also p. 24.

3. Cited by Abdul-Hai, *Conflict and Identity*, pp. 40–41.

4. *Ghadhbat al Hababy* (Beirut, 1968); Abdul-Hai, *Conflict and Identity*, p. 52.

5. Boutros-Ghali, interviewed by author in Cairo, 1985.

6. V. A. Panadiker and P. K. Umashaker, "Politics of Population Control in a Diverse, Federal Democratic Polity: The Case of India," conference paper presented at the international symposium on "The Politics of Induced Fertility Change," sponsored by the University of Michigan, Villa Serbelloni, Rockefeller Foundation Conference Center, Bellagio, Italy, February 19–23, 1990.

7. See Mahmoud Muhammad Taha's book, *The Second Message of Islam* (Evanston, Ill.: Northwestern University Press, 1987).

8. John R. Weeks, "The Demography of Islamic Nations," *Population Bulletin* (a publication of the Population Reference Bureau, Inc.) 43, no. 4 (December 1988), p. 15.

9. Ibid., p. 20.

10. It is widely believed in African Muslim circles that Islam is already the majority religion on the African continent. This claim was often repeated at an international conference on "Islam in Africa" held in Abuja, Nigeria, in November 1989. See *Africa Events* (London) 6, no. 2 (February 1990).

11. *Young India, 1924–1926* (Madras: S. Ganesan, 1927), pp. 839–840. Consult also Pyarelal, "Gandhi and the African Question," *Africa Quarterly* 2, no. 2 (July-September 1962). See as well the selection from Gandhi entitled "Mahatma Gandhi on Freedom in Africa," *African Quarterly* 1, no. 2 (July-September 1961). For a more extensive discussion by Gandhi on nonviolence, consult Gandhi, *Non-Violence in Peace and War*, 2d ed. (Ahmedabad: Navajivan Publishing House, 1944).

12. Jawaharlal Nehru, "Portuguese Colonialism: An Anachronism," *Africa Quarterly* 1, no. 3 (October-December, 1961), p. 9. See also Nehru "Emergent Africa," *Africa Quarterly* 1, no. 1 (April-June 1961), pp. 7–9.

13. *Harijan*, October 14, 1939. This essay is also indebted to Ali A. Mazrui, *The Africans: A Triple Heritage* (New York: Little, Brown, and London: BBC Publications, 1986).

14. See Colin M. Morris and Kenneth D. Kaunda, *Black Government? A Discussion between Colin Morris and Kenneth Kaunda* (Lusaka, Zambia: United Society for Christian Literature, 1960).

15. Kwame Nkrumah, *Ghana: The Autobiography of Kwame Nkrumah* (New York: International Publishers, 1957), p. 112.

16. *Morning Telegraph*, June 27, 1949.

17. See *Uganda Argus*, May 29, 1964, and Ali A. Mazrui, *Africa's International Relations: The Diplomacy of Dependency and Change* (London: Heinemann Educational Books, and Boulder: Westview Press, 1977), pp. 117–121.

18. Albert Schweitzer, *Indian Thought and Its Development*, trans. by Mrs. C.E.B. Russell (New York: Henry Holt and Co., 1936), pp. 231–232. Consult also George Seaver, *Albert Schweitzer: The Man and His Mind* (London: Adam and Charles Black, 1951), p. 275.

19. See Ali A. Mazrui, "The Bondage of Boundaries," *The Economist*, 328, 7828 (September 11–17, 1993), pp. 28–30.

5

Dependent by Default: Africa's Relations with the European Union

JOHN RAVENHILL

IN THE GROWING SPECULATION in the early 1990s about the emergence of three giant trading blocs, the natural assumption was that Africa would be a component of a bloc centered on the European Union (EU).[1] Trade patterns change only slowly. They are determined not only by geographical proximity but also by historical links that facilitate commerce: by patterns of investment, by the presence of trading companies with knowledge of local production, by the use (in this instance) of European languages, and by tariff preferences.[2] But Africa's dependence on Europe also arises by default, that is, from the failure of African countries to diversify to any significant degree their trading links in the three decades since most states received their independence. Ideas of continental economic self-reliance have come to naught. The disparity between the enormous bureaucratic investment in the promotion of African regional integration and the meager results achieved has merely increased cynicism. And Africa's economic decline makes the continent an unattractive prospect as a trading partner.

The causes of economic decline are multiple.[3] Africa's recent dismal economic performance is partly explained by the lack of attractiveness of the continent as an economic partner. Many African governments have been very wary, in general, of immersion in the world economy and, in particular, of foreign investment. Foreign investors were further deterred by political instability and economic mismanagement. The 1980s were characterized by disinvestment as foreign corporations sought to disengage from what was perceived as an increasingly hopeless situation. With the ending of the Cold War, the principal motivation for non-European involvement in the continent disappeared.[4] In the 1990s, African countries had to rely primarily on humanitarian factors for motivating foreign involvement on the continent, factors that historically have seldom carried much weight in foreign policy bureaucracies faced with problems that are perceived to be central to the national interest.

Europe, preoccupied with its own internal problems as it moved toward the establishment of a single integrated market in 1992 and with the growing instability on its eastern borders following the disintegration of the Soviet bloc, appeared, in the early 1990s, to have lost enthusiasm for its development compact with Africa. Although European publics continued to give generously to charities seeking to mitigate the effects of disasters in Africa, aid fatigue appeared to be affecting European governments. Disillusioned with the meager effects of project aid, donor governments increasingly tied their aid to political reform and often to the adoption of an IMF-approved structural adjustment program. Even France, long the champion of increased assistance to Africa within the European Union, seemed to be tiring of the costs of supporting its sphere of influence. The data on Africa's share in European trade illustrate one reason for Europe's decreasing interest in the continent.

Trade Between Africa and the European Union

More than twenty years have passed since the beginning of the negotiations for the first Lomé Convention. At the time of those negotiations, the initial success of the Organization of Petroleum Exporting Countries (OPEC) in forcing up the price of oil raised fears among industrialized countries about the future security of the supply of raw materials. A partnership with raw-materials-rich Africa appeared attractive to European governments. But OPEC's success was short-lived. Not only did the price of oil tumble, its downward spiral was followed by similar movements for the prices of other primary commodities. New sources of minerals were opened up—often in countries (Australia, Canada, and even Brazil and Chile) that were regarded as far more secure sources of supply than their African competitors. Meanwhile, the raw materials intensity of industrial production declined significantly. In 1975, commodities constituted 26 percent of EU imports; by 1980, their share had fallen to 22 percent, and six years later, it was just 17 percent. The scramble of less developed countries to increase their export earnings in the 1980s produced an oversupply of most tropical agricultural products. With the collapse of international commodity agreements, there was nothing to prevent significant price falls.

The combination of reduced demand for their primary product exports, lower prices, and often reduced supply as a consequence of economic mismanagement has produced a marked diminution in Africa's importance as a trade partner for the European Union. The data in Table 5.1 document this decline.

The magnitude of the collapse of Africa's share of the European market, particularly since 1980, is quite staggering. For the European Union as a whole, Africa's share of extra-European Union imports in 1992 was only 3.2 percent, less than half the level of a decade before. For individual European countries, Africa's share

TABLE 5.1   Sub-Saharan Africa's Share of European Union Imports (in percentages)[a]

	1960	1965	1970	1975	1980	1985	1990	1992
Belgium	8.6	5.1	5.3	2.8	3.2	3.4	2.3	2.2
France	9.2	7.3	5.4	5.1	5.1	4.7	2.3	1.8
Germany	3.8	3.4	2.8	2.9	2.9	2.6	1.1	0.8
Italy	3.6	4.2	3.6	2.4	2.9	3.3	1.4	1.0
Netherlands	3.8	2.7	3.2	3.4	5.0	2.5	1.5	1.2
Portugal	15.3	16.5	15.0	6.1	4.1	7.3	4.2	3.0
United Kingdom	5.1	7.2	5.4	3.5	2.3	2.2	0.9	1.0
European Union[b]	8.3	8.9	8.4	6.7	6.6	6.9	3.8	3.2

   [a] The group "Sub-Saharan Africa" in Tables 5.1 through 5.6 does not include South Africa.

   [b] Excludes intra-European Union trade. Calculations for individual countries include imports from other European Union member states.

Source: International Monetary Fund, *Direction of Trade* (Washington, D.C.: IMF, various years, accessed through the International Economic Data Bank, Australian National University).

of total imports (including those from other European Union countries) exceeded 2 percent only for Belgium and Portugal. Africa's share in French imports was barely a third of the 1980s' level.[5]

A similar decline in Africa's share in European Union exports is reflected in the data in Table 5.2. Between 1960 and 1980, Africa's share in the exports of the European Union (excluding trade with other European Union countries) fell by only one-half of 1 percent. By 1992, however, the share was less than half of the 1980 level. In that year, there were only two countries, France and Portugal, for which Africa provided markets for more than 2 percent of their total exports. To be sure, some African markets continued to be of significance to European exporters; Nigeria is the obvious example. But even here, economic decline took its toll on the value of commerce with the African country, for Nigeria was by far the single most important source of bad debts for the export insurance schemes of both the

TABLE 5.2   Sub-Saharan Africa's Share of European Union Exports (in percentages)

	1960	1965	1970	1975	1980	1985	1990	1992
Belgium	3.2	2.5	2.2	2.0	2.2	1.6	1.2	1.1
France	8.4	7.7	5.8	6.3	6.0	4.7	3.2	3.1
Germany	2.5	2.0	1.7	1.9	1.9	1.1	0.7	0.7
Italy	2.7	2.9	2.5	2.4	2.6	1.9	1.2	1.0
Netherlands	3.1	2.7	1.9	2.4	2.5	1.5	1.1	1.0
Portugal	28.1	25.8	24.9	9.2	6.6	4.7	3.7	5.9
United Kingdom	6.8	6.4	5.1	5.1	5.1	2.7	1.7	1.6
European Union[a]	8.0	8.2	7.0	7.0	7.5	4.9	3.7	3.7

   [a] Excludes intro-European Union trade. Calculations for individual countries include exports to other European Union member states.

Source: International Monetary Fund, *Direction of Trade* (Washington, D.C.: IMF, various years, accessed through the International Economic Data Bank, Australian National University).

United Kingdom and West Germany. The cumulative losses for Britain's Export Credit Guarantee Department on trade with Nigeria amounted to £1.9 billions (approximately $3 billion) in 1992, nearly four times the value of all British exports to Nigeria in the previous year.[6] Trade with Nigeria increasingly took on the character of a form of outdoor relief for British industry as the British government had to pick up the bills on which Nigeria defaulted. The poor credit rating of many African countries made them ineligible for European export insurance schemes—further adding to the risk and lack of attractiveness of Africa as a market for European firms. Africa's declining significance as an outlet for European exports has given European governments and corporations, pursuing more rapidly growing markets elsewhere, little reason to preserve, let alone extend, the advantages in market access (such as the tariff preferences offered by the Lomé Convention) that Africa enjoys compared with other less developed countries.

The asymmetry in the relationship is evident when the data on Africa's dependence on Europe as a market and as a source of imports are examined. The data in Table 5.3 show that despite a drop in Africa's dependence on the European market since independence, the European Union still accounts for close to one-half of Africa's exports and supplies a similar percentage of Africa's imports.[7]

Aggregating data at the European level does, however, obscure the diversification that has occurred within the European Union. In particular, the shares of the former metropoles in the exports of their former colonies declined markedly. For instance, Britain's share of the exports of its former African colonies dropped from an average of 36 percent in 1958–1963 to under 10 percent in 1974–1986. Perhaps more surprising, given France's continued close ties with its former colonies, was the decline in the importance of the French market for the exports of francophone African states. The percentage of exports from former French colonies absorbed by France fell from an average of 56 to 25 percent in the years 1958–1963 to 1974–1986. Similarly, the most marked reduction in Belgian and Portuguese shares of African exports occurred in those of their former colonies. Meanwhile, the share of the former colonial powers in the exports of other African countries rose significantly. This diversification of markets within the European Union reflects both the ending of traditional colonial spheres of preferential trading and the improved access to the markets of nontraditional trading partners that was provided to African states by the Lomé Conventions.[8]

Even with the postindependence decrease in Africa's export market concentration, Europe as a whole, particularly the European Union, remains by far the sin-

TABLE 5.3   European Union's Share in Sub-Saharan Imports and Exports (in percentages)

	1960	1965	1970	1975	1980	1985	1990	1992
Imports	61.9	52.7	51.1	50.3	50.2	46.6	46.4	44.8
Exports	65.0	59.5	54.8	45.8	46.4	55.2	44.5	45.1

Source: International Monetary Fund, *Direction of Trade* (Washington, D.C.: IMF, various years, accessed through the International Economic Data Bank, Australian National University).

gle most important export market. In contrast to the European Union's 45 percent share of African exports, the next most important market is the United States, which absorbed 25 percent of all African exports in 1992 (and a far smaller percentage still if Nigeria is removed from the analysis). The third of the major trading giants, Japan, is a pygmy as far as African exports are concerned. In 1992, it provided a market for only 2.7 percent of Africa's total exports and has never been above the 3 percent level. Despite the emphasis given to south-south trade in general and to African regional integration in particular, other developing countries absorbed 12 percent and African countries absorbed only 8 percent of all African exports. The asymmetry of the trade relationship with Europe makes Africa's dependence on—and thus its vulnerability to leverage from—the European Union all the more acute.

The Aid Relationship

Africa's dependence on the European Union for foreign aid is equally pronounced. The data in Table 5.4 show that the European Union's share in the total aid receipts of Africa has remained fairly steady over the last twenty years, at about 50 percent. Europe's share in Africa's aid receipts is higher than its share in global overseas development assistance.

For many years, France has been by far the largest single source of aid to Africa. In 1991, its aid to Africa, at close to $3 billion, was more than 60 percent above that of the second largest donor, the International Development Association (IDA), the World Bank's soft-loan arm (Table 5.5). The European Development Fund (EDF), the European Union's multilateral aid fund, now a component of the Lomé relationship, was close behind the World Bank; its aid to Africa far exceeded that from all the U.N. agencies (such as the United Nations Development Program [UNDP], the United Nations International Children's Emergency Fund [UNICEF], the United Nations High Commission for Refugees [UNHCR], and the World Food Program [WFP]) combined. The EDF together with four EU member states made up five of the top nine donors to Africa; the only non-European donors on the list besides the World Bank were the United States and Japan.

The data in Table 5.6 show that most of the major European Union aid donors in the last decade directed between one-third and one-half of their total foreign

TABLE 5.4   European Union's Share in Africa's Total Net ODA Receipts (in percentages)

1970	1973	1977	1981	1985	1987	1991
53	53	48	47	43	52	45

Source: Derived from data in Organization for Economic Co-operation and Development, *Geographical Distribution of Financial Flows to Developing Countries* (Paris: Organization for Economic Co-operation and Development, various years).

TABLE 5.5   Major Aid Donors to Africa in 1991 (in millions of US$)

Donor	Amount
France	2,973
International Development Association	1,839
European Development Fund	1,557
Germany	1,371
United States	935
Japan	757
United Kingdom	710
Sweden	626
Italy	589

Source: Organization for Economic Co-operation and Development, *Development Co-operation: 1992 Report* (Paris: OECD, 1992).

aid to Africa. For several of the countries, however, Africa's share declined in the early 1990s. This was true of Belgium, Denmark, Italy, and the Netherlands, with the United Kingdom being the only country with a pronounced move in the other direction in 1991. Generalizations on the basis of data for an individual year are extremely hazardous, particularly for data on aid disbursements, which tend to be "lumpy" in that they may be distorted by payments for a single large project. One might speculate, nevertheless, that the trends in Table 5.6, viewed in conjunction with a similar downward tendency in the data in Table 5.4, may provide a preliminary indication of a growing aid "fatigue" in the European Union's relations with Africa. Certainly since 1990, when the European Union has become particularly preoccupied with the promotion of democratization and privatization in less developed countries, there has been far less tolerance of African governments perceived as recalcitrant. Aid programs have increasingly been coordinated at the European level and frequently made subject to African governments' reaching agreement on a structural adjustment program with the International Monetary Fund and the World Bank. Aid programs to countries that

TABLE 5.6   Sub-Saharan Africa's Share in Net Disbursements of ODA by European Union Countries (in percentages)

	1973	1977	1981	1985	1990	1991
Belgium	69	68	67	67	54	42
Denmark	54	53	52	50	43	45
France	44	47	50	45	55	51
Germany	20	26	31	30	31	31
Italy	19	34	61	57	52	27
Netherlands	18	28	31	33	34	24
United Kingdom	31	27	37	35	36	42

Source: Organization for Economic Co-operation and Development, *Development Co-operation* (Paris: OECD, various years).

were previously major recipients, such as Ethiopia, Kenya, Malawi, Sudan, Togo, and Zaire, were suspended at various times in the early 1990s.[9]

Relations Between Individual European Countries and Africa

Britain

Britain's loss of interest in Africa has been more pronounced than that of the other major former colonial powers. The strong Africa lobby of the 1950s and 1960s has largely disappeared from the British political scene, and African events—except for crises and disasters—seldom receive detailed attention in the media. The economic problems that Britain experienced since the 1960s led to a general turning inward and to an attempted redefinition of its role within Europe; as far as Africa is concerned, there has been a great deal of impatience and disappointment in political circles with Africa's economic and political evolution.[10] British politicians, particularly in the period of Conservative party government since 1979, have given the impression that the colonial legacy is something of an embarrassment, a situation in which they are unwilling to invest any significant political energies.

British capital, with the exception of rather maverick corporations like Lonrho, has generally seen little advantage in attempting to increase ties with black Africa (Nigeria was an exception during the oil boom), given the region's poor economic performance and the capricious attitudes displayed by several former British colonies in the 1970s toward foreign investment. In contrast, British corporations maintained their role as the single most important source of foreign investment in the Republic of South Africa, accounting for over 40 percent of the total. Britain broke ranks with its European Union partners in 1990 by unilaterally lifting the voluntary ban on new investments in South Africa (the EU lifted the ban at the end of that year).

The preoccupation of Conservative governments with cutting public expenditure reduced the value of the aid program by more than 20 percent in the early 1980s. Britain's ratio of overseas development assistance to GNP fell from 0.47 percent in 1965 to a low of 0.27 percent in 1990 before picking up to 0.31 percent in 1991.[11] Since Britain has traditionally given a major portion of its aid to African countries (although India has been the largest single recipient overall), the decline in the aid budget has reduced Britain to being a second-tier player in Africa. British aid to Africa had been exceeded by that from Japan in 1986; in 1990, aid from Britain to Africa was lower than that of Italy, the Netherlands, and Sweden. The government's niggardly attitude was maintained in multilateral institutions: Britain initially refused to support the World Bank's Special Facility for Africa but eventually made a contribution in 1985; in 1993, Britain refused to provide any financing for the replenishment of the International Monetary Fund's Enhanced Structural Adjustment Facility (which provides low-interest loans to countries, the majority of which are in Africa, embarked on structural adjustment programs).

The Conservative governments have insisted that greater weight in the aid program be given to British commercial and political interests. This has led to a rise in the share of "mixed" credits (which typically combine grants or loans on concessionary terms with export credits tied to purchases from the donor country) in Britain's aid. The program was criticized by the Foreign Affairs Committee of the House of Commons for moving away from agricultural projects to large construction projects intended to enhance British prestige abroad. At the Commonwealth Heads of Government Meeting in Harare in October 1991, Prime Minister John Major stated that British aid in the future would be linked to good government; the Harare Declaration emphasized the promotion of democracy, human rights, and equality for women.

On issues relating to debt and structural adjustment, the Conservative governments, under pressure from Britain's significant development assistance lobby, have adopted a more progressive stance than some of their European counterparts. Britain was one of the first countries to convert all outstanding loans to thirteen of the poorest African countries into grants. The government supported the replenishment of IDA and the trebling of the capital of the African Development Bank. Chancellor of the Exchequer Nigel Lawson deserves much of the credit for the plan for African debt relief devised at the Toronto economic summit of industrialized countries. At the Trinidad meeting of Commonwealth finance ministers in 1990, his successor, John Major, called on Western governments to write off two-thirds of the debts of the least developed countries and to extend the repayment period for other loans. Britain pioneered the purchase of surplus food from African countries to be given as aid to their neighbors; it subsequently succeeded in convincing its European Union colleagues of the merit of this idea for EEC-financed food aid.

Although Margaret Thatcher's government was closely associated with the hard-line "globalist" posture on international affairs pursued by the Reagan administration,[12] the globalist approach surprisingly did not spill over into attitudes on a number of key African issues. The government ignored both the calls of right-wing critics for a termination of aid to the government of one longtime critic of Britain, Milton Obote, then president of Uganda, and their protests at British assistance for Angola and Mozambique. The government's agreement to provide British training for Mozambique's army angered many within the Conservative party. Thatcher was insistent—despite pressure from various sporting bodies in Britain—on upholding the Gleneagles agreement on a Commonwealth sports boycott against South Africa; in general, the government also observed the U.N. arms embargo against the republic. Again somewhat surprisingly, Thatcher opposed the linkage made by the Reagan administration between a settlement of the Namibian issue and the withdrawal of Cuban troops from Angola.

The most controversial of the African policies of the Thatcher era was the stance taken on the Republic of South Africa. Throughout most of the 1980s, the government encouraged an expansion of Britain's already strong economic ties with the republic. Initially, it appeared that some British companies would seek to fill the gap left by U.S. disinvestment—although certain larger British companies began to pull out by the end of the decade. The government permitted the state-owned Central Electricity Generating Board to continue to purchase uranium from South Africa (probably extracted in Namibia). Thatcher expressed a good deal of sympathy for the modest reform efforts undertaken by the South African government prior to the release of Nelson Mandela; her personal opposition to sanctions left Britain isolated in the Commonwealth Heads of Government Meetings through much of the 1980s.

The Commonwealth continues as the principal institutional embodiment of the colonial legacy and is undoubtedly still valued by Britain as a lingering reminder of its former status as a great power. But in the 1980s, the Commonwealth Heads of Government Meeting served primarily as a forum in which the former colonies voiced their grievances about British policies, particularly those toward South Africa. With Thatcher's removal from office, coincidental with a movement toward constitutional reform in South Africa, relations with the Commonwealth improved. In September 1993, however, the government of John Major angered other members of the Commonwealth by its decision to discontinue funding for the Commonwealth Institute in 1996.

Thirty years after independence, Britain's political influence in most of its former African colonies appears negligible. An intervention by British troops to put down a military revolt—as happened in East Africa in 1964—is unthinkable today. The decline of British influence in Africa mirrors the country's loss of stature as a world power.

Germany

In Germany, Margaret Thatcher had a reliable ally in her efforts to oppose the imposition of sanctions against South Africa and to resist any significant restructuring of international economic regimes. Germany, like Japan, has placed business above politics in its relations with other countries; its objective has been to maintain good relations regardless of the type of regime in power in its trading partners. Africa (again with the exception of South Africa) has been very low on the German political agenda, even more so given the financial difficulties of reunification. Since the abandonment of the Hallstein Doctrine, under which the former West Germany broke diplomatic relations with countries that recognized East Germany, political developments on the continent have seldom been permitted to interrupt economic ties.

Germany sells a smaller percentage of its exports to African markets than do any of the other larger economies in the European Union. Although not the most important trading partner for any African country, Germany has been successful in establishing itself across the continent in francophone, anglophone, and lusophone countries. Rolf Hofmeier noted that Germany is consistently the second, third, or fourth most important business partner for African countries and thus has a wider geographical spread of trading and investment interests on the continent than either the United States, Britain, or France.[13] Although Germany devotes a smaller proportion of its aid budget to Africa than do most other European Union countries, this share has risen from 20 percent in the mid-1970s to over 30 percent presently. Coupled with the increase in the size of its foreign aid program, this has raised Germany to the position of the second most important bilateral donor to Africa, with total aid close to double that supplied by Britain. German aid also tends to be more widely dispersed geographically throughout Africa than that of other major donors.

Over the past thirty years, Tanzania and the Sudan have been the most favored recipients of German aid, followed by Kenya, Ghana, Cameroon, Zaire, Togo, Mali, and Niger.[14] The presence of Tanzania (a pre–World War I German colony) at the top of the list belies the normal German preference for countries with pro-Western sympathies that are pursuing market-oriented policies. With the installation in 1982 of a conservative coalition government in Bonn, however, responsibility for the Ministry for Economic Cooperation passed to the Bavarian-based Christian Social Union (CSU), which utilized its control of the ministry as a means of attacking the foreign policy pursued by its larger coalition partner, the Christian Democratic Union (CDU). A prolonged debate was initiated on the political suitability of some African aid recipients, most notably Tanzania, Ethiopia, and Mozambique. Tanzania's economic reforms in the 1980s and especially its willingness to comply with an IMF adjustment program quickly led, however, to its being restored as one of the more privileged recipients of German aid. To appease conservative interests, however, aid to Zaire was stepped up.

After 1982, in order to placate domestic constituencies, the conservative coalition placed a greater emphasis than its predecessor had on the use of aid to serve the interests of German industry. An increase in the percentage of aid given as mixed credits occurred (which has the effect of automatically tying the aid to purchases from German suppliers). Since 1978, however, German aid to the least developed countries has exclusively taken the form of grants; the Federal Republic of Germany has also canceled all interest and repayment obligations from earlier credits for nineteen African countries.

The Bonn government has been among the most intransigent of the industrialized countries in north-south negotiations, insisting on the superiority of market mechanisms to interventionist schemes. Germany initially refused to support the World Bank's Special Facility for Africa when it was proposed in 1985. It has consistently opposed any significant improvement of the Lomé Conventions (except where there is an obvious benefit to Europe—Germany was a principal advocate of the SYSMIN scheme, which provides support for maintaining mineral exports to the European market). In recent years, the Federal Republic has placed a great deal of emphasis on policy dialogue and conditionality in its aid relations. Germany has also joined Britain on a number of occasions in criticizing that part of the European Union's aid to Africa that had no strings attached.

Germany was adamantly opposed to the imposition of economic sanctions against South Africa. Like Britain, it reluctantly went along with the limited sanctions imposed by the European Union in 1986 in order to preserve a facade of European unity, but it succeeded in preventing imports of South African coal from being added to the European boycott. The Bonn government was also reluctant to cancel the cultural agreement that had existed with South Africa since 1962; this was eventually allowed to lapse in 1986. The governing CDU party, however, did resist the urging of the CSU (in particular, that of its former leader, Franz-Josef Strauss) to adopt an even more conservative stance on South African issues. The CSU had voiced its support for the rebel Mozambique National Resistance Movement (MNR, also known as RENAMO) in Mozambique; its political foundation, the Hans Seidel Foundation, provided support for the office of the National Union for the Total Independence of Angola (UNITA) in Munich.[15]

German industry has been one of the largest investors in the Republic of South Africa. In the 1980s, there were a number of political scandals regarding illegal German arms exports to South Africa, including the sale of construction plans for an advanced submarine. Successive governments did not pursue those accused of illicit arms sales with any vigor.

France

France's determination not only to maintain but also to expand its sphere of influence in Africa has set it apart from the other European former colonial powers. French policy toward Africa is best understood as one of the most important components of France's claim to middle power or mini-superpower status (together with its independent nuclear arsenal and its efforts to play a leading role in promoting European integration) and of its determination to pursue an independent and active foreign policy.[16] Only in Africa does France enjoy the relative autonomy to pursue a dominant political (and often economic) role, in large part unhindered by other countries. The second crucial factor motivating French policy toward Africa is the determined promotion of French language and culture. The countries of francophone Africa constitute more than half of the states worldwide in which French is an official language.[17]

French policy toward Africa, like its foreign policy in general, has been characterized by a striking continuity. Some would argue that this has been true over the centuries; certainly, it is apparent for the whole period of the Fifth Republic. Gaullism in foreign policy has long outlived de Gaulle. France's continuing quest for prestige and glory (*rayonnement*) stands at the heart of the policy. As Guy Martin pointed out, francophone African states have always been considered to be part of the French sphere of influence because of their historical links and geographical proximity: Francophone Africa is often considered as a French preserve (*domaine réservé or pré carré*) from which other foreign powers are to be excluded.[18]

Regardless of the political complexion of the government of the day, there has also been a marked continuity in procedures for foreign policy decisionmaking. Ultimate responsibility for foreign policy lies in the hands of the presidency—a matter that has not been seriously disputed even during the two periods in which the Socialist presidency of François Mitterrand has had to "cohabit" with non-Socialist governments. On African policy, successive presidents have always maintained their own advisers; for much of the Fifth Republic, this was the rather shadowy figure of Jacques Foccart.[19] Mitterrand's principal African adviser has been his own son, Jean-Christophe Mitterrand, known disrespectfully throughout francophone Africa by the nickname *PapaMaDit* (Daddy said). Although the elder Mitterrand came to office in 1981 with a pledge to "liberalize" policy toward Africa, the weight of entrenched bureaucratic, economic, and political interests has ensured that African policy during his presidency generally has been marked more by continuity than by change. By the early 1990s, however, there was increasing domestic criticism of the policy toward Africa, particularly its role in propping up corrupt dictatorships. With Africa's economic decline, French business has lost interest in the *pré carré*, and substantial disinvestment occurred in the second half of the 1980s. Although there are signs of changes in French policy and a general diminution of interest in Africa, the evidence is yet far from conclusive.

To the extent that France's African policy has been successful, this has resulted from the significant resources—economic, diplomatic, and military—that have been devoted to the continent. As noted earlier, France is the largest single aid donor to sub-Saharan Africa. Even if one discounts the half of this sum that, as Martin noted,[20] supports the more than 10,000 French technical assistance personnel in Africa, the residue of French aid would still place France at the top of the list of bilateral aid donors to Africa.[21]

Perhaps as significant as—and possibly more so than—the relatively generous assistance program has been the willingness of French governments to devote the diplomatic resources necessary not only to maintain political influence within the francophone states but also to expand it to other African countries. The key to French success has been the time and energy expended to convince African leaders that they enjoy a special relationship with Paris and that their views are taken seriously. This is reflected in data on state visits to African countries by French presidents, foreign ministers, and presidential advisers on African affairs and, similarly, on the number of visits by African heads of state to Paris. Martin reported that President Mitterrand made 13 state visits to Africa during the course of his first presidency; the former presidential adviser for African affairs, Guy Penne, undertook 81 missions in Africa and met privately with francophone heads of state on 205 occasions during his five-year tenure in office.[22] The contrast with the lack of interest that British and German governments have displayed in black Africa is striking.

The focal point of French relations with Africa is the Franco-African summit, inaugurated by President Georges Pompidou in 1973. Such summits were held annually until the late 1980s when it was decided that they would be convened biennially, alternating with the summit of francophone states. With rare exceptions, such as the 1984 summit following the French decision to terminate its military involvement in the Chadian imbroglio, these have been significant diplomatic successes for France. The number of African states attending has risen over the years to an average of 38 during the Mitterrand presidency. In 1986, for example, besides the 25 full members (Benin, Burundi, Cape Verde, Central African Republic (CAR), Chad, Comoros, Congo, Ivory Coast, Djibouti, France, Gabon, Gambia, Guinea, Guinea-Bissau, Equatorial Guinea, Mali, Morocco, Mauritius, Mauritania, Niger, Rwanda, Senegal, Seychelles, Togo, and Zaire), there were 14 other countries with observer status in attendance (Angola, Botswana, Egypt, Liberia, Mozambique, Nigeria, Sao Tome, Sierra Leone, Somalia, Sudan, Tanzania, Tunisia, Zambia, and Zimbabwe).[23] The list of full members attests to France's success in extending its sphere of influence beyond former French colonies: Besides the former Belgian colonies of Burundi, Rwanda, and Zaire, the list includes the former Portuguese colony Cape Verde, the former Spanish colony Equatorial Guinea, and the Gambia, a former British colony.

The very success of French diplomacy in extending its influence beyond the francophone group has itself been a source of problems. The African francophone states were quick to express their displeasure at what they perceived to be the dilution of a privileged relationship with Paris. These feelings came to a head shortly after Mitterrand's election when the Ministry for Cooperation and Development was subordinated to the Foreign Office and when its minister, Jean-Pierre Cot, attempted to fashion a broader role to include the supervision of development aid for all Third World countries. Cot's resignation at the end of 1982 after only eighteen months in office was widely perceived as a victory for the old guard. The 1983 Franco-African summit was preceded in Paris by a dinner for the heads of state of francophone countries; in 1985, the summit was preceded for the first time by a full-day meeting between Mitterrand and francophone delegations, a meeting dubbed *une réunion de famille*. African francophone states and conservative opposition parties within France alike had sought for special status to be given to the francophones. Finally, under the Chirac government, the Ministry of Cooperation was restored to a full-fledged ministry, with its responsibilities to be confined to francophone states.

The jealousies that emerged over the broadening of the francophone summit are indicative of the problems that France faces in playing an interventionist role in Africa. French attempts to maintain good relations throughout the continent frequently necessitate an attempt to be all things to all states—ranging from the very conservative regimes of the late Houphouet-Boigny in Ivory Coast and Omar Bongo in Gabon to those of radicals such as the late Thomas Sankara in Burkina Faso. Inevitably, France becomes drawn into disputes between African states; the decision to admit Morocco as a full member of the francophone group, for instance, caused friction with Algeria, given the latter's support for the Polisario Front that is in dispute with Morocco over the future of the Western Sahara. At times, France's relations with its extended family have resembled a soap opera—characterized by feuds over the activities of French-based exile groups and former emperors ensconced in French chateaux and over disclosures by French journalists of the extramarital affairs of the wives of African leaders. The usual solution to such family squabbles has been to dispatch the president's African adviser to soothe feelings in the appropriate African capital.

France has been particularly astute in portraying itself as a champion of Third World interests in international negotiations. Paris frequently voiced support for Third World proposals, safe in the knowledge that another Western power—the United States, Britain, or West Germany—would block any significant changes to international economic regimes. France is the classic free rider on other states' conservatism—but what often appear to others as cynical French maneuvers still enable Paris to take the kudos as the West's Third World champion. To some extent, a similar statement can be made about French policy toward South Africa.[24] Paris excelled in voicing slogans and taking symbolic actions that won it favor with black African states, but it was much more reticent about taking effective action (for example, imposing trade and investment sanctions against South Africa) that might have had a negative impact on its commercial interests. During the Giscard presidency, France supplied a nuclear reactor to South Africa's Koeberg station. Repeated accusations were made about French corporations breaking the U.N. arms embargo toward the republic. Yet France continued in the sanctions period to be one of South Africa's major economic partners. Certainly, the Mitterrand presidency went further than its counterparts elsewhere in Europe in arguing for stronger sanctions against South Africa—but again, the government could rely on West Germany or Britain to veto effective EU action.

France's economic influence in Africa is sustained by the membership of fourteen former French colonies, plus Equatorial Guinea, in the CFA franc zone. The franc zone consists of two currency unions with a common currency—the CFA franc. The CFA franc was, until August 1993, freely convertible, and it is guaranteed by the Bank of France at the exchange rate of 1 French franc to 50 CFA francs. In return, CFA members are required to hold 65 percent of their foreign exchange reserves in French francs with the Bank of France. By participating in the CFA, countries relinquish a great deal of control over their monetary policy: The central bank of each of the two currency unions determines how much may be borrowed by individual countries. Devaluation is not a policy option open to individual countries.

Balanced against this loss of control is a stability lacking in the financial affairs of many other parts of Africa. Until the mid-1980s, the franc zone countries had consistently lower rates of inflation than other African countries; the convertibility of the CFA franc was also attractive to foreign investors. Quantitative studies showed that until the mid-1980s, the economic performance of franc zone countries was no worse than that of other developing economies and significantly better than the average for sub-Saharan Africa.[25] From the mid-1980s onward, however, the situation was reversed. The economic performance of franc zone member states deteriorated, whereas that of the rest of sub-Saharan Africa improved. Most observers agree that the problem lies with the overvalued exchange rate: The rate of conversion of the CFA franc against the French franc has remained unchanged since 1947. Although most of the other countries in black Africa undertook (often massive) devaluations of their real exchange rate, the CFA appreciated in real terms.[26] This divergence of exchange rates made it very difficult for franc zone countries to sell their export crops on world markets. This was a complete contrast, for instance, to the situation in the 1970s when Ivory Coast successfully expanded its cocoa exports—to a considerable degree at the expense of neighboring Ghana, whose currency was overvalued at the time. In addition, the overvaluation of the CFA franc has encouraged smuggling from neighboring countries, with a resultant outflow of francs.

The unwillingness of either France or the members of the CFA to agree to devaluation has prompted substantial criticism from the World Bank, the International Monetary Fund, and the U.S. government. The French head of the IMF, Michel Camdessus, has been particularly outspoken, claiming that the overvaluation of the CFA franc has primarily benefited African elites who have been sending capital to Europe. In a deepening crisis in August 1993, the central banks of the two currency unions that constitute the CFA announced that they would no longer repurchase CFA francs from outside the franc zone. This move was designed to halt smuggling of goods from and currency to neighboring countries. The CFA franc henceforth was no longer fully convertible. But neither France nor the CFA member states showed any inclination toward devaluation. In fact, French officials have repeatedly questioned the effectiveness of devaluation as a policy tool for African economies. Certainly, an initial devaluation would encourage speculation that further devaluations would occur, posing the danger that expectations would become self-fulfilling.[27] Whatever its current negative influence on the performance of francophone economies, there is little doubt that the franc zone facilitates continued French influence and certainly provides an advantage to French traders.[28]

France's considerable military presence remains a potent tool of French influence in Africa. France maintains close to 8,000 troops on a permanent basis in the Central African Republic, Chad, Ivory Coast, Djibouti, Gabon, and Senegal. In addition, over 1,200 French military advisers are stationed in twenty-six African countries. In some countries, French advisers retain control over military communications networks.[29] To back up its personnel stationed in Africa, the Mitterrand government created a 47,000-strong rapid deployment force (*Force d'Action Rapide*) that can be quickly airlifted into African trouble spots. France has also had defense agreements with thirteen African countries. Bilateral agreements were signed with Benin (terminated 1974), Cameroon, Central African Republic, Chad (terminated 1978), Congo (terminated 1972), Ivory Coast, Djibouti, Gabon, Madagascar (terminated 1975), Mauritania (terminated 1972), Niger (terminated 1972), Senegal, and Togo. In addition, there are multilateral agreements between France and the three original members of the *Conseil de l'Entente* (Ivory Coast, Benin, and Niger) and with three countries of equatorial Africa (Central African Republic, Congo, and Chad). Of the former French colonies, only Mali and Guinea have never signed a defense agreement with France. All francophone African countries except Guinea (including the former Belgian colonies of Burundi, Rwanda, and Zaire) have military assistance agreements with France, and French troops frequently conduct joint exercises with local armed forces. Special protocols on "strategic" raw materials and products were concluded with Central African Republic, Gabon, Madagascar, Mauritania, Senegal, and Togo, providing French forces with privileged access to "strategic" materials in African states.[30]

France has not hesitated to intervene militarily when it believed its interests were threatened. Over the years since independence, it has deployed military forces in the Central African Republic, in Chad on five occasions, and in Djibouti, Gabon, Mauritania, Togo, Zaire, and, most recently, Rwanda. During the Giscard presidency in particular, France happily assumed the mantle of the defender of Western interests in Africa, most notably in the dispatch of troops to support President Mobutu Sese Seko of Zaire following the Shaba invasions—an action that prompted *Le Nouvel Observateur* to dub Valéry Giscard d'Estaing the "gendarme of Africa." Within French political circles, there was a widespread perception that France was standing alone in Africa in defense of stability against externally induced unrest.[31] Through its intervention in Chad to support the forces of Hissene Habré against those backed by Libya in the mid-1980s, the Mitterrand administration showed that it was no less willing than its predecessor to deploy French forces in Africa. The decision not to intervene to back Habré in November 1990 when he was eventually overthrown by the army of Idriss Deby thus seemed all the more surprising and was taken by some as a signal of a change in policy. As *Marchés Tropicaux* noted,[32] this was the first time that France had not intervened to support a government in an African country where French troops were stationed. Subsequently, however, French troops were dispatched to shore up the regime in Rwanda. Ostensibly, their mission was to protect French civilians, but the 600 to 700 troops supplemented by special forces from the Direction Générale de la Securité Exterieure outnumbered the French civilians they were supposed to be protecting.

Most francophone African governments (with the exception of the more radical regimes in office at one time in Burkina Faso, Guinea, and Mali) have welcomed the presence of French troops in their own or in neighboring countries. There have been efforts in recent years to establish regional and even pan-African forces to undertake peacekeeping efforts. But the reality, as the francophone states fully realize, is that any such forces, especially a regional west African force, will inevitably be dominated by Nigeria—as has been seen with the Economic Community of West Africa's Monitoring Group (ECOMOG), dispatched in an attempt to bring an end to the conflict in Liberia. Nigeria's leading role in ECOMOG caused resentment and suspicion among francophone states. Mali and Togo withdrew from the group, and several francophone states aided the rebel forces that ECOMOG was attempting to contain. A continued French military presence thus is valued by many francophone states as a means of offsetting what are perceived to be Nigeria's regional hegemonic aspirations.

The problem for many African governments is that they can no longer be assured that French forces will be used to support them, regardless of how good a friend they believe they have been to France in the past. This is where a shift of policy does, indeed, appear to have taken place. With the new emphasis on the promotion of democratization in Africa (discussed later in this chapter), France has been less willing to prop up regimes whose resistance to liberalization has provoked civil unrest. In November 1991, for instance, French troops were sent to Benin to be available for intervention in Togo if needed to support the elected government of Prime Minister Koffigoh and thus stand against the Togolese military, loyal to longtime French ally President Gnassingbe Eyadema. Again, it is too early to judge whether there has been a decisive shift in policy: The right-wing victory in the French elections in March 1993 brought new hope to dictators such as Eyadema.

If there has been a turning point in French policy, it may be dated to 1990. Then-Prime Minister Michel Rocard commissioned a report by a former ambassador, Stephane Hassel, on the country's development cooperation policies. The report concluded that: "Sub-Saharan Africa is a sub-continent in a state of structural crisis, threatened by marginalization. It is not suffering from a temporary crisis nor from a passing slump in its raw materials, but from a lasting inability to make itself part of the world economy and to hold on to its share of the market there—let alone increase its share."[33]

Hassel recommended that the distinction in cooperation between francophone and nonfrancophone countries should end. The report was very much in accord with contemporary French public opinion. With the new wave of democratization sweeping Eastern Europe, there was increasing disquiet regarding the way in which French policies were propping up corrupt, dictatorial regimes in Africa. What were previously regarded as policy indiscretions—for example, the use of 16 million francs from the French aid budget to refurbish the private DC-8 jet of President Bongo of Gabon—were no longer tolerable.

The response of the French presidency was to advocate democratization at the La Baule Franco-African summit in June 1990. Although Mitterrand took great pains to assure African countries that France had no intention of abandoning them now that the Cold War was over, he was insistent that political liberalization in francophone countries would have to occur. Former African heads of state were quoted as saying that they regarded the speech as "subversive."[34] In the subsequent period, only half-hearted attempts have been made at promoting democratization. As usual with French policy, the new thrust has been subordinated to traditional *raison d'état*. Neither democratization nor economic liberalization prevails in the event of a clash with perceived French interests. Thus, even though franc zone countries were told in September 1993 that they would no longer receive balance-of-payments support unless they undertook structural adjustment programs negotiated with the International Monetary Fund and World Bank, the French government's previous record of propping up favored regimes would have comforted African heads of state. And as noted earlier, the

1993 election of a right-wing government, traditionally more enthusiastic about links with Africa and more hospitable toward Africa's dictators, suggested that African policy in the mid-1990s would be characterized by substantial continuity.

Belgium, Portugal, and Spain

Even Belgium's considerable patience with the Mobutu regime in Zaire appeared to have been exhausted in June 1990 when it suspended aid following Mobutu's refusal to hold an international inquiry into an alleged massacre at Lubumbashi University. Although an agreement was reached to lift these sanctions at the beginning of 1992, relations were frozen again when Belgium refused to recognize the government appointed by Mobutu in April of that year. Subsequently, relations remained frozen as Zaire descended rapidly toward anarchy. Mobutu had previously been extremely adept at exploiting the desire of the Belgium government to maintain its influence in the largest of its former colonies in Africa. Despite the repeated humiliations to which Belgian interests in Zaire were subjected, successive governments in Brussels had not abandoned their enfant terrible, and they resisted French attempts to muscle in on their preserve. Thus, despite its frustrations with Mobutu, Belgium continued to champion his interests in consultative group meetings. Most of Belgium's aid is directed to its former colonies in Africa, and there is no doubt that Belgium will be anxious to resume its role in Zaire once Mobutu is finally forced from office.

Spain and Portugal were both preoccupied in the 1980s, first with preparation for and then with adaptation to their entry into the European Union. Relations with Africa have generally had a low priority, and neither country has clearly articulated an African policy. Spain's Socialist government, in power since 1982, continues to be embarrassed by its only former colony in black Africa, Equatorial Guinea. Spain had broken diplomatic relations with the country's notorious dictator, Francisco Macias Nguema, before his overthrow in 1979 but propped up the country's bankrupt economy and the only moderately more enlightened successor regime until the mid-1980s. Madrid was greatly relieved by the admission of Equatorial Guinea to the Union Douanière Economique de l'Afrique Centrale (UDEAC) in 1984 and to the franc zone in the following year, and it has given every indication that it is delighted that France wishes to include this unfortunate territory within its sphere of influence. Although it continued to be the largest single recipient of Spanish aid, funding to the former colony has leveled off since the mid-1980s.

Spanish economic, diplomatic, and cultural ties elsewhere in black Africa are extremely limited. Until the mid-1980s, Spain had no foreign aid or technical assistance program outside of Equatorial Guinea; subsequently, a very modest effort was begun in Mauritania, Senegal, and Zimbabwe. Spain's primary commercial interests in black Africa are in oil exploration (Gabon and Nigeria) and in fishing. It has few interests in South Africa; indeed, the Socialist government was prominent in calling for sanctions against Pretoria. Spain's primary interests in

Africa lie in the north part of the continent, where its enclaves of Ceuta and Melilla are among the last remnants of the old Spanish empire. These cities on the Moroccan coast, the majority of whose populations are Spanish, have been ruled continuously by Madrid since the sixteenth century. Both have been claimed by Morocco, which has drawn the obvious comparison between the situation of Ceuta and Melilla and that of Gibraltar. Spain has generally been successful in maintaining good relations with the regime of King Hassan in Morocco, to which it has provided military and other aid. Hassan has been regarded as the most reasonable leader that Morocco is likely to produce as far as Spanish interests are concerned.[35]

Spain has become the principal spokesman in the European Union for Central and Latin American interests. Inevitably, these interests sometimes conflict with those of African countries. For instance, Spain promoted the admission of the Dominican Republic to the Lomé Convention, against the wishes of several European and many African, Caribbean, and Pacific (ACP) states. Spain has also generally been opposed to any strengthening of the Lomé relationship, favoring a reduction in the trade preferences enjoyed by the ACP countries over other developing (including, of course, Latin American) states and supporting more European aid to countries outside the ACP group.

Portugal has effected a remarkable reconciliation with its former African colonies in the two decades since its precipitous exit following the military coup in Lisbon.[36] The Lisbon government occasionally served as an intermediary between Mozambique and Angola, on the one hand, and South Africa, on the other. Relations between Portugal and these two largest of its former African colonies have been complicated by the activities of exile groups in Lisbon and by accusations that support has been given to UNITA in Angola and the MNR in Mozambique. Portugal played a major role, with the support of the United States and the former Soviet Union, in mediating a cease-fire in the Angolan civil war in 1991, which opened the way for elections.

As the European Union's weakest economy, Portugal is not well placed to offer substantial assistance to African economies. Its small aid program is concentrated on its former territories, but Lisbon has also extended assistance to the Southern African Development Co-ordination Conference (SADCC). Attempts have been made to capitalize on its relations with Angola and Mozambique to extend trade ties with other frontline states. Portugal is not in a position to take advantage of economic opportunities, however, and has steadily lost economic influence in its former colonies to other European countries. In particular, Guinea Bissau and Cape Verde grew much closer to France in the late 1980s. Portugal responded by renewed diplomatic efforts, and in January 1990, Guinea Bissau announced that it had withdrawn the application it lodged in 1985 to join the franc zone and that its currency would be tied to the Portuguese *escudo*.[37]

Portugal was unwilling to take a strong stand on the issue of sanctions against South Africa. A principal reason for this was the size of the Portuguese settler community in the republic. Estimated at over 600,000, or approximately 14 percent of the white population, it is the third largest population group, behind the Afrikaners and the British. In addition to the actual numbers of Portuguese citizens involved, the fact that their remittances are one of Portugal's major sources of foreign currency earnings was important to Lisbon.

South Africa and the European Union

The lifting of sanctions against South Africa as the country moved toward free elections brought to an end a particularly shabby episode in European diplomacy. The European Union had been able to agree on a program of sanctions against South Africa only on the basis of the lowest common denominator—in this case, the opposition of Britain and Germany to any meaningful action. A voluntary code of conduct for the subsidiaries of European transnational corporations operating in South Africa was adopted in 1977 after the Soweto massacre. But only a small percentage (about 200 of the total of 1,000 subsidiaries) of the firms complied with the code by filing an annual report. In 1985, a new program of sanctions was adopted that reaffirmed the EU's support of the 1977 U.N. arms embargo. European states, however, failed to prevent the export of material that had possible dual (i.e., civilian and military) purposes. Machinery was exported that enabled South Africa to manufacture armaments domestically, thereby circumventing the arms embargo.

Meanwhile, individual European firms broke the arms embargo with impunity. British Aerospace supplied missiles to the republic, French technicians helped South Africa establish its own production of combat helicopters, Spain sold it arms in 1987, and Germany signed an agreement in 1984 on the supply of troop-carrying aircraft. Germany was to be further embarrassed by the revelation of the sale of construction plans for a sophisticated submarine by the state-owned Howaldtswerke-Deutsche Werft shipyard in Kiel. European oil companies (most notably Total, Shell, and British Petroleum) supplied petroleum. And British, French, and German banks agreed to a moratorium on South African debt in 1985. European Union member states had a similarly shabby record on supplying aid to the black population of southern Africa: The $8 million budgeted for the black population of South Africa, Namibia, and the SADCC countries was redirected in September 1990 to refugees from the Iraqi invasion of Kuwait.[38]

Although the lifting of sanctions by the international community has relieved the European Union from continuing embarrassment on this particular issue, it has raised another difficult question: What trading arrangement should be offered to the republic after the elections that were held in April 1994?[39] South Africa poses a problem for the EU because its economy is so much larger, more industrialized, and more diversified than any of the other countries of sub-Saharan Africa. Its gross domestic product in 1991 was estimated to be over $90 billion, or three times greater than that of Africa's next largest economy, Nigeria. A quarter of South Africa's GDP is derived from manufacturing, a figure matched only by Zimbabwe. Its per capita GNP at $2,560 was second only to that of Gabon

($3,780). Only Botswana joins these two in the World Bank's definition of upper-middle-income countries.[40]

Despite their limited effectiveness, there is no doubt that sanctions did have some impact in distorting the South African economy and its trading patterns in the last decade. And financial sanctions contributed to the republic's very poor economic performance in the second half of the 1980s. The available data on the value of South African trade must be treated with extreme caution, not only because they may well underestimate the potential of the South African economy but also because in the sanctions era, neither South Africa nor its trading partners were willing to reveal the true extent of potentially embarrassing relationships.

The data in Table 5.7 show that the pattern of South Africa's trade with the European Union mirrored that of other African countries: The republic declined in significance as a trading partner, especially since 1980.

Rather than focusing on South Africa's low shares in total European trade, it is more relevant to compare the shares with those of other African countries. South Africa was nominally doubly disadvantaged: It did not enjoy the trade preferences in the European Union market available to other African countries, and it also had to contend with economic sanctions. Despite this, however, the European Union's total imports from South Africa in 1991 were close to one-third of the value of imports from all other sub-Saharan countries. Moreover, imports of manufactures from South Africa were over half the value of all imports of manufactures from all other African countries.[41]

The simplest solution to the trade relationship dilemma might seem to be to accord South Africa full membership in the Lomé Convention, for this would provide the republic with the same access to the European market as that enjoyed by neighboring states, and it would thus facilitate economic cooperation within the southern African region.[42] But whether this move would be acceptable to the European Union or, indeed, to all of the existing members of the ACP Group is questionable. When the Lomé Convention was first negotiated, following Britain's admission to the European Union, the six members of the union at the time were emphatic in stating that a relationship similar to that enjoyed by the former Belgian and French colonies would only be made available to countries of "comparable economic structure" (thereby ruling out the more developed former British colonies such as India and Pakistan, and the soon-to-be-former colony of

TABLE 5.7 South African Customs Union's Share in European Union's Imports and Exports (in percentages)[a]

	1960	1965	1970	1975	1980	1985	1990	1992
Imports	2.2	2.4	2.2	2.2	1.9	1.8	1.4	1.3
Exports	2.9	3.8	3.4	2.8	2.3	1.5	1.3	1.2

[a] Excludes intra-European Union trade.

Source: International Monetary Fund, *Direction of Trade* (Washington, D.C.: IMF, various years, accessed through the International Economic Data Bank, Australian National University).

Hong Kong). Whether South Africa could be regarded as being of "comparable economic structure" to the remainder of sub-Saharan Africa is debatable. Certainly, its inclusion within the Lomé relationship would pose potential problems in the trade field (both for "sensitive" European industries such as textiles and for European producers of apples and citrus) and also would require a significant expansion of the aid commitment if South Africa were to be given access to all the various dimensions of the convention (such as STABEX, SYSMIN, and the European Development Fund, discussed in the final section of this chapter).

South Africa's admission to the Lomé Convention might also be opposed by existing members of the ACP Group and by other trading partners of the European Union. The obvious fear of other ACP countries is that providing additional aid to accommodate South Africa's claims will inevitably mean depleting funds that they would otherwise have received. The presence of South Africa would also completely change the delicate balance that currently exists within the ACP Group, which has always been afflicted by tensions between francophone and anglophone and between Caribbean and African members. The interests of other trading partners of the European Union might also be adversely affected. For instance, the Mediterranean and Maghreb countries have agreements that permit access to the European market for specific quantities of citrus and other agricultural products that currently provide them with a competitive advantage over South Africa. And Australia, a country with a similar mix of exports to South Africa, might also object if it was placed on a disadvantageous footing in the European market.

Multilateralized Relations Between Africa and the European Union: The Lomé Conventions

With successive enlargements of the European Union, Africa's trade relations with most of Western Europe have been increasingly regulated by Brussels rather than the individual European capitals. Africa's initial association with the European Union came through the Treaty of Rome at a time when France and Belgium maintained formal political control over their black African territories; with independence, the relationship was maintained with only minimal modification in the Yaoundé Conventions. Finally, British accession to the union in 1973 led to the association of former British colonies in Africa, the Caribbean, and the Pacific, accompanied by Ethiopia and Liberia, through the first Lomé Convention, signed in 1975. Subsequently, the agreement has been extended to all independent countries in black Africa.

As the EU is fond of reminding its ACP partners, the convention is the most comprehensive economic agreement offered by industrialized countries to a group of developing countries. Besides a trade chapter, which grants free access to European markets on a nonreciprocal basis to most of the exports of the ACP countries,[43] it includes a scheme to stabilize ACP earnings from the export of agricultural commodities (STABEX), measures to encourage ACP mineral production for the European market (SYSMIN), arrangements for specific quantities of ACP sugar to be purchased by the EC at prices close to those paid to European producers, institutions to promote cooperation in the fields of agriculture and industry, and funding for financial and technical assistance through the European Development Fund.

The intention of the ACP Group in entering the Lomé relationship was primarily a defensive one: first, to utilize the "special relationship" they enjoyed with their former colonial powers to safeguard their position in the European market, and second, to maintain their status as privileged recipients of European aid—a strategy that I characterized as "collective clientelism."[44] Fifteen years after its initial signature, the Lomé Convention has disappointed those who held high hopes for what it might achieve. Launched with the heady rhetoric of interdependence and equality expressed by the Third World in its demands for a new international economic order, the convention has been routinized into what is primarily an aid relationship—albeit one that is of considerable value to Africa. As data in Table 5.5 show, the EDF has become the third largest donor to sub-Saharan Africa, which was contributing $1.5 billion annually by the early 1990s. And though the increase in the funding of the EDF over the years may have come at the expense of some of the member states' bilateral aid programs, the share of ACP countries in general and of Africa in particular in the bilateral programs has not declined—suggesting that the ACP Group might well be receiving more aid than it would have had the EDF not been established. There is, of course, no way of definitively determining whether this is so.

The most disappointing aspect of the convention has been the poor results (from the ACP perspective) in the trade sphere.[45] The ACP Group has not been able to persuade the European Union to maintain its margin of preference over third countries on a number of products of particular interest to the group. The EU has gradually enlarged the Generalized System of Preferences (GSP) scheme that it offers to other developing countries, often placing their market access on a par with that of the ACP Group. The World Bank estimates that Africa receives an average tariff preference in the European Union market of 2 percent over other developing countries. This margin may be reduced further as a result of the Uruguay Round of the General Agreement on Tariffs and Trade (GATT) negotiations.[46] The preferential margin hardly offsets the disadvantages African countries have in competition with more advanced developing countries such as Malaysia.

European representatives have argued that the primary benefit of the convention's trade provisions lies in the security they provide. Whereas the ACP Group enjoy a "contractual" arrangement in their trade with the EC, other developing countries are dependent upon a unilaterally administered GSP scheme that changes from year to year. In reality, the contractual element of the convention is largely illusory: The agreement contains a number of escape clauses that enable the union to take safeguard action should it perceive that ACP imports are damaging domestic producers. While negotiations for the second convention were in progress, the European Commission threatened to take safeguard action against Mauritius unless it agreed to a voluntary export restraint on its sales of sweaters to the European market—despite the minuscule share of European imports that Mauritius supplied. This action sent a clear signal to investors that exports of "sensitive" products from the ACP Group would not be treated any differently than those from other suppliers. Confidence in the security of access provided by the convention was undermined. The EU has also taken a very mean-spirited approach toward ACP agricultural products that compete with domestic production.

The convention cannot be blamed for the relatively poor trade performance of most ACP states. This owes far more to economic mismanagement and to adverse developments in the world economy, especially the collapse of commodity prices. In fact, a plausible argument can be made that the trade record of African states might have been even worse were it not for the convention's provisions. On the other hand, the margin of preferences that the convention provides has ensured that it simply has not had a major effect on the trade relationship.

As I have argued elsewhere,[47] the Lomé relationship has largely been routinized, ritualized, and marginalized—routinized in that the energies of the parties are concentrated on the day-to-day implementation of aid and trade procedures that, for the most part, are now well established; ritualized in that the parties periodically (especially at the time of the convention's renegotiation) confront one another with demands that have changed little since the signature of the first convention (particularly true of the ACP Group) and that produce equally predictable and ritualized responses; and marginalized in that the ACP countries in general and the institutionalized relationship with them through Lomé in particular have become less and less important to the European Union. Inevitably, the rhetoric about the convention being an equal partnership has been exposed as hollow. The asymmetry in the relationship has been underlined by the European insistence on a greater element of policy dialogue in the aid relationship and on greater conditionality to be attached to those transfers (e.g., from the STABEX scheme) that were originally intended to be made automatically to ACP governments once the relevant criteria were met.

The Lomé relationship, for all its limitations, nevertheless represents the best deal available to African states. Therein lies the second dimension of dependency by default: Not only have African countries failed in significantly reducing their dependence on the European Union, but no other major industrialized country has had any interest in adopting them as clients.

Notes

I am grateful to Lyn Fisher and David Sullivan for research assistance on successive versions of this chapter.

1. On November 1, 1993, the Maastricht Treaty on European Union entered into force between the twelve members of the European Community, which thereafter was known as the European Union. For the sake of consistency, references in this chapter will be to

the European Union (EU). Unless otherwise stated, *Africa* in this chapter refers to sub-Saharan Africa, with the exception of South Africa.

2. In this case, I refer to those provided under the Lomé Convention, which links the European Union with sixty-nine African, Caribbean, and Pacific countries. The convention is discussed in more detail in the last section of this chapter.

3. See Thomas M. Callaghy and John Ravenhill, eds., *Hemmed In: Responses to Africa's Economic Decline* (New York: Columbia University Press, 1993).

4. Even Japan's aid to Africa was determined in the first half of the 1980s, largely by strategic considerations, with emphasis being given to East Africa.

5. Although I anticipated a decline in Africa's share of Europe's trade, I was so surprised by the magnitude recorded that I recalculated all the figures for the previous years. Some minor differences are reported from the data in the tables that appeared in the first edition of this book. These variations could be caused by corrections made by the IMF to the earlier data or by different definitions of the sub-Saharan or European Union group, among other things. Data in these tables, for instance, refer to the twelve member states of the European Union, whereas those in the tables of the earlier edition excluded the most recent members of the European club, Spain, Portugal, and Greece. The overall trend in the tables is the same, however, showing a dramatic decline, especially in the past decade, in Africa's importance as a trading partner for Europe.

These tables use European data rather than the notoriously unreliable African data. For discussion of the problems of African data, see Alexander J. Yeats, "On the Accuracy of Economic Observations: Do Sub-Saharan Trade Statistics Mean Anything?" *The World Bank Economic Review* 4, no. 2 (May 1990), pp. 135–156.

6. *Africa Research Bulletin: Economic, Financial and Technical Series* (January-February 1993), p. 11123. In 1987, Nigeria's bad debts to the West German government's Hermes export guarantee scheme amounted to DM658m. Rolf Hofmeier, "West Germany's Year in Africa: Politicians Suddenly Discover Africa," in Colin Legum and Marion E. Doro, eds., *Africa Contemporary Record: Annual Survey and Documents 1987–88* (New York: Africana Publishing, 1989), p. A88.

7. These data must be interpreted with some caution, for they are supplied by African reporting countries. Trends in aggregate exports for Africa are also determined overwhelmingly by a limited number of commodities, of which petroleum is by far the most important. Much of the diversification in markets for African exports in the 1970s was the result of a very large increase in the value of oil exports to the United States.

Aggregate data also obscure the variation in dependence on the European market by commodity and by country. African countries are generally less dependent on the European Union for their exports of fuels and minerals than they are for agricultural exports. Country dependence on Europe varies from about one-third of the exports of Ethiopia to about 90 percent of the exports of Senegal, Niger, Sierra Leone, and Equatorial Guinea. For data, see Alfred Tovias, *The European Communities' Single Market: The Challenge of 1992 for Sub-Saharan Africa*, World Bank Discussion Paper no. 100 (Washington, D.C.: World Bank, 1990), statistical annex table A1.

8. A similar diversification in trade patterns with individual European Union partners occurred for imports. For more detailed discussion, see Joanna Moss and John Ravenhill, "Trade Diversification in Black Africa," *Journal of Modern African Studies* 27, no. 3 (September 1989), pp. 521–545.

9. With the ending of the Cold War, African governments are no longer able to play the security card in attempting to attract aid. Meanwhile, the increasing coordination

between donors has reduced the (rather limited) capacity of African governments to play donors off against one another. A united front, however, is not always maintained by European donors. France has most frequently broken ranks to provide aid to countries that are otherwise on donors' blacklists. An example is the substantial French aid in the early 1990s to Cameroon and Senegal, countries that failed to adhere to the terms of their structural adjustment programs. In January 1993, for instance, France gave Cameroon a loan to meet the arrears in payments that the African country owed the World Bank, thus enabling Cameroon to avoid being added to the bank's blacklist of countries ineligible for credits. European countries also often play significant roles as champions of particular African governments in the board meetings of international financial institutions or in the meetings of creditors' consultative groups; they also sometimes assume the lead position as providers of finance once agreement has been reached in a consultative group meeting. France and the United Kingdom typically continue to be the major players and champion the interests of some of their former colonies. For a useful discussion of trends in Europe's aid to Africa, see Roger Riddell, "Aid Performance and Prospects," in I. William Zartman, ed., *Europe and Africa: The New Phase* (Boulder: Lynne Rienner Publishers, 1993), pp. 139–158.

10. See the very useful surveys by Colin Legum that have appeared annually in *Africa Contemporary Record* (New York: Africana Publishing, various years).

11. Organisation for European Co-operation and Development, *Development Co-operation* (Paris: OECD, various years). Britain's ratio was far below the U.N. target of 0.7 percent, and among OECD countries, it only exceeded the ratios of Ireland, New Zealand, and the United States. Of the other European Union donors, only Denmark and the Netherlands (at 0.96 and 0.88 percent, respectively) exceeded the U.N. target in 1991. France, however, had exceeded the target between 1985 and 1990.

12. "Globalists" typically perceive local confrontations in terms of the overall East-West struggle. For a discussion of the globalist nature of the Reagan administration's African policies, see Donald Rothchild and John Ravenhill, "Subordinating African Issues to Global Logic: Reagan Confronts Political Complexity," in Kenneth A. Oye, Robert J. Lieber, and Donald Rothchild, eds., *Eagle Resurgent? The Reagan Era in American Foreign Policy* (Boston: Little, Brown, 1987), pp. 393–430.

13. Rolf Hofmeier, "Aid from the Federal Republic of Germany to Africa," *Journal of Modern African Studies* 24, no. 4 (December 1986), p. 577.

14. For a more complete listing of the geographical distribution of German aid to Africa in the 1980s, see ibid., pp. 588–589, and Brigitte Schulz and William Hansen, "Aid or Imperialism? West Germany in Sub-Saharan Africa," *Journal of Modern African Studies* 22, no. 2 (June 1984), p. 304.

15. For further details, see the articles on West Germany and Africa by Rolf Hofmeier in successive issues of *Africa Contemporary Record* (New York: Africana Publishing).

16. Stanley Hoffman, "La France face a son image," *Politique étrangère* 51 (1986), pp. 25–53.

17. For further discussion of *francophonie,* see Robert Aldrich and John Connell, "Francophonie: Language, Culture or Politics?" in Aldrich and Connell, eds., *France in World Politics* (London: Routledge, 1989), pp. 170–193.

18. Guy Martin, "France and Africa," in ibid., p. 104.

19. Tamar Golan, "A Certain Mystery: How Can France Do Everything It Does in Africa—And Get Away with It?" *African Affairs* 80, no. 318 (January 1981), pp. 6–7.

20. Martin, "France and Africa," p. 108.

21. In recent years, an increasing amount of French aid has been given as mixed credits in an attempt to utilize aid for export promotion purposes. The United States has been particularly critical of French subsidization of its exports to Third World countries in this manner.

22. Martin, "France and Africa," p. 122, n. 47.

23. Claude Wauthier, "France and Africa in 1986: Cohabitation and Its Ambiguous Consequences for French Policy," in Colin Legum, ed., *Africa Contemporary Record: Annual Survey and Documents 1986–87* (New York: Africana Publishing, 1988), p. A199.

24. For instance, in May 1987, France abstained on a U.N. vote that would have imposed mandatory sanctions against South Africa over its illegal occupation of Namibia. The resolution was vetoed by the United Kingdom and the United States.

25. Patrick Guillaumont, Sylviane Guillaumont, and Patrick Plane, "Participating in African Monetary Unions: An Alternative Evaluation," *World Development* 16, no. 5 (May 1988), pp. 569–576; see also Shantayanan Devarajan and Jaime De Melo, "Evaluating Participation in African Monetary Unions: A Statistical Analysis of the CFA Zones," in ibid., pp. 483–496. For a critical appraisal of the franc zone, see Guy Martin, "The Franc Zone: Underdevelopment and Dependency in Francophone Africa," *Third World Quarterly* 8, no. 1 (January 1986), pp. 205–235.

26. Shantayanan Devarajan and Jaime de Melo, "Relative Performance of CFA Franc Zone Members and Other Countries," in I. William Zartman, ed., *Europe and Africa: The New Phase* (Boulder: Lynne Rienner Publishers, 1993), pp. 121–138.

27. After this chapter was completed, the CFA franc was devalued by 50 percent in January 1994.

28. The monetary links between France and its former colonies again stand in marked contrast to anglophone Africa: By the middle of the 1980s, no African currency was linked to the pound sterling.

29. Golan, "A Certain Mystery," p. 8. In Gabon, French pilots reportedly fly most of the air force planes. See Michael C. Reed, "Gabon: A Neo-Colonial Enclave of Enduring French Interest," *Journal of Modern African Studies* 25, no. 2 (June 1987), p. 284.

30. Edmond Kwam Kouassi and John White, "The Impact of Reduced European Security Roles on African Relations," in I. William Zartman, ed., *Europe and Africa: The New Phase* (Boulder: Lynne Rienner Publishers, 1993), pp. 29–31; and Martin, "France and Africa," citing John Chipman, *French Military Policy and Africa Security,* Adelphi Paper no. 201 (London: International Institute for Strategic Studies, 1985).

31. Pierre Lellouche and D. Moisi, "French Policy in Africa: A Lonely Battle Against Destabilization," *International Security* 3, no. 1 (Spring 1979), pp. 108–133.

32. Quoted in *Africa Research Bulletin: Political, Social and Cultural Series* (November 1990), p. 9888.

33. *Le Monde,* March 31, 1990, quoted in *Africa Research Bulletin: Economic, Financial and Technical Series* (April 1990), p. 9898.

34. *Africa Research Bulletin: Political, Social and Cultural Series* (July 1990), p. 9713.

35. Aaron Segal, "Spain and Africa: The Continuing Problem of Ceuta and Melilla," in Colin Legum and Marion E. Doro, eds., *Africa Contemporary Record,* vol. 20, *Annual Survey and Documents 1987–88* (New York: Africana Publishing, 1989), pp. A71–A77.

36. Norman MacQueen, "Portugal and Africa: The Politics of Re-Engagement," *Journal of Modern African Studies* 23, no. 1 (April 1985), pp. 31–51.

37. *Africa Research Bulletin: Economic, Financial and Technical Series* (February 1990), p. 9841.

38. See Valérie Hugues, "La CEE et L'Afrique du Sud," *Année Africaine* (1990–91), pp. 61–85; Martin Holland, *The European Community and South Africa* (London: Frances Pinter, 1988).

39. On September 29, 1993, the European Union agreed on a "rolling program" for the normalization of relations with South Africa but delayed negotiation of a new trade accord until after the elections.

40. Data from World Bank, *World Development Report 1993* (New York: Oxford University Press, 1993), statistical annex.

41. Author's calculations using data from U.N. trade tapes from the International Economic Data Bank, Australian National University. These data refer to the South African Customs Union (comprising the Republic of South Africa, Botswana, Lesotho, and Swaziland). The existence of the Customs Union is a further complication in any analysis of South Africa's trade.

South Africa's dependence on the European Union for imports and exports is less than that of other sub-Saharan African countries. In 1992, the European Union consumed 25 percent of South African exports and provided 37 percent of South African imports. Japan and the United States each provided a market for about 6 percent of South Africa's exports; they supplied 9 and 13 percent, respectively, of the republic's imports. These data are based on South African reporting and can only be taken as rough approximations of the relative importance of the various trading partners.

42. If South Africa negotiated a trade treaty with provisions different from those of the Lomé Convention, cooperation with neighboring countries might be impaired by difficulties in complying with the convention's rules of origin (which specify that a certain percentage of the value of a product must be added locally for it to be classified as originating within that country). For a useful discussion of the various trade options available in the EU–South African relationship and their possible pitfalls, see Christopher Stevens, Jane Kennan, and Richard Ketley, "EC Trade Preferences and a Post-apartheid South Africa," *International Affairs* 69, no. 1 (January 1993), pp. 89–108.

43. Special protocols and other specific provisions in the convention apply to "sensitive" products, most notably those included within the European Union's Common Agricultural Policy.

44. John Ravenhill, *Collective Clientelism: The Lomé Conventions and North-South Relations* (New York: Columbia University Press, 1985).

45. The convention's provisions for reducing the instability of earnings from the export of primary commodities, STABEX, have also proved disappointing. The collapse of prices for African commodity exports has exhausted the funds available to STABEX on several occasions, with the consequence that beneficiary countries sometimes received less than half the compensation to which they were entitled. This exhaustion of funds occurred despite a particularly ungenerous interpretation during the third convention of the rules for calculating transfers. In this period, export earnings were calculated in local currencies. Where African countries had, in line with the recommendations of the international financial institutions and Western donors, significantly depreciated their currencies, the local currency equivalents from commodity exports were sometimes sufficient to deny them eligibility for STABEX transfers, even though the foreign currency earnings were a fraction of previous levels. Uganda, for instance, was denied transfers because of the effects of devaluation on local currency earnings. This anomaly was removed in the fourth convention when it was agreed that eligibility for STABEX would be determined by earnings calculated in European currency units (ECUs).

46. -Figure cited in Tovias, *The European Communities' Single Market*, p. 5. In principle, the reductions in duties, particularly on tropical agricultural products, in the Uruguay Round should offer new opportunities to ACP exporters. To exploit them, however, they will have to be competitive with alternative sources of supply. Tovias estimated that the elimination of the German excise tax on tropical beverages will lead to an increase in domestic consumption of about 8 percent, equivalent to a rise of 3 percent in overall EU demand. On past patterns, about one-quarter of this increase will benefit African exporters.

47. John Ravenhill, "When Weakness Is Strength: The Lomé IV Negotiations," in I. William Zartman, ed., *Europe and Africa: The New Phase* (Boulder: Lynne Rienner Publishers, 1993), pp. 41–62.

PART THREE

Regional Theaters of African International Relations

6

Post–Cold War Politics in the Horn of Africa: The Quest for Political Identity Intensified

JOHN W. HARBESON

THE FIRST YEARS of the post–Cold War era have wrought a fundamental transformation in the political contours of the Horn of Africa and in the nature of its participation in international politics beyond its borders.[1] Eritrea has emerged as an independent state from its long war with Ethiopia, and Somaliland is bidding to disengage from the wreckage of Somalia to do so as well. Whether Somalia's warlords, residual legatees of Siad Barre's autocratic regime, or anyone else can resurrect a new Somalia state in some form remains an open question. Meanwhile, Ethiopia is in transition from Mengistu Haile Mariam's military dictatorship to what its new leaders have pledged will be a democratic state founded on self-determination for its component ethnic communities. Southern Sudan's civil war with the fundamentalist Islamic north rages on with little prospect of resolution, while leadership struggles within the south have themselves approached civil war dimensions. The delicate ethnic balance holding Djibouti together has been threatened by moves to entrench Issa predominance.

On the heels of its first multiparty elections in thirty years of independence, historical ethnic conflicts over land in neighbor-state Kenya have become the most serious since the Emergency years of the 1950s. International cooperation between the leaders of Ethiopia, Eritrea, and Kenya has gained international recognition as perhaps the most promising venue for promoting a restored Somalia. Finally, externally supported insurgency in the name of Islamic fundamentalism carries the potential to replace the Cold War in the Horn of Africa as the rationale for subordinating economic and political form to the requirements of domestic and regional international security.

What are the connections, if any, between cessation of the Cold War and these tumultuous and profound political transformations on the Horn? The hypothesis of this chapter is that the end of the Cold War removed artificial restraints on profound, long-simmering, and overlapping struggles over political identity—struggles whose courses and outcomes cannot yet be discerned with any degree of clarity. Colonial powers were always far less successful in the Horn than elsewhere in defining political communities on the basis of structures fashioned after their African communities. Moreover, because the foundations of the Western nation-state have been more shallow than elsewhere, the processes and ultimate outcomes of the Horn's struggles over political identity have been correspondingly less predictable in Western terms than they might otherwise be.

Bilateral and multilateral campaigns for more open societies, multiparty democracies, and market-led economies, hallmarks of a unipolar post–Cold War international order, have done more to date to further fuel the Horn's struggles over political identity than to guide them toward the realization of those goals. The major powers have linked their demands that African governments reduce their domination of political and economic life with programs to strengthen their governmental capacity and effectiveness. But these measures may not have offset the effects of somewhat shrunken public sectors on the governments' capacities to shape struggles over political identity in constructive directions by peaceful means.

In global terms, what is at issue in the region's strife is whether, in what ways, when, and on what terms the Horn will participate in an order still resting theoretically and empirically on realist-neorealist assumptions: That there continue to be secure nation-state actors functioning within an international system that shapes the interests of its participating nation-state actors. In addition, neorealist theory postulates that the international system of nation-states will emerge and prevail over the Hobbesian anarchy that would otherwise obtain.[2] One consequence of the limited impact of European imperialism on the Horn is that in the post–Cold War world, the area may continue to defy neorealist notions about the universality of these underlying premises. The conceptual and empirical implications of this state of affairs remain to be fully explored.[3]

The Horn's burgeoning struggles over political identity venture into largely uncharted terrain in both theory and practice. The literature on democratic transitions, based heavily on Latin American experience, generally tends to focus on transitions from authoritarian to democratic regimes where the question of legitimacy and viability of the state itself is not in question. But it is precisely the nature and viability of the state as we know it that is at issue in the civil wars on the Horn. In a region where Western notions of the nation-state are much less deeply rooted than elsewhere, rulers have undermined the legitimacy of those ideas, along with their own regimes, by their heavy-handed tactics. Thus, the shrinking of the spheres of such governments that has occurred under structural adjustment programs has simply further opened the floodgates to underlying contests over political identity that may ultimately lead to alternative political formations. It follows that the institutionalization of democracy and market economies can, at best, occur parallel to ongoing debates over political identity.

It is probably more realistic to suggest that whether, how, and what kind of economic and political liberalization is institutionalized will depend on the outcomes of those struggles.

In international terms, the Horn countries' preoccupation with profound internal questions of political identity creates the same political vacuum that the Cold War gladiators rushed to fill in this part of the world. Now, however, Islamic fundamentalism seeks to fill this political space, and, unlike the situation in the Cold War, countervailing campaigns have yet to be defined and implemented. From a base in Sudan where Islamic fundamentalism has been institutionalized, at least in the north, observers have spotted its advanced guards in parts of southern Ethiopia, Eritrea, Kenya, and Somalia where Islamic moderation has historically prevailed.

In the pages that follow, I will explore these themes, first by outlining the historical, political, and socioeconomic dimensions of the region that frame the searches for political identity and community there. Second, I will review briefly the history of the region's engagement with major world powers, with a view to exploring the interaction between regions that do not equally exemplify the assumptions of neorealist international relations theory. Third, I will explore the flourishing contemporary struggles over political identity and consider their implications for the Horn of Africa as a regional international system.

Defining the Horn of Africa

One direct consequence of the incomplete process of establishing the stable, settled identity of the major international actors in the Horn of Africa is that the boundaries of the region itself are somewhat inchoate, even shifting, and defined differently by various individuals. Ethiopia, Eritrea, Djibouti, and Somalia would be included in almost any definition of the Horn. If one sets as a criterion for inclusion a thin, even nonexistent line between domestic and international politics, Sudan should probably be included. Egypt and Kenya should probably be treated as important participating neighbors in the international politics of the Horn.

In the region's struggles over the geographic and juridical identities of its actors, the boundaries between "domestic" and "international" spheres have remained unusually permeable. Disputed boundaries have both reflected and fueled complex, revolutionary conflict over who the legitimate rulers are and whom they are entitled to rule. Sudan's long-running civil war has influenced and been influenced by the Eritrean civil war and the Tigrean-led insurgency leading to the overthrow of the Mengistu government. The collapse of the Somalian state simply dramatizes the fact that what was at stake in its conflicts with Ethiopia was far deeper than simply boundary disputes; it was the survival of the Somali state itself. For Ethiopia, the withdrawal of ethnic Somalis would compound the loss of Eritrea, setting a bold precedent for the Oromo and other peoples inhabiting 75 percent of the land annexed to the ancient empire by the conquests of Emperor Menelik II around the turn of the century.[4] Finally, tiny Djibouti is composed of peoples closely identified with their kin in Ethiopia and Somalia. Its continued existence as an independent state since 1977 has rested on a rough power balance between Ethiopia and Somalia and on a continued French military presence. In other words, more fundamental even than the constitution of the state is at least a rudimentary, minimal consensus on the shared cultural and political identity of those who allow themselves to be united juridically.

Recent and contemporary boundary struggles reflect the continuation and, in some cases, the intensification of just those multiple, overlapping, and perhaps conflicting struggles regarding political identity. Sudan's struggle has been made increasingly complex by more and more violent divisions within the north and especially the south over the objectives and conduct of the civil war. Sudan and Ethiopia have provided refuge and support for each other's opponents throughout the Mengistu years and, to some extent, even beyond. During that same period, Sudan vacillated between supporting the Eritrean liberation movement against Ethiopia and seeking to employ its good offices to reconcile the conflict.

The overthrow of Siad Barre's regime in Somalia ended over twenty years of a generally successful suppression of the most basic questions of political identity left unresolved during the colonial era. The issue of the political identity of Somalis residing in Ethiopia, arbitrated primarily on the battlefield with superpower involvement during the Cold War, has resurfaced. This occurs even as many other ethnic communities have been reexamining the meaning and terms of their participation in Ethiopia, with at least the qualified encouragement of the new Ethiopian People's Revolutionary Democratic Front (EPRDF).

At issue has been not only their claims for greater political and cultural equality in the present but also historical issues of equity arising from their conquest by the expeditionary forces of Emperor Menelik II. The fragile balance in Djibouti between the Afars and Issas has been further tested and magnified by the effects of the renewed contests over the definition of postimperial Ethiopia and the collapse of Somalia, respectively.

A defining feature of the Horn is the region's qualitatively different exposure to European influence during the colonial era. Although the machinations of European powers complicated, disrupted, and profoundly altered the politics of the Horn, their impact on the region's socioeconomic and culture structures was, in many respects, less intensive and profound than elsewhere on the continent. The peoples of the Horn displayed a singular capacity to resist imperial intrusions. The prior spread of Islam in the Horn and the political strength of Coptic Christianity in Ethiopia appear to have stiffened local peoples' resistance to European socioeconomic, cultural, and political influences.[5] Largely as a result, substantial areas of all the Horn countries—southern Sudan, the interior of Somalia, and 80 percent of the land area of Ethiopia—have remained essentially unpenetrated by roads and other modern means of communication longer than has been the case in much of the rest of Africa. Mountainous terrain in Ethiopia has also impeded the spread of transport and other communication networks.

This prolonged inaccessibility has helped the region resist European political influences, perpetuated strongly centrifugal domestic political tendencies in all the countries (with the possible exception of Djibouti), and limited Western socioeconomic impact. To this generalization, Gezira in the Sudan, the Chilalo (later Arsi) Agricultural Development Unit in Ethiopia, and somewhat higher educational levels in Italy's former colony Eritrea appear to be the major exceptions. Otherwise, the per capita incomes and educational levels in the region have remained among the lowest in the world.

With some significant localized exceptions, primarily in Ethiopia, the region has attracted much less overseas private investment than other parts of the continent. One aspect of this underinvestment has been that relatively little attention has been paid to technologies that might help the region cope with its precarious ecology. Although the region is by no means lacking in economic potential, desertification and deforestation have been endemic. At present, large areas are basically suitable only for pastoralism, others cannot be cultivated intensively, and still others have suffered from centuries of deep erosion. Areas of significant irrigation potential—notably along the Nile, the Awash, and the Wabe Shebelle Rivers—remain underdeveloped.

The underlying struggle over political identity in the region has been greatly accentuated by the Horn's enormous and complex ethnic diversity. As its present state of collapse makes clear to all, this is true even in Somalia, where a common Islamic faith and the Arabic language have been ineffectual as bases for a shared political destiny. Politically dominant groups, such as the Amhara and the Oromo in Ethiopia, have remained internally divided along territorial lines. Innumerable small communities with distinct dialects and traditions, many of them still relatively isolated, are found throughout the region. The indifference of pastoralists, a sizable and distinctive constituency, to political boundaries has further complicated the international politics of the region. The historical bases of ethnic conflict in Ethiopia, further deepened by involvement with European powers, have magnified and been enlarged by recurrent drought and famine. One of the largest movements of refugees in the world has resulted, further complicating and burdening the already troubled processes of political formation and development in the region.

The Modern History of International Politics on the Horn

The international politics of the Horn and those of Europe began to converge in the nineteenth century, although this was preceded much earlier by the region's exposure to external influence from Islam. In the sixteenth century, the Portuguese remained to apply their technological capabilities after having helped Ethiopia survive the jihad of Ahmed Gran. However, they overextended their welcome and were expelled when they sought to convert the Coptic kingdom to Roman Catholicism.[6] On the heels of this international triumph followed by domestic trauma came an external challenge from another source: Oromo expansion from the south. The combined effect of the Amhara kingdom's wars with and more peaceful interpenetration by the Oromo was to reduce the authority of the monarchy to little more than symbolic proportions by the end of the eighteenth century. During this period of radical decentralization (known as the "era of princes"), Ethiopia nevertheless successfully preserved its independence. Sven Rubenson has argued persuasively that national identity, not merely forbidding topography (as Arnold Toynbee asserted), enabled the Ethiopian state to survive, although the nature of that political identity and how it was perceived by the actors themselves remain subjects for further historical research.[7]

The beginnings of European imperial intrusion in the Horn as a whole roughly coincided with the renaissance of the Ethiopian state under Teodros and Johannes, followed by the state's threefold expansion under Menelik II. In this process, the interests of Ethiopia collided with those of its neighbors. Simultaneously, all the countries of the region were struggling to come to terms with the expanding European powers, whose competition with each other reflected the dynamics of the European balance of power.

European imperial competition on the Horn profoundly influenced but did not decisively determine the parameters of international politics in the region. The rivalry centered first on Egypt. The French invasion and occupation of Egypt under Napoleon Bonaparte awakened long-dormant European interest in the region, provoking a fundamental transformation in relations among the peoples of the region. In the disarray following France's departure, Muhammed Ali emerged not only to consolidate his rule in Egypt and promote European-influenced reforms but also to extend his rule over much of what is now Sudan by the middle of the nineteenth century. Within a generation, Egyptian influence expanded further south and east, extending to what is now Eritrea and the Somali coast.[8] In the first decades of the nineteenth century, meanwhile, Great Britain began to make increasing use of the Red Sea as a pathway to India. Within a generation, France and Italy responded by acquiring their own outposts on the Red Sea coast. With the further decline of the Ottoman Empire, highlighted by Serbian and Bulgarian revolts, the resulting political vacuum led to a major clash of interests among the expanding, competing European powers. Meanwhile, at the high point of Egypt's territorial expansion, unrepaid Egyptian external debt prompted British and French administrative intervention and led, in 1882, to a British military strike.

The dynamics of the European balance of power shaped the manner in which Britain employed its enhanced influence in the region. To avoid upsetting increasingly strained and frayed international relations within the European theater and in response to domestic pressures, the British government chose to prop up and exert influence through the existing Ottoman rulers rather than to establish more formal colonial authority. That pattern of limited, indirect involvement was to continue and to shape fundamentally the impact of European international relations upon those of the Horn. Elsewhere in Africa and in the Third World, colonial powers ultimately excluded European competition in their respective spheres through formal colonization.

By contrast, Britain's constrained role in Egypt and in the Sudan, controlled by Egypt on behalf of the Ottoman rulers, imposed no limits on a major international struggle within the Horn itself or on other European powers pursuing their own interests in the region. While Egypt was preoccupied with escalating European involvement in its affairs and competition in its neighborhood that involved Italy as well as France, the Mahdist revolution broke out in the Sudan, fueled by a combination of religious idealism and resentment of heavy-handed Egyptian administration.[9] The Mahdist revolution challenged not only a weakened Egypt and limited British presence but also Ethiopia, where Emperor Johannes IV wrestled with centrifugal tendencies integrally related to his country's growing involvement with European powers and their international competition. Johannes died leading his armies against Mahdist forces with whom one of his principal rivals, Teclehaimanot of Gojjam, was suspected of collaborating. Simultaneously, the other rival, Menelik, who was to become Johannes's successor, was beginning the vast expansion of the Ethiopian empire made possible, in large part, by his arms trade with Italy. Meanwhile, France as well as Italy challenged Britain's claim to control of the upper Nile, producing the Fashoda crisis at the end of the century.

This pattern of constrained European imperial intervention and competition, stirring up rather than suppressing "international" conflict and competition among rulers within the Horn itself, strongly influenced the pattern of state formation within the region long after the European powers formally withdrew. The fundamental outcome was that the importation of Western state structure in the Horn was far more superficial than elsewhere. Correspondingly, local and preexisting political formations have remained important bases of political identity, notwithstanding efforts of regimes in the postindependence era to employ the trappings of Western forms of statehood and thereby entrench their positions. The weakness and/or collapse of these successor regimes has deepened the crisis of Western-style state formation and highlighted the question of its utility in the cultivation of enduring political identity in the Horn. The cases of Sudan, Ethiopia, and Somalia illustrate the point.

The Sudan

The memory of the Mahdist revolution lived on to influence Sudanese nationalist politics during the colonial period. At the time, however, the embryonic Mahdist state failed to establish itself as an autonomous actor capable of joining and sustaining its own interests in the European competition for power in the region. Preoccupied with a bitter and violent struggle to consolidate his power among rivals who united behind the Mahdi, Abdallahi (the Mahdi's successor) chose to continue the jihad rather than establish an embryonic territorial state through attempted negotiations with European powers. His eventual defeat by Anglo-

Egyptian forces was to perpetuate both Egyptian and British influence through the Condominium.

As a consequence, ambivalence on the issue of whether Sudan would or should be an independent state or, alternatively, merge with Egypt remained centrally important to Sudanese politics throughout the colonial period. Egyptian nationalists encouraged nationalism in Sudan. Britain sought to manage regional international relations through divide-and-conquer tactics against both Sudanese and Egyptian nationalist movements. In the former case, Britain sowed divisions between pan-Arab nationalists, who sought a common cause with Egypt, and the Mahdists. Although the Mahdists preferred an independent course, they found it prudent to unite with Britain against both Egypt and their domestic rivals, who viewed such an unholy alliance with contempt. It was Nasser's renunciation of Farouk's pretensions to be king of both Egypt and Sudan and his recognition of Sudanese self-determination—not any rapprochement with the Sudan itself—that cleared the way for Sudanese independence in 1956.

Meanwhile, the British had set out to cordon off the southern provinces from the influence of either the Mahdists or their rivals; this policy was not abandoned until less than a decade before Sudan's independence, by which time the fruits of separate development had ripened into glaring socioeconomic inequalities. Thus, in important ways, British recognition of Sudan's independence may be said to have represented a juridical fig leaf, poorly concealing the sacrifice of emergent Sudanese statehood to Britain's manipulation of regional politics on the Horn to serve its imperial ends. On the one hand, the long-standing de facto partition of the Islamic north from the Christian-animist south weakened the position of those within the north who might have preferred a more independent role for the country vis-à-vis the Muslim states of the Middle East. On the other hand, cordoning off the south was not sufficient by itself to stimulate a durable nationalism that embraced the entire area. The fissures in southern resistance to integration with the north on the north's terms bear further witness to a superficial sense of statehood in the Western context, even within this region. Thus, limited as well as divisive British colonial politics in Sudan prepared the way for the civil wars that have dominated Sudan's history since independence and for the possibility that the idea of the state itself, as understood in the West, may yet be a casualty in both the south and the north.

Ethiopia

From the mid-nineteenth to the late twentieth centuries, Ethiopia's rulers courted international recognition both to confirm the country's historical independence in a world of intensifying international conflict and to buttress the domestic legitimacy of their regimes. However, the most lasting consequences of Ethiopia's engagement with expanding European competition in the Horn was a multifaceted, thirty-year struggle over the existence and definition of the Ethiopian state, culminating in Eritrea's independence in 1991.

In the mid-nineteenth century, Teodros emerged from obscurity to initiate the revival and reunification of the Ethiopian empire. His shining vision was secular, though the Mahdi's was sacred, but its revolutionary fervor was no less intense.[10] Teodros sought to purify the Ethiopian state from the corrupting influences of the clergy and of the nobility and their armies. He pursued this vision with a militancy that undermined the unity he at first began to build and the international recognition that he sought. Thus, he left to his successor, Johannes, the twin tasks of consolidating a reunited Ethiopia and preserving its integrity and independence in the face of imperial competition.[11]

Ethiopia both gained and lost in the international competition of European and regional actors on the Horn. As *negusa negast*—king of kings—Johannes succeeded diplomatically in consolidating Ethiopian unity on the basis of a federal-like relationship with the kings of Gojjam and Shoa, Teclehaimanot and Menelik, respectively. But it was a fragile unity, given Teclehaimanot's suspected collaboration with the Mahdi against Johannes and Menelik's expanding power base vis-à-vis the "king of kings" through his conquests. Italy judged that its trade in arms with Menelik for this purpose weakened any effort Johannes might make to obstruct its incursion into what is now Eritrea.

Early in Johannes's reign, his own military strength was sufficient to expel a weakened Egypt and defeat a small Italian force in Eritrea in pursuit of his kingdom's historical claim to be a Red Sea power. In the complicated politics of the European balance of power, however, Britain found it was in its interests to encourage Italian advances in the Horn as a means of checking French pretensions. Johannes's diplomacy was not sufficient to prevent Italy's inheritance of Massawa from a retreating Egypt—with British concurrence. In the 1880s, Italy expanded its sphere to include most of what is now Eritrea. Emperor Menelik, accepting realities, confirmed this with his erstwhile partner, Italy, in the Treaty of Ucciali in 1889. From that time on, Eritrea proceeded on a course separate from that of Ethiopia, laying the foundations for its civil war with and eventual independence from Ethiopia.[12]

Italy's imperial thirst, encouraged by Britain for its own purposes, was not quenched. Menelik renounced the Treaty of Ucciali when French diplomats pointed out to him that the Italian version of the treaty suggested he had agreed to an Italian protectorate over all of Ethiopia, allowing Italy to represent him in international negotiations. The resulting war, climaxed by an Ethiopian victory at Adwa in 1896, brought Ethiopia a stature in Eurocentric international relations enjoyed by no other African power. However, this newly won status counted for little when, forty years later, Emperor Haile Selassie appealed to the League of Nations for support in a new Italian war against Ethiopia. Italy occupied Ethiopia from 1936 until British armies liberated the country and restored Haile Selassie to his throne in 1941. Britain, however, had its own colonial designs on Ethiopia, but these were to be thwarted primarily by the emperor's own determined efforts and by a lack of U.S. encouragement for British pretensions.[13]

Undeterred by past experience, Haile Selassie calculated that the enhancement of Ethiopian interests—the interests of his regime—and Ethiopia's standing in world affairs dictated his country's active participation in both regional international relations and in the Cold War on the side of the Western alliance. As a historically independent state in an otherwise still-colonized continent, Ethiopia came to symbolize African liberation even to national leaders a generation removed and a pole apart politically from Selassie. In cultivating his new role, Selassie gained a measure of legitimacy among African leaders bent on rolling back European imperialism, an irony that Somalia, with its claims to the Ogaden, has never successfully impressed on the OAU or other African leaders individually.

Selassie's domestic traditionalism brought him important patronage from the United States, which feared that the Soviet Union would capitalize on nationalism in northeastern Africa and the Middle East to expand its influence. U.S. patronage allowed Ethiopia to present a more modern image internationally. This included training Selassie's armed forces and building a communications base in Asmara, Eritrea, which was used for monitoring activities in the Soviet Union and the Middle East until it became technologically obsolete in the early 1970s.

Haile Selassie may also have calculated that such international prestige would both dampen criticism of his transparently superficial measures to convert his empire to a Westminster constitutional monarchy and quell adverse international reaction to his deliberate cashiering of the Eritrean federation in favor of full incorporation with Ethiopia.[14] In this, he largely succeeded but only until just before the end of his reign in 1974.

In this respect, Cold War détente in the 1970s prefigured the end of the Cold War itself less than two decades later. Ethiopia's strategic value to the United States diminished with the technological obsolescence of the Kagnew communications base and the beginnings of a more "evenhanded" approach to the Arab-Israeli conflict in the Kissinger years. Ethiopia's unwillingness to confront its massive drought and famine in 1972–1973 shattered Selassie's carefully crafted international image, and his seeming inability to address the crisis betrayed both his personal decline and the flimsiness of his alleged guidance of the country toward a Westminster-style constitutional monarchy. Particularly in retrospect, it is clear that his dethroning in 1974 not only set Eritrea on an inevitable course to independence but also seriously undermined the Ethiopian national unity that had been restored by the exertions of Teodros and Johannes. The successor regime of Mengistu Haile Mariam remembered Teodros's vision but not the lesson his regime bequeathed its successors. The regime of Meles Zenawi today wrestles with the consequences—that is, party-supported ethnic challenges to national unity continue.

Somalia

In contrast to Ethiopia and Sudan, the future Somalian state was affected more directly by the expanding Ethiopian empire than by European empires, which, for the most part, limited their activities to coastal Red Sea beachheads. Strengthened by success at Adwa, Menelik won acceptance from all three European powers for Ethiopia's claims to and appropriation of much of the Ogaden region. Inland Somalia rallied to the oratory and vision of Muhammed Abdille Hassan in launching a jihad against alien incursions.[15] The Sayyid, as he was known, proved adept in playing European powers against one another, gaining some German assistance in his war with Britain and—during an interlude in the war—finding protection from the Italians. In the end, British military power established its superiority over his forces. Although the Sayyid made an enduring contribution to Somali nationalism, the nascent state he started to build did not survive his death. Just as the Mahdi's had, his vision for his people survived but without any structure to lend it operational permanence. Italy, France, Britain, and Ethiopia parceled among themselves the domain of the Somali nation he envisaged, most of which was temporarily reunited as Italian East Africa during World War II.

The reinstatement of these colonial territorial divisions after World War II by the United Nations included the restoration to Italy of its Somalia holdings as a trust for a ten-year term. The renewed divisions spurred the Somali Youth League to demand the incorporation in a single independent state of all Somalis residing in the three European colonies, the Ethiopian empire, and British colonial Kenya. The league's vision has proved elusive from that day to the present. While the Italian and British territories were reunited, Djibouti was to become independent, and intermittent irredentist wars with Kenya and Ethiopia have never been successful. Currently, the former British colony seeks to separate from the rest of Somalia and become the Somaliland republic. Never directly connected to colonially defined boundaries or to the embryonic postindependence successor states, the vision of a Somali nation has sustained neither fleeting postindependence democracy nor the nearly quarter century of military dictatorship under Siad Barre. At this writing, it remains unclear at best whether and how, if at all, this vision will serve as the foundation of a new Somali political formation.

The Contemporary Crisis of Political Identity

The shallow foundations of Western-style state forms in the Horn of Africa lay bare fundamental issues of political construction in Africa—issues that are more clear here than in other parts of the continent. The tendency of autocratic rulers to identify their governing regimes with the state and pervasive tendencies in the academic literature to equate state and government conflate two distinct matters: (1) the legitimacy of a particular government and its policies, and (2) the consensus (or lack of consensus) on how the state itself should be constituted.[16] At the same time, external pressures for economic and political liberalization also merge two distinct issues: the constitution of the state, establishing rules for the structure and operation of government—and here elements of democracy are generally uncritically presumed to enjoy universal legitimacy across cultures— and the consensus among peoples to exist as one political community on the

basis of which to construct a state. This most fundamental of all political issues—
the question of the contours and geography of political identity—defines the
contemporary political crisis of the Horn of Africa.

There is, I think, an unspoken and unexamined assumption in the campaigns
for economic and political liberalization that, in the absence of Cold War external pressures, the wellsprings of entrepreneurial initiative and political expression thus liberated will be asserted in an orderly fashion. That is, it is generally
tacitly assumed that market systems of exchange will emerge, behaving as Adam
Smith expected, as will analogously orderly political marketplaces of ideas, as ex-
tolled by Oliver Wendell Holmes and many others.

If that were the case, one would expect civil society, understood as a network
of nongovernmental associations mutually supportive in their common task of
exercising and defending a political community's dominant (in this case, democratic) values, to emerge more or less spontaneously. However, the crises of political communities seeking definition and identity in the contemporary Horn of
Africa have afforded stark demonstrations that such orderly systems of entrepre-
neurship and expression do not necessarily emerge spontaneously. Rather ironically, their birth requires skilled midwifery, the nature and sources of which remain as speculative and experimentally determined as they are urgently required
and sought after—in no place more urgently than in the Horn of Africa.

"Domestic" Politics

The contemporary crisis of political identity in the Horn of Africa occurs at two
different political levels, "domestic" and "international." At the "domestic" level,
the very survival of colonially defined state structures forcing ethnic groups
within common political frameworks is currently more at issue in the Horn than
at any time in the past.[17] The end of support for regimes that tended to treat
themselves as synonymous with the states they governed—support justified by
the Cold War—has removed a major barrier to popular determination of the legitimacy of (1) those state structures, and (2) the suitability of the underlying
political communities that the state structures were presumed to establish. Conflicts and debates over this issue have the potential to lead to a reformation of
political communities and new forms of state structure to give them expression—
or they may lead to near chaos, as exemplified by Somalia.

There are several ways to deal with these profound crises of political reconstruction: existing governments can sustain (in Eritrea), reconstruct (in Djibouti
and Ethiopia) or impose (in Sudan) bases of identity for the establishment or
reestablishment of political community; external theocratic ideologies (fundamentalist Islam) can be imported; or a political community can be "grown" from
the bottom up through the exertions of survivors of Hobbesian-like wars of all
against all—the antithesis of the orderly formations tacitly assumed by policymakers and rather explicitly projected in liberal theories of political economy. All

five countries are subject to donor pressure of varying severity to move toward market economies and pluralist democracies by forced marches. This is true even in Somalia, partly as a consequence of the U.S. decision to remove its troops by March 31, 1994, in order to escape, at least partially, the Damoclean sword of Vietnam-like entanglements and all the searing domestic consequences. It is by no means clear, however, which forms, combinations, and tactics of agency are most suitable in any particular circumstance.

At one end of the spectrum, Somalia is a classic example not only of a failed state, in the Western sense, but also of the seeming dissolution of the political community itself to which the Somali state was presumed to give expression. As of mid-1994, there was little clarity on the issue of what viable bases or means, if any, might exist for putting the Somali Humpty-Dumpty back together again, that is, for reestablishing political community (or communities) and reconstructing a political order (or orders). Working against a self-imposed deadline of March 31, UNOSOM (United Nations Operations in Somalia) undertook to reconstruct local councils as a foundation for reestablishing a national government. It also attempted to rebuild a Somali police force. The local legitimacy of the councils was uncertain in terms of their personnel, their structure and/or the means employed to create them.

The overthrow of Siad Barre signified his regime's inability to capture or sustain existing bases of political community. The regime's demise demonstrated its failure to establish, sustain, or legitimately reformulate a connection between a historical vision of Somali political identity, as expressed by the Sayyid and reasserted by the Somali Youth League, and the territory it governed. Siad Barre's residual legatees are clan leaders whose respective credentials and bases of legitimacy to lead Somalia out of a Hobbesian state are thus varied and uncertain. Based on his role in the overthrow of Siad Barre, augmented by the stature he gained by eluding UNOSOM efforts to arrest him in connection with the killing of two dozen Pakistani soldiers, Mohammed Farah Aideed claimed that, under his leadership, clan leaders would reach a consensus on restoring a Somali political community. Indeed, his party, the Somali National Army, claimed that it had the support of a majority of the clan leaders.

How such negotiations might produce a restored basis of political community and define the parameters of a new democratic constitution remained unclear as of mid-1994. There were no overt indications that the clan leaders collectively enjoyed enough legitimacy to reconstitute a Somali political order. To the extent that they lacked legitimacy, the prospect of renewed civil war loomed—perhaps more properly, a Hobbesian war of all against all and of indefinite duration. To the extent, however, that they did enjoy the requisite legitimacy, the question of what kind of political order they might fashion remained open. With the collapse of the colonially inherited state following the overthrow of Siad Barre, there was no guarantee nor even necessarily a presumption that negotiations among clan leaders, if successful, would yield consensus on the reestablishment of the preexisting structure. Those negotiations would be just as likely to produce a distinctly Somali political order, departing in significant ways from the Western model inherited from colonial times.

External midwifery in Somalia has been founded on a series of demonstrably and empirically false assumptions, thus confusing and probably delaying, rather than assisting, the process of re-creating a Somali political community.

1. Humanitarian intervention to feed Somalis was initially based upon the demonstrably false presumption that globally based humanitarianism and local political reconstruction could be divorced from one another. In fact, the effort to establish the security necessary to distribute food unavoidably embroiled external forces in the very civil war that obstructed humanitarian assistance in the first place.

2. UNOSOM tacitly assumed Somalis would accept or share its claim that its efforts to avenge the killing of two dozen Pakistani comrades by Somali combatants was apolitical. In fact, General Aideed's successful resistance to this UNOSOM campaign greatly enlarged his stature among Somalis and competing clan leaders beyond what it otherwise might have become.

3. UNOSOM has appeared to assume that its efforts to begin reconstruction of a Somali state, via the local councils and the creation of a new police force, are apolitical and autonomous from the clan leaders' struggles for political preeminence.

In reality, the civil war is about both the reconstruction of a Somali political order and the leadership within it.

Sudan is a fractured political community wherein the divisions between north and south increasingly appear to be so deep and permanent that the possibility of a truly "multinational" state seems remote. Within the north, the existence of a political community does not yet appear to be in doubt. Rather, the political fissures there relate to the constitution of a state appropriate to that community; that is, the issue is whether Sudan should, in fact, be an Islamic theocracy. In the south, the bases of political community, the appropriateness of a separate state, the structure of such a would-be state, the bases (if any) for reconciliation with the north, and the shape of a Sudanese political order that would make such a reconciliation possible all remained unresolved and barely addressed issues. In short, as in Somalia, the future of the Sudanese state bequeathed from the colonial era and both the shape and the very possibility of a successor state or states all remained indeterminate as of mid-1994.

The newly independent state of Eritrea stands at the other end of the spectrum from Somalia and Sudan. In its first three years of independence, a sense of political identity, seemingly indelibly forged in the thirty-year war of liberation from Ethiopia, has, to date, more than sufficed to overlay and subordinate potential ethnic, religious, and territorial bases for centrifugal politics. Led by President

Issayas Afewerki, the Government of Eritrea has initiated a cautious and pragmatic transition to what it had led its people to expect will be a democratic state in the long run. The thirty-year civil war enabled the Eritrean People's Liberation Front (EPLF) leadership to think deeply and carefully about the design of an independent Eritrea and to hone an unusually deep sense of and commitment to disciplined self-reliance. In Eritrea, by contrast to other newly independent states, expectations for realizing economic well-being and participatory democracy may have been less intense at the outset simply because the long civil war imbued the EPLF government and the Eritrean people with a long-term perspective.

The independence and viability of the new Eritrean state, however, are by no means assured or inevitable. Given the region's chronic food deficit, even when it was part of Ethiopia, the new EPLF government must confront the challenge of repatriating hundreds of thousands of refugees from neighboring countries, particularly Sudan, and demobilizing and integrating most of its large army into civilian life—at a time of serious war-related deficiencies in food production. Indeed, the numbers of displaced civilian and military individuals may exceed a third of the country's entire population.

The birth of the Eritrean state itself suggests that the new governments of both Eritrea and Ethiopia have tacitly recognized the limitations of the sovereign nation-state to which the former emperors Menelik II and especially Haile Selassie made largely symbolic political commitments.[18] The EPRDF government accepted the EPLF's offer of its good offices to mediate its internal conflict with its erstwhile ally, the Oromo Liberation Front, which represented much of the territory brought into the empire by the conquests of Menelik II. The EPLF has accepted Ethiopian duty-free use of the vital port of Assab. And the EPRDF government has accepted the continued presence of numerous Eritreans in its government, even in high places, as well as within the private sector.

Some Ethiopian commentators have indignantly asked what the point of the Eritrean war of "independence" was if the nation is going to continue these practices of interdependence and why, in fact, Ethiopia continues to indulge in such practices. The real answer may be that both the Meles and Issayas governments, for all their nationalist pride, recognize the necessity for more porous boundaries between their respective internal political orders than the inherited model of the autonomous nation-state presumes.

Between the failed and fractured states of Somalia and Sudan, respectively, and the newly minted state of Eritrea, with its buoyant nationalism, stands Djibouti. This country seeks to restructure the basis of political identity on which the state can rest without falling into the traps experienced by Somalia and Sudan. Long carefully balanced between the majority Issa and the minority Afar, Djibouti now appears determined to redefine itself as an Issa, rather than a multinational, political community.

This fundamental and high-risk attempt to transform Djibouti as a political community has occurred because of a changing balance of power in the region at two levels. At one level, the end of the Cold War largely eliminated the importance of Somalia and Ethiopia to the two superpowers and their interests in sustaining client governments. The subsequent rapprochement between Siad Barre's and Mengistu Haile Mariam's regimes facilitated their joint preoccupation with profound internal transformations that would soon lead to the fall of both regimes and the independence of Eritrea. Thus, at a second level, both regimes were relatively inattentive to the regional balance of power that undergirded Djibouti's delicate internal balance between the majority Issa, with roots in Somalia, and the Afar, whose roots lie in Ethiopia—notwithstanding the economic importance of the port of Djibouti. In this sense, therefore, the transformation of Djibouti's political community now under way derives, in effect, from those occurring in Ethiopia and Somalia.

An even more profound attempt to redefine the basis of political community is under way in Ethiopia. Since the "era of princes" and throughout its modern history from Teodros through Haile Selassie and the successor regime of Mengistu Haile Mariam, Ethiopia has survived several potential breakdowns of the empire into component nationalities and numerous localized rebellions.[19] Students of Ethiopian political history have looked in different directions to find the glue that underlay this durability.[20] However, a fundamental consequence of the Mengistu regime's relentless and ultimately failed campaign to subdue Eritrea militarily has been a heightened ethnic consciousness in a country where, at least at elite levels, ethnic differentiation has historically been more muted and crosscut by territorial identities than perhaps anyplace else in Africa.[21]

The Tigrean-led Ethiopian Peoples Revolutionary Democratic Front government has elected to reinforce ethnic consciousness by pursuing its vision of Ethiopia as a multiethnic postimperial political community. It has implicitly cast the previous survival of imperial Ethiopia in ethnic terms, in contradiction to the national consciousness others have discerned—that is, as based on the hegemony of the Amhara peoples as both cause and consequence of the survival of the Menelik and Haile Selassie governments. The EPRDF has redefined the country's administrative regions in ethnic terms, a contrast to their previous predominantly territorial basis. It has also proposed a measure of autonomy for these ethnically defined regions, which was considered but never implemented during the Mengistu regime.

In this way, the EPRDF government purports to change fundamentally the basis of Ethiopian political community reestablished by the country's modern emperors. This is a high-risk-high-gain strategy, risking stronger separatist movements following the Eritrean model but seeking to strengthen the basis of postimperial Ethiopian political community by creating greater interethnic equality.

At the same time, however, it is unclear to what extent the EPRDF's plan goes beyond symbolism. Regions will be permitted to elect their own governments and to conduct business in the dominant languages.[22] But economic policy will likely continue to be closely controlled from the center.[23] The Amhara and others who decry what they see as Balkanization assume that the new program goes beyond symbolism; the Oromo and others who stand to be among the major beneficiaries of greater interethnic equality appear unprepared to accept what they see as only symbolic official steps in that direction. Meanwhile, grassroots initiatives, in the form of interregional trade barriers and de facto modifications of land tenure traditions unauthorized by the central government, suggest that the government may have difficulty maintaining leadership as it attempts to institutionalize its vision of a postimperial Ethiopian political community.

The fundamental question in Ethiopia and, indeed, in all five countries is the extent to which transformations and/or collapses of political community will destroy the institutionalized remnants of Western nation-states or, conversely, the extent to which peoples of the region will rally behind Western state structures or fashion some alternative as the best hope of rationalizing and institutionalizing restructured political communities.

"International" Politics

The contemporary crisis of political identity in the Horn of Africa also occurs at the level of "international" politics. Two different sets of questions have arisen at this level. First, the superficial grounding and uncertain status of the state in this region, as the term *state* is understood in the West, suggests the need for bases for a regional "supranational" system within which political conflicts can be resolved. A key test of such a system is its capacity to serve as a basis for peace and security internally. The efforts of Presidents Meles of Ethiopia, Issayas of Eritrea, and Moi of Kenya to mediate the Somali crisis, which carries potentially destabilizing implications for all three governments, suggest the hypothesis that "international" peace and security can be maintained by governments even as the boundaries and definitions of the political orders over which they preside are in flux. Indeed, their interdependence as a result of that very flux may help to facilitate their disposition, if not necessarily their capacity, to maintain a viable, regional international system.

Second, a further test of a regional international system is its capacity to moderate and defend itself against external influences that are perceived as threatening. For the Horn, the reality of a unipolar post–Cold War world in military terms at the global level does not necessarily translate as an absence at regional levels of challenges to the West's agendas of economic and political liberalization. In the Horn of Africa, the spread of fundamentalist Islam is regarded as a serious challenge both by major Western powers and by Horn governments themselves. A fear of Islamic fundamentalism may yet replace the Cold War as a rationale for submerging contests over political identity at the "domestic" level, as governments seek to reduce their vulnerability to such threatening "external" forces.[24] Scarcely a factor in the Horn in prior years, Islamic fundamentalism now appears to have made inroads (partly because of the conversion of Sudan to an Islamic state) in southern Ethiopia, Kenya, and perhaps Somalia. Eritrea, in particular, is very concerned that it, too, will be affected via refugees returning from Sudan.

The dimensions and impacts of this threat to the stability of the Horn should differ from those of the Cold War in two respects. First, the nature of the threat is less military than cultural and political; hence, its effects on defense budgets are likely to be limited. Second and far more important, Islamic fundamentalism offers a preordained, universal, theological answer to the problem of redefining political communities and their identities even as the Horn countries are absorbed by this very crisis. For some governments, the temptation may be to resort to counterproductive, illiberal policies in order to protect the integrity of their own "internal" processes of political reconstruction. Western governments, also hostile to the spread of Islamic fundamentalism, may be caught in the same dilemma insofar as they continue to press Horn governments to establish more open political and economic orders, animated by market systems both for allocating goods and services and for determining political values and public policies.

Conclusion

The fundamental thesis of this chapter has been that the end of the Cold War has accelerated processes of redefining the bases of political community and identity in the Horn of Africa. These processes were submerged initially by colonialism but subsequently by the continuation of the Cold War. International pressures on Horn countries for economic and political liberalization fuel these processes of political reconstruction. The prospects for a radical reconstruction of the bases of political community are apparent not only in Somalia but also throughout the region. The essential legitimacy of these efforts is tarnished by the resort to armed conflict to arbitrate the underlying issues. It is also diminished by the twin dangers that the efforts may decay into Hobbesian wars of all against all and that a fresh external threat in the form of Islamic fundamentalism will short-circuit processes of reconstructing political communities and identities.

Notes

1. The terms "domestic" and "international" are frequently put in quotes in this chapter to highlight precisely what is at issue in the region: the viability of the nation-state in this context.

2. Major sources on realist and neorealist theories of international relations include Robert Keohane, ed., *Neo-Realism and Its Critics* (New York: Columbia University Press, 1986); Hedley Bull, *The Anarchical Society: A Study of Order in World Politics* (New York: Columbia University Press, 1977); J. E. Dougherty and Robert Pfaltzgraff, *Contending Theories of International Relations,* 2d ed. (Philadelphia: Lippincott, 1981); Robert Jervis, *Per-*

ception and Misperception in World Politics (Princeton: Princeton University Press, 1976); and Kenneth Waltz, *The Theory of International Politics* (Reading, Mass.: Addison-Wesley, 1979).

3. The extent to which it is appropriate to define an international system in terms of the characteristics of its component actors is one of the prime issues between Kenneth Waltz and his critics. See Keohane, *Neo-Realism,* and Waltz, *Theory of International Politics.* The argument here is that the Horn provides an opportunity to advance theory on this point.

4. References to Ethiopia as not including Eritrea historically are made for the sake of clarity only and are not to be assumed to imply my position on that issue.

5. Sven Rubenson, *The Survival of Ethiopian Independence* (London: Heinemann, 1976).

6. An excellent source is A. M. Jones and E. Monroe, *A History of Ethiopia* (London: Clarendon Press, 1955).

7. Rubenson, *The Survival of Ethiopian Independence.*

8. A good source is P. Vatikotis, *The Modern History of Egypt* (New York: Praeger, 1969).

9. On the Sudan, see P. M. Holt and M. W. Daly, *The History of Sudan: From the Coming of Islam to the Present,* 3d ed. (Boulder: Westview Press, 1979).

10. Rubenson, *The Survival of Ethiopian Independence.*

11. Harold Marcus, *The Life and Times of Menelik II* (London: Clarendon Press, 1975); Kofi Darkwah, *Menelik and the Ethiopian Empire 1813–1880* (London: Heinemann, 1975).

12. Rubenson, *The Survival of Ethiopian Independence.*

13. Harold Marcus, *Ethiopia, Great Britain and the United States: The Politics of Empire* (Berkeley: University of California Press, 1983).

14. This was painstakingly crafted via the U.N. in 1951.

15. On Somalia, see David Laitin, *Politics, Language, and Thought: The Somalia Experience* (Chicago: University of Chicago Press, 1977); also I. M. Lewis, *A Modern History of Somalia: Nation and State in the Horn of Africa* (London: Longman, 1980).

16. *Regime* is used as the equivalent of *administration,* as in *the Clinton administration.*

17. Again, for purposes of this analysis, I treat the regimes of Emperor Haile Selassie I and his immediate predecessors as analogous to the colonial regimes comprising the European empires in Africa.

18. John Markakis, *Ethiopia: Anatomy of a Traditional Polity* (London: Oxford University Press, 1974).

19. Rubenson, *The Survival of Ethiopian Independence;* John W. Harbeson, *The Ethiopian Transformation: The Quest for the Post-Imperial State* (Boulder: Westview Press, 1988); Richard Greenfield, *Greater Ethiopia: A New Political History* (New York: Praeger, 1965).

20. Ibid.; also Donald Levine, *Greater Ethiopia: The Evolution of a Multicultural Society* (Chicago: University of Chicago Press, 1974).

21. Young, *The Politics of Cultural Pluralism* (Madison: University of Wisconsin Press, 1976).

22. As of mid-1994, the EPRDF government had not yet come to terms with the difficulties and potential problems of attempting to integrate a federal system permitting separate official languages at regional levels with the continuation of Amhara as the language of power at the national level.

23. Satish Mishra, "Public Expenditure Implications of Regional Economic Develop-

ment," paper, June, 1993. Also see Transitional Government of Ethiopia Proclamations 7/1992, 33/1992, and 41/1993.

24. Indeed, the distinction between domestic and international politics, as well as the bases for distinguishing between political jurisdictions, disappears in Western parlance to the extent that the nation-state as understood in the West does not constitute the core political formation.

7

South Africa and Southern Africa After Apartheid

JEFFREY HERBST

THE TRANSITION to nonracial rule in South Africa will have important implications for the evolution of regional politics in all of southern Africa. When the elimination of apartheid was still a distant dream and then again immediately after State President F. W. deKlerk unbanned the African National Congress (ANC) in February 1990, there was considerable euphoria about what the transition to nonracial rule might mean for the region. However, as the realities of the transition come into focus, it is now clear that the move to nonracial rule will pose both new opportunities and new challenges to the roughly fifty million people in the countries surrounding South Africa. In this chapter, I will try to analyze the potential benefits and disadvantages to the region. Offering a perspective absent from most accounts of regional politics, I will place particular emphasis on the fact that the countries bordering South Africa will reap very different "apartheid dividends" given their own security, economic, and political conditions. I will also reverse the customary analytic causality and ask how regional politics will affect South Africa's own development prospects.

Southern Africa as a Region

Since 1968, analysts have taken as a given that southern Africa is, as Larry Bowman put it in his pioneering article, a subordinate state system.[1] The economic and military dominance of South Africa as well as the regionwide project of Africans to physically overthrow institutionalized white rule meant that analyzing regional politics was an absolute necessity for understanding the fate of any one country. Over the last twenty-five years, an enormous amount of analysis was devoted to South Africa's destabilization of the region,[2] as well as the collective response of southern African countries to Pretoria's security and economic challenge.[3] Indeed, future scholars may well be bewildered at the amount of attention devoted to the Southern Africa Development Community (SADC, formerly the Southern African Development Coordination Conference) in particular, given its meager accomplishments. Beyond the absolute importance of understanding regional politics, many scholars were drawn to writing about the interactions between Pretoria and its neighbors because they could not do research in South Africa, and because they hoped to draw attention to the evils of apartheid and give support to the various ideological projects (especially socialism in Mozambique) that were seen as threatened by South Africa.

In light of apartheid's demise, all the old analytic certainties are being challenged. The abolition of minority rule in South Africa marks the successful end of the long effort to end the settler colonialism that structured so much of international politics in Africa since 1960. No longer will countries of the region be able to claim that they are a separate group simply because they are governed by blacks, nor are they any longer on the front line of any conflict. Indeed, the countries of the region will never have as much in common in the future as they did in the 1980s when they could reasonably suggest that they were all under threat from Pretoria. With the normalization of politics in South Africa, there is no longer an obvious organizing principle around which countries in the region can coalesce.

Further, there are now new economic and technological forces at work that will challenge the notion that southern Africa remains both a coherent and an interesting analytic unit.[4] In a world where billions of dollars are transmitted across borders instantly and where countries are encouraged to export for the world market, it is unclear that regional politics should be considered a priori important simply because countries share a geographic proximity.

However, such changes are often slow to make an impact on policy discussions. Indeed, much of the analysis of southern Africa's prospects is simplistic, based on little more than an assumption that the transition in South Africa will be as simple as throwing a switch: The old South Africa was destabilizing for the region, and the new South Africa will therefore be an unmitigated good for the entire region. For example, the World Bank is extraordinarily optimistic about the prospects for southern Africa after the transition: "It is reasonable to assume that solutions will be found to the problems that have divided the peoples of that region [southern Africa] and that South African economic cooperation will eventually transform the prospects for the whole of southern Africa."[5] More generally, the bank has now made regional integration a priority, partially in response to complaints about its calls for structural adjustment. Indeed, the bank argues that "progress toward market integration and increased cooperation in a whole range of areas—economic, technical, environmental, food security, educational, and research—is central to Africa's long-term development strategy."[6]

And in South Africa, the country's leaders discuss the region as if it will have the same relevance to the national interest as it had in the 1980s. For instance, Nelson Mandela, in an article that attempted to lay out a framework for the

ANC's future foreign policy, argued that "democratic South Africa will . . . resist any pressure or temptation to pursue its own interests at the expense of the subcontinent."[7] This point was stated emphatically because Mandela wanted to stress that the ANC's policy toward the region would be friendly, as opposed to the hostile destabilization that characterized the 1980s.

The greater likelihood, as I will argue, is that the region will, in many traditional ways, matter less to South Africa's foreign policy than ever before and that many regional considerations will simply fade into the background. Indeed, far from finding a strong new ally in union building now that the ANC has come to power, the countries of the region may find that they simply do not matter that much to the "new" South Africa. However, South Africa's policies and fortunes will still be consequential to most countries in the region. This asymmetry will be played out in economic, political, and military relationships.

Economic Relations

Given the primacy of development for the region, future economic relations within the subcontinent must be discussed first. One of the constants in southern Africa has been South Africa's economic dominance. Table 7.1 presents the best available evidence of how the shares of the gross regional product changed between 1960 and 1991. All the usual caveats about data from Africa are applicable; however, the table does present a picture consistent with observable trends in the region. South Africa's share of economic activity in the region was about 75 percent in 1991, a significant increase over the 1960 figure of 65 percent. The increase

TABLE 7.1   Share of Gross Regional Product, by Country[a]

	1960	1970	1980	1991
Angola	6	NA	3	6
Botswana	NA	0.4	1	3
Lesotho	0.3	0.3	0.3	0.5
Malawi	2.	1	1	2
Mozambique	8	NA	2	1
Namibia	NA	NA	2	2
South Africa	65	77	77	75
Swaziland	NA	NA	1	1
Tanzania	5	6	5	2
Zambia	6	8	4	3
Zimbabwe	7	7	4	5

[a] I have rounded to the nearest integer (except when the number was below 0.5) to emphasize the problematic nature of many of these statistics. The table should only be taken as a rough guide to the economic fortunes of individual countries. Data are for year closest to that actually reported.

Source: World Bank, *World Development Reports* (New York City: Oxford University Press, various years).

in South Africa's share came about because of the collapse of the Mozambique, Tanzanian, and Zambian economies and the significant absolute decline experienced by Zimbabwe. Of course, Angola's economy also collapsed during that period; however, the dominance of oil (the one sector that has not suffered from the almost constant warfare in the country since 1960) in its measurable national accounts has meant that, in statistical terms, Angola's economy seems relatively robust. Of the countries in the region, only Botswana, which increased its share of the regional economy tenfold between 1970 and 1991, performed well in both relative and absolute terms. Indeed, the region as a whole performed poorly, with its share of the global economy decreasing from 0.76 percent in 1970 to 0.56 percent in 1991.[8]

Even this cursory review of the regional economy makes clear the central economic reality of southern Africa: South Africa is the absolutely critical country for the region because its economy dwarfs those of its neighbors. Correspondingly, as noted earlier, the region is increasingly irrelevant to the economic fortunes of South Africa. The region's total economic product without South Africa amounted to only 0.14 percent of the global economy in 1991. The absolute size of the regional economy without South Africa is roughly equivalent to the economy of Egypt or Romania; Hong Kong's economy alone is approximately 235 percent larger than the regional economy excluding South Africa.[9] Obviously, if South Africa hopes to develop, especially by exporting more, the regional economy will be of only marginal help. It is true that there are fifty million people in the countries near South Africa, but their extraordinarily low per capita income means that the effective market they represent is tiny. It is therefore extremely questionable whether increased regional trade, presumably the main reason for greater economic cooperation in the region, will be important for South Africa or, indeed, for most other southern African countries.

In fact, the regional economy is even less attractive to South Africa than it would be if that nation bordered Romania or Egypt because the market, such as it is, is divided among ten countries. Table 7.2 shows the breakdown of shares of

TABLE 7.2   Share of Regional Product Outside South Africa in 1990, by Country

	Percentage
Angola	27
Botswana	13
Lesotho	2
Malawi	7
Mozambique	4
Namibia	7
Swaziland	2
Tanzania	8
Zambia	13
Zimbabwe	19

Source: World Bank, *World Development Reports* (various years).

the regional economy excluding South Africa. The most important market is Angola, partially due to the statistical artifact explained earlier but also due to the fact that the constant stream of oil revenue is a source of wealth unmatched throughout the region. Of course, as long as Angola is in turmoil, it will be very difficult to export to Luanda, and much of the country's wealth will have to be devoted to weapons and disaster relief. The remainder of the region's wealth is divided among many different markets, with Zimbabwe, Zambia, and Botswana accounting for approximately 45 percent of the remaining economic activity.

Further, the region will not be particularly attractive to South Africa because it already dominates what economic activity there is. Exact statistics are a particular problem in understanding South Africa's commercial relations with the region because many African countries did not want to publicize their trading relationship with the apartheid regime and because South Africa reciprocated by not disaggregating its trade statistics. However, the penetration of South Africa is immediately obvious in the statistics from those countries honest enough to admit they were trading with South Africa. Table 7.3 documents that South Africa already accounts for approximately one-quarter of total imports in Malawi, Zambia, and Zimbabwe, and this figure is probably higher in the neighboring countries. It is hard to believe that South Africa will be able to increase these market shares significantly, especially given that imports of fuel, which South Africa cannot provide, probably account for a substantial portion of the import profile in all countries in the region.

Somewhat surprising are the very low totals for exports to South Africa. Countries in the region have not been able to export to South Africa because of a fundamental mismatch in their development profiles. As is typical for middle-income countries, South Africa imports mainly capital goods and manufactured products. In 1990, machinery and transport equipment alone accounted for 43 percent of its total imports, and chemicals, manufactured goods, and miscellaneous manufactured goods accounted for another 35 percent of the total import bill.[10] On the other hand, the other countries of the region are mainly exporting a few raw materials. South Africa simply does not need that much of Zambia's copper (79 percent of its total exports), Malawi's tobacco (67 percent of its total exports), or Zimbabwe's tobacco, gold, or ferro-alloys (48 percent of its total exports).[11] What South Africa does need in terms of basic raw materials it proba-

TABLE 7.3   South African Regional Trade

	Percentage of Total Exports to South Africa	Percentage of Total Imports from South Africa
Malawi	8	28
Zambia	0.1	25
Zimbabwe	9	24

Source: International Monetary Fund, *Direction of Trade Statistics Yearbook 1993* (Washington, D.C.: IMF, 1993).

bly buys already, suggesting that the immediate scope for increased regional exports to South Africa will mainly be a function of economic growth rather than increasing market share.

Indeed, given the fundamental mismatch between South Africa's import profile and what the region is currently exporting, the critical question becomes whether southern African countries can transform their economies so that they are more than mere raw material producers and actually make products that South Africa will buy. Thus, prospects for increased exports from the region to South Africa, which would be an important component of any regional economic resurgence, hinges far less on the transition in South Africa than on the success of economic reforms in the countries of the region. Given the degree of transformation required, there is probably little hope that any of the countries in the region except for Zimbabwe will soon develop new industries that could count South Africa, among other places, as a significant market. Accordingly, in contrast to much of the literature,[12] the critical variable, at least for interregional trade, is not the attitude of South Africa's new rulers toward the regions but the decisions made by the leaders of the other countries.

Regional Economic Diplomacy

The new South African government will undoubtedly become involved in the extensive array of regional institutions, notably the SADC, the much larger Preferential Trade Area (PTA) that spans east and southern Africa, and the recently muted East and Southern Africa Economic Community. Especially in the early years after the transition, the new government in Pretoria may appear to energetically engage these organizations in order to reassure its neighbors about its intentions and to signal the nature of the transition. However, over the long term, these organizations simply will not play a major part in the new South Africa's diplomacy. First, as noted, South Africa is already fully engaged in the regional markets. Consequently, the new South Africa must become more engaged in the international economy outside of the region if it is to make substantial gains in exports and thereby promote economic growth.

Second, it is unlikely that either organization or any other regional structures that are likely to emerge from the region in the foreseeable future (such as the recently proposed common market for Africa by the year 2000) will promote substantial trade liberalization that might be of interest to South Africa. Regional trade agreements work best with countries at roughly the same level of development who can share in the gains from trade. Given South Africa's technological dominance, regional agreements to promote trade would probably only increase the regional trade imbalance, as more efficient South African firms outcompete with companies in the region that are currently protected by tariff and nontariff barriers.

However, many are not willing to countenance the prospect of creative destruction. Somewhat bizarrely, Mandela, whose country would benefit from a quick decrease in trade controls, argued that "any move toward a common market or economic community must ensure that industrial development in the entire region is not prejudiced. It is essential therefore that a program to restructure regional economic relations after apartheid be carefully calibrated to avoid exacerbating inequities."[13] Of course, the countries in the region would benefit from a liberalized trade regime by being able to buy goods that were cheaper than if they had produced them themselves. However, the political problems caused by this new South African economic dominance, combined with the economic dislocation, would probably abort any regionwide trading agreement. The European Community has only managed to avoid the problem of including countries with different development profiles (compare Germany and Portugal) by institutionalizing huge side payments from the rich to the poor that mitigate the losses caused by trade.[14] However, funds for softening the impact of increased regional trade will not be available in the poor region of southern Africa. Given the political realities, regional integration as it has traditionally been conceived will play only a relatively minor role if the countries of southern Africa are to turn their economies around.

South Africa's economic diplomacy will undoubtedly be concentrated on sources of funds needed for its enormous development tasks: the IMF, the World Bank's regular-loan window, the African Development Bank (ADB) regular-loan window, and the major bilateral donors. In addition, unique among sub-Saharan African countries, South Africa will probably be a recipient of at least some funds from money managers eager to invest in emerging markets. Thus, the new South Africa will travel in markedly different circles than most African countries that are now limited to the soft-loan windows of the World Bank and the ADB. Especially if it is successful, the new South Africa will quickly see that the region is not fundamentally relevant to its future.

Finally, it is likely that the SADC in particular will not be nearly as attractive to foreign donors as it has been in the past. The very limited record of the SADC will be difficult to justify in a world where a seemingly endless number of countries have legitimate demands on foreign aid. Also, part of the reason why the SADC was so successful as an aid platform during the 1980s was because many Western countries used their donations to the regional organization to signal their distaste for apartheid and to compensate for their failure to impose sanctions. There is no other way to justify the international attention given to an organization that, in Anthony Hawkins's words, had little to show for itself after ten years other than a secretariat in Gaborone.[15] Now that the transition in South Africa has begun, donors will be able to signal their desire to end the legacy of apartheid directly by donating money to projects in South Africa. SADC funding will not disappear overnight. However, over the long term, the SADC will probably revert to its nominal importance in international affairs—simply one of literally dozens of regional organizations worldwide that are seeking aid. The prospects for outside aid are the same for any other regional arrangement that may emerge from east and southern Africa.

Investment

There has also been a hope that normalization of relations between South Africa and the region might lead to increased South African investment in neighboring countries. It is true that given the financial sophistication of the South African financial sector, the country has underinvested in foreign markets, primarily because of exchange controls imposed to halt the flow of capital caused by divestiture in the 1980s and to counteract sanctions. Although the ANC says it is committed to eliminating those capital controls, it is unlikely that the region will see a burst of South African-sponsored investment.

Since no one else is investing in the region, any hope that new funds will be provided by South Africa must rest on the assumption that either (1) South African investment managers are less averse to risk for a given rate of return than those investing capital from other countries, or (2) that the South Africans have special knowledge of business opportunities that have escaped the rest of the world. The first assumption seems implausible because in post-apartheid South Africa, business will be able to participate in the same instruments and opportunities as other investors worldwide. Thus, their risk-averseness should not deviate from the international norm. South African business should have been more prone to invest in the region during the sanctions era when many major markets were closed to them. Indeed, despite the regional politics of the 1980s, the South Africans had no problem investing in projects such as the soda-ash factory in Botswana, the Lesotho Highland Waters Project, and the Cahora Bassa hydroelectric plant. Ironically, investing in the poor and unstable region of southern Africa in the post-apartheid period may actually be less appealing to South Africans because they will no longer be constrained in their choice of markets or countries to enter.

Since almost all the countries in the region are making efforts to attract foreign investment, it also seems unlikely that the South Africans have any special knowledge of potentially lucrative investments that have been mistakenly overlooked by foreigners. In fact, many South African businesses are remarkably ignorant of developments just across their border.

Also, it appears that some of the South African foreign investment is little more than capital flight by businesses who were unwilling to risk their money during the transition. They would hardly want to put their money in the risky countries of southern Africa when the safe harbors of Europe and Asia beckon.

In the end, South African investment is probably no different than foreign investment by businesses in other countries. If southern African countries offer lucrative opportunities to invest in a secure environment, then South Africans and other foreigners will invest in them. If those opportunities are not present, there is little chance of attracting outside capital from any country. Once again, the transition from apartheid is probably less important to southern African countries than the decisions they themselves make in regard to structuring their own economies.

The Peace Dividend

There will presumably be an economic boon from the transition in terms of the peace dividend, for South African destabilization of the region will end. However, the peace dividend's magnitude will vary considerably. As Table 7.4 demonstrates, perhaps contrary to the conventional wisdom, many countries in the region do not spend an enormous amount on the military, at least compared to the African average. The countries that can benefit by bringing their military spending down at least to the African average are Zimbabwe, Lesotho, Mozambique, and Angola. The first two countries will, if their internal politics permit, certainly be able to redirect military spending elsewhere. Whether Mozambique and Angola will be able to reap their potentially much larger peace dividends, given how much more they spend on defense, is unclear. Obviously, ratcheting down military expenditures will depend on the evolution of the conflicts in those nations. Simply because the regime in Pretoria may be more favorably disposed to the governments in Angola and Mozambique does not mean there will be an automatic end to the threat posed by UNITA and the MNR. Those two movements have many weapons of their own, can steal easily from the army they face, and can purchase weapons on an international market that has been flooded by supplies dumped by the countries of Central Europe and the Commonwealth of Independent States (CIS) region.

Southern Africa will obviously benefit from an overall decrease in tensions. The problems in transshipping goods that countries sometimes experienced with South Africa will disappear, as will a myriad of other difficulties that arose when the conflict on apartheid spilled over into normal commercial relations. However, once again, it is likely that the onetime gains that emerge from a decline in

TABLE 7.4   South African Defense Investment[a]

	Defense as Percent of the Government Budget	Defense as Percent of GNP	Soldiers per 1,000 Citizens
Zambia	8.4	1.4	2.2
Swaziland	5.5	1.7	4.9
Malawi	8.2	2.3	0.8
Botswana	6.0	2.8	5.0
Tanzania	10.0	4.1	1.6
African average	14.7	4.5	2.8
Zimbabwe	15.0	6.7	5.1
Lesotho	10.0	9.4	1.2
Mozambique	40.7	9.7	4.6
Angola	16.1	28.8	12.9

[a] Statistics are for the most recent year available. In the case of Angola, statistics are from the mid-1980s. Also, many statistics are only a very rough approximation of reality.

Source: U.S. Arms Control and Disarmament Agency (ACDA), *World Military Expenditures and Arms Transfers 1990* (n.p.: ACDA, 1992).

regional tensions will soon dissipate unless the countries of the region reform themselves so they can begin to grow again.

Political Interests

Regional interests were paramount to the South African government during the 1970s and 1980s because neighboring states were providing sanctuary to the ANC's armed wing, Umkhonto we Sizwe, whose declared goal was the violent overthrow of the white state. In addition, Pretoria had a strong interest in seeing that the majority-ruled countries failed in order to emphasize its argument that a transition in South Africa would be detrimental to all its citizens. In the post-apartheid future, these considerations are irrelevant. Indeed, paralleling the future economic relations, South Africa will probably never again have as great an interest in the region again as it did in the 1980s.

The primary interest the new nonracial government will have in the region is to prevent regional instability from spilling over into South Africa and making the transition from minority rule even more difficult. When South Africa's new rulers look at the region, they will see what is, in many ways, an unlimited supply of very poor people who, if they were tempted to move to South Africa, could, as refugees, pose extraordinary demands on an already overstretched state and potentially exacerbate ethnic politics. These refugee flows could start for any number of reasons: the continuation of conflict in Angola and Mozambique, eruption of domestic battles elsewhere, further economic deterioration across the region, or a collapse of the social fabric in several countries due to AIDS.

South Africa will have a strong interest in the stability of the region so that these many poor people do not flood across its borders. Ironically, this is exactly opposite to the interest of the last, white government, which saw instability in the region as a way of stabilizing the domestic situation.

Helping promote stability in the region involves several sets of difficult issues, and the new South Africa will be able to affect only some of these. One issue for South Africa's future regional diplomacy is how it will address the conflicts occurring in Angola and Mozambique as well as other armed conflicts that could break out across the continent. The country's new authorities will obviously hope that the international community will facilitate peaceful relations, as appears to be happening in Mozambique, so that it will have to do little more than applaud. However, some problems, notably Angola, may not be resolved by the international community and will therefore have to be faced by the ANC.

In contrast to the proliferation of statements on how ANC foreign policy will promote the global good, South Africa's former putative leaders did not focus on the question of conflict resolution in southern Africa or the continent generally. The difficult domestic issues affecting the transition had first call on the prior leadership's attention. In addition, South Africa's foreign policy apparatus, almost completely dominated by whites in the past, will undergo a massive transformation in the next few years that will seriously hinder the new leaders' ability to understand events in foreign countries and how they can affect them. A regional foreign policy that seriously addresses these conflicts will not come quickly. As they formulate a policy, South Africa's new leaders will have to face the same kind of difficult choices that U.S. foreign policy leaders have encountered in Bosnia and Somalia: Does a tragedy in a distant land that involves the deaths of thousands of people really affect the national interest? When is foreign intervention useful? How many lives can be sacrificed to end a conflict in another country? Can a military apparatus designed to preserve the physical integrity of a country really evolve into a force for peacekeeping?

At first, perhaps before a full calculation of the national interest is made, South Africa's future leaders may be surprisingly willing to commit their troops to peacekeeping and peacemaking operations, for several reasons. First, especially given the decades of exile when the United Nations provide crucial sanctuary and constant support in the struggle against apartheid, many ANC officials may feel that they owe the international community a degree of participation that is disproportionate to the country's interests and resources. Certainly, many individual ANC officials have literally grown up within the culture of the U.N. and accordingly see involvement in its affairs in a much more positive light than do leaders in many other countries that have had far more difficult encounters with the U.N. Further, the international community, constantly looking for a way to share burdens and save money, is likely to pressure South Africa, the richest country in southern Africa and the only one besides Nigeria able to project force a considerable distance, to immediately become involved in many of the conflicts in the region and across the continent. Contrary to Mandela's assumption that the international community will try to divide South Africa from the region, Western countries in particular will pressure South Africa's new leaders to find southern African responses to the region's problems. The unwillingness of the international community to commit troops to difficult situations, underlined by the crises in Bosnia and Haiti, may prompt considerable pressure on Pretoria to intervene in the region.

The domestic politics of the new South African Defense Force may also encourage the new government to be relatively adventurous. The new army will be relatively large, at least in terms of manpower, because it will be used both as a sponge to absorb ANC cadres who fought against the white regime and as one means of addressing the unemployment problem. It will also be very much a force in search of a mission because there will be no immediate external threats against South Africa. Therefore, there may be considerable pressure from military leaders to allow the force to be deployed under U.N. auspices.

However, much of the regional instability that may be of interest to South Africa's leaders will not be solved by deploying troops. For instance, if the social fabric of some countries is threatened by AIDS, South African troops will not stem the flow of refugees. Thus, South Africa's new leaders may find themselves increasingly involved in many aspects of the domestic politics of neighboring countries in order to promote stability. Whether they will be successful by any measure cannot be predicted. However, becoming involved in the region's troubles will necessarily divert the leadership's attention from South Africa's own extraordinarily difficult domestic problems.

Migration

Although trade and investment flows may only slowly increase between South Africa and its neighbors in the post-apartheid period, the flow of people may increase quite rapidly. As noted earlier, given the great number of poor people in the region, there is the real possibility that significant poverty-alleviation efforts on the part of the new government could be overwhelmed by floods of refugees or simply by a large number of poor people seeking better opportunities. Just between 1990 and 1993, as the immigration and influx control systems broke down, there was a very significant increase in the number of African traders from as far as Zaire trading their wares on the once lily-white streets of Johannesburg. Of course, such flows are especially likely if the neighboring countries experience natural disasters or continued economic decline or if AIDS begins to erode the social fabric of the region.

At the same time, South Africa will have a strong interest in attracting skilled black manpower from the region, especially the anglophone countries. South Africa's economy suffers from an absolute shortage of skilled people, and there will also be considerable pressure on the new regime to increase the number of blacks visible in all aspects of every institution in society.[16] Since the number of skilled South African blacks will only rise slowly because the entire educational system will have to be dramatically expanded, many companies, universities, and other organizations will naturally look to the region for immediate placements. This is not to say that the new government will have an explicit policy of poaching black talent from the region. Indeed, the new government may publicly speak out against this practice at the request of the small South African black elite. However, the individual offers made to citizens of the region from South African firms and other organizations may, in an uncoordinated fashion, greatly accelerate the already significant brain drain to South Africa. Of course, to middle-class Zambians or Zimbabweans especially, the new South Africa could be a tempting land of opportunity because they will probably be paid far better there than in their own, declining countries. For close to a century, South Africa organized vast flows of untrained labor from the region, in part to forestall dependence on trained manpower within the country. Now it will want to stop the flow of untrained people into the country and will gladly encourage trained blacks to immigrate.

The contradiction in this practice is obvious. All the countries in the region desperately need their meager cadres of skilled workers in order to adjust their economies and begin to grow again. Given modern business practices, countries arguably compete in terms of the quality of their workforces. However, if South Africa is continually attracting significant numbers of trained Africans from its neighbors, the economies of those countries may suffer, propelling many poor people to cross the border into South Africa in search of a way to fulfill their basic needs. It may not be an exaggeration to say that the threat from the brain drain will seriously reduce any gains from trade between South Africa and the region.

The other migration issue that will have to be resolved concerns foreign mineworkers in South Africa. The number of Africans from other countries legally working in South African mines has decreased from 388,000 in 1973 to 165,000 in 1991 because of the deliberate strategy of some countries (notably Zimbabwe) to keep their citizens from working on the mines, the decreasing profitability of mining gold in South Africa, and the increasing capital-intensiveness of the industry.[17] With the employment crisis inside South Africa, the long-term prospects for foreign miners hoping to continue to work in South Africa are dim. However, South Africa will probably embark on a gradual downsizing of the foreign workforce because the new leaders will be aware that precipitous actions on their part could have a profound effect on the economies of Lesotho and Mozambique in particular.

Boundaries

It is tempting to try to analyze a future southern Africa by assuming that everything will remain the same except for the political structure inside South Africa. However, there is good reason to believe that the domestic transition may set off a chain of events that could lead to boundary changes in the subcontinent. The end of the Cold War, the growing respect accorded to the right to ethnic self-determination, and the demonstration effect of boundaries being changed elsewhere has created an atmosphere where the potential for changes in national demarcations is much greater than before.[18] In reality, boundary change would be a much greater form of regional integration than was ever suggested by the southern African countries in the 1980s. The SADC proposals mainly involved consolidating economic ties between nations, rather than questioning the very rationality of national design.

Boundary change in southern Africa is especially likely for three reasons. First, three of the states—Lesotho, Swaziland, and Botswana—were specifically designed by the British to protect Africans from the perils of institutionalized racism being created by the Afrikaners. Second, both Lesotho and Swaziland are so obviously not viable that incorporation into a nonracial South Africa must sooner or later become the major question on their national agenda. In particular, there is no obvious justification for Lesotho—landlocked and utterly dependent on South African infrastructure—to continue to exist. Finally, incorporation into South Africa would be particularly easy for Lesotho and Swaziland because the hard part of merging countries—allowing the free movement of people and adopting one currency—has already been done. South Africa, Swaziland, and Lesotho are already much more integrated than members of the European

Union, and they could move toward creating one nation much more quickly than any combination of countries in Europe could.

Of course, the major obstacle to national integration in southern Africa, even among South Africa, Lesotho, and Swaziland, has been the interests of the elites. Even if Lesotho and Swaziland do not make sense constructed as nations, their small elites benefit greatly from all the trappings of government: ministries, ambassadorial postings, and control over the flow of government spending and foreign aid to reward followers and build constituencies. These elites would lose out if their countries were to become integrated with South Africa because there would no longer be a need for such prerogatives.

Still, over the long term, there will probably be considerable pressure on Lesotho and Swaziland (Botswana, due to its outstanding success, is obviously in a different category) to fundamentally alter their relationship with South Africa through outright incorporation or some kind of increasingly broad, supranational federal arrangement.[19] Much of this pressure will probably come from the international community, which provided significant aid to Lesotho and Swaziland during the 1980s as a way of showing the world's solidarity with the struggling people of southern Africa when little could be done inside South Africa.[20] Inevitably, international attention will now focus on aiding people inside South Africa, to the detriment of Lesotho and Swaziland. Indeed, a key signal will be if aid agencies start distributing their assistance in Lesotho and Swaziland from Pretoria, a logical step given the short distances involved and the desire on the part of all donors to avoid administrative duplication. Such a step would be the first in a process whereby the international community—which did so much to legitimate the creation of these microstates in the first place—now demands a regional reorganization in light of the changes inside South Africa. Of course, the nature of the pressure on the two countries will depend greatly on perceptions of how successfully the South Africans are managing their economic and political transition. However, the prospect for much more radical changes in regional design than was ever contemplated by SADC should not be ignored.

Conclusion

In the short term, southern African countries may be surprised at how little they are affected by the transition in South Africa. As I have noted, the transition does not hold out the prospect of immediate, short-term gains for Africans in the region. Over the long term, decisions made by governments within the countries surrounding South Africa will determine how consequential the move away from white rule will be for their countries. If the leaders of the region are able to transform their own economies, they have at least the prospect of a large market that could absorb a considerably greater percentage of exports than it does now. However, if economic stagnation and social decline continue in the region, South Africa's transformation may become a threat as increasing numbers of skilled people from the region head for greener pastures. At the same time, leaders within the region may find that the new government in South Africa is more willing to intervene in the domestic affairs of other countries than they might have expected. For the smallest countries in the region, the transformation should mean the start of an important national debate about the very design of their nations. Thus, the transformation in South Africa will dramatically affect regional politics, if not in the manner originally expected.

Notes

1. Larry Bowman, "The Subordinate State System of Southern Africa," *International Studies Quarterly* 12 (September 1968), pp. 231–261.

2. See, for instance, Joseph Hanlon, *Beggar Your Neighbors: Apartheid Power in Southern Africa* (London: James Currey, 1986); Phyllis Johnson and David Martin, eds., *Destructive Engagement: Southern Africa at War* (Harare: Zimbabwe Publishing House, 1986); Elipha G. Munkonoweshuro, *Zimbabwe: Ten Years of Destabilization, A Balance Sheet* (Stockholm: Bethany Books, 1992); Robert S. Jaster, "War and Diplomacy," in Robert S. Jaster et al., *Changing Fortunes: War, Diplomacy, and Economics in Southern Africa* (New York: Ford Foundation, 1992); United Nations, *South African Destabilization: The Economic Cost of Frontline Resistance to Apartheid* (New York: United Nations, 1989).

3. See, for instance, Olayiwola Abegunrin, *Economic Dependence and Regional Cooperation in Southern Africa: SADCC and South Africa in Confrontation* (New York: Edwin Mellen Press, 1990); Reginald H. Green and Carol B. Thompson, "Political Economies in Conflict: SADCC, South Africa and Sanctions," in Phyllis Johnson and David Martin, eds., *Frontline Southern Africa: Destructive Engagement* (New York: Four Walls, Eight Windows, 1988); Moletsi Mbeki and Morley Nkosi, "Economic Rivalry and Interdependence in Southern Africa," in Robert S. Jaster et al., *Changing Fortunes: War, Diplomacy, and Economics in Southern Africa* (New York: Ford Foundation, 1992).

4. See, for instance, Richard O'Brien, *Global Financial Integration: The End of Geography* (London: Pinter Publishers, 1992).

5. World Bank, *Sub-Saharan Africa: From Crisis to Sustainable Growth* (Washington, D.C.: World Bank, 1989), p. 61.

6. Ibid., p. 162.

7. Nelson Mandela, "South Africa's Future Foreign Policy," *Foreign Affairs* 72 (November-December 1993), p. 91.

8. Calculated from World Bank, *World Development Report 1993* (Washington, D.C.: World Bank, 1993), pp. 241–242.

9. Calculated from ibid.

10. Calculated from Republic of South Africa, *South African Statistics 1992* (Pretoria: Republic of South Africa, 1992), pp. 16.6–16.9.

11. Statistics are from the Economist Intelligence Unit reports, published in London: *Zambia and Zaire,* 3d quarter 1993, p. 3; *Mozambique and Malawi,* 3d quarter 1993, p. 5; and *Zimbabwe,* 4th quarter 1993, p. 3.

12. See, for instance, Baron Boyd, "South Africa and Its Neighbors: Continuity and Change in the Post-Apartheid Era," in James Chipasula and Alifeyo Chilivumbo, eds., *South Africa's Dilemmas in the Post-Apartheid Era* (Lanham, Md.: University Press of America, 1993), p. 139.

13. The quote suggests that the ANC's leadership has yet to complete the transition from a liberation movement with no national responsibilities to an administration that makes tough calculations about the national interest. See Mandela, "South Africa's Future Foreign Policy," p. 92.

14. For instance, in 1992, transfers from the EU to Portugal accounted for 4 percent of that country's gross domestic product. *The Economist,* October 30, 1993, p. 56.

15. Anthony M. Hawkins, "Economic Development in the SADCC Countries," in Gavin Maasdorp and Alan Whiteseid, eds., *Towards a Post-Apartheid Future: Political and Economic Realities in Southern Africa* (London: Macmillan Press, 1992), p. 105.

16. These issues are discussed in the Commonwealth Expert Group, *Beyond Apartheid: Human Resources in a New South Africa* (London: James Currey, 1991), esp. pp. 17 and 94–95.

17. Statistics from Elling N. Tjønneland, *Southern Africa After Apartheid* (Bergen, Norway: Chr. Michelsen Institute, 1992), p. 87.

18. I have elaborated on this argument in "The Challenges to Africa's Boundaries," *Journal of International Affairs* 46, no. 1 (Summer 1992), pp. 17–31.

19. There has been relatively little analysis of this issue. For a very good discussion, see R. Southall, "Lesotho and the Re-Integration of South Africa," in Sehoai Santho and Mafa Sejanamane, eds., *South Africa After Apartheid: Prospects for the Inner Periphery in the 1990s* (Harare: Southern Africa Political Economy Series Trust, 1991), pp. 209–227.

20. World Bank, *African Economic and Financial Data* (Washington, D.C.: World Bank, 1989), p. 196.

8

Francophone Africa in the Context of Franco-American Relations

GUY MARTIN

FRANCOPHONE SUB-SAHARAN Africa (FSSA) today consists of twenty-one countries of west, central, and eastern Africa and the Indian Ocean region where the
French language has an official status.[1] Among the factors that make FSSA
unique and distinctive are: (1) a common (French or Belgian) colonial experience; (2) the adoption of the French language as the official language of administration and education; (3) a broad cultural unity (or "francophone African culture") resulting from a fusion of French and African cultures; (4) a tradition of
moderation and compromise arising out of a peaceful transfer of power at independence; and (5) the perpetuation of Franco-African relations characterized by
a pattern of continuing French political, economic, and cultural power and influence in FSSA.[2]

Francophonie is the concept used to organize the world's French-speakers and
the countries sharing, at least partly, in French civilization. For some, *francophonie* means only the use of the French language; for others, it refers to countries where this language has an official status. Generally, most users of French
see *francophonie* as an element of shared identity by which citizens of countries
with no indigenous national language (such as most francophone African states
[FAS]) can communicate with each other inside the state and in their regions.
Promoters of *francophonie* in Africa also see it as demarcating a distinctive Latin
world—inclusive of the Portuguese- and Spanish-speaking African elites—that is
separate from the English-speaking world; they also believe it is a way of guarding
against encroachment from Anglo-Saxon civilization. In its nationalistic extreme, *francophonie* becomes *francité*, the distinguishing mark of French civilization.[3] Ultimately, *francophonie* appears as a postcolonial modernization of the
French colonial policies of assimilation (the total political, economic, and cultural absorption of colonies and colonial peoples into France) and association
(which recognized the autonomous identity of African colonies and cultures).

Thus, to the extent that it implies the inclusion of people outside France in the culture of France itself, *francophonie* is a truly neocolonial concept.

The purpose of this chapter is fourfold: (1) to outline the cultural, ideological, and historical foundations of francophone Africa; (2) to analyze in some detail the political, diplomatic, economic, and security dimensions of Franco-African relations since independence (that is, between 1960 and 1994) with a view toward ascertaining the extent of residual French power and influence in Africa, as well as the degree of autonomy of FSSA in regional and world politics; (3) to review francophone African security arrangements in order to assess their potential for successful regional cooperation; and (4) to assess the prospects for the survival of FSSA in light of recent developments in Franco-African relations.

The Cultural and Ideological Foundations of Francophone Africa

France prides itself on being the home of a particularly rich culture and on having a vocation to spread this culture overseas. Stimulated by the universalist ideals of the French Revolution of 1789 (i.e., *Liberté, Egalité, Fraternité*), this vocation in the nineteenth century became a *mission civilisatrice* (civilizing mission), intimately linked with French imperialist expansion and colonialism in Africa. Even after decolonization, France retains its claim to be the center of an international culture and to pursue a policy of cultural *rayonnement* (diffusion). Underlying this quest is a belief in the innate value of the French language. According to French historian Fernand Braudel, "La France, c'est la langue française."[4] But cultural pride has also been mixed with a need to spread the culture beyond France and a claim to share with Africans—via association or assimilation— the ideals of French civilization by imparting to them the essentials of that language and culture. Cultural diffusion thus entails elements of an ideology (*France-Afrique* and *Eurafrique*) and a policy (*francophonie*) that can be used to reinforce France's presence overseas.

Assimilation and association were the main doctrines that dominated French colonial thought and practice during most of France's imperial rule (1880 to 1960).[5] The concept of assimilation refers to a process by which Africans were to be incorporated into the French nation, taught its language, and indoctrinated in its culture. They were to become French through an acculturation process. The policy of assimilation assumed that the colonies were a natural extension of the metropole and that they should become a part of it formally. The concept of assimilation relates to the idea of a *France d'outre-mer* (overseas France) that could be created by a successful *mission civilisatrice*. In its most extreme version (never actually achieved), assimilation could lead to the granting of French citizenship to colonial peoples. The alternative French colonial policy of association— favored by General Lyautey in Morocco and Savorgnan de Brazza in central

Africa—recognized the separate cultures and institutions of African peoples and established protectorates over them. According to Jules Harmand, one of its main advocates, association was "indirect administration, with the preservation but improved governance of the institutions of the conquered peoples, and with respect for the past."[6] Although neither of these doctrines was ever really practiced, they both implied an intimate link between France and its colonies that survives (albeit in a modified form) to this day.

The colonial doctrines of assimilation and association offered guidelines to colonial administrators and insights into the aims of French colonial policy. But neither of these doctrines could inspire a bold French policy in Africa. When the concept of a "larger France" was focused on Africa, reference was made to a Franco-African entity that would symbolize the greatness of France. The idea of *France-Afrique* as a single geopolitical whole was offered as the goal of a continued French presence in Africa. Sometimes, the ideal of *Eurafrique* was propounded by French individuals who believed that France should be the leading European power in Africa. The concepts of *France-Afrique* and *Eurafrique* symbolized the intensity with which the French believed that links with Africa were indissoluble.[7]

The first Eurafricanists appeared among French interest groups that had a stake in the colonial venture (the *parti colonial,* or colonial lobby): politicians, soldiers, and business people. These individuals attempted to justify and to rationalize the colonial venture on the grounds of the natural complementarity and resultant unavoidable "interdependence" of the two continents: Africa as provider of raw materials and Europe as supplier of finished goods. Prominent members of the French colonial lobby argued that to preserve and manage this intercontinental complementarity, it was necessary to unite Africa and Europe and to link the future of the two continents together, thus ensuring the economic prosperity of both.[8] Thus, from its inception, the ideology of Eurafrica appeared as a convenient justification of the colonial policies of the European powers— and particularly of France—in Africa and as a rationalization of the inherently unequal and fundamentally exploitative economic policies implemented by the metropoles in their African colonies.

The central tenets of the Eurafrican ideology (complementarity, solidarity, and interdependence) continued to be invoked by postcolonial Eurafricanists (such as Leopold Senghor). According to this updated Eurafrican ideal, the creation of *Eurafrique* appeared as a strategic and economic necessity for those countries and regions (such as Europe, France, and Africa) trying to combat the influence of the superpowers (the United States and the Soviet Union) on the continent.

However, the tensions created by the question of which should be given pre-eminence—bilateral relations between France and its former colonies or multi-lateral relations between Europe and Africa—would always remain. Although France retains a special relationship with its former colonies, Europe presents a coherent and largely favorable image of itself in the developing world through the Lomé Convention. This comprehensive trade and aid agreement between the twelve member states of the European Community (EC) and seventy African, Caribbean, and Pacific (ACP) states has constituted the framework of economic relations between Europe and Africa since 1975.

The Historical Basis of Francophone Africa

In the aftermath of World War II, French policymakers initiated a process of decolonization from above in Africa as they came to realize that the loss of formal control would not necessarily be accompanied by a loss of real power and influence on the continent. By establishing the principle of territorial autonomy, the *Loi-cadre* adopted by the French National Assembly in June 1956 (and effective April 1957) in effect encouraged each of the fourteen constituent territories of the Fédération de l'Afrique Occidentale Française (French West African Federation, or AOF) and the Fédération de l'Afrique Equatoriale Française (French Equatorial Africa Federation, or AEF) to seek independence separately rather than within the preexisting federations. France's successful pursuit of this age-old strategy of divide and rule and implementation of its associated policy of balkanization in its African colonies eventually resulted in "the break up [of] former large united colonial territories into a number of small, nonviable states, which are incapable of independent development."[9]

Shortly after assuming power as the first president of the Fifth French Republic (in June 1958), General Charles de Gaulle, who was trying to revive French *grandeur*, nurtured a special relationship with francophone African nationalist leaders who thought that if they could share in the creation of a new France, they would also have a part in its success. De Gaulle's personal conception of *France-Afrique* was translated into his project for a Franco-African community that would grant autonomy and internal self-government to the African colonies while France retained control over essential areas such as defense, foreign affairs, and economic, monetary, and strategic minerals policy. This Gaullist proposal was presented to the African people in the September 28, 1958, referendum that, although formally offering the option of immediate independence, in effect strongly discouraged it. In any event, all French African territories voted overwhelmingly in favor of the Franco-African community, except Sekou Toure, who had intimated to de Gaulle that the people of Guinea preferred "poverty in liberty to wealth in slavery" (which, with hindsight, proved to be a sadly prophetic statement).[10]

However, following the independence of Ghana in March 1957 and that of Guinea in October 1958, the movement toward independence—in spite of the delaying tactics of such diehard francophiles as Ivory Coast's Felix Houphouet-Boigny and Gabon's Leon M' Ba—proved irresistible. Following the independence of the short-lived Mali Federation (Senegal and Mali) in June 1960, all former French African colonies—including Ivory Coast and Gabon but excluding Comoros and Djibouti—had become independent by August 1960.[11] Thus, the Franco-African Community, as originally constituted, became moribund.

Francophone Africa: The Political and Diplomatic Dimensions

Independence and Cooperation

As suggested earlier, one of the characteristic features of francophone African countries is the peaceful transfer of power they experienced at independence, which explains the emphasis placed on such values as moderation and compromise in their foreign policies. This peaceful transfer of power, however, resulted in the perpetuation of French power and influence in Africa with a corresponding loss of power, autonomy, and sovereignty of FSSA both in Africa and in the world.

The ideologies of *Eurafrique* and *France-Afrique* that had been used to justify French colonialism and the stillborn Franco-African Community became applicable, *mutatis mutandis,* to postindependence Franco-African relations, now conveniently renamed "cooperation." As noted, with the prominent exception of Guinea, the independence of the African territories in 1960 was more the result of French goodwill and magnanimity than of the pressure of African nationalist movements. The transition from colonization to cooperation was smoothed before the formal granting of independence by the negotiation of comprehensive bilateral agreements between France and each African state, covering such areas as defense and security; foreign policy and diplomatic consultation; economic, financial, commercial, and monetary matters; and technical assistance. Through the linkage established between the accession to international sovereignty, the signing of model cooperation agreements, and the wholesale adoption of the French constitutional model of the Fifth Republic, France managed to institutionalize its political, economic, monetary, and cultural preeminence over its former African colonies, which thereby remained excessively dependent on France. Though the first generation of cooperation agreements were subsequently revised in the mid-1970s at Africa's request, the new agreements still gave exorbitant privileges to France.[12]

The small group of francophone African political elites—carefully nurtured through fifteen years of on-the-job training as members of various French legislative bodies, advisory councils, and even cabinets—had earlier enthusiastically adhered to de Gaulle's Franco-African Community; now they unreservedly acquiesced to the new cooperation agreements insofar as these helped sustain their own power base and gave them a degree of influence over the French political agenda. Given their stake in the Franco-African system, one understands why—except in the cases of Sekou Toure's Guinea and Modibo Keita's Mali—the francophone African elites opted for a gradual process of decolonization rather than a revolutionary break with the past.

France's African Policy: Exclusivity, Stability, and Continuity

France's African policy is characterized by exclusivity, stability, and continuity.[13] During the heyday of imperial expansion, France's economic dynamism and level of industrial development never quite matched that of its major European competitors (Britain and Germany). This explains why protectionism and autarky were systematically applied to France's African empire and continued to shape its colonial and postcolonial policies. France's heavy reliance on explicit legal instruments is codified in the form of a highly normalized set of binding documents (the cooperation agreements), supported by a number of multilateral agencies (such as the franc zone and Franco-African summits). To this day, FSSA is perceived as belonging to the French traditional sphere of influence by virtue of historical links and geographic proximity. According to this French version of the Monroe Doctrine, francophone Africa is seen as constituting a natural French preserve (*domaine réservé, ou pré-carré*), off limits to other foreign powers, whether perceived as friends (the United States, Canada, Great Britain, Germany) or foes (the former Socialist states, Libya). Indeed, France has, on several occasions, shown a deep suspicion of the motives and actions of these powers in Africa.[14] Although camouflaged under the mantle of "cooperation," France's African policy is, in fact, primarily motivated by a narrow conception of its national interest, and it blatantly disregards African concerns and interests. As former President Valéry Giscard d'Estaing once bluntly declared, "I am dealing with African affairs, namely with France's interests in Africa."[15]

Because they are said to be based on historical links, geographical proximity, and linguistic and cultural affinity, relations between France and francophone Africa are invested with a special quality in the sense that they are particularly close and intimate, almost familial. According to former Minister of Cooperation Jean-Pierre Cot, "The relationship between France and its francophone African partners is based on traditional complicity, on a background of common friendship and references which facilitate contact and dialogue."[16] Thus, although family feuds may occasionally erupt, differences are never such that they cannot be quickly reconciled within the informal, warm, and friendly atmosphere of Franco-African institutions. This explains the extraordinary resilience and stability that characterize Franco-African relations.

One of the most striking features of France's African policy is its continuity throughout the various political regimes of the Fifth French Republic, from 1958 to 1994. There is no doubt that an autonomous and permanent policy exists, transcending the traditional political cleavages, the various regimes, and individual political leaders. The successive governments of Charles de Gaulle, Georges Pompidou, and Valéry Giscard d'Estaing have initiated and nurtured this African policy.

Although François Mitterrand had proclaimed his intention to decolonize this policy, his Socialist regime (inaugurated in May 1981) found its room for maneuver strictly limited by historical constraints and by the weight of economic, political, and strategic interests. Mitterrand was thus left to manage, rather than to radically transform, this inheritance.[17] Paradoxically, the two periods of government cohabitation during which Mitterrand has been forced to share power with a rightist parliamentary majority and prime minister (Jacques Chirac, 1986–1988;

Edouard Balladur since March 1993) revealed the broad agreement that exists across party lines on the substance of France's African policy.

The Institutional Framework of Franco-African Relations

French political power and influence in FSSA is exercised through an elaborate institutional network. A careful analysis reveals that the African policy decision-making structures are characterized by three main features—centralization, secrecy, and specialization.

Ever since the de Gaulle administration, the formulation and implementation of major African policy decisions has always been the quasi-exclusive preserve of the president of the republic, acting through a small advisory unit on African affairs (The Cellule Africaine de l'Elysée, or Presidency's Africa Bureau). According to the principle of reserved competence, other ministries and government departments involved in African affairs act strictly and exclusively by delegation of presidential authority in this area. The proliferation of decisionmaking units responsible for Africa within the French administration—the presidency, its advisory unit on African affairs, the Ministry of Cooperation, the Ministry of Foreign Affairs's Directorate for African Affairs, the Ministry of Francophonie, the Ministry of Defense, the Treasury (Ministry of Finance), and the French Development Agency (Caisse Française de Développement or CFD)—might give the impression that France speaks with far too many voices in African affairs. Yet thus far, the maestro (François Mitterrand) has somehow managed to mute the dissonance of this growing cacophony.[18]

Regarding secrecy, decisionmaking in African affairs is based on a complex and elaborate intelligence network initiated by de Gaulle's influential and ubiquitous adviser on African affairs, Jacques Foccart. This network is characterized by close personal relations and loyalty based on common cultural and ideological references, business partnership, and membership in secret societies (freemasonry), as well as by the permanent intervention of official or unofficial "special action" agencies.[19]

As for specialization, relations with francophone Africa (the *pays du champs*, or countries within the domain) has always been the responsibility of a special ministry, the Ministry of Cooperation (familiarly known as Rue Monsieur because of its location in Paris). It is interesting to note in this regard that Mitterrand's first minister of cooperation, Jean-Pierre Cot, unsuccessfully attempted to broaden the functional and geographic competence of the ministry to include all the developing world (usually referred to as *pays hors-champs*, or countries outside the domain), thus making it into the Ministry for Development. Cot was eventually forced to resign (in December 1982) by a coalition of rival bureaucracies, the French African lobby, and certain African heads of state, all of whom had particular reasons for feeling threatened by his proposed reforms. Similarly, soon after taking charge of the Ministry of Cooperation in April 1993, Michel Roussin (the seventh to occupy this post in the Mitterrand administration) tried in vain to modify the ministry's geographic competence to include the French-speaking countries of the Maghreb (Algeria, Morocco, and Tunisia). Thus, more than thirty years after its creation, Rue Monsieur very much remains the Ministry of Franco-African Affairs.[20]

At a more general level, one of the constant preoccupations of French policy-makers in Africa has always been to inspire and sustain formal or informal institutions bringing together all the francophone African states under the aegis of the former metropole. It is such concerns that have led to the creation of the Conseil de l' Entente (Entente Council) by Ivory Coast, Dahomey (Benin), Niger, and Upper Volta (Burkina Faso) in May 1959, followed by the Organisation Commune Africaine et Malgache (Common African and Malagasy Organization, or OCAM), which brought together all the moderate FAS in February 1965. It was partly to make up for the deficiencies of the rather ineffectual and dormant OCAM that President Pompidou initiated the Franco-African summit conferences in November 1973. Since then, seventeen such conferences have been held biannually, alternatively in France and in Africa.[21]

In spite of their progressive inclusion of an ever greater number of nonfrancophone African participants (a fact that has prompted some observers to suggest that they act as a kind of surrogate Organization of African Unity), these meetings essentially retain their familial character and constitute the centerpiece of the Franco-African institutional edifice. More generally, the Franco-African summits constitute a form of institutionalization of the permanent tête-à-tête maintained between the French president and each of the francophone African heads of state, either directly or via the presidential advisory unit on African affairs, conveniently headed (from October 1986 to March 1992) by Mitterrand's own son, Jean-Christophe.[22] Such intimate contacts are also preserved through the frequent (official, working, or private) visits of the francophone African presidents to France, as well as the numerous reciprocal visits undertaken by the French president.

At a lower level, a number of ad hoc conferences periodically bring together the French and African ministers who deal with similar areas of competence in their respective countries—foreign affairs, economy and finance, telecommunications, justice, education, culture, health, sports, and so on. Finally, a wide network of intergovernmental organizations and conferences—whose hub is the Agence de Coopération Culturelle et Technique (Agency for Cultural and Technical Cooperation, or ACCT)—tries, under the label of *francophonie*, to institutionalize the linguistic, cultural, educational, and communication links existing between France and its African partners. President Mitterrand's decision to revive this concept led to the creation, in June 1988, of a full-fledged Ministry of Francophonie and to the organization of five annual summit conferences of francophone heads of state and government, inaugurated in Paris in February 1986.[23]

During the Cold War, France was generally perceived by most FAS as a respectable middle power, free from superpower hegemony, truly nonaligned, and thus a natural ally of the Third World. In this perspective, francophone Africa constituted a base from which France was able to develop relations with countries located outside its traditional sphere of influence. Thus, France has recently developed political and economic relations with a number of nonfrancophone African states, notably Nigeria, Angola, Mozambique, Kenya, Zimbabwe, and South Africa. The recent broadening of the participation in Franco-African summits to include nonfrancophone African countries derives from the same policy. And though all the FAS nominally belonged to the Non-Aligned Movement (NAM), they effectively retained close political, military, and economic ties with France throughout the Cold War. In reality, France was acting in Africa not only in defense of its own national interest but also as a proxy gendarme of the West. In the post–Cold War era, Africa remains the only area of the world where France retains enough power and influence to support its claim to medium-power status in the international system.[24]

The Economics of Franco-African Relations: From the *Pacte Colonial* to the Franc Zone

Among neo-Cartierist academics and policymakers, it has become fashionable to argue that France never derived any substantial economic benefits from its African colonies, which were perceived as costing, rather than earning, money and which—so the argument goes—actually contributed to slowing down the modernization of France's productive capacity and retarded the development of French capitalism.[25] As one former French foreign minister succinctly put it, "Black Africa is not an indispensable source of raw materials for France. Our investments there are minimal and our trading relations remain fairly limited."[26] In reality, Africa was and is an important economic partner for France as a source of strategic raw materials, as a market for its manufactured goods, as an outlet for its capital investment, and as a prop to its currency.

Strategic Raw Materials

The perennial question of assured access to strategic raw materials places Africa squarely at the center of French geopolitical designs. Europe in general and France in particular are highly dependent on the import of strategic raw materials—those minerals vital to the functioning of their high-technology industries—from Africa. Thus, in the early 1980s, France's rate of dependency on mineral imports from Africa ranged from 100 percent for uranium (Gabon and Niger) to 90 percent for bauxite (Guinea); 76 percent for manganese (Gabon and the Republic of South Africa [RSA]); 59 percent for cobalt (Zaire and Zambia); 57 percent for copper (Zaire and Zambia); 56 percent for chromium (Madagascar and RSA); 55 percent for phosphate (Morocco and Togo); and 31 percent for iron ore (Liberia and Mauritania).[27] More generally, France's energy dependency increased from 30 percent in 1950 to 80 percent in 1988–1989. Furthermore, the postindependence cooperation and defense agreements concluded between France and the FAS contain special provisions concerning exclusive French access to such strategic raw materials as oil, natural gas, uranium, thorium, lithium, beryllium, and helium. According to the defense agreements, these raw materials must be sold to France on a priority basis—and restricted to third countries—as required by "the interests of common defense."[28]

Uranium is an interesting case in point. France's ambitious program to expand its nuclear power industry makes it greatly dependent on long-term African sources of supply. Thus, uranium plays a prominent role in France's African policy. From 1981 to 1987, Africa's total production of uranium amounted to 94,025 tons. Total African uranium exports increased from 17,000 tons (76 percent of world uranium exports) in 1980 to 23,000 tons (50 percent of world exports) in 1990. France's uranium imports from Africa amounted to 6,048 tons (38.5 percent of its total uranium imports) in 1986. During that year, France's major African uranium suppliers were Niger (3,708 tons), South Africa-Namibia (1.301 tons), and Gabon (1,039 tons). Gabon and Niger alone provided 36.7 percent of all French uranium imports in 1987. Evidently, a select group of (mostly francophone) African countries play a crucial role in the production and export of uranium to France, thus substantially contributing to the continuing prosperity of the French economy.[29]

Franco-African Trade

Geographically, Africa's foreign trade remains extremely polarized on Europe in general and on France in particular. Some 45 percent of African exports and 50 percent of the continent's imports are with the European Community (EC). In addition, France's share in FSSA's total trade remains as high as 38 percent. Furthermore, most trade, marketing, and shipping activities in the FAS are still monopolized by the old colonial trading companies—notably the Compagnie Française de l'Afrique Occidentale (CFAO) and the Société Commerciale de l'Ouest Africain (SCOA)—that have recently diversified into import-export activities and that operate within the vast protected market circumscribed by the franc zone. Thirty-three years after independence, the foreign trade of francophone African countries is still largely functioning according to the rules of the *économie de traite* (trade economy), according to which Africa is restricted to the function of commodity producer, and the European metropoles retain exclusive control over the production and export of manufactured goods. According to a recent study, 20 percent of France's imports from Africa in 1991 were made up of agricultural and food products, and 45 percent comprised energy and fuel products.[30]

France's main trading partners remain the chosen few who still constitute the core of the Franco-African "family," namely, Cameroon, Congo, Ivory Coast, Gabon, Niger, and Senegal. In 1992, these six countries together accounted for 22 percent of France's imports from Africa and for 26 percent of its exports to the continent. It is noteworthy that France's balance of trade, which is in chronic deficit with the rest of the world, has always been positive with Africa (+20,337 million French francs [FF] in 1986; +10,369 million in 1991; +14,000 million in 1992). Thus, in spite of a gradual decline in Franco-African trade since 1985, French exports to Africa have (particularly since 1988) stabilized or even increased, amounting to FF 72 billion in 1992 (with Africa ranking as France's third main export market behind Europe and North America).[31]

French Aid and Investments in Africa

French official development assistance (ODA) to sub-Saharan Africa (SSA) has increased from FF 12.1 billion (representing 70 percent of total ODA to the region) in 1985 to 18.1 billion (85 percent of total ODA) in 1990 and 18.3 billion (81 percent of total ODA) in 1991. During 1989–1990, France allocated 54 percent of its total ODA to sub-Saharan Africa. Although the amount of French aid to Africa has increased, the quality of this aid has substantially deteriorated. Thus, over the last fifteen years, the degree of concessionality of French ODA has steadily decreased: Grants, which represented 80 percent of French ODA to sub-Saharan Africa in 1975, only accounted for 65 percent of such aid in 1985. In 1992, 59.4 percent of French ODA was allocated to economic, social, educational, and administrative infrastructure; 10 percent to industrial production; 7 percent to agriculture; and 2.6 percent to food aid. In keeping with France's policy of *rayonnement culturel* (cultural influence) and promotion of *francophonie*, French bilateral aid to Africa is heavily biased in favor of cultural and technical cooperation. Thus, in 1991, France still maintained over 7,000 French technical assistance personnel in FSSA.[32]

Judging by its modus operandi, French ODA acts more as a form of export credit facility for French firms than as an instrument of development aid. Indeed, the two main French public aid agencies, the Fonds d'Aide et de Coopération (Cooperation and Aid Fund, or FAC) and the Caisse Française de Développement (French Development Fund, or CFD, formerly Caisse Centrale de Coopération économique, or CCCE) actually operate as conduits for the transfer of French public capital to the beneficiary African state agencies and from the latter to the French firms operating in these countries. Thus, about 60 percent of total French ODA is tied, which explains why some 70 percent of FAC and CFD aid allocated to Africa actually returns to France in the form of purchases of goods and services. Not surprisingly, the main beneficiaries of French aid are France's traditional economic partners. Thus, in 1989–1990, 20 percent of French ODA went to eight African countries, including Cameroon, Ivory Coast, Gabon, Mali, Senegal, and Zaire.[33]

Since the mid-1980s, a gradual process of multilateralization of French aid has been under way, whereby increasing amounts of French ODA are channeled either through the EC-ACP Lomé Convention's European Development Fund or through the various financial facilities of the International Monetary Fund and the World Bank. Though purporting to be the advocate of the FAS in north-south fora and in the international financial institutions, France, in fact, increasingly defers to the dominant (neoliberal) development ideology of these institutions as reflected in the Structural Adjustment Programs (SAPs) that they impose on the African countries.[34]

With regard to French private investment overseas, the available data indicate that during the decade 1980 to 1990, private capital flows to other developed countries increased substantially (from FF 10 billion in 1983 to about 140 billion in 1990), and such flows to sub-Saharan Africa decreased markedly (from FF 5,800 million in 1985 to 300 million in 1990). One should note, however, that investments by French firms in the west and central African oil sector (not included in the preceding estimates) remain significant, totaling FF 3,037 million in 1990. Furthermore, total CFD commitments (loans and subsidies) to Africa for the period 1987–1991 amounted to some FF 35.5 billion (including 31.7 billion for francophone SSA). During this period, the major beneficiaries of these commitments were Ivory Coast (FF 5,177.5 million), Cameroon (3,266.3 million), Senegal (2,710.3 million), Gabon (2,533.6 million), Zaire (1,897.2 million), Madagascar (1,682.4 million), Burkina Faso (1,640 million), Mali (1,634.9 million), and Congo (1,438 million), together accounting for 61 percent of total CFD commitments.[35]

Monetary Dependency: The Franc Zone and After

Thirty-three years after independence, France continues to play a dominant role in the formulation and implementation of monetary policies in francophone Africa. Through the franc zone—a monetary cooperation arrangement set up between France and thirteen former colonies in SSA (plus Equatorial Guinea) following their independence in the early 1960s—France controls their money supply (i.e., the issuance and circulation of their currencies), their monetary and financial regulations, their banking activities, their credit allocation, and, ultimately, their budgetary and economic policies. Through their acceptance of the draconian membership rules of the franc zone—such as the joint management of all foreign exchange reserves by the French treasury and the quasi-veto right retained by French administrators in the African central banks' decisionmaking process—the African member states of the franc zone have entrusted all their monetary and financial responsibilities to France in what amounts to a voluntary surrender of sovereignty. Similarly, because of the links established between the two currencies, any modification in the value of the French franc against other currencies automatically and fully affects the CFA franc (the legal tender in the African member states of the franc zone)—and the SSA governments are not consulted prior to any French devaluation decision. Ultimately, the CFA franc appears to be a mere appendage of the French franc, with no real autonomy.[36]

Following an extraordinary Franco-African summit meeting in Dakar, Senegal (January 10–11, 1994), the CFA franc was officially devalued by 50 percent, effective January 12, 1994. The French decision—apparently arrived at in July 1992 but delayed for political reasons—is motivated by several factors. One is the obvious fact (belabored by the IMF and the World Bank) that the CFA franc, whose exchange rate had remained unchanged since 1948, was grossly overvalued; this made CFA zone goods uncompetitive on African markets and encouraged cross-border smuggling with non-CFA franc countries. Second, capital transfers between the African CFA zone and European banks amounting to several million French francs had sharply increased in 1992 and 1993, prompting the franc zone monetary authorities to suspend the free convertibility of the CFA franc as of August 2, 1993. Third, the French treasury had been repeatedly called upon to bail out francophone African states on the verge of financial bankruptcy (notably, Cameroon, Congo, Ivory Coast, Gabon, and Senegal) either by providing direct budgetary support or by paying these states' arrears to the IMF and the World Bank. Such short-term aid relief amounted to more than FF 1.5 billion over the six-month period from December 1992 to May 1993; in July 1993, France allocated an additional FF 650 million to Cameroon on that account.

Ultimately, the deepening economic and financial crisis in francophone Africa, coupled with a severe recession in the former metropole, led to the sobering realization that France could no longer afford to foot the bill. As Prime Minister Balladur candidly admitted, "France alone cannot solve all the economic and financial problems of all the African countries. The international [financial] institutions must become much more involved in Africa than they are at present."[37] This explains the French government's decision to make any new French aid commitment to franc zone countries conditional upon a prior agreement with the IMF and the World Bank as of January 1, 1994. From the French government's perspective, the devaluation of the CFA franc is a perfectly rational economic decision in the sense that it transfers the burden of the huge foreign debts of such countries as Cameroon and Ivory Coast from the French treasury to the international financial institutions.[38] And though its full impact is yet to be felt, the devaluation is certain to have disastrous economic and social consequences for the African countries and peoples concerned in terms of sharply reduced foreign exchange earnings, household incomes, and general standards of living. Recent proposals for reform of the franc zone center around the strengthening of intraregional monetary, financial and economic unions in Africa and on the creation, within the framework of the EC-ACP Lomé Convention, of a new Eurafrican monetary zone (superseding the franc zone) in which the European currency unit (ECU) would replace the French franc as the monetary unit of reference. This severing of the link between the CFA franc and the French franc would, in effect, signal the end of the franc zone.[39]

French Military Presence and Intervention in Africa

Since independence, France has maintained 8 defense agreements and 24 military technical assistance agreements, both with its former African colonies (including those in North Africa) and with African countries situated outside the traditional French sphere of influence (such as Burundi, Rwanda, Zaire, and Zimbabwe). Furthermore, France maintains a significant permanent military presence in Africa, with 8,650 troops deployed in the following countries: CAR (1,200), Chad (1,000), Ivory Coast (500), Djibouti (4,000), Gabon (550), Rwanda (200) and Senegal (1,200). A further 960 French military advisers are currently assigned to 23 African countries. In addition to its military bases on the continent, which have been gradually phased out since independence, France has, since August 1983, set up a rapid deployment force (force d'action rapide, or FAR), composed of five units totaling 44,500 men, that is capable of intervening on short notice almost anywhere in Africa from its bases in France. This elaborate network of defense and military assistance agreements and logistical support structures enabled the French army to intervene thirty times in Africa over a thirty-year period (1963–1993), an average of one intervention per year. According to the official French doctrine, military interventions in Africa are ad hoc, always conducted at the concerned government's specific request, operated within the framework of an existing defense agreement, and designed to counter actual or potential external aggression.[40]

French leaders tend to link the concepts of security and development by arguing that their help in creating strong national armies has contributed to the stability and hence to the economic benefit of all concerned. In fact, the French government's objective in creating African national armies at the time of independence was to build up units that could work closely with French units and effectively serve as branches of the French army overseas. The French Ministry of Cooperation continues to subordinate particular African requests in this sector to France's general strategy for Africa. In this area, as in others, continuity has prevailed over change. Although the preelection Socialist policy paper on Africa stated that the whole question of the French military presence on the continent would have to be reviewed, the Mitterrand government decided to intervene in Africa on eight separate occasions between 1981 and 1993.[41] France's military cooperation policy in Africa, which has so far produced some 40,000 African military officers, enables it to control the size and capabilities of most francophone African armies—and hence the defense systems of the FAS—and helps to further exacerbate these states' already acute dependence on Paris.

In the final analysis, France's military presence in Africa is determined by three main factors: the size and degree of its economic interests and involvement, the number of French residents, and the nature of the links existing between France and the national ruling elites. It is interesting to note in this regard that the core countries of the Franco-African defense system (linked to France by defense agreements) are precisely those that are central to France's economic interests, namely, Cameroon, CAR, Ivory Coast, Gabon, Senegal, and Togo. Ultimately, one suspects that the main objective is to help pro-French regimes stay in power, as the remarkable political stability and exceptional elite longevity of these FAS seem to indicate.

Regional Security in Francophone Africa

In the early 1990s, most FAS—which have initiated comprehensive economic and political reform programs—remained economically, politically, and militarily fragile. These states suffered from various internal and external disturbances that directly affected their stability and security. Although the Franco-African security system covers most of the francophone African security concerns, regional security structures have recently taken on increased responsibilities in this area. In West Africa, the Economic Community of West African States (ECOWAS), set up in May 1975 by the Lagos Treaty, includes sixteen member states and aims at establishing a common market and economic union. It took another six years for thirteen of the member states to sign the Defense Protocol (May 1981). Some FAS (notably Ivory Coast and Niger) feared that the influence of Nigeria in ECOWAS would be overwhelming. Indeed, the vast majority of FAS continue to view Nigeria with suspicion, while the Nigerians believe that the continuing French presence in Africa impedes their own progress toward regional power status. The ECOWAS Defense Protocol provides a collective security system under which member states pledge to give mutual aid and assistance against an armed attack of aggression from a nonmember state and to provide a peacekeeping force in cases of conflict between member states.[42]

An elastic interpretation of this protocol enabled ECOWAS to directly intervene in an attempt to resolve the Liberian civil war. At their Banjul (Gambia) summit meeting of May 1990, the organization's heads of state decided to set up a five-member Standing Mediation Committee (SMC) (Gambia, Ghana, Mali, Nigeria, and Togo) that would intervene promptly whenever a conflict threatened the stability of the region. However, the old anglophone-francophone divisions threatened to undermine the ECOWAS initiative. Eventually, these differences were resolved, at least momentarily, and on August 24, 1990, a peacekeeping force known as the ECOWAS Monitoring Group (ECOMOG)—initially composed of 3,000 troops (now 16,000) from five (predominantly anglophone) countries (Gambia, Ghana, Guinea, Nigeria, and Sierra Leone)—was sent to Liberia with the mandate of "keeping the peace, restoring law and order and ensuring that the cease-fire is respected." At the first ECOWAS extraordinary summit in Bamako, Mali (November 27–28, 1990), a cease-fire agreement was signed between the warring Liberian factions, an interim government was installed in Monrovia, and a national conference was planned. From the outset, the francophone West African states appeared to be reluctant to get fully involved in the ECOMOG initiative. Burkina Faso (and, to a lesser extent, Ivory Coast and Senegal) expressed reservations about the intervention of the ECOMOG peacekeeping force in the Liberian conflict. Neither Mali nor Togo (the two francophone representatives on the SMC) contributed to the force. The subsequent creation in July 1991 of the Committee of Five (Ivory Coast, Senegal, Togo, Guinea-Bissau, and Gambia), chaired by Felix Houphouet-Boigny and effectively supplanting the SMC, restored a major diplomatic role to the francophones. Eventually, with U.S. encouragement and financial support, the Senegalese government agreed to contribute a contingent of about 1,500 peacekeepers to ECOMOG as of October 1991. As a result of a variety of domestic political problems and external (mostly French) pressures, however, Abdou Diouf decided to repatriate the Senegalese troops by January 15, 1993. Thus, although ECOMOG constitutes a unique effort at regional peacekeeping in Africa, the particular circumstances of francophone-anglophone frictions that surrounded Senegal's entry into (and departure from) ECOMOG once again revealed the absence of a strong political consensus among the parties involved.[43]

The existence of the Communauté Économique de l'Afrique de l'Ouest (CEAO)—a seven-member organized trade zone moving toward a common market, created in April 1973—is, in itself, testimony to the fact that the FAS remain suspicious of Nigerian power and are more comfortable dealing with each other than with nonfrancophone states in the region. As early as 1977, the CEAO member states (plus Togo) signed a defense protocol, the Accord de Non-agression et d'Assistance en Matière de Défense (ANAD). It was only in 1981, however, that the ANAD states were able to come to an agreement with respect to the protocol of application. The objective of the ANAD protocol is to reinforce defense measures of the member states in order to increase stability in the sub-region. Member states also agree not to use force to resolve their disputes. Though a standing army has not yet been created, some work is being done to establish an interallied command, and member states have agreed to create an intervention force by assigning units of their own armies to ANAD. By far the most innovative aspect of the ANAD is the attempt to set up a system of confidence-building measures to ensure that states are informed on potential threats to their security. Additional protocols dealing with nonaggression and civil defense were subsequently adopted by the ANAD member states (in December 1982 and October 1983, respectively). In October 1984, the ANAD states agreed to establish both a commission for the peaceful settlement of disputes between member states and a peacekeeping force. In April 1987, a Comité Régional d'Assistance en Matière de Protection Civile (as agreed in October 1983) was formally established. Until 1985, ANAD was still very much an idea in search of funds and political will. But the success it had in the establishment of a cease-fire in early 1986, after the "Christmas war" between Mali and Burkina Faso, demonstrated its potential utility in helping to solve regional conflicts. However, to the extent that its member states maintain close bilateral relations with France and because of its limited ability to serve as a regional peacemaker, the existence of ANAD in no sense challenges French power in Africa.[44]

New Trends in Franco-African Relations: Between Democratization and Authoritarian Reaction

Democratic Transition in Francophone Africa

Since 1990, the winds of change have swept throughout Africa, signaling the dawn of a new era variously referred to as the "second independence," the "second liberation," or the "Springtime of Africa."[45] After three decades of authoritarian, one-party rule characterized by political repression, human rights abuses, economic mismanagement, nepotism, and corruption, democracy is spreading like bushfire throughout francophone Africa. A recent evaluation of the Carter Center's African Governance Program noted that eight FAS may be described as "democratic," three are under "directed democracy" regimes, one (Zaire) remains "authoritarian," and nine are in transition to democracy, with various degrees of commitment.[46] Recent changes in the structure of the international system (notably, the successful democracy movements in Eastern Europe and the former Soviet Union) have created a generally favorable and supportive environment for the development and maturation of popular struggles for democracy in francophone Africa.

The transition to democracy in this region is taking different forms and is proceeding at various speeds with different outcomes, depending on the nature of external inducements and on the configuration of domestic sociopolitical forces. In this regard, it is possible to identify four types of democratic transition, from the smoothest to the most problematic. The first type includes cases of normal transition from military dictatorship to civilian, multiparty democracy, primarily via a national conference, as in Benin, Congo, Gabon, Mali, and Niger (CAR and Madagascar are exceptions to this). In this (essentially francophone) scenario, a broad coalition of the civil society invests itself with sovereign and supreme constitutional powers; appoints a transitional government with a dual executive (a figurehead president and a prime minister responsible for managing the transition); and organizes (within a year) local, legislative, and presidential elections culminating in the installation of a democratically elected head of state, who forms a new government.

A second type include cases of managed military transitions: A military regime retains virtually complete control over the transition process (which is deliberately complex and prolonged) and is thus assured of an outcome favorable to its own corporate interests; Burkina Faso, Ghana, Guinea, and Mauritania are cases in point. A third category includes extreme cases of authoritarian military reaction (as in Nigeria, Togo, and Zaire) in which the ruling military autocrats have been able, through deceit, manipulation and fraud, to subvert the democratically constituted institutions and processes. In the fourth scenario—co-opted transitions—the incumbent (civilian) president acts in time to allow multiparty elections. With control over the media and electoral machinery and superior financial resources, the president is able to defeat the opposition at the ballot box and to stay in power despite widespread allegations of fraud. This has happened in Cameroon, Ivory Coast, Ethiopia, Gabon, Kenya, and Senegal.[47]

France and the Promotion of Democracy in Francophone Africa: The Politics of Creative Ambiguity

France initially observed with some trepidation a process of democratization that it had not initiated and over which it had no control unfolding in its former African colonies. However, French leaders soon realized the inevitability of that process and promptly initiated a policy of "political conditionality." This policy establishes an explicit linkage between the provision of economic and financial assistance and the initiation of political reforms leading to liberal, multiparty democracy. Thus, at the June 1990 Franco-African summit meeting of La Baule (France), Mitterrand stressed the link between democracy and development and declared that "French aid [to Africa] will be lukewarm toward authoritarian regimes and more enthusiastic for those initiating a democratic transition."[48] However, a review of the evidence seems to suggest that France has not actually matched its deeds with words and that, as is often the case, official pronouncements have not been followed by concrete and appropriate policy measures.

Total French ODA to FSSA in 1991 amounted to FF 8 billion. A country-by-country breakdown reveals that the French aid share of countries in transition to democracy (such as Benin, Mali, and Niger) has actually been reduced (as in Benin, from FF 588 million in 1989 to 300 million in 1990), and African authoritarian regimes or reluctant democrats saw their share increase during the same period (from FF 628 to 963 million in Cameroon, from FF 305 to 519 million in Togo, and from FF 669 to 1,002 million in Zaire).[49] Similarly, the only concrete decision of the Libreville Franco-African summit meeting (October 5–7, 1992) was the creation by France of a Debt Conversion Fund for Development, endowed with FF 4 billion to provide debt relief to Cameroon, Ivory Coast, Congo, and Gabon where (except in Congo) the democratization process has been either blocked or derailed. Although France officially discontinued ODA to Zaire following the 1991 popular riots, "humanitarian assistance" to that country continues. And barely two months after having been reelected to office in seriously flawed elections, president Paul Biya of Cameroon was allocated FF 600 million in French economic aid.[50]

The recent oil war between Congo and the French state oil corporation Elf-Aquitaine perfectly illustrates the ambiguity of French African policy and is worth recounting in some detail. The August 1992 presidential elections in Congo saw the defeat of incumbent President Denis Sassou Nguesso (a close associate of France and of Elf-Aquitaine) and brought to power Pascal Lissouba (a respected scientist and former UNESCO official) and his radical Union Panafricaine pour la Démocratie et le Progrès Social (UPADS). Lissouba inherited from Sassou Nguesso a disastrous economic and financial situation: Civil service salaries and pensions were no longer paid, the state coffers were empty, the oil revenues were mortgaged until 1999 to the tune of FF 1.8 billion, and the country's foreign debt amounted to a staggering U.S. $5 billion. More critically, Lissouba urgently needed some $200 million to pay the civil servants' salaries before the legislative elections of May 2, 1993. He naturally turned to Elf-Aquitaine (which controls 80 percent of the country's oil production) and his chief executive officer (CEO) Loik Le Floch-Prigent, for help on two separate occasions: first, on February 24, 1993, when he requested a $300 million loan, and again on March 9, 1993, with a request for $200 million mortgaged on the future production of three promising new off-shore oil deposits.

Having met with a categorical refusal from Elf-Aquitaine and Le Floch-Prigent, Lissouba then initiated (with the assistance of former President Jimmy Carter) secret negotiations with one of the most enterprising U.S. "minors," Occidental Petroleum Corporation (OXY). In Brazzaville on April 27, 1993, OXY (represented by its CEO David Marten) and the Congolese government concluded a purchase agreement according to which Congo is committed to deliver to OXY 75 million barrels of Elf-Congo's projected share of the three new off-shore oil deposits in exchange for a cash down payment of $150 million. The money reached Brazzaville on May 1, just in time to pay the salaries of the 80,000 Congolese civil servants.

In the first round of parliamentary elections on May 2, Lissouba's "presidential majority" obtained 62 out of 125 seats in the National Assembly. Three lessons can be drawn from this revealing story. First, Elf-Aquitaine and its CEO exhibited a total lack of empathy for and sensitivity to their Congolese partners' priorities and needs, and they generally acted in a most paternalistic and neocolonial fashion. Second, paranoid French senior officials tended to view the Congo-OXY agreement as yet another inadmissible intrusion of U.S. capitalism into a region (central Africa) considered as an exclusive French preserve. Third, by denying Lissouba's government financial resources vital to its survival, Elf-Aquitaine (and, by extension, the French state) could rightly be perceived as favoring opposition leaders that were close to them (such as Sassou Nguesso and Energy Minister Jean-Pierre Thystère Tchicaya) against the democratically elected (but noncompliant) Lissouba. The much publicized dismissal of Elf-Aquitaine's CEO Le Floch-Prigent by Mitterrand on August 3, 1993, cannot obscure the fact that in this particular case, France, true to its economic and strategic interests, deliberately chose to back the forces of authoritarian reaction against those in favor of democratic change.[51]

Not only does France financially support nondemocratic regimes, it also comes to their rescue whenever their internal security and stability are seriously threatened. Thus, France embarked on ten military interventions in support of these regimes between 1986 and 1993 (in Chad, Togo, Comoros, Gabon, Rwanda, Ivory Coast, and Zaire). The total cost of French military interventions between October 1990 and October 1991 has been conservatively estimated at FF 6 billion, an amount almost equivalent to total French ODA to FSSA during that year. Indeed, French military aid is increasingly redirected to satisfy the urgent internal security needs of the embattled African military dictatorships attempting to resist popular pressure for democracy. Thus, France has recently launched a vast program of internal security assistance involving the deployment of 700 officers of the French *Gendarmerie* to eight countries (Benin, CAR, Chad, Comoros, Congo, Madagascar, Niger, and Togo) as well as technical assistance, material and logistical support to the police forces, riot control units, presidential guards, secret services, and intelligence agencies of these countries. In 1991, FF 990 million were earmarked for that program to the benefit of twenty-four FAS linked to France by defense and/or military technical assistance agreements.[52]

Implicitly recognizing the ambiguity of France's African policy, the Balladur government has recently downplayed political conditionality—the linkage between the provision of French aid and the initiation of democratic reforms—in favor of the prevailing norm, namely, economic conditionality. Thus, Balladur now insists that the African states should work toward the establishment of definite and stable political and social norms and rules (*L' état de droit*, or the rule of law) and that the African democratization processes should not be externally induced according to a presumed ideal model but should be allowed to follow their own individual course.[53]

Conclusion

The preceding analysis illustrates the perennial tension between continuity and change in Franco-African relations. While officially proclaiming support for democratization and human rights in francophone Africa, France continues, in reality, to support the regimes and leaders of the core countries in terms of French economic and politico-strategic interests in Africa, such as Cameroon's Paul Biya, Ivory Coast's Konan Bedie, Gabon's Omar Bongo, Togo's Gnassingbe Eyadéma, and Zaire's Mobutu Sese Seko. France thus maintains a deliberate (though recently toned-down) "creative ambiguity" in its African policy pronouncements and actions. In this regard, continuity and stability tend to prevail over justice and equity. In the post–Cold War era, Africa remains the only area of the world where France retains enough power and influence to support its claim to medium-power status in the international system.

On the other hand, two recent events of great symbolic significance point toward profound change—and possibly even a new era—in Franco-African relations. The first is the death (on December 7, 1993) and solemn state funeral (on February 7, 1994) of President Felix Houphouet-Boigny of Ivory Coast, one of the last of a generation of African nationalist leaders. Houphouet-Boigny's close personal ties with several generations of French leaders were reflected in the level and size of the French delegation to the funeral, which included President François Mitterrand and Prime Minister Edouard Balladur, former President Valéry Giscard d'Estaing, six former prime ministers, and more than seventy other dignitaries. As the New York Times reporter rightly observed, "Mr. Houphouet-Boigny's death is not only the end of a political era here, but perhaps as well the end of the close French-African relationship that he came to symbolize."[54] The second event is the 50 percent devaluation of the CFA franc of January 12, 1994, signaling the demise of the Franco-African preferential monetary and trading area known as the franc zone. In a context of increasing globalization of the world economy and European integration, France no longer has the wherewithal and the political will to maintain an autonomous African policy distinct from that of its Western partners. Thus, the devaluation of the CFA franc is likely to result in a gradual (but substantial) loss of political, diplomatic, and economic power and influence for France in francophone Africa. This will probably lead to a long-overdue economic rapprochement between the francophone African states and major world economic powers (such as the United States and Japan), as well as with nonfrancophone African regional powers (notably, Nigeria and South Africa). In this regard, as Albert Bourgi cogently remarked, "the devaluation of the CFA franc will ultimately have a cathartic effect, that of mentally decolonizing the African leaders in their relations with France, thus finally cutting the umbilical cord that, for more than three decades, has tied them to their former metropole."[55]

Notes

1. These countries are: Benin, Burkina Faso, Ivory Coast, Guinea, Mali, Mauritania, Niger, Senegal, and Togo in west Africa; Burundi, Cameroon, Central African Republic, Chad, Congo, Gabon, Rwanda, and Zaire in central Africa; Djibouti in east Africa; and Comoros and Madagascar in the Indian Ocean region. The following countries have, for obvious reasons, been excluded from the purview of this article: the Maghreb countries of north Africa (Algeria, Morocco, and Tunisia); the Indian Ocean states of Mauritius and Seychelles; and the Indian Ocean French overseas territories of Mayotte and Réunion.

2. See Patrick Manning, *Francophone Sub-Saharan Africa 1880–1985* (New York: Cambridge University Press, 1988), pp. 1–3.

3. On *francophonie,* see, in particular, Robert Aldrich and John Connell, "Francophonie: Language, Culture or Politics?" in R. Aldrich and J. Connell, eds., *France in World Politics* (New York: Routledge, 1989), pp. 170–193; Xavier Deniau, *La Francophonie* (Paris: Presses Universitaires de France, 1983); and Michel Guillou, *La Francophonie, nouvel enjeu mondial* (Paris: Hatier, 1993).

4. Quoted by Mort Rosenblum, *Mission to Civilize: The French Way* (San Diego, Calif.: Harcourt, Brace, Jovanovich, 1986), p. 8.

5. See John Chipman, *French Power in Africa* (Cambridge, Mass.: Basil Blackwell, 1989), pp. 53–59; Manning, *Francophone Sub-Saharan Africa,* pp. 59–62; and Francis T. McNamara, *France in Black Africa* (Washington, D.C.: National Defense University Press, 1989), pp. 33–39.

6. Jules Harmand, *Domination et Colonisation* (1910); quoted in R. F. Betts, *Uncertain Dimensions: Western Overseas Empires in the Twentieth Century* (Minneapolis: University of Minnesota Press, 1985), p. 68.

7. See Chipman, *French Power,* pp. 61–84; Max Liniger-Goumaz, *L'Eurafrique: Utopie ou réalité?* (Yaoundé: Editions CLE, 1972); and Guy Martin, "Africa and the Ideology of Eurafrica: NeoColonialism or Pan-Africanism?" *Journal of Modern African Studies* 20, no. 2 (June 1982), pp. 221–238.

8. Eugène Guernier, *L'Afrique: Champ d'expansion de l'Europe* (1933); quoted in Chipman, *French Power,* pp. 71–72.

9. Kwame Nkrumah, *Neo-Colonialism* (London: Heinemann, 1965), p. xiii; see also Martin, "Africa and the Ideology of Eurafrica," pp. 227–228.

10. Georges Chaffard, *Les Carnets secrets de la décolonisation,* vol. 2 (Paris: Calmann-Lévy, 1965), p. 197; see also Chipman, *French Power,* pp. 85–102; and McNamara, *France in Black Africa,* pp. 67–93. In his recently published memoirs, the then French governor of Guinea (later prime minister under de Gaulle), Pierre Messmer, reveals that Guinea was deliberately made to suffer the consequences of its fateful decision; he personally issued specific orders for the speedy withdrawal of all French personnel (within two months) and

the rerouting of two rice cargo shipments and of several billion newly printed CFA francs from Conakry to Dakar; see Pierre Messmer, *Après tant de batailles* (Paris: Albin Michel, 1992), pp. 240–242.

11. The Comoros became independent in July 1975, as Djibouti did in June 1977.

12. Albert Bourgi, *La Politique française de coopération en Afrique* (Paris: Librairie Générale de Droit & de Jurisprudence, 1979); Chipman, *French Power*, pp. 102–113; Guy Martin, "The Historical, Economic, and Political Bases of France's African Policy," *Journal of Modern African Studies* 23, no. 2 (June 1985), pp. 189–192; McNamara, *France in Black Africa*, pp. 95–99.

13. Much of the information in this section is drawn from my chapter on "France and Africa" in Robert Aldrich and John Connell, eds., *France in World Politics* (New York: Routledge, 1989), pp. 101–105, 110–113.

14. France has recently expressed serious concern about alleged "American activism" in francophone Africa, following the appointment of George Moose (former ambassador to Senegal) as assistant secretary of state for African affairs; Washington's discreet support of prodemocracy forces in Cameroon, Congo, and Togo; the signature of the Congo-OXY purchase agreement of April 27, 1993; and the resounding success of the second African/African-American Summit in Libreville (May 24–28, 1993), attended by eighteen francophone African heads of state and government, see "France-Etats-Unis: George Moose inquiète," *Jeune Afrique*, no. 1688 (May 13–19, 1993), p. 19; Géraldine Faes, "Etats-Unis-Afrique: Les Conseilleurs ne sont pas les payeurs," *Jeune Afrique*, no. 1692 (June 10–16, 1993), pp. 22–26; Philippe Triay, "Deuxième Sommet Africain/Africain-Américain: La Consécration d'une idée," *Jeune Afrique Economie*, no. 169 (July 1993), pp. 17–33).

15. Televised interview of Valéry Giscard d'Estaing, quoted in T. Jallaud, "La Coopération militaire," in *La France contre l'Afrique* (Paris: Maspéro, 1981), p. 105.

16. Jean-Pierre Cot, *A L' Epreuve du pouvoir* (Paris: Editions du Seuil, 1984), p. 63.

17. Much the same argument is made by Jean-François Bayart, who goes so far as to assert that it was, in fact, Mitterrand himself who initiated a new deal for Africa when he became minister for overseas France in 1954: "The real continuity actually starts with Mr. Mitterrand and was passed on to General de Gaulle and to his successors;" see J. F. Bayart, *La Politique africaine de François Mitterrand* (Paris: Karthala, 1984), p. 52.

18. On the principle of the "reserved competence" of the presidency in African affairs, see Brigitte Nouaille-Degorce, *La Politique française de coopération avec les etats africains et malgache au Sud du Sahara* (Bordeaux: Center d'étude d'Afrique noire/IEP, 1982), pp. 104–155. On institutional proliferation in African affairs, see J. F. Bayart, "Fin de partie au Sud du Sahara? La Politique africaine de la France," in Serge Michailof, ed., *La France et l'Afrique: Vade-mecum pour un nouveau voyage* (Paris: Karthala, 1993), pp. 112–129. On recent political and institutional developments in Franco-African relations, see François Gaulme, "France-Afrique: Une Crise de coopération," *Etudes* 3801 (January 1994), pp. 41–52.

19. On this issue, see, in particular, Antoine Glaser and Stephen Smith, *Ces messieurs Afrique: Le Paris—Village du continent noir* (Paris: Calmann-Lévy, 1992); McNamara, *France in Black Africa*, pp. 186–208; Pierre Péan, *Affaires africaines* (Paris: Fayard, 1983); and P. Péan, *L'Homme de l'ombre: Eléments d'enquête autour de Jacques Foccart* (Paris: Fayard, 1990). It is interesting to note that Foccart made a remarkable comeback as adviser on African affairs to *cohabitation* prime minister Jacques Chirac on two occasions (1986–1988 and again after March 1993); see Péan, *L'Homme de l'ombre*, pp. 471–486.

20. On Cot's *déboires*, see Bayart, *La Politique africaine de François Mitterrand*, and Cot,

A L'Epreuve du pouvoir. On more recent developments, see François Soudan, "Michel Roussin: Gendarme, 'espion,' ministre," *Jeune Afrique* 1699 (July 29–August 4, 1993), pp. 14–19.

21. The 17th Conference of the French and African Heads of State and Government was held in Libreville (Gabon), October 5–7, 1992, with thirteen heads of state in attendance. The same city hosted the interim ministerial conference (July 29–30, 1993), attended by some thirty ministers of foreign affairs.

22. See "Jean-Christophe Mitterrand, le conseiller," in Antoine Glaser and Stephen Smith, *Ces messieurs Afrique,* pp. 209–235, and François Soudan, "Le 'vrai-faux' départ de Jean-Christophe," *Jeune Afrique* 1630 (April 2–8, 1992), p. 10.

23. The most recent francophone summit was held in Mauritius, October 16–18, 1993. An interesting overview of the foreign policy of *francophonie* from the perspective of one of its first ministers is Alain Decaux, *Le Tapis rouge* (Paris: Librairie Académique Perrin, 1992).

24. See Zaki Laïdi, *The Super-Powers and Africa, 1960–1990* (Chicago: University of Chicago Press, 1990); Guy Martin, "France and Africa," in Robert Aldrich and John Connell, eds., *France in World Politics* (New York: Routledge, 1989), pp. 115–117; and Guy Martin, "The Theory and Practice of Non-Alignment: The Case of the Francophone West and Central African States," in L. Adele Jinadu and Ibbo Mandaza, eds., *African Perspectives on Non-Alignment* (Harare, Zimbabwe: Jongwe Press/AAPS, 1986), pp. 20–38.

25. The classic exposé of this argument can be found in Jacques Marseille, *Empire colonial et capitalisme français: Histoire d'un divorce* (Paris: Albin Michel, 1984); see also Chipman, *French Power in Africa,* pp. 186–192. Cartierists (and their contemporary followers, the neo-Cartierists) are people who, following French journalist Raymond Cartier's series of articles in the early 1950s in the weekly *Paris-Match,* believe that French economic assistance should be primarily directed within (to the underdeveloped French regions) rather than without (overseas), according to the famous motto *La Corrèze avant le Zambèze!*

26. Louis de Guiringaud, "La Politique africaine de la France," *Politique étrangère,* no. 2 (June 1982), p. 443.

27. Statistical data are from Jacques Adda and Marie-Claude Smouts, *La France face au sud: Le Miroir brise* (Paris: Karthala, 1989), p. 98, table 10.

28. Pierre Lellouche and Dominique Moisi, "French Policy in Africa: A Lonely Battle Against Destabilization," *International Security* 3 (1979), p. 116, n. 15.

29. On this issue, see Guy Martin, "Uranium: A Case-Study in Franco-African Relations," *Journal of Modern African Studies* 27, no. 4 (December 1989), pp. 625–640, also published in *Australian Outlook* 43, no. 3 (December 1989), pp. 89–101.

30. On Franco-African trade relations, see Elsa Assidon, *Le Commerce captif: Les Sociétés commerciales françaises de l'Afrique noire* (Paris: L'Harmattan, 1989), and Adda and Smouts, *La France face au sud,* pp. 81–103. Franco-African trade statistics are taken from "France-Afrique: L'Afro-pessimisme ne passera pas," *Jeune Afrique* 1598–1599 (August 14–27, 1991), pp. 128–141; F. Dorce, G. Faes, and R. Godeau, "France-Afrique: Le Temps du réalisme," *Jeune Afrique* 1649–1650 (August 13–26, 1992), pp. 130–135; "Rapport Prouteau 1992: Les Entreprises françaises et l'Afrique," *Jeune Afrique* 1659 (October 22–28, 1992), pp. 47–55; "Rapport Prouteau 1993: Les Entreprises françaises et l'Afrique," *Jeune Afrique* 1712-1713 (October 28–November 10, 1993), pp. 53–98.

31. Dorce, Faes and Godeau, "France-Afrique: Le Temps du Réalisme," op. cit.; "Rapport Prouteau 1992," op. cit.; "Rapport Prouteau 1993," op. cit.

32. On French aid to Africa, see Adda and Smouts, *La France face au sud,* pp. 27-60.

French aid statistics are taken from "Rapport Prouteau 1992," pp. 13–22, 37–44, "Rapport Prouteau 1993," pp. 94–98, and OECD, *Development Assistance Committee Report 1991* and *1992* (Paris: OECD, 1991 and 1992).

33. "Rapport Prouteau 1992," pp. 16–17; "Rapport Prouteau 1993," pp. 94–96.

34. See Adda and Smouts, *La France face au sud*, pp. 50–60; Zaki Laïdi, *Enquête sur la Banque Mondiale* (Paris: Fayard, 1989), pp. 313–337.

35. See "Rapport Prouteau 1992," pp. 17–22, 39–41; Caisse Centrale de Coopération Economique, *Annual Report 1991* (Paris: CCCE, 1991), pp. 36–37.

36. On the franc zone, see Adda and Smouts, *La France au sud*, pp. 62–79; Shantayanan Devarajan and Jaime de Melo, "Relative Performance of CFA Franc Zone Members and Other Countries," in I. W. Zartman, ed., *Europe and Africa: The New Phase* (Boulder: Lynne Rienner Publishers, 1993), pp. 121–137; Patrick and Sylvianne Guillaumont, *Zone franc et développement africain* (Paris: Economica, 1984); Guy Martin, "The Franc Zone, Underdevelopment and Dependency in Francophone Africa," *Third World Quarterly* 8, no. 1 (January 1986), pp. 205–235; and Olivier Vallée, *Le Prix de l'argent CFA: Heurs et malheurs de la zone franc* (Paris: Karthala, 1989). On recent developments in Franco-African economic relations, see François Gaulme, "France-Afrique: Une Crise de coopération," *Etudes* 3801 (January 1994), pp. 41–52; and Philippe Leymarie, "Inexorable effritement du 'modèle' franco-africain," *Le Monde Diplomatique* 478 (January 1994), pp. 4–5.

37. Quoted in J. P. Bechtold, Z. Limam and F. Soudan, "Balladur: Ce que veut la France," *Jeune Afrique* 1720–1721 (December 23, 1993–January 5, 1994), p. 55. Balladur earlier made similar statements in *Le Monde,* September 23, 1993, and *Le Point,* October 16, 1993.

38. Pierre Messmer, "Il faut dévaluer le franc CFA," *Jeune Afrique* 1689 (May 20–26, 1993), pp. 26–27; see also Géraldine Faes, "Franc CFA: Comment éviter l'inévitable," *Jeune Afrique* 1701–1702 (August 12–25, 1993), pp. 47–50; Rémi Godeau, "La Dévaluation en douze questions," in ibid., pp. 50–58; and Jones Dowe, "Du Rififi a CFA City," in Serge Michailof, ed., *La France et l'Afrique* (Paris: Karthala, 1993), pp. 461–488.

39. See Patrick and Sylvianne Guillaumont, "La Zone franc à un tournant vers l'intégration régionale," in Serge Michailof, ed., *La France et l'Afrique* (Paris: Karthala, 1993), pp. 411–422; Marie-France L'Hériteau, "Intégration régionale en Afrique et coopération monétaire euro-africaine," in ibid., pp. 449–458. On the CFA franc devaluation of January 12, 1994, see, in particular, "Franc CFA: La Déchirure," *Jeune Afrique* 1724 (January 20–26, 1994), pp. 36–52; George Ola Davies, "The Devaluation Bombshell," *West Africa* 3982 (January 24–30, 1994), pp. 116–117; Frederic Dorce, "Dévaluation du Franc CFA: Un Piège sans fin," *Jeune Afrique Economie* 176 (February 1994), pp. 10–13; and Kenneth B. Noble, "French Currency Move Provokes Unrest in Africa," *New York Times,* February 23, 1994, pp. A1, A6.

40. On the French military presence in Africa, see John Chipman, *French Military Policy and African Security,* Adelphi Paper no. 201 (London: International Institute for Strategic Studies, 1985); Chipman, *French Power,* pp. 114–167; Lellouche and Moisi, "French Policy in Africa," pp. 108–133; Robin Luckham, "French Militarism in Africa," *Review of African Political Economy,* no. 24 (May 1982), pp. 55–84; McNamara, *France in Black Africa,* pp. 143–182; and George E. Moose, "French Military Policy in Africa," in W. J. Foltz and H.S. Bienen, eds., *Arms and the Africans* (New Haven: Yale University Press, 1985), pp. 59–97. The statistical data are from P. M. de la Gorce, "Pourquoi la France est sur tous les fronts," *Jeune Afrique* 1636 (May 14–20, 1992), pp. 30–31, and Philippe Leymarie, "Les Voies incertaines de la coopération franco-africaine," *Le Monde Diplomatique* 463 (October 1992), pp. 22–23.

41. *Le Parti socialiste et l'Afrique Sub-Saharienne* (Paris: Secrétariat général du Parti Socialiste, 1981). French military interventions during the period 1981 to 1993 include Chad (1983, 1986–1989), Togo (1986), Comoros (1989), Ivory Coast (May 1990), Gabon (May 1990), Rwanda (October 1990), and Zaire (September 1991).

42. "Protocol Relating to Mutual Assistance on Defense," in *Official Journal of ECOWAS* 3 (June 1981); see also Chipman, *French Power*, pp. 175–177, and B. Eyo Ate, "The Presence of France in West-Central Africa as a Fundamental Problem to Nigeria," *Millenium* 12, no. 2 (Summer 1983), pp. 110–127. On the economic dimension of ECOWAS, see Guy Martin, "Regional Integration in West Africa: The Role of ECOWAS," in Emmanuel Hansen, ed., *Africa: Perspectives on Peace and Development* (London: Zed Books, 1987), pp. 171–182; and Guy Martin, "African Regional Cooperation and Integration: Achievements, Problems and Prospects," in Ann Seidman and Fred Anang, eds., *Twenty-First Century Africa: Towards a New Vision of Self-Sustainable Development* (Trenton, N.J. and Atlanta, Ga.: Africa World Press/ASA Press, 1992), pp. 78–79.

43. On the role of ECOWAS in the Liberian conflict, see Terry Mays, "Nigeria and the ECOWAS Peacekeeping Mission to Liberia," paper presented at the annual convention of the ISA, Atlanta, Ga., March–April 1992; Robert A. Mortimer, "ECOMOG, Liberia and Regional Security in West Africa," paper presented at the conference on "The End of the Cold War and the New African Political Order," JSC African Studies Center, University of California–Los Angeles, February 17–19, 1994; and Abiodun Williams, "Regional Peacekeeping: ECOWAS and the Liberian Civil War," in David D. Newson, ed., *The Diplomatic Record 1990–1991* (Boulder: Westview Press, 1992), pp. 213–231. On the role of the francophone countries (and particularly of Senegal) in the Liberian crisis, see Robert Mortimer, "Senegal's Role in ECOMOG: The Francophone Dimension in the Liberian Crisis," unpublished paper, 1993.

44. The ANAD member states are Burkina Faso, Ivory Coast, Mali, Mauritania, Niger, and Senegal; Togo is a signatory, and Benin is an observer state. The text of the ANAD protocol is reproduced in *African Defense Journal* (May 1983), and that of the Civil Defense Protocol is in ibid. (December 1983). For details of the other agreements, see *Journal officiel de la République du Sénégal*, February 13, 1988, and February 20, 1988. On the economic dimension of CEAO, see Martin, "African Regional Cooperation and Integration," pp. 76–77.

45. On the concept of "second independence," see Georges Nzongola-Ntalaja, *Revolution and Counter-Revolution in Africa* (London: Zed Books, 1987), p. 92; on that of "second liberation," see George Ayittey, *Africa Betrayed* (New York: St. Martin's Press, 1992), pp. 305–334. The term "Springtime of Africa" was coined by Albert Bourgi and Christian Casteran in *Le Printemps de l'Afrique* (Paris: Hachette, 1991).

46. *Africa Demos* 3, no. 2 (July–August 1993), p. 19.

47. I develop this typology in a forthcoming article on "Democratic Transition in Francophone Africa." For slightly different typologies, see Richard Joseph, "Africa: The Rebirth of Political Freedom," *Journal of Democracy* 2, no. 4 (Fall 1991), pp. 13–18, and Guy Martin, "Democratic Transition in Africa," *Issue: A Journal of Opinion* 21, nos. 1–2 (1993), pp. 6–7.

48. Quoted in Christian Casteran and Hugo Sada, "Sommet de La Baule: L'Avertissement," *Jeune Afrique* 1539 (June 27–July 3, 1990), p. 15.

49. Data provided by Jean-Pierre Alaux, "Les Contradictions de la coopération française en Afrique," *Le Monde diplomatique* 456 (March 1992), p. 4.

50. See Elimane Fall, "Le Sommet des désillusions," *Jeune Afrique* 1658 (October 15–21,

1992), p. 4; and "La Coopération et les processus démocratiques en Afrique" (an interview with French Minister of Cooperation Marcel Debarge), *Le Monde,* February 17, 1993, pp. 1, 6.

51. This revealing story is chronicled in some detail in Francis Kpatinde, "La Guerre du Petrole," *Jeune Afrique* 1690 (May 27–June 2, 1993), pp. 12–15, and Zyad Limam, "La Guerre du petrole est-elle finie?" *Jeune Afrique* 1705 (September 9–15, 1993), pp. 52–55. Apparently under intense French pressure, President Lissouba later reneged on the April 1993 Congo-OXY agreement by retroactively recognizing, through a special law passed in December 1993, Elf-Aquitaine's exclusive exploitation rights over the new Nkossa offshore oil field; see Francis Kpatinde, "Lissouba dit tout," *Jeune Afrique* 1729 (February 24–March 2, 1994), pp. 68–69.

52. See, in particular, J. P. Alaux, "Les Contradictions de la coopération française en Afrique"; Mongo Beti, *La France contre l'Afrique* (Paris: La Decouverte, 1993), pp. 152–198; and P. Leymarie, "Les Voies incertaines de la coopération franco-africaine."

53. See Edouard Balladur's statements as reported in *Le Monde,* September 23, 1993, and *Le Point,* October 16, 1993. See also P. Leymarie, "Inexorable effritement du 'modèle' franco-africain," p. 5, and F. Gaulme, "France-Afrique: Une Crise de coopération," pp. 46–47.

54. Kenneth B. Noble, "Ivory Coast Buries Its Father of Freedom," *New York Times,* February 8, 1994, pp. A1, A5.

55. Albert Bourgi, "Dévaluation, Emancipation," *Jeune Afrique* 1724 (January 20–26, 1994), pp. 46–47.

9

The Lagos Three:
Economic Regionalism
in Sub-Saharan Africa

CAROL LANCASTER

SUB-SAHARAN AFRICA is currently engaged in the most extensive experimentation in regional economic cooperation of any region in the developing world. According to the World Bank, intergovernmental organizations in Africa, many of which have an economic focus, exceed two hundred.[1] These organizations include service, research, and professional organizations, such as the African Center for Monetary Studies or the West African Rice Development Association; the monetary unions, including the Union Monétaire Ouest Africaine, development finance and coordination organization, such as the African Development Bank and the Southern African Development Conference (SADC); and eight regional integration experiments, the most prominent of which is the Economic Community of West African States.

This chapter focuses on the three largest experiments in regional economic integration: ECOWAS, the Preferential Trade Area of East and Southern Africa (PTA), and the Economic Community of Central African States (ECCAS). These organizations, together with the Arab Maghreb Union of North African Countries, are intended as the first steps toward the creation of a continent-wide common market, which is called for in the Lagos Plan of Action. The Lagos Plan, signed by African heads of state at the Organization of African Unity meeting in 1980, sought to promote Africa's long-term industrialization and development through the creation, first, of larger, subregional markets and, by the year 2000, of a continent-wide market through merging the subregional markets.

By 1985, the subregional organizations had all been set up. But relatively little progress had been made in any of them toward economic integration, despite repeated commitments of the part of African leaders to move toward that integration. The first half of the 1990s brought further changes in the world and raised further uncertainties about the means and ends of economic integration in sub-Saharan Africa. There was an appreciable loosening in the ties with Europe, especially with France after the death of President Houphouet-Boigny of Ivory Coast and the subsequent 50 percent devaluation of the CFA franc. The gradual loosening of ties with France opened up the possibility of closer ties among francophone and anglophone African states and an easier path to integration among them in west and central Africa. The ending of apartheid in South Africa and the election of a nonracial government in 1994 also opened up possibilities for integration among all states in southern Africa, though at the same time, it raised concerns on the part of some officials and experts in the region that closer economic ties with South Africa—with its relatively developed industrial base—could turn neighboring states into hewers of wood and drawers of water for their more industrialized neighbor.

Other changes in the world and in Africa also promised to affect the prospects for integration, though the net effect of all these changes remained unclear. Economic reforms, particularly in making currencies more convertible and in liberalizing trade, opened up African markets to world and regional trade and eroded the argument for preferential trade areas and the ability to create regional trade blocs. At the same time, however, the establishment of the North American Free Trade Area (NAFTA) gave new life to debates on regional integration and set a model for such integration—around a major, developed country market—which did not go unnoticed in Africa. In this chapter, I argue that although the creation of the Lagos Three and other experiments in economic integration in Africa was intended primarily to advance the economic goals—more rapid development through economic integration—what persuaded African governments to join the experiments and participate in them were the diplomatic and political objectives they helped fulfill. And whether the organization proved to be a relatively vibrant one (where heads of state attended annual meetings and gave at least verbal support to the organization's goals and activities, as in the case of Economic Community of West African States), it was able to provide a venue for member states to pursue openly or behind closed doors their diplomatic and political objectives. Where the diplomatic benefits were small, these organizations atrophied, as in the case of the Economic Community of Central African States.

The first section of this chapter explores the rationales as well as the politics behind the establishment of these three organizations and examines how the organizations have actually performed. The second section examines the lessons provided by the Lagos Three regarding economic regionalism in sub-Saharan Africa. The third section peers into the possible future of economic regionalism in sub-Saharan Africa.

Economic Integration In Sub-Saharan Africa: History, Rationales, Politics, And Performance

Regional economic ties in Africa have a long history. Long-distance trade throughout Africa existed before the Europeans arrived. With the coming of European colonialism, economic activities of many kinds—trade, finance, monetary affairs, administrative responsibilities, transport, and communications networks—were organized on a regional basis during the colonial period. A number of those arrangements extended into the independence period, including the monetary unions between francophone countries and France as well as the East African Common Services Organization among Kenya, Uganda, and Tanzania.

Africans gained independence at a time when regional economic cooperation was popular among developing countries in other parts of the world. The Latin Americans, supported by the Economic Commission for Latin America, were experimenting with their own schemes of regional cooperation, including the Central American Common Market and the Latin American Free Trade Area.[2] The Asians soon followed with the creation in 1967 of the Association of South East Asian Nations (ASEAN).[3] The European Economic Community (EEC), initiated with the signing of the Treaty of Rome in 1957, was already functioning and provided a model and source of encouragement for groups of developing countries wishing to create their own regional integration schemes.

In addition to a history of long-range economic contacts and regional economic organization during the colonial period, Africans brought to independence their own aspirations toward continental or regional unity. The most vocal advocate of pan-African unity was Kwame Nkrumah, the first president of Ghana. Other leaders of the new states affirmed their commitments to pan-Africanism, even if few supported Nkrumah's vision of immediate political union among themselves. Several groupings of states—Senegal and Mali and, later, Ghana, Guinea, and Mali—experimented with political unions. These soon proved unworkable and were abandoned.

Also, in the early 1960s, African states began to organize themselves in loose political organizations, such as the Monrovia and Brazzaville groups, based primarily on the ideological orientations of member states. In 1963, the Organization of African Unity was created to include all African countries. The OAU was, in part, an expression of the aspiration of unity among Africans, although it was not given the authority to make decisions that were binding on member states. It was also intended to head off the increasing division of Africa into ideological blocs, which threatened to introduce Cold War tensions into the continent. After the OAU was set up, the Monrovia and Brazzaville groups were dissolved, and no further formal subregional organizations based primarily on shared ideological orientations or political goals were established. Regional cooperation among African governments thereafter centered primarily on achieving common economic objectives.

There are at present eight experiments in regional economic integration among sub-Saharan African states.[4] The three largest and most ambitious are the Economic Community of West African States, with sixteen member countries; the Preferential Trade Area with nineteen member states; and the Economic Community of Central African States, with ten member countries. The goal of these experiments is to create economic unions among member states. There are typically three stages in the process of creating such a union: the establishment of a preferential or free trade area through the reduction or elimination of barriers to trade among member states; the creation of a customs union or common market involving free or preferential trade among members plus the erection of a common external tariff on imports from nonmember states; and the initiation of a full economic union among members, involving the removal of barriers to the movement of goods, services, capital, and labor, the unification of customs regulations, the harmonization of macroeconomic policies, and the creation of a common currency and a common central bank.

Regional integration schemes may aim at achieving any one of the stages or at achieving all three, usually in successive steps. In addition, ECOWAS, the PTA, and the ECCAS each has a secretariat, and ECOWAS and the PTA have established development banks to finance regional projects and to compensate member states for losses resulting from membership in the organizations—for example, losses in government revenues from tariff reductions. The ECCAS plans to establish its own development bank in the future. ECOWAS and the PTA also have currency clearinghouses—organizations responsible for facilitating the settlement of trade payments among member states. The ECCAS plans eventually to establish its own clearinghouse. The objective of these houses is to encourage and facilitate the use of local currencies in trade financing among members and, thus, to encourage expanded intraregional trade.

What are the Lagos Three and other African regional integration experiments intended to accomplish? The answers to this question are of two kinds: economic and diplomatic. The existence and functioning of these organizations cannot be understood unless both are taken into account.

The basic rationale for regional economic integration has traditionally been the promotion of trade and economic welfare among member states. This rationale has evolved primarily with developed economies in mind.[5] The establishment of a free trade area or customs union among previously separate economies will result in the most efficient producers among them expanding their production and sales. Trade among member states will be created as less competitive producers are forced out of business. Economic resources in participating states will be employed more productively, and consumers will benefit through lower prices. This reasoning is drawn from international trade theory based on comparative advantage. Its main focus is on improving economic welfare through a more efficient use of resources. Its analysis is static. It is not focused on the dynamics of long-run growth or development, although a consequence of improved economic welfare may be stimulation of that growth.

However, economic development rather than resource efficiency has been the principal preoccupation of developing countries. The objectives for creating expanded markets among them have therefore focused mostly on promoting rapid growth through expanded investment. Although the links between economic integration and development have not always been clearly articulated by developed country economists, their reasoning has been based on the following assumptions: (1) Industrial development is a key element in overall economic development; (2) efficient industrial development typically requires producers to be large enough to achieve economies of scale;[6] (3) most industrial producers in the smaller, developing countries will require markets larger than their home markets to achieve economies of scale; (4) hence, it makes sense to merge smaller markets into larger markets that will encourage expanded investment, production, trade, national income, and growth; (5) however, the larger markets must be protected for a time from competitive imports from third countries while producers expand their investments to achieve scale efficiencies and benefit from the learning process associated with new or expanded investments.

This rationale is, in effect, a growth strategy based on import substitution within multicountry integration schemes. Efficiency is not its highest priority, and—indeed—at its initial stages, greater inefficiencies in resource use might occur as trade is diverted from more efficient producers within it. In theory at least, some of the less efficient producers in the scheme will, with sufficient market size and protection, eventually become both efficient and internationally competitive.

In contrast to economic integration among developed countries, the critical element in regional integration as a strategy for promoting industrial growth among developing countries is not its expansionary impact on trade. Indeed, most developing countries—particularly in Africa—have only limited potential for expanding trade with one another, given the similarities in what they produce—mainly, primary products. What is much more important to them is the stimulus integration can provide for expanded investment. Increased trade may be a consequence of greater capacity utilization by existing producers or of new investment, but it is not the ultimate end of regional integration schemes. This fact has too often been confused in discussions of regional integration among African countries.

A second rationale—more in the area of ideology than economic reasoning—often used to justify regional integration in Africa has been the importance of achieving collective economic self-reliance among African states. A major symbol of the limitations on African self-reliance has been the heavy dependence of African countries on international trade, primarily with Western developed countries and—in southern Africa—with the Republic of South Africa. Most African countries produce and export a few types of primary products, such as groundnuts, copper, or cotton. They must import almost all of their manufactured goods. Their trade dependence on the rest of the world has heightened their sense of economic vulnerability and fed their desire to become economically self-reliant. However, most African countries are too small to become economically self-sufficient on their own. (There are at present twenty-one countries with a population of six million or less. Ten of these have a population of one million or less.[7]) They must rely on others. But Africans have often preferred to rely on other Africans in various forms of economic union, which they feel is less risky and more supportive of their dignity than relying on non-African powers.[8]

A further rationale behind regional integration schemes has been more strictly political in nature. It involves the bargaining power of African states vis-à-vis the rest of the world. Africans have long recognized that acting together in economic groupings enhances their bargaining power with foreign governments, international institutions, and multinational corporations. Together, they have more to offer or to deny others in terms of size, economic potential, and political weight. Alone, their small size, narrow range of exports, poverty, and reliance on external financing combine to make them weak and vulnerable to the pressures from external powers.

In addition to these general economic and political rationales, Africans have pursued specific diplomatic goals in joining regional integration schemes. A recounting of the circumstances leading to the creation of these schemes, the stated or apparent purposes of their members in joining them, and their functioning once established will illustrate this important point.

The Economic Community of West African States, established in 1975 among sixteen states of West Africa (see Table 9.1 for membership), is perhaps the most visible and certainly the most studied of the current experiments in regional integration in sub-Saharan Africa.[9] The creation of ECOWAS was in large measure

TABLE 9.1   The Lagos Three: Member States and Organizations

	Established	Members	Major Institutions
Economic Community of West African States (ECOWAS)	1975	Benin, Burkina Faso, Cape Verde, Gambia, Chana, Guinea, Guinea-Bissau, Ivory Coast, Liberia, Mali, Mauritania, Niger, Nigeria, Senegal, Sierra Leone, Togo	secretariat, ECOWAS fund, West Africa Clearing House
Preferential Trade Area of East and Southern Africa (PTA)	1981	Burundi, Kenya, Comoros, Djibouti, Ethiopia, Malawi, Lesotho, Mauritius, Rwanda, Somalia, Swaziland, Uganda, Tanzania, Zambia, Zimbabwe, Zaire, Sudan, Namibia, Mozambique	trade and development bank, clearinghouse, secretariat
Economic Community of Central African States (ECCAS)	1983	Gabon, Chad, Cameroon, Central African Republic, Congo, Zaire, Burundi, Rwanda, São Tomé and Principe, Equatorial Guinea	secretariat, development bank

a result of Nigerian diplomacy.[10] From the early years of independence, the Nigerian government had supported the idea of an African common market. This idea was inevitably put aside during the Biafra conflict. In the wake of that conflict, however, the Nigerian president, General Yakubu Gowan, made economic integration a cornerstone of his regional diplomacy. In addition to believing in the economic importance of integration for the region, General Gowan wished to reduce his country's isolation from other West African countries, to regain and expand its influence, and to reduce the influence of France in the region. (The French had supported Biafra during the Nigerian civil war, while the Ivory Coast had recognized Biafra. Both France and the Ivory Coast were uneasy about the potential economic and political influence of Nigeria in West Africa and were hoping that a breakup of Nigeria would limit that influence.) Nigerian businessmen also supported the creation of ECOWAS, seeing it as providing them with opportunities for expanding their markets in West Africa. (A key provision of the ECOWAS treaty ensured that only products from businesses owned primarily by Africans would be eligible for preferential treatment with ECOWAS. This "rules of origin" provision effectively excluded the products from French-owned businesses in francophone countries from the benefits of intra-ECOWAS trade.[11])

Nigeria pursued a carefully planned strategy of persuading its often-reluctant neighbors to support the creation of ECOWAS. It recognized that agreement by the francophone countries was essential, and so it focused its efforts first on Togo, with which it had close relations. With Togo's support, Benin—which is sandwiched between Nigeria and Togo—would feel compelled to join to avoid being surrounded and isolated by pro-ECOWAS governments. It was expected that Niger (another neighbor with strong economic ties to Nigeria) would be unable to resist supporting ECOWAS if Benin and Togo agreed. These countries' support would begin to create a momentum among francophone states in support of ECOWAS and, Lagos hoped, would persuade the two key francophone states—Senegal and the Ivory Coast—to join.[12]

In seeking the support of these and other countries, Nigeria used "spray" diplomacy, offering interest-free loans, grants, concessionally priced oil, [13] and equity investment in projects in neighboring countries. Nigerian efforts at persuasion, plus its effective leadership of the African, Caribbean, and Pacific countries in their negotiations with the EEC on the first Lomé Convention (associating the ACP countries economically with the EEC through special trade, investment, and aid arrangements), finally bore fruit when the francophone countries along with nine other West African governments signed the Lagos Treaty in 1975, which established ECOWAS. The Communauté Economique de l'Afrique de l'Ouest (CEAO)—an already-established integration experiment among francophone countries—would continue to exist, and its separate status was acknowledged in the Lagos Treaty.

Economic union among ECOWAS countries was planned to occur in three stages. In the first two-year period, members were to freeze their tariffs on primary products produced by other members and on manufactured goods eligible for preferential treatment in intra-ECOWAS trade. The second period, which was to last eight years, was to end with the elimination of import duties in intra-ECOWAS trade. The final stage would last five years and involve the erection of a common external tariff. The ECOWAS Treaty called for the free movement of labor as well as goods, services, and capital. However, at the request of the Nigerians, who feared a large influx of labor into their country, it was decided that free movement of labor would be implemented over a period of fifteen years.[14]

To provide compensation for the poorer members of ECOWAS for the costs of participation in the community, the Fund for Cooperation, Compensation, and Development was set up. ECOWAS members were to contribute to the fund on the basis of their relative income levels and gains from new investments in the community. The fund was also authorized to accept contributions from nonmember governments. Finally, the West African Clearing House was set up in association with ECOWAS to facilitate the use of local currencies in financing intra-ECOWAS trade.

ECOWAS has achieved few of its goals. The first stage of the integration scheme—involving the consolidation of customs procedures (including the freezing of tariffs)—has been approved by governments, but little action appears to have been taken to implement this stage. The *Annual Report* of ECOWAS in 1985 observed that "despite the impressive number of agreements reached and decisions taken regarding the harmonization of customs documents, the adoption of common procedures, and the program for deregulating non-manufactured crude goods, traditional handicrafts and industrial products, the Economic Community of West African States has not made tangible progress in practical terms."[15] The second and most critical stage of trade liberalization among member states was to have been completed by 1985 but has been postponed repeatedly; it was rescheduled to commence in 1990. By 1994, member states had not yet begun to liberalize their trade with one another. The protocol on the free movement of labor was finally signed in 1986, but few states have actually ratified it, and "systematic and flagrant violations" by member states continue. Member governments remained in arrears in their contributions to the secretariat and the fund.[16] The record of the West Africa Clearing House was also regarded as disappointing, with member states financing a small and declining proportion of their intraregional trade through the institution.[17] Finally, the existence of ECOWAS has had no impact on the proportion of trade among ECOWAS states, which has remained at its level of just over 5 percent of their total trade for decades.

Despite the continuing failure of member states to implement agreements reached at ECOWAS meetings or to pay in full their contributions to the community's institutions, most heads of state continue to attend the annual meetings, vociferously reaffirm their commitment to the goals of the organization, and frequently approve new and often ambitious schemes for ECOWAS to undertake. In 1987, the heads of state approved a three-year Economic Recovery Programme for the region, which was estimated to cost nearly $1 billion; they agreed to develop a common approach to debt negotiations; and they adopted a

Monetary Cooperation Program aimed at creating a monetary union among member states.

The pattern of well-attended annual meetings, adoption of new initiatives, and inaction on past commitments has provoked criticism in the African media and among the heads of states. *West Africa* magazine commented on the 1989 ECOWAS summit in the following words:

> There is a pattern to ECOWAS summits which in some respects has become all too familiar, after 14 years of the organization's existence and 12 summits. There are the sterling calls to action, the urgent pleas for member states to carry out the protocols they have happily signed, and above all to pay the arrears in their membership subscriptions . . . ECOWAS may be facing a make-or-break phase. Unless some sign of progress can be registered in sectors that matter, the imperatives that led to the Community's creation back in 1975 may be called into question.[18]

The failure of ECOWAS to achieve its goals of integration versus the continuing support (both in words and attendance at its annual meetings) among heads of member states and their tendency to approve new initiatives is puzzling. Why, on the one hand, do member governments fail to implement their commitments under the agreement and, at the same time, lament that failure, attend annual meetings, affirm the value and importance of ECOWAS, and adopt additional initiatives? ECOWAS, despite its failure to achieve its stated goals, is clearly viewed by heads of state as benefiting them and their governments; otherwise they would stop attending its meetings.

Two benefits, both political, derive from ECOWAS's annual meetings. One is the exposure heads of state receive in their own media and in the media of other west African states from participating in a meeting with a large number of other heads of state. These annual ECOWAS meetings are media events, even reported at times in the world press. But probably more important are the opportunities offered by these annual meetings for the political leadership of west Africa to deal with regional issues of importance to them that could not easily be dealt with in the much larger annual meetings of the Organization of African Unity or at the bilateral level. In several recent instances, the annual ECOWAS heads of state meeting has provided an opportunity for reducing tensions between member governments. In 1988, the attendance of the head of state of Ghana, Flight Lt. Jerry Rawlings, at the ECOWAS summit in Togo gave him and President Eyadema of Togo an opportunity to smooth the strained relations between them. In 1989, the presidents of Senegal and Mauritania met for the first time since the mutual expulsions of their citizens from the other country, and relations between them were reconciled. This increasingly important function was officially recognized at the 1990 ECOWAS heads of state meeting when a Nigerian proposal to create a standing mediation committee was adopted.

The venue of a regional heads of state meeting, with participants attempting to mediate difficulties between member states, can play a useful role in African diplomacy, where personal relations between political leaders can greatly influence relations among their countries. ECOWAS is the only regional organization in west Africa that includes francophone, lusophone, and anglophone states and that can, therefore, mediate disputes among these countries. It also has the advantage of being smaller than the OAU, and so it can focus its efforts on regional issues without involving large numbers of governments outside the region.

ECOWAS appears to be becoming a regional diplomatic or political organization, and this evolution may sustain it even in the face of its failure to realize its formal goals of economic integration. There is, however, a serious danger to the future of ECOWAS as it becomes more active in mediating regional disputes, particularly where concerted action among member states is involved. An example is the ECOWAS intervention force in Liberia (ECOMOG). ECOMOG at one point nearly provoked a break with the ECOWAS states, with Burkina Faso and the Ivory Coast openly opposing the intervention force, fearing it was a stalking horse for Nigerian policies supporting President Samuel K. Doe of Liberia. (The bulk of the ECOMOG forces were Nigerian, along with several of the senior officers.) Should this or any other concerted ECOWAS action set member states against one another, the organization may break apart. This is true for other regional organizations where there may be a temptation to help resolve disputes.

In 1981, the Preferential Trade Area of East and Southern Africa was formed. It is the largest regional integration scheme, with nineteen members (see Table 9.1 for membership). The PTA treaty is modeled on that of ECOWAS, with an economic union among member states to be achieved in stages through the freezing and then progressive elimination of tariffs and nontariff barriers on eligible goods produced in member states. A regional common market was to be fully established by 1992, with the first reductions in tariffs to commence in 1984. There is a restrictive rules of origin provision in the PTA treaty, which requires that goods eligible for preferential trade among member states be produced by firms with majority African ownership. There is no compensation mechanism to offset the costs of membership in the PTA for poorer member states. All states are permitted to impose temporary tariffs or quotas on imports from other member states when they are suffering from persistent balance-of-payments problems or wish to protect their own infant industries. The Trade and Development Bank has been set up to finance development projects in members states, and a currency clearinghouse has been established that is run by the Central Bank of Zimbabwe.

The origins of the PTA have less to do with the regional diplomatic policies of member states than with the ideology of regional integration in Africa and the pressures from the Economic Commission for Africa for the creation of integration schemes. The proposals in the Lagos Plan of Action were developed by the ECA, which, since its creation in 1958, had promoted the idea of regional economic integration in Africa. In approving the Lagos Plan, African heads of state implicitly approved the creation of the subregional integration schemes recommended in the plan. ECOWAS already existed in west Africa; what remained was to create the subregional market integration schemes in central and east Africa.

The PTA was the designated scheme for east and southern Africa, and its midwife was the ECA.

Negotiations under ECA auspices on the creation of a regional integration scheme for east and southern Africa began in 1978 soon after the collapse of the East African Community. Nevertheless, a number of states had serious reservations about the new scheme based on its wide geographical spread, the poor transportation network shared by member states, and the lack of complementarity among member states' economies. Tanzania and Mozambique delayed signing the PTA treaty for several years. (Tanzania was also reluctant in the early 1980s to reopen its border with Kenya, as it would have to do as a member of the PTA. It had closed that border in the disputes with Kenya over sharing the assets of the failed East African Community.) The government of Zimbabwe needed to be persuaded to join by Kenya, Zambia, and its own business community.[19] Lesotho and Swaziland had to make sure the Republic of South Africa had no objections to their joining before they could sign the treaty.

It is not hard to understand why the more advanced states in the region supported the creation of the PTA. Both Kenyan and Zimbabwean businesses stood to benefit from improved export opportunities in the region. But it might well be asked what the poorer states hoped to gain, especially with the absence of any compensating mechanism to offset the costs of their membership in the PTA. The Somali government, according to one of its officials, joined primarily to avoid economic and political isolation. Siad Barre, the president of Somalia, decided to sign the PTA treaty (without consulting his staff) once it was clear that Somalia's neighbor, Ethiopia, was going to join.[20] Avoidance of isolation may have been a motivating factor for other of the smaller and poorer member states, such as Djibouti, Rwanda, Burundi, and Malawi.

The experience of the PTA has begun to echo the pattern of other African regional integration schemes.[21] Problems among member states have arisen on several issues. Objections were raised by Kenya and several other states over the rules of origin provision of the treaty; these states argued that the provision penalized their producers—many of which were more than 51 percent foreign-owned. The provision was ultimately eased. Poorer members have objected to the absence of any compensation mechanism; a study of the problem was undertaken, but no action was agreed upon. Meanwhile, it appears that although a degree of trade liberalization has occurred within the PTA, a number of member states delayed implementing agreed tariff reductions, forcing a postponement of the final date for achieving a common market until the year 2000. The currency clearing arrangement has yet to be fully utilized, although utilization is reported to have increased recently. Although the institutions of the PTA have suffered less than those of other integration schemes from the unwillingness of member states to provide agreed financing, there have been some shortfalls in the past. Trade among PTA member states remains at an average of 6 percent of their total trade worldwide. Meanwhile, PTA members have begun discussions of grandiose schemes that appear even less likely to be realized than their basic commitments under the PTA treaty, including the creation of a monetary union among themselves and the possibility of creating a PTA airline. Member states have agreed to impose economic sanctions against South Africa.

It is not yet clear whether the PTA will follow ECOWAS in the latter's failure to implement fully its economic integration policies and simply become something of a political umbrella under which member states conduct regional diplomacy. Although an increasing number of states have joined the PTA, members have thus far used it relatively little as a venue for regional diplomacy. The PTA may already be too large to serve such a purpose effectively, as its nineteen member states represent central, southern, and east Africa.

The most recently created integration scheme is the Economic Community of Central African States, with a total membership (see Table 9.1) of ten.[22] The treaty of the ECCAS, like that of the PTA, was modeled on the ECOWAS treaty. A common market was to be completed in stages by the year 2000. With the commitment of African heads of state to the Lagos Plan and the pressures from the ECA to establish the third regional integration scheme envisaged by that plan, the creation of the ECCAS was probably inevitable. However, several potential member states strongly supported its creation. Zaire, for example, would now belong to a major integration scheme. (Its request to join the SADC had been turned down, and it had not yet joined the PTA.) Chad and São Tomé and Príncipe would also end their isolation joining such a scheme.

The ECCAS has gotten off to an exceedingly slow start. Only six of the ten heads of state attended the fifth summit in 1989, and their conclusion at that time was that "significant obstacles prevent an immediate and real economic integration of the countries."[23] No agreement was reached on the details of how a customs union and tariff liberalization should proceed, and members have not yet frozen existing tariff barriers on goods produced by member states. The free movement of labor also remains to be settled. Only four of ten member states have paid their contributions to ECCAS institutions. Thus far, the ECCAS has made little progress even in establishing its institutions and its plan for integration. It also does not appear to have given member states a venue for pursuing regional diplomacy.

Economic Regionalism: Theory And Experience In Sub-Saharan Africa

What methodology or theories can give us insights into the experience of the Lagos Three in sub-Saharan Africa? The most obvious place to look for relevant theories is in the political science literature on political and economic integration. Most of this literature is functionalist or neofunctionalist in orientation—that is, it focuses on the process by which "political actors in several distinct national settings are persuaded to shift their loyalties, expectations and political activities toward a new center, whose institutions possess or demand jurisdiction over the preexisting national states."[24] Functionalists have posited that successful cooperation among independent states on "technical" issues can spill over into areas that are more political, providing key elites with benefits or the expectation of benefits that derive from integration and a learning experience of effective international cooperation, which predisposes them to further cooperation.

Much of the functionalist and neofunctionalist literature of the 1960s is not very helpful in understanding economic integration efforts in the developing world.[25] Based primarily on the experience of the EC, this literature focuses on the process by which integration occurs. But although a certain amount of technical cooperation has taken place in Africa, it has not yet led to greater integration among African states. However, some of the later work in this area has begun to examine the experience of economic integration in developing countries and to emphasize the role of economic costs and benefits from integration in the success of integrative schemes.[26] The concept of costs and benefits deriving from integration schemes is the most helpful in explaining the experience of the Lagos Three. But, unlike much of the literature on integration among developing countries, the experience of these schemes tells us that we must consider diplomatic as well as economic costs and benefits.[27]

One of the basic problems of regional integrative schemes is that the economic costs of participation for member states can be immediate and concrete, while the economic benefits typically accrue only after a long period and are uncertain and often unevenly distributed among member states. The costs include, first, a decrease in government revenues when tariffs are reduced. For developing countries, many of which rely on tariffs for a substantial proportion of their revenues, this cost can be substantial. Another cost may be the collapse of local firms as they find themselves unable to compete with firms in other member countries, resulting in a loss in national income, production, and employment.

Benefits from integration may include immediate opportunities for expanding production and trade for eligible firms located in member countries. Most important, the major benefits sought from regional integration schemes among developing countries are the new investments stimulated by the larger markets and potential scale economies deriving from the schemes. But even when such investment occurs, it can bring costs as well as benefits. New investors will usually locate in better-off members of a union, where economies are more vibrant, transport and communications facilities more developed, and living conditions more pleasant. This is the polarization effect of economic integration. The poorer members of an economic union often perceive that they are losing opportunities for industrialization, and they demand compensation. This was the fundamental problem with the East African Community, in which Tanzania felt it was not being properly compensated when new investment located in Kenya—permitting Kenya to expand its income, employment, and trade. Poorer countries in an economic union typically fear that they will become and remain the "hewers of wood and drawers of water" for the more advanced member states and, in the end, be worse off in an integration scheme than they would have been without it.

Most integration schemes contain arrangements to compensate poorer states for losses from membership, including direct payment of compensation as in ECOWAS. However, new investment has not been stimulated by the Lagos Three, so these problems have yet to arise. Several added problems in Africa make the investment benefits of integration even less certain than in other parts of the world. The rules of origin restrictions in some of the schemes were intended to ensure that African-owned rather than foreign-owned firms reaped the benefits of integration. But there are few African-owned firms of any size in these schemes (except those owned by Nigerians), and there is relatively little capital owned by Africans who are willing to invest it in their own countries. The only alternative for new investments may be foreign-owned capital. Yet, the Africans have effectively discouraged that capital through the rules of origin requirements. A second factor discouraging foreign or domestic investment in sub-Saharan Africa is the economic malaise that has afflicted the region for over a decade, deriving from economic mismanagement by Africans themselves, a sharp deterioration in the terms of trade, a heavy debt burden, and a slowing of growth. Private investors are understandably reluctant to risk their capital under such circumstances. Moreover, political instabilities also undermine the confidence of potential investors. Coups, demonstrations, strikes, internal conflicts, and other uncertainties exist in Africa to a greater degree than in Europe, Asia, or even most of Latin America. Investors have many attractive opportunities elsewhere in the world.

One more peculiarity of African integration schemes has added to the challenges facing them. Within ECOWAS are two other regional integration schemes: the CEAO and the Mano River Union among Sierra Leone, Liberia, and Guinea. Within the ECCAS, there is the Union Douanière et Economique de l'Afrique Centrale, composed of six mainly francophone states of central Africa, and the Communauté Economique des Pays de Grands Lacs (CEPGL) among Zaire, Rwanda, and Burundi. In west Africa in particular, something of an Alphonse and Gaston act has been going on between the CEAO and ECOWAS over which organization adjusts its trade preferences to fit the other first.[28] ECOWAS states that are nonmembers of the CEAO argue that they cannot reduce their tariffs on one another's products if another preferential trade area is within their membership. The CEAO members argue that they cannot reduce their tariffs on ECOWAS goods if other ECOWAS states are not prepared to do the same. The ECCAS has not yet reached the stage of conflict with the UDEAC, but this may come in the future. In fact, the dispute between ECOWAS and the CEAO, the latter now weakened by internal scandals and its progress toward trade liberalization stalemated, would not present a decisive barrier to progress toward integration within ECOWAS if key member states were prepared to move forward on trade liberalization.

The basic problem of regional economic integration schemes in Africa has been and remains that the economic costs of participation in such schemes are immediate, while the economic benefits are long-term and uncertain. Political leaders in Africa, like political leaders elsewhere in the world, are unwilling to sustain the immediate costs of integration for uncertain benefits available—if at all—only in the long run. This explains why member governments have mostly failed to implement trade liberalization and other agreements and why the schemes have failed to achieve their goals. However, it does not explain why Africans have continued to create such schemes, join them, attend their meetings, and repeatedly approve new initiatives for the faltering organizations.

Here, the answers are political and diplomatic. ECOWAS was a case where an aspiring regional hegemon—Nigeria—was willing and able, for diplomatic reasons, to sponsor (and pay for) the creation of ECOWAS. Nigeria, with its economic problems and absorption in its domestic political changes, is no longer willing or able to play the role of a regional hegemon in maintaining the momentum of integration in ECOWAS. In fact, there are no regional hegemons in black Africa today that are able and willing to sponsor effective economic integration schemes.

However, these schemes—even when they are ineffective in achieving their goals—have diplomatic value for member states. For some states, membership in and attendance at annual meetings of such schemes is a form of defensive diplomacy—the avoidance of isolation and an expression of regional solidarity. For others, such membership and attendance have become useful means of conducting quiet regional politicking under the guise of discussing economic matters. Since the creation of the OAU in 1963, Africans have been reluctant to set up regional political organizations that would challenge this symbol of continent-wide political unity. But they have been encouraged to set up regional economic cooperation schemes, and some of these, such as ECOWAS, have begun to become convenient venues for the conduct of regional diplomacy in cases where the OAU would be too large and too public a forum for such diplomacy. In order to provide these integration schemes with legitimacy and a raison d'être in the face of the obvious unwillingness of member governments to proceed with trade liberalization, however, heads of state repeatedly commit themselves to ambitious new initiatives.

The Future of Economic Regionalism
In Sub-Saharan Africa

The prospects for effective economic cooperation among African states for the remainder of this century are not bright. Economic cooperation among sub-Saharan African states makes sense, as it ultimately promises them improved prospects for industrial development, enhancement of their bargaining power vis-à-vis the rest of the world, and greatly strengthened economic self-reliance. Africans will continue to believe in the value of regional cooperation. And if regional economic organizations provide diplomatic benefits to member states, these organizations may continue to be active, although repeated failure to follow through on old and new commitments may eventually destroy their credibility among African opinionmakers.

However, until the calculus of economic costs and benefits shifts in favor of the benefits, the organizations will fail to achieve their economic objectives. And the economic costs and benefits appear unlikely to change dramatically any time soon. The costs will remain immediate and the benefits long-run and uncertain. It is possible that the World Bank and other aid-giving institutions and governments will attempt to push African governments toward economic integration through conditioning a proportion of their lending on progress in this area. Foreign aid in sufficient quantities might be helpful in promoting trade liberalization in individual integration schemes, but unless the integrative process itself begins to generate economic benefits for member states, that aid will have been an ineffective palliative. In any case, it seems unlikely that sufficient foreign aid would be available—in addition to what is already being provided to African governments—to make a significant difference in the major integration schemes in sub-Saharan Africa.

Looking beyond the year 2000, the future of economic regionalism in sub-Saharan Africa may depend on the emergence of regional hegemons with the will and the resources to promote economic cooperation and integration. A post-apartheid South Africa may eventually play that role in southern Africa. A politically stable and prosperous Nigeria could play that role in west Africa. Some day, a politically stable and prosperous Zaire could also claim that role in central Africa. But these are indeed long-term speculations, and their prospects are uncertain.

Notes

1. World Bank, *Sub-Saharan Africa: From Crisis to Sustainable Growth* (Washington, D.C.: World Bank, 1989), p. 152.

2. There is a large body of literature on experiments in economic integration in Latin America. See, for example the InterAmerican Development Bank (IADB), *Economic and Social Progress in Latin America: Economic Integration* (Washington, D.C.: IADB, 1984).

3. There is also ample literature on ASEAN. See, for example, the *ASEAN Economic Bulletin,* a monthly publication.

4. Other than the Lagos Three, there are the Communauté Economique de l'Afrique de l'Ouest among seven francophone countries and the Mano River Union among Sierra Leone, Liberia, and Guinea. In central Africa, there is the Union Douanière et Economique de l'Afrique Centrale with six member states, mostly francophone; and the Communauté Economique des Pays de Grands Lacs among Zaire, Rwanda, and Burundi. In southern Africa, there is the South African Customs Union among the Republic of South Africa, Botswana, Lesotho, and Swaziland. SADC is often thought of as a regional integration scheme. Although regional economic integration is among its major functions, it has never been a driving one. SADC has functioned much more as a regional development financing scheme, channeling aid to its member states. For an overview of integration schemes in Africa, see Elliot Berg, *Strategies for West African Economic Integration* (Bethesda, Md.: Development Alternatives, 1991), and Facrek Foroutan, *Regional Integration in Sub-Saharan Africa: Past Experience and Future Prospects* (Washington, D.C.: World Bank, 1992).

5. For discussions of the economic rationales for establishing customs unions among

developed economies, see, for example Jacob Viner, *The Customs Union Issue* (New York: Carnegie Endowment for International Peace, 1950), and Bela Belassa, *The Theory of Economic Integration* (Homewood, Ill.: Richard D. Irwin, 1961).

6. Economic integration is primarily an industrialization strategy, as agricultural production does not usually require large home markets to reach scale economies. For efforts to apply integration theory to the case of developing countries, see C. A. Cooper and B. F. Massell, "Towards a General Theory of Customs Unions for Developing Countries," *Journal of Political Economy* 73, pp. 461–476, and Peter Robson, *The Economics of International Integration* (London: Allen & Unwin, 1980).

7. See World Bank, *Sub-Saharan Africa: From Crisis to Sustainable Growth* (Washington, D.C.: World Bank, 1989) for population and other statistics.

8. This is a belief rather than an established fact. Neighboring countries can be as disruptive and destructive of economic progress as can distant countries. One has only to remember the number of African countries expelling foreign workers at one time or another or erecting trade barriers against one another.

9. There is a large body of literature on ECOWAS. A good introduction is Uka Ezenwe, *ECOWAS and the Economic Integration of West Africa* (St. Martin's: New York, 1983).

10. See Olatunde Ojo, "Nigeria and the Formation of ECOWAS," *International Organization* 34, no. 4 (Autumn 1980), pp. 571–604, and Daniel Bach, "The Politics of West African Economic Cooperation: CEAO and ECOWAS," *Journal of Modern African Studies* 21, no. 4 (Autumn 1983), pp. 605–623.

11. This provision was included in response to pressures from Nigerian businesses and to ensure their support of the organization. See Ojo, "Nigeria," pp. 585ff. It is also in accord with the Nigerian Policy of *indigenization*—that is, of requiring that between 40 and 60 percent of Nigerian firms be owned by Nigerians.

12. This strategy by Nigeria is recounted in detail in ibid. Francophone states in west Africa had already created their own regional economic integration scheme—the Communauté Economique de l'Afrique de l'Ouest (CEAO).

13. See Olajide Aluko, "Oil at Concessionary Prices for Africa: A Case-Study in Nigerian Decision-Making," *African Affairs* 75 (October 1976), p. 430.

14. For details on this issue of particular sensitivity to Nigeria, see Ralph Onwuka, "ECOWAS Protocol on Free Movement of Persons," *African Affairs* 81 (April 1982), pp. 193–206.

15. Quoted in Makhtar Diouf, "Evaluation of West African Experiments in Economic Integration," in World Bank, *The Long-Term Perspective Study of Sub-Saharan Africa, Background Papers, Volume 4: Proceedings of a Workshop on Regional Integration and Cooperation* (Washington, D.C.: World Bank, 1990), pp. 22–23.

16. *Africa Research Bulletin*, Economic Series 26 (July 31, 1989), p. 9593.

17. Bernadette Cole and Oudjoe Kpor, "A House in Need of Attention," *West Africa* (March 19, 1990), pp. 440ff.

18. *West Africa* 3751 (July 10, 1989), p. 1119.

19. Douglas Anglin, "Economic Liberation and Regional Cooperation in Southern Africa: SADCC and PTA," *International Organization* 37, no. 4 (Autumn 1983), p. 689. For more background on the PTA, see Ngila Mwase, "The African Preferential Trade Area," *Journal of World Trade Law* 19 (1985), pp. 622–636.

20. Interview with Somali permanent secretary for the PTA, Ministry of Commerce and Industries, Mogadishu, December 1986. Barre apparently did not ask the opinion of any of his economic officials before he signed the PTA treaty.

21. For a review of the history and experience of the PTA, see Guy Martin, "The Prefer-

ential Trade Area (PTA) for East and Southern Africa: Achievements, Problems, Prospects," *Afrika Spectrum* 2 (1989), pp. 157–171.

22. There is little written on the ECCAS. See Laurent Zang, "L'Integration Economique en Afrique Centrale: De Nouvelles Perspectives avec la CEEAC?" *Le Mois en Afrique* (February 1987), pp.253–259, for one analysis.

23. "Fifth Summit (Bangui),"*Africa Research Bulletin*, Economic Series 26 (April 30, 1989), p. 9491.

24. Ernst B. Haas, *The Uniting of Europe* (Stanford: Stanford University Press, 1958), p. 16.

25. There is a large body of literature on international integration, functionalism, and neofunctionalism. See, for example, Leon Lindberg and Stuart Scheingold, eds. *Regional Integration: Theory and Research* (Cambridge, Mass: Harvard University Press, 1971); Ernst Haas, *Beyond the Nation State* (Stanford: Stanford University Press, 1964); Charles Pentland, *International Theory and European Integration* (London: Faber and Faber, 1973); and the set of articles in *International Organization* 24, no. 4. (1970). Most of this work focuses on the experience of integration in Europe.

26. See particularly Joseph Nye, "Comparing Common Markets: A Revised Neo-Functionalist Model," *International Organization* 24, no. 4 (Autumn 1970), pp. 796–834, for an effort to apply the theory to the experience of developing countries. See also Lynn Mytelka, "The Salience of Gains in Third World Integrative Systems," *World Politics* 25, no. 2 (January 1973), pp. 236–250.

27. Diplomatic factors also played a role in the creation of the EEC. Germany was willing to join because it saw membership as a means of restoring its international credibility; France and the rest of Europe (and the United States) wanted Germany in the EEC to constrain its future ability to pursue a militaristic foreign policy.

28. For more details, see Daniel Bach, "Francophone Regional Organizations and ECOWAS, or What Is Economic Co-operation About in West Africa," in S. Wright and J. Okolo, eds. *West Africa Regional Cooperation and Development* (Boulder: Westview Press, 1989), pp.53–65.

PART FOUR

Major Issues

10

The United States and Conflict Management in Africa

DONALD ROTHCHILD

By THE LATE 1980s, the Cold War had come to an end, and Africa, left increasingly to its own devices, turned its attention to the problems of governance and economic survival. A number of Africa's old, authoritarian regimes, no longer of strategic importance to their superpower patrons, were forced by their societal leaders to accept political reforms. In some instances, such liberalization has led to open, multiparty elections, resulting in a reconnection of state and society and a greater regularity in their reciprocities and political exchanges.

But if some African countries have been fortunate in finding new bases for legitimate political relations, others have been plagued by grave irregularities in their state-society interactions. This has led in worst-case situations to insurgency, civil war, and the breakdown of state and society. "Old identities," wrote Francis M. Deng, "undermined and rendered dormant by the structures and values of the nation-state system, are reemerging and redefining the standards of participation, distribution, and legitimacy."[1] Africa, like many other parts of the world, is undergoing a search for new, legitimate units of authority, a turbulent process that disrupts old intergroup linkages and state norms. When internal connections are torn asunder and innocent civilians are threatened by rival gangs and armies, the international community cannot remain aloof and allow the situation to deteriorate.

In the case of the United States, senior-level foreign policy makers, concerned with promoting a stable international order in which democratic regimes and economic trade and investment can be nurtured, have found themselves with little choice but to become involved in internal conflicts in many Third World countries. The end of the intense rivalry between the superpowers has allowed the United States to return "to its natural position as order's conservator."[2] Consequently, as the sole remaining great power (in military terms, at least), it cannot stand aside while separatist demands and destructive regional conflicts jeopardize effective governance.

The U.S. diplomatic involvement in Africa's conflict resolution processes during and after the Cold War has taken many forms: conflict prevention (the assemblage of information, measures of reconciliation, and pressure for human rights and democratization); behind-the-scenes support for the mediation of disputes by African third-party actors (Nigeria in Sudan, Zaire in Angola); the backing of a regional actor (ECOMOG in Liberia, OAU in Rwanda); assistance for an extra-continental actor (Britain in Zimbabwe, support for Portugal in negotiating the internal settlement in Angola and for Italy in the Mozambican negotiations); the promotion of an international organization's initiative (the U.N. in Congo, Somalia, Rwanda, Liberia, Namibia, and Angola—after the signing of the Bicesse accords); pressure on local actors to negotiate (South Africa, Sudan); humanitarian intervention and diplomatic facilitation (Somalia); the organization of a regime transition (Ethiopia); and direct third-party mediation between internal parties (Sudan 1989–1992, Zaire 1992) as well as between international parties (Angola-Namibia). To some extent, then, the United States has become a part of the attempted resolution of these African conflicts, seeking to use its political and economic resources to move the peace ahead.

In examining the American role in peacemaking, I will address three interlinked issues. First, to what extent did the status and power of the United States contribute to the successful promotion of an understanding or peace accord? In conflict situations involving highly antagonistic parties, the negotiation process is inevitably a difficult one. Key actors view one another's intentions in belligerent terms and often advance nonnegotiating demands at the bargaining table. Yet despite these unpropitious circumstances, third-party mediators, whether acting on a direct or indirect basis, have sometimes prevailed—partly by being in a position to manipulate pressures and incentives in an effective manner. Second, why, after a laborious effort crowned by a measure of success, have some of these agreements dissolved? And third, following the collapse of these accords, what options are open to U.S. diplomats to bring about a return to constructive state-society encounters? In examining these questions, I will try to establish two general propositions: first, that the United States will increasingly tend to conduct its peacemaking initiatives indirectly, under the auspices of the U.N., OAU, or other official and unofficial actors, and second, that U.S. diplomats should view implementation (or postagreement peace-building) as a critical part of the larger mediation process.

The United States as Facilitator of African Peace Accords

The necessity for international negotiations and mediation efforts arises as a consequence of the failure of global and regional collective security mechanisms and the decline of domestic norms of conflict resolution. Where the weak state lacks the capacity to regulate society effectively and the relations between ethnic and nationality groups become irregular and possibly warlike, an imbalance between conflict and stability becomes apparent, often "exact[ing] a terrible toll on help-less people."[3] One option open to state elites is to attempt to eliminate the opposition or to force its capitulation, as happened, according to Stephen Stedman's data, in forty-one out of sixty-eight civil wars in the twentieth century, including Uganda (1966, 1987), Burundi (1972), and Nigeria among the African cases.[4] Another option is to seek to reestablish a balance between conflict and stability by negotiating with subnational interests, as was the case with twenty incidents identified by Stedman, including Zaire (1965), Sudan (1972), Angola (1975), Zimbabwe (1979), and Namibia (1989). Clearly, recently compiled data lead to rather low expectations regarding successful mediation of civil wars.

The difficulty of mediating substate insurgencies becomes even more pronounced when insurgencies have an ethnic or nationality dimension. No doubt, this reflects the high level of emotion surrounding these encounters and the great reluctance that state authorities have for dealing with the leaders of guerrilla movements, fearing that such diplomatic contacts may accord them a measure of international respectability or even legitimacy.[5] Concluding that interstate conflicts tend to be more amenable than state-insurgent struggles to mediation, Daniel Frei commented that "it might be argued that governments of states are in a better position to agree to the compromise suggested by the mediator rather than the leadership of insurgent groups because their legitimacy is usually not questioned."[6] The general prospects of mediating Africa's civil wars therefore seem limited. Even so, where certain circumstances prevail (such as the emergence of identifiable bargaining parties, a mutually hurting stalemate, leaders determined to find a political solution, external pressures to reach agreement, and a mediator actively on the scene), third-party intervenors have at times prevailed.[7]

One of the key variables at play would appear to be the status and power of the third-party actors. Various African leaders, singly or jointly, have undertaken mediatory initiatives in African state-substate conflicts: Emperor Haile Selassie proved an effective arbiter during particular confrontations over the 1972 Sudanese peace accord, an OAU peacekeeping force (replaced by a U.N. peacekeeping force under the August 1993 agreement) worked alongside a Tanzanian diplomatic team to facilitate negotiations between the Rwanda government and the rebel Rwandese Patriotic Front, and a six-state ECOMOG force has had some success in stabilizing the situation in Liberia. Other African leaders have been less successful. For example, President Daniel arap Moi's efforts to mediate the Uganda civil war in 1985–1986, President Mobutu Sese Seko's peacemaking initiative at Gbadolite in 1989, President Kenneth Kaunda's attempts to mediate between South Africa's African National Congress and the Inkatha Freedom Party in 1992, and the various attempts by Moi, President Robert Mugabe, and President Hastings Banda to intercede in the ongoing civil war in Mozambique softened the perceptions that the adversaries held about one another but produced little deci-

sive change.[8] Although leaders such as Moi displayed considerable skill in bringing the Uganda rivals to the bargaining table and then hammering out a logical
plan of action, they were constrained from the outset by the unwillingness of the
negotiating parties to shift their preferences and perceptions to the extent necessary to make the agreement stick.

Certainly, where a decolonizing state was prepared to mediate between internal
parties (as in Ghana, Kenya, and Zimbabwe) or where the great powers changed
their perceptions and cooperated to facilitate the negotiations (as in the Angola-
Namibia accords), the prospects for successful conflict management were greatly
enhanced. On the other hand, where middle-range European countries such as
Portugal and Italy, lacking the political and economic resources needed to or-
chestrate a settlement on their own, stepped into the Angolan and Mozambican
conflicts as mediators, their success in the final analysis proved contingent upon
their ability to secure great-power backing. The ability of strong third-party
actors to use pressures and incentives to alter the choices of conflicting parties
may not prove sufficient (as in Jonas Savimbi's renewal of the Angolan civil war
following the 1992 elections in Angola), but there is little doubt as to the necessity
of such measures.

Some Key U.S. Diplomatic Initiatives

To gain an understanding of the extent of the U.S. role in peacemaking activities,
it is important to note the interconnections between the various stages of this
process. Thus, the prenegotiation stage is linked in important ways to the negotiating stage, and these, in turn, are tied to the implementation of agreements.
Looked at broadly, then, the onset of negotiations is part and parcel of what preceded and what followed them. In this sense, it is possible to break down the
third-party peacemaking initiatives taken by U.S. diplomats in Africa into five
basic types: pressures on internal actors to negotiate, indirect mediatory action,
direct mediation, military-diplomatic interventions, and the implementation of
agreements. In this section, I will concentrate upon the prenegotiation and negotiation stages.

Pressure on Internal Actors to Negotiate

It is more and more accepted as doctrine that states have a right to intervene in
the domestic affairs of other states to pursue humanitarian objectives and advance the peace process. It is therefore not surprising that a powerful international actor such as the United States will intercede in various state-subnational conflicts that pose a serious threat to the stability and well-being of the world
community. In doing so, the United States has aligned itself with various state or
insurgent leaders, with very real consequences in terms of the resulting levels of
conflict. Thus, by aligning the United States with Haile Selassie's Amharic-domi-
nated state and building up and equipping his armed forces, U.S. officials were

firming up state power at the expense of other, less powerful ethnic peoples. Conversely, economic and military support for the Ovimbundu-based National Union for the Total Independence of Angola (UNITA) insurgency in Angola has weakened the capacity of the central government in Luanda to penetrate and regulate its society.

In addition, the United States has, at times, protested, sometimes in an unpublicized manner, abusive actions directed at ethnic minority peoples. It has long been recognized that such protests represent "a legitimate exercise of the law of humanitarian intervention";[9] however, their ability to change practices in the target states remains somewhat hazy. The American role in publicly protesting the Amin government's harassment of its Asian citizens or South Africa's apartheid practices is well known. More recently, the U.S. Senate has taken a strong stand on human rights violations in the Sudan, forcefully criticizing the Sudanese government for engaging in a campaign of "ethnic cleansing" against the Nuba people in Kordofan Province and opposing the extension of further World Bank or IMF loans while this situation persists.[10] And in September 1993, the United States and European Community countries urged an end to the Kenya regime's practices of ethnic cleansing in the Rift Valley, linking the cessation of such human rights violations to any discussions on the resumption of multilateral economic assistance.[11] To the extent that these statements of principle help to establish international standards of appropriate behavior, they may represent a contribution to actual policies and behavior.

Pressures of a nonmilitary type have also been invoked by U.S. administrations to raise the costs on governments seen to be abusing the civil and political rights of their disadvantaged peoples. In pressing African governments to observe the civil rights of their citizens and to accept democratic forms of governance, the United States is practicing a kind of preventive diplomacy. Its policies have the effect of structuring political relations in such a way as "to diffuse potential ethnic conflicts";[12] they make conflict more manageable by establishing norms and routines of relationship that act as a general incentive for intergroup cooperation.[13] Moreover, the Kampala Forum, in an important declaration of May 1991, anchored its "security calabash" on several principles, starting with measures "to prevent or contain [a] crisis before an eruption into violent confrontation."[14] The forum's emphasis on timely OAU mechanisms of mediation and reconciliation to deal with conflicts before they escalate into internal strife and military encounters is clearly in line with current American preferences on encouraging regional organizations to take the lead in dealing with tensions in their area.

In addition to general U.S. pressures for human rights and democracy, the United States has used its influence on various occasions to intercede in a variety of internal conflicts. Such actions include the closure of an American embassy (Uganda), the temporary cessation of bilateral aid projects (Uganda), termination of programs by such U.S. government agencies as the Export-Import Bank or the Overseas Private Investment Corporation (Uganda, Rhodesia, South Africa), and economic sanctions (South Africa, Rhodesia, and Uganda).[15] In the case of Uganda, the 1978 trade embargo on coffee imports was a congressional initiative designed to protest human rights violations by the government against both disadvantaged African groups and Ugandan Asians. Examples of mixed nonmilitary-military U.S. pressures include limitations on the use of military assistance (Sudan) and a ban on the export of military equipment (South Africa, Rhodesia, and Uganda).

U.S. diplomats have been increasingly energetic in attempting to alter group preferences within African countries regarding the need to enter into negotiations. In the case of South Africa, according to former Assistant Secretary of State for African Affairs Chester A. Crocker, "our role was to facilitate negotiation."[16] American pressure was directed mainly at South Africa's white ruling establishment, seeking to raise costs on further inaction in coming to the negotiating table and to ensure that no backsliding took place in its commitment to a negotiated settlement. By the time the Reagan administration took office, the struggle for progressive change in South Africa had emerged as something of a domestic issue in American politics. Despite the Reagan team's resistance to placing sanctions on South African trade and on its access to certain technology and services, Congress passed the 1986 Comprehensive Anti-Apartheid Act into law. This law made the South African government's acceptance as a legitimate member of the world community conditional upon its reevaluation of the need for political reform. Such international sanctions have had at least a limited impact upon South Africa's economy. The ban on new loans and investments was damaging, as was the denial of access to world markets for certain goods, technology, and services. Real growth has slackened, leading to a continuing rise in unemployment (some 2 million by 1991) and an estimated fall in average incomes of some 15 percent.[17]

As was true with earlier administrations, the Bush team continued to place a high priority on all-party negotiations. Thus, in the summer of 1992, as the talks at the Convention for a Democratic South Africa (CODESA) were suspended, the United States took steps to encourage a return to the bargaining table. President Bush wrote to ANC President Nelson Mandela, President de Klerk, and Inkatha Party leader Chief Mangosuthu Buthelezi encouraging them to address the immediate issue of violence and indicating American preparedness to assist in creating a climate conducive for negotiations.[18] At the same time, the Bush administration seemed ambivalent about utilizing sanctions against South Africa. Restrictions were eased in 1990 on iron and steel and the sale of Boeing 747s. Then, in an effort to provide an incentive for further acts to dismantle the apartheid state, Bush declared himself convinced in 1991 that the transition process was irreversible and terminated federal economic sanctions; however, pressures were maintained at the state or local levels, for the Bush action had little effect on these governments. Clearly, the U.S. ability to influence the pace of the reform process was ebbing.

Although South African editorialists spoke of their concern that the new Clinton administration would be tougher on their nation than its predecessor had been,[19] the period immediately after Clinton's inauguration actually witnessed little substantive change. The Clinton administration gave continuing support to the idea of all-party negotiations, and it encouraged CODESA to reassemble and get on with negotiating a settlement. President Bill Clinton, determined to use his remaining influence to spur the process of negotiations, made it clear that his administration would only relax the country's remaining sanctions when "it bec[ame] clearer that the day of democracy and guaranteed individual rights [was] at hand."[20]

Some Americans have been active on a private basis in South Africa, helping the Conflict Management Group run workshops on negotiations and constitutional options, and the U.S. Agency for International Development (USAID) has given support for training in conflict resolution. Moreover, a small U.N. observer group is on the scene, actively making recommendations to local officials on the handling of security matters and urging participation by the Pan-Africanist Congress and others in the nationwide peace commission. The ANC has gone on record favoring use of an election monitoring team from abroad,[21] and the Azanian People's Organization has expressed an interest in appointing a neutral convener.[22] Other than these efforts to keep the negotiating process on track, however, the United States seemed to have a marginal role to play. For the most part, the negotiations have been an internally driven dialogue with all the major South African parties rebuffing proposals for formal third-party mediation. Nevertheless, the Commonwealth Group was able to mediate in Natal, and the U.N. mission led by former U.S. Secretary of State Cyrus Vance engaged in some quiet mediatory activities between ANC Secretary General Cyril Ramaphosa and Minister of Constitutional Development Roelf Meyer in August 1992. And with the change of regimes, there will certainly be an urgent need for a U.S. and allied initiative to encourage the process of democratization and to help in the reconstruction of South Africa's economy and society. Only such an undertaking can lay the framework for black empowerment in the years immediately ahead.

Indirect Mediatory Activity

As used in this context, indirect mediatory activity refers to United States backing for a formal mediatory effort mounted under the auspices of another actor. This approach can involve U.S. support for a private, informal mediator (as in former President Jimmy Carter's attempts to mediate between the Ethiopian government and the Eritrean People's Liberation Front [EPLF] in 1989) or for a formal third-party undertaking led by another state or regional or international organization. The line between indirect mediatory activity and direct mediation is sometimes quite blurred. In Somalia following the U.S. humanitarian intervention in 1992–1993, for example, American diplomats mediated certain local conflicts on their own. However, in the critical negotiations of March 1993, where the fifteen factional leaders agreed in Addis Ababa to set up the Transitional National Council, U.N. and Ethiopian government leaders played a prominent third-party role, facilitated by a behind-the-scenes American diplomatic effort.

There are numerous instances of indirect mediatory action by the United States under the auspices of other state actors. In the case of Rhodesia (Zimbabwe), where Britain was still recognized throughout the world as the colonial power, U.S. diplomats appropriately played a supporting role during the critical Lancaster House peace negotiations in 1979. The conference was organized and guided by Britain's Foreign Secretary Lord Peter Carrington, whose firm direction of the sessions prompted one author to describe his leadership style as "dominant third-party mediation."[23] Carrington and his team controlled the conference agenda, set deadlines, dealt with issues on a step-by-step basis (each partial agreement providing the basis for the next set of deliberations), and submitted drafts that served as the basis for further deliberations. The British intermediaries used various pressures and incentives to push the negotiation process ahead, threatening the Patriotic Front by declaring that they would accept an internal settlement if the conference broke down, promising Bishop Abel Muzorewa that his delegation's interests would be protected during the transition, and vowing fair elections prior to turning over power. The pledge on elections was regarded as a credible undertaking by the Mozambican leadership (especially President Samora Machel and Fernando Honwana), who did not see any reason for using their territory as a safe sanctuary for Patriotic Front forces any longer. The Mozambicans, in turn, pressured Patriotic Front leader Robert Mugabe to trust the British-orchestrated process.

Not everything proceeded according to plan, however, and at one critical juncture when the future constitutional arrangements were being discussed, it became necessary for the British to try to overcome the impasse by offering to grant financial assistance for land resettlement and redistribution to an independent Zimbabwe if the Patriotic Front leadership agreed to the proposed arrangements. At this time, U.S. diplomats, who had been observing the procedures closely, came to the support of the British mediators, offering financial grants to an independent Zimbabwe for such broad purposes as agriculture and education. This offer proved very timely, for it helped to keep the conference from breaking down over the land issue. The American money was not, as described in the press, specifically intended for a buyout of white farmers, although everyone knew that money was fungible and could, in fact, be used for such a purpose. By enabling the Patriotic Front negotiators to save face, the American side payment made an important contribution to the overall success of the British-led peacemaking effort.

Although U.S. mediators played the central role in facilitating an Angolan peace settlement among the international actors (the Luanda government and the four major external intervenors—South Africa, Cuba, the Soviet Union, and the United States), they followed the lead of two middle-power mediators when it came to negotiating an agreement between the internal parties—the Popular Movement for the Liberation of Angola (MPLA) government and the UNITA insurgents.[24] With the rapid withdrawal of Cuban and South African forces after the signing of the 1988 accord, the internal adversaries were left increasingly on their own and had little prospect of winning a decisive victory. Under these circumstances, a political solution was necessary, but it was not easily managed.

The first such peacemaking effort was undertaken by Zaire's President Mobutu Sese Seko, with the quiet backing of the Soviet Union and the United States. Mobutu, with encouragement from a number of governments in the region, sought to organize an African summit initiative aimed at bringing the Angolan civil war to a conclusion. In all, twenty countries were represented at the Gbadolite summit in June 1989, eighteen of them by their heads of state. Throughout the seven-hour, closed-door meeting, Mobutu met separately with Angolan President José Eduardo dos Santos and UNITA leader Savimbi in order to procure an agreement on the summit declaration. After that, he presented the rivals before the gathering of Africa's respected leaders, securing a handshake between the arch adversaries as well as an agreement in principle on a cease-fire and moves to promote national integration. Given the hasty way in which the agreement was hammered out and the vagueness of the resulting principles, it was not surprising that the accord proved extremely hard to implement. The antagonists differed in their interpretations of Savimbi's agreement to go into exile and on the integration of UNITA's civilian and military elements into the MPLA-state and MPLA-party organizations. Negotiators in a series of minisummits attempted to thrash out the differences, but it was not long before heated military engagements again occurred in the Mavinga area.

The American role in this crisis was never sufficient to deal with the needs on the ground. Although supportive in principle of the Gbadolite peace process, U.S. policymakers did not put sufficient pressure on Savimbi to change his preferences and perceptions at that juncture. The United States continued to provide military aid to the insurgents and to refuse to recognize the legitimacy of the MPLA-led government (thus enabling it to exert some influence over Savimbi through the implied threat of a policy shift on this issue). Such backing provided the United States with sufficient leverage to help get Savimbi to cooperate in attending Gbadolite but not enough to assure that he would appear at the Kinshasa minisummit or move toward a compromise agreement.

With the failure of the minisummits, it became apparent to dos Santos that the Gbadolite process had stalled. He therefore called for the acceptance of a new third-party intermediary. Portugal, the former colonial power, stepped into the situation, and from mid-1990 onward, it chaired a series of talks between representatives of the Angolan government and UNITA. U.S. Assistant Secretary Herman Cohen, with Soviet approval, gave quiet assistance to Portuguese Deputy Foreign Minister Durao Barroso's efforts to work out a set of basic principles acceptable to both sides. The United States and the Soviets were continuing to supply their local allies with extensive military aid, giving them considerable leverage in the negotiating process. And in contrast to their lack of urgency over the Gbadolite initiative, the two great powers took a very active stance this time in support of the Portuguese mediators.

In seeking to buttress the Portuguese mediation effort, U.S. Secretary of State James Baker met publicly in December 1990 with the Angolan foreign minister while Soviet Foreign Minister Eduard Shevardnadze conferred with Savimbi. Then, the two great powers jointly sponsored a meeting in Washington, D.C., attended by the Angolans and the Portuguese, which produced the so-called Washington Concepts Paper, a conceptual framework for the Portuguese-mediated talks. Under the terms of this paper, a cease-fire would be followed by: a cessation of exports of lethal matériel to the parties by the United States, the USSR, and all other countries (the "triple zero option"); an amendment of the constitution to provide for multiparty democracy; free and fair elections; the creation of a national army; and the installation of an international monitoring force. The Washington agreement of basic negotiating principles gave a new impetus to the flagging deliberations at Bicesse. With U.S. and Soviet observers in attendance at the subsequent rounds of discussions, the negotiators came to an agreement on such knotty issues as the formation of a national army, the setting of dates for the cease-fire, the timing of multiparty elections, and the international monitoring process. Not only did they play an important role in pushing the parties to sign the interim cease-fire accord, they also took part in the Joint Political-Military Commission that oversaw the transition process.

U.S. indirect mediatory action was also evident during the critical phase of the 1992 Mozambican negotiations between the government and the Mozambique National Resistance (RENAMO). With the arrival of the Reagan administration in 1981, U.S. policymakers, concerned over increased Soviet-Cuban involvement in the armed struggle there, sought to establish better relations with the Mozambican government and to encourage a dialogue between government authorities and both RENAMO and the government in South Africa. In this respect, the 1984 Nkomati pact of nonaggression signed by the Mozambican and South African governments was viewed positively by American authorities, who described it as a "prominent symbol of a broader process."[25]

In the period that ensued, the Reagan administration continued a policy of quiet diplomacy toward Mozambique, striving, as a 1985 Defense Department memorandum put it, "to replace Soviet influence with our own, to reduce regional violence vis-à-vis South Africa, and to induce [President Samora] Machel's FRELIMO [Mozambique Liberation Front] Government to enter into substantive negotiations with the very active RENAMO insurgents."[26] In seeking improved ties with the Mozambican government and national reconciliation between the warring parties, U.S. diplomats worked with the major regional leaders to facilitate a settlement of the civil war. An abortive effort by Kenya's President Daniel arap Moi and Zimbabwe's President Robert Mugabe to mediate the conflict in August 1989 soon lost its impetus as RENAMO demanded recognition as a condition for negotiations while the FRELIMO government sought recognition as the valid ruling authority in the country.[27] With the gap between adversaries remaining wide, the two African mediators, allied as they were with one of the local rivals, soon lost the confidence of the opposing party.

In these circumstances, a new intermediary acceptable to both sides became essential, and the rival parties agreed, in the summer of 1990, to begin direct talks in Rome under the joint mediation of the Italian government, the Roman Catholic Lay Organization Sant Egidio, and the Roman Catholic archbishop of Beira. The United States, as Assistant Secretary of State for African Affairs Herman Cohen testified, "played a prominent facilitative role" in advancing the agenda of the talks, getting the parties to the bargaining table, and consulting with the mediators and rival interests in the two years of talks that ensued.[28] In its capacity as an official observer, the United States sent legal and military experts to Rome to help iron out the details and was in regular consultation with the contending parties regarding the cease-fire and military-related issues.[29] In addition, the United States agreed to participate in the U.N.-supervised effort to implement the peace agreement. Inevitably, this proved a challenging undertaking, for under the terms of the October 4, 1992 settlement, the Supervision and Monitoring Commission had a general responsibility for verifying the cease-fire and demobilization process, overseeing the formation of unified military forces, and guiding the economic and social reintegration of refugees and demobilized combatants. The costs of this are not insubstantial, for $320 million were pledged by a group of donors in Rome for the transition process and the cost of the U.N. monitoring operation (UNOMOZ, the United Nations Operations in Mozambique) was estimated at $260 million.[30] After a brutal war of sixteen years, involving more than an estimated one million lives and millions of displaced people, the peace treaty signed by President Joaquin A. Chissano and RENAMO leader Afonso Dhlakama seemed a major achievement in overcoming a destructive deadlock. The timetables set for demobilization, disarmament, and the unification of forces seem somewhat unrealistic, probably requiring further negotiations. Even so, a successful consolidation of this shaky agreement through externally facilitated monitoring and supervision would no doubt add significantly to the likelihood of a constructive outcome.

Direct Mediation

As noted, U.S. third-party mediation of African conflicts can involve unofficial or official actors or a combination of these. Illustrative of the interconnection between individual and state initiatives was former President Jimmy Carter's efforts to promote a dialogue between the Ethiopians and Eritreans in 1989. Certainly, Carter, as a past president of the United States, had exceptional entrée to people in high places as well as an aura of power associated with his former office. In addition, his attempt to bring the main protagonists together took place with the tacit approval of the U.S. government and against a backdrop of increasing superpower cooperation on regional issues.[31] Despite their very different conceptions of the negotiating process, the Ethiopian and the Eritrean People's Liberation Front delegations did come to the Carter Center in Atlanta prepared to talk about internal issues. The results represented a hopeful beginning, for agreement was reached on ten out of thirteen points, including the agenda for the follow-up .

meeting, the nature of the delegations, and the official languages to be used at the meetings. Unfortunately, the more substantive issues on the role of the chair, the nature of the mediation process, and the number and composition of the observers were left unsettled and contributed to the breakdown of the dialogue when the follow-up Nairobi conferees assembled. The Carter effort had displayed considerable creativity by bringing the rival parties together for a useful exchange of views; with the two sides still convinced that a military victory was not out of the question, however, there was little leeway for the Carter team to overcome the issues of principle dividing them.[32]

After that, the U.S. authorities became more directly involved in mediating between the various parties. In October 1990 and February 1991, Assistant Secretary Cohen held talks in Washington with Ethiopian government and EPLF delegations but again proved unable to narrow the differences. Then, as the insurgent Ethiopian People's Revolutionary Democratic Front (EPRDF) forces approached the perimeters of Addis Ababa, and President Mengistu Haile Mariam fled the country in May, the United States interjected itself into the unfolding crisis. At the request of the caretaker government and the opposition movements in the field (the EPRDF, EPLF, and the Oromo Liberation Front), Cohen convened a meeting of these parties in London on May 27 to work out a cease-fire and transition to a new regime. The situation on the ground was deteriorating rapidly. EPRDF troops remained on the outskirts of Addis Ababa, honoring a pledge to Cohen that they would not enter the city prior to the commencement of negotiations. Upon learning that the interim government was losing control of its troops and anxious to spare the city the destruction that accompanies house-to-house combat (as in Somalia), Cohen seized the initiative and publicly recommended that the EPRDF be allowed to move into the capital "in order to reduce uncertainties and eliminate tensions."[33] The interim government, unable to prevent the occupation of the city by EPRDF troops, watched helplessly during the night of May 27–28 as the insurgents took charge. By sanctioning the EPRDF takeover, Cohen contended that he acted as the "conscience of the international community," sparing Addis Ababa from certain havoc and then conditioning aid to the future government on its good faith in putting democratic reforms into effect.[34]

Again involving both official and nonofficial actors, American mediators intervened actively at various points in the Sudanese civil war, both to protect the distribution of relief supplies and to facilitate the peace process. Upon taking office in 1989, the Bush administration decided upon a concerted effort to settle the long-running conflict in the Sudan. In February, Secretary James Baker publicly urged the Sudanese government and the Sudan People's Liberation Movement and Sudan People's Liberation Army (SPLM/SPLA) to put peace first and agree to an early cease-fire. Significantly, with the Cold War ebbing and the U.S. administration more prepared to speak out on human rights abuses than the previous administration had been, Baker supported calls by the Democratic Unionist party, the SPLA, and other internal groups calling for a constitutional convention and urging that the government take "no preemptive moves to revise or implement Sharia laws pending the conference."[35] Seeking to give a new impetus to the peace process, State Department officials carried on a dialogue with Soviet diplomats regarding a new cooperative effort to end the civil war. These efforts were spurned by Prime Minister Sadiq al-Mahdi, however, who told his Constituent Assembly that the Sudan did not need external involvement in its domestic affairs.[36]

In the months that followed, the al-Mahdi government came under increasing international pressure to allow various public and private aid agencies to deliver food to the rebel-controlled areas in the south. In the end, the government consented and allowed Operation Lifeline Sudan to go forward.[37] Various U.S. government agencies contributed food aid and logistical support to the 1989 relief effort. Food assistance inevitably became intertwined with new U.S. calls to negotiate an end to the war—the source of the problem in the area. Assistant Secretary Cohen met separately with John Garang, the chairman of SPLA and commander in chief of SPLM, and Prime Minister al-Mahdi, and separately, former President Jimmy Carter laid plans for a new peacemaking exploration. This meeting was delayed by the military coup led by General Omer al Bashir; nevertheless, after considerable effort, Carter did manage to bring representatives of the al Bashir government and the SPLM/SPLA together in Nairobi in late December. Although the insurgents responded in a conciliatory manner regarding the government's proposed federal scheme, they balked over Khartoum's insistence on applying Sharia law and its firm resolve to control the country's oil reserves.[38]

Additional American (and other) peace initiatives were to follow. In March 1990, Herman Cohen undertook a new peace initiative, involving a cease-fire and disengagement of forces, the establishment of a monitoring force, and the convening of a national constitutional conference. As initially conceived, Cohen argued that disengagement involved the maintenance of law and order in the vacated area by the police, with no SPLA forces being permitted to enter this zone.[39] The thought, Cohen reasoned, was

> that a disengagement, structured in a way to make the resumption of fighting much more difficult, would in itself provide a greater impetus to peace talks. By creating new facts on the ground, the two parties would be forced to confront the political facts, and come up with some realistic ideas. So we suggested that the government withdraw a large number—perhaps half—of its troops in the South. At the same time the SPLA would pull back to a set distance from all government-held areas in the South. . . . Both the government and the SPLA initially agreed with this idea, but could not agree on how a disengagement could be carried out so that neither side would be disadvantaged.[40]

By contrast, southerners interpreted it as entailing a pullback of government forces, with the SPLA occupying the area vacated by the withdrawing government troops. As reformulated and formalized, the notion of disengagement held up, but its content was altered, they argued, to convey the idea of a mutual withdrawal of forces.[41] Although southerners were very disappointed by what they viewed as a significant change in Cohen's original ideas, they nonetheless met with the assistant secretary again and urged a reactivation of the original recommendations. Proposals were followed by counterproposals—Khartoum, for example, offered to institute a cease-fire. With Sudanese military authorities suspicious of intrigues between the SPLA and the Americans, the process of peacemaking gradually stalled.

Further variants of the 1990 proposals, including federalism, disengagement, and multiparty democracy, were subsequently presented by Cohen and other nonofficial intermediaries but to no avail.[42] Southerners were particularly insistent upon American championship of the notion of multiparty democracy in the negotiations, something that Cohen hesitated over because he assumed that Khartoum would reject this idea on principle. Cohen also raised the idea of demilitarizing Juba, attempting to bring about a cessation of hostilities in this area to protect the beleaguered city and its many inhabitants. Achieving little success in negotiating a Sudanese government-insurgent peace through a direct approach, the United States appeared to resign itself to indirect mediatory activity. It gave quiet support to the Abuja peace process in 1992–1993 (mediated by Nigerian authorities on behalf of the OAU).[43]

Other inconclusive U.S. mediatory initiatives can be cited. For instance, Cohen mediated an agreement in Zaire between President Mobutu Sese Seko, Archbishop Laurent Monsengwo (the president of the High Council of the Republic), and Prime Minister Etienne Tshisekedi wa Mulumba on a sharing of power during the 1992–1994 transition period. The Cohen initiative represented a kind of high-risk, preventive diplomacy, inevitably fragile in the face of immoderate demands. In fact, the results proved most disappointing, for Mobutu, after accepting the compromise, refused to abide by its terms. This led to a breakdown of the agreement and a continuance of disorder.[44] Obviously, diplomatic "activism" is not always productive.

Even so, the *international* negotiations in Angola and Namibia show that U.S. initiatives can sometimes result in settlements that endure. From independence in November 1975 to the signing of the Angola-Namibia agreements in December 1988, the conflict among the Angolan nationalist movements (UNITA, MPLA, and, until the early 1980s, the National Front for the Liberation of Angola [FNLA]) was a civil war exacerbated by the ties that these nationalist movements had to various external powers. Whereas the MPLA government was bolstered by Soviet military equipment and Cuban combat troops, UNITA and, for a time, FNLA received Chinese military equipment following decolonization and U.S. military assistance around independence and after 1985 as well as South African military assistance and combat units during all phases of the war. As the civil war continued into the 1980s and as the MPLA and UNITA forces, backed by their external allies, became locked into a costly stalemate, the various local and international actors showed themselves to be increasingly responsive to proposals for international—but not internal—negotiations. The inability of UNITA and South African forces to achieve a decisive victory at Cuito Cuanavale and the

Cuban military strike at the Calueque Dam, with its accompanying evidences of Cuban air superiority, represented a change in the balance of military power in Angola that raised the costs on further South African offensives.[45] Moreover, the opportunity for a serious peace initiative was greatly advanced by the change that took place in the mid-1980s in the perceptions that the great powers had about one another. With Moscow and Washington shifting from adversarial to cautiously cooperative relations, it was time to make a new concerted effort to settle outstanding regional conflicts.[46]

The critical negotiations to end the deadlock and bring about an international settlement gained momentum in late 1987 as the Angolan government accepted the idea of linking a phased withdrawal of Cuban forces from Angola with Namibia's independence. The Angolans and the South Africans were far apart in their thinking on the timetable for Cuban redeployment and withdrawal, aid for the UNITA insurgents, and the terms for South Africa's disengagement from Namibia, but Assistant Secretary Crocker nonetheless concluded that the moment was ripe for a major third-party peace initiative. What followed was an eight-month effort to overcome the regional deadlock through peaceful means. With Crocker in the chair, the representatives of Angola, Cuba, and South Africa met in secret in London in May 1988 to explore the Angolan proposal for a four-year withdrawal of Cuban forces. This was followed by sessions in Brazzaville, Cairo, and New York, where persistent behind-the-scenes Soviet and American communications between these adversaries and even some pressures on their allies resulted in the acceptance of general principles on Namibia's independence, a phased Cuban withdrawal, verification, and formal recognition of the United States role as mediator. "Momentum," Crocker wrote, "helped keep our flock headed in the right direction."[47]

At the Geneva talks that followed, the conferees issued a joint statement announcing a de facto cessation of hostilities and a series of steps, including proposed dates for Namibia's independence and for the exit of Cuban and South African troops from Angola. At successive meetings in the fall, the parties narrowed the gaps between them on the issue of Cuban troop withdrawal, agreeing that the pullout would take place over a twenty-seven-month period and that two-thirds of these soldiers would leave during the first year, with the remainder being redeployed by stages to the north. With this thorny question behind them, the conferees tackled the remaining points of contention still outstanding—the verification procedures and the language of the protocol. Although the MPLA government and the various external intervenors remained antagonists, they had nonetheless managed to act in a pragmatic manner with respect to the issue of regional peace in southern Africa. A shift in the balance of military power on the ground, a sense of war weariness, and a change of perceptions on the part of the great powers combined in a fortuitous way to advance the possibilities of a settlement. But these positive preconditions did not carry over to the related task of reconciling the MPLA-UNITA civil war. Only as the great powers came to recognize the urgency of reaching an internal agreement and, under the auspices of a Portuguese mediator, to exert significant influence on their respective allies did a fragile and largely ineffective peace agreement materialize.

Military-Diplomatic Intervention

In the period ahead, the United States seems likely to remain actively involved in helping resolve African conflicts, exerting diplomatic pressure and mediating directly or under the auspices of other countries or international organizations. However, the Clinton administration is likely to avoid new, large-scale humanitarian interventions in Africa. Rather, it can be expected to emphasize multilateral diplomacy through regional organizations or the United Nations. In this respect, the U.S. role in Rwanda in 1992–1993, where American diplomats gave financial support for the OAU monitoring efforts and where they have participated as observers in the Tanzanian-mediated negotiations at Arusha, appeared to be a harbinger of preferred policy styles in the immediate future. Further evidence of such preferences appears in the case of Liberia, where the United States has encouraged and backed the dispatch of Senegalese peacekeepers and has contributed $29 million to the ECOMOG peacekeeping operation.[48]

The Somali humanitarian intervention may be something of an exception in terms of unilateral action. In the Somali case, the Bush administration dispatched a 25,000-person U.S. military force to an African country in 1992–1993 to ensure a safe environment for the delivery of relief supplies and to begin the process of national reconciliation.[49] The exception here is in the will of U.S. policymakers to intervene in situations where the state fails. State loss of influence, even breakdown, is also evident in Liberia and the Sudan, and it appears a distinct possibility in Zaire, Zambia, and Mozambique. Yet, with the possible exception of Liberia, the international community appears reluctant to become actively involved in the internal affairs of these countries, in part because domestic publics in the United States and elsewhere are disinclined to shoulder the burden.

Although Somalia is mostly a precedent in terms of the successful military effort to ensure food deliveries to the starving, there was a question of the mission's ability to disarm the militias and restore order in Mogadishu, to cope with the threat of national disintegration, and to undertake the diplomatic initiative necessary for political healing. In essence, the problems in Somalia, with its clan-based rivalries and ethnoregional antagonisms (i.e., the Isaak rebellion and separatism in northern Somalia), are essentially political in nature.[50] The U.S. military could not be expected to create political legitimacy through the use of force. All that could be asked of it was to utilize the momentary opportunity of its overrule to create the conditions in which diplomacy could take place. It did secure the main transportation routes, pacify a sizable area of the country, and, to a limited extent, disarm the main factional leaders. However, the peace talks that took place under its aegis have proved a tenuous basis for peace.

In effect, American and U.N. diplomats had two basic choices regarding the peace process: to promote negotiations among the powerful warlords on the scene or to reach out and encourage the development of civil society—that is, traditional leaders and authorities, religious leaders, professionals, women's organizations, intellectuals, and others. Inevitably, the first route was attractive to American authorities because it was quicker and easier to put into effect. On the downside, it also meant dealing with the very people who had been the source of the breakdown and ending with some kind of pacted arrangement that was likely to be far less democratic than the civil society route. As Ken Menkhaus and Terrence Lyons commented on this dilemma:

> In the initial phase of the U.S. intervention, Ambassador Robert Oakley opted to accept the authority of the two major rival leaders in the capital, Ali Mahdi and [General Mohamed Farah] Aidid. As a tactical move, this was probably unavoidable, because the United States wished to secure the capital without engaging in hostilities with either faction. In the long run, however, the bestowal of such recognition and credibility on political figures with dubious legitimacy in their own community may distort the process of national reconciliation.[51]

The diplomatic process that followed the U.S. military intervention represented a cautious effort to contain the most destructive elements of the conflict—in particular, seizing some of the weapons controlled by the warlords and thereby forcing them into the political arena. Although the American team did mediate some of the local conflicts on their own, such as that between Ali Mahdi and Aidid, the main task of negotiating a national agreement fell to Ethiopian leader Meles Zenawi and the U.N., with the Americans playing a supporting role. In March 1993, the fifteen main factional leaders met in Addis Ababa under U.N. sponsorship. They agreed to establish a transitional national council that would have included the various clan leaders plus three elected representatives (one of whom has to be a woman) from the country's eighteen regions. The council would have served as a legislative body, and it would have set up an independent judiciary as well as provide for the establishment of elected and regional councils.[52] All this appeared to come apart in the ensuing months as violence flared up anew and the U.N. high command declared the provisional framework null and void.[53] In this situation, the clan leaders remain powerful, and the situation on the ground is still highly fluid and uncertain; yet at some point in the future, new efforts will have to be undertaken by external third-party actors to reconcile the clan leaders and to expand the ranks of the ruling coalition.

The Extent of U.S. Leverage

It is now time to see what light the foregoing analysis sheds on the three issues raised at the outset of this chapter. First, as the data on termination of civil wars through mediation suggest, one would have every reason to anticipate that the

American record in facilitating negotiated settlements would be a mixed one. Mediation is essential but not necessarily sufficient for the task of overcoming perceptions of menace and intense internal conflicts. If U.S. indirect mediatory action played a supportive role in Zimbabwe and in the shaky Mozambican, (internal) Angolan, and Rwandan agreements and if U.S. direct mediation in Ethiopia and (the international) Angola-Namibia accords proved largely successful, the record in Sudan, Zaire, and elsewhere attests to the inherent difficulties of such diplomatic initiatives.

Clearly, a great power has an enormous potential capacity to alter the preferences of weaker states through the use of a variety of pressures and incentives. Sanctions applied against South Africa and financial side payments offered to Zimbabwe's nationalist leaders have helped to alter choices. Moreover, in the international negotiations on Angola, Crocker was in a position to exert some influence on South African thinking regarding the urgency of reaching an agreement with its regional adversaries. Not only did he make further moves to implement the sanctions legislation, he also bypassed the South African government to give support to anti-apartheid groups on the scene; in addition, he pointedly lodged no protest when the number of Cuban troops was increased in 1987.[54]

Even though American status and power, used in cooperation with the Soviet Union, contributed to the settlement of a number of regional encounters left over from the days of the Cold War, the windup of great-power confrontations in Africa has created a changed situation. Internal wars are proliferating; yet the great-power dimension is less and less in evidence. The effect of this on American diplomacy is likely to be quite significant in the years ahead. Rather than take the lead in dramatic formal negotiations of the Angolan type, U.S. officials can be expected to engage increasingly in behind-the-scenes contacts with prominent local actors and to work increasingly under the auspices of regional, continental, and global organizations. Such a team effort is likely to prove more effective in preventing and dealing with conflicts in the twenty-first century and to contribute to another U.S. objective: building the capacity of these regional and international organizations "to engage early and effectively."[55]

Complications During the Phase of Extended Negotiations

It should come as no surprise that some of the agreements that have been laboriously worked out through U.S.-brokered or U.S.-backed diplomatic efforts have weakened or dissolved during the implementation stage. After all, implementation is not separate from the negotiation of agreements but part of the larger peacemaking process. Hence, to understand the partial or total breakdown of the Bicesse accords, the various Liberian agreements (prior to August 1993), or the political compromise in Zaire, it is necessary to link negotiations to reach agreements with negotiations aimed at putting them into operation.

In a number of instances, the United States seems better at facilitating peace accords than implementing them. A number of possible explanations for this come to mind, including the legalistic faith that many Americans have in the sanctity of agreements, absorption in the drama of negotiations, impatience with long-term implementation processes, domestic bureaucratic politics, and the costs associated with long-term peace enforcement activities. The most dramatic illustration of this gap between negotiating and administrative concerns thus far is the orchestration of the Bicesse settlement and its tragic aftermath. At the 1991 negotiations at Bicesse, the Angolan government sought to lengthen the period prior to national elections but agreed, at UNITA's insistence, on a Portuguese-recommended compromise of eighteen months. Both sides continued to hold grim perceptions of one another's intentions, but each went ahead with the elections—assuming it would be victorious. With dos Santos receiving 49.57 percent of the presidential vote (and Savimbi 40.6 percent), Savimbi charged electoral fraud and, recognizing the likelihood of defeat in a second round, refused to proceed with the run-off election. Heavy fighting resumed, with UNITA gaining the initiative in the early months.

One aspect that clearly went amiss in Angola was a flawed U.N.-administered transition. With the U.N. trying to resolve conflict on the cheap, it provided too thin a presence on the ground to dissuade Savimbi from defecting. In all, there were only 400 cease-fire monitors in Angola, an insufficient number to assure the disarming of the combatants and to verify that the troops had actually gathered at the prescribed assembly points. Related to this, the integration of the two military forces was incomplete prior to the election, and there were questions over whether the armies would have remained loyal to the new command structure in the event that the civil war flared up again. Finally, there was no means of breaking a deadlock at the meetings of various observer organizations set up to oversee the elections.[56]

This lamentable experience contrasts markedly with that in Namibia in 1989 where the U.N. effectively controlled the transition process, dispatching a total of 4,650 troops to oversee the elections. The U.N. peacekeeping and monitoring operation in Namibia cost $430 million; in Angola, the expenses came to a mere $132 million.[57] It is also important to note that the contending parties in Namibia adopted essentially pragmatic perceptions of one another; indications of this can be seen in the fact that national elections came after agreement on a constitution and that the constitution provided protections for minority interests and dispersed power among the rival parties.[58] It seems apparent that the United States and other international observers have learned the lesson of the Angola administrative failure, for in Mozambique, where the United Nations presides over another transition process following a peace accord, there were plans to send 7,500 monitors (5,500 troops and 2,000 civilians) to enforce the demobilization and disarmament of the combatants and the creation of a unified army prior to the elections.[59]

Diplomatic Options After Negotiations Fail

Finally, where implementation fails, as in Angola, Zaire, and Cambodia, the options open to U.S. and other diplomats are extremely narrow. The third-party actor has limited influence and is reluctant to mobilize the force necessary to keep the situation from spiraling out of control. The call made by some African observers for U.S. military intervention in Zaire may be logical at this juncture,[60] but it is not likely to elicit a positive response from a country that views itself as overburdened with global commitments. In the case of Cambodia, Khmer Rouge leaders, who gave signs of honoring the peace treaty they negotiated in 1991, appeared to be motivated by a desire to be included within the new ruling coalition. Although Chinese influence on Khmer Rouge decisionmakers was not to be discounted, the decisionmakers' own desire to participate in affairs of state likely proved the critical factor.[61]

The limits on the U.S. capacity to influence recalcitrant leaders after the collapse of an agreement are well illustrated by the situation in Angola following Savimbi's resumption of military action after the elections. Savimbi's ability to take the offensive was demonstrated clearly in the year that ensued. His forces were disciplined and well armed and, by all accounts, received additional supplies from South Africa.[62] Yet even the remote Savimbi cannot insulate himself entirely from American and allied pressures. In May 1993, after UNITA rejected a peace plan drawn up by the United States and the U.N. during negotiations in Abidjan (and accepted by the Angolan authorities), the Clinton administration ended old animosities and recognized the Angolan government. At this point, Washington's preferred course would appear to be the dispatch of an envoy to UNITA headquarters where a series of diplomatic pressures could be articulated. The United Nations Security Council, frustrated over UNITA's failure to put a cease-fire in place or to implement the Bicesse accords, voted arms and oil sanctions into effect in September 1993. But what other pressures could the United States bring to bear on Savimbi? Analysts on the scene speak of various possible options at this time, including an appeal to abide by the constitutional rules, a warning that the United States might provide military equipment to the Angolan government, declaring UNITA a terrorist organization, cutting off its satellite telephones, sharing intelligence with the Angolan government, and augmenting Namibia's capacity for air traffic surveillance. The Portuguese and Russians have been calling on the United States to allow a lifting of the ban on weapons sales, thus undercutting the Bicesse accords' provisions on military sales and assistance to either of the rival forces. For the time being, Washington resists this alternative, but if exhortation or appeasement will not bring Savimbi to compromise, then some kind of coercive pressure may be decided upon to force him to comply with the rules of the Bicesse accords.

Conclusion

As a strong third-party intermediary, the United States has made a significant difference in the peaceful settlement of a number of African internal conflicts and civil wars in the Cold War and post–Cold War years. With enormous resources at its disposal, it has facilitated agreements in Namibia, Angola (the international settlement), Zaire, Ethiopia, and Somalia and played an important supporting role in Zimbabwe, Rwanda, Liberia, South Africa, Mozambique, and Angola (the internal accords). In a world caught up by increasing economic scarcity, political factionalism, and national assertiveness and hostility, great-power pressure and efforts to promote conflict management seem likely to remain a necessary, even if not always sufficient, reality on the African scene. In this respect, the Clinton administration gives every indication of continuing to play an activist role in helping to cope with Africa's internal and external conflicts, undertaking confidence-building initiatives as well as engaging actively in efforts of conciliation and mediation.

This chapter has pointed up two main aspects about the changing American policy on dealing with conflict resolution issues in Africa in the post–Cold War period. First, the U.S. approach is currently undergoing a shift from direct to indirect mediatory activity. With the end of the Cold War struggle and the weakening of the superpowers' hegemony over their African allies, the international stakes at play have declined and the complexity of coping with inter- and intra-African disputes has increased noticeably. U.S. urgency over African conflict issues has remained, but the strategic significance that galvanized Americans in earlier periods has declined. As a consequence, the tendency to become directly involved in highly consuming diplomatic initiatives, as in the case of Angola, gradually gave way in the post–Cold War period to a preference for conflict resolution efforts under the auspices of regional and international organizations or friendly powers. In this, the Somali intervention seems something of an exception to the rule; it was taken for humanitarian purposes and involved no critical U.S. national interest. Yet even here, public disappointment over the outcome of the military intervention in that country became evident as the casualties and costs mounted, and little progress seems evident in dealing with the underlying political dimensions of the crisis. The result, therefore, is to encourage the drift toward indirect mediatory efforts, whether consciously or unconsciously.

Second, with the failure of the Bicesse accords to hold up following Angola's national elections, American policymakers are now less inclined to see the negotiation of agreements as representing the end of a highly charged encounter. Increasingly, these diplomats have come to see the implementation (or postagreement peace-building) phase as critical to consolidating the gains made at the bargaining table. For the most part, then, conflict management is now viewed in more inclusive terms, emphasizing the gathering of data; preventive diplomacy; pressure; conciliation, mediation, and arbitration; and the processes of implementation (including unifying the military and demobilization, the monitoring of elections and democratization, the return and resettlement of refugees, and the revival of the economy). The United States cannot be expected to achieve such broad and difficult tasks on its own in post–Cold War times, but success in the peacemaking effort requires that it continue to be actively engaged at every stage.

Notes

This chapter is a revised and updated version of a paper presented at the Fourth Annual East-African American Studies Colloquium, Thika, Kenya, July 19–24, 1993. I wish to express my appreciation to Terrence Lyons, Timothy Sisk, Daniel Volman, John Harbeson, Caroline Hartzell, Khalid Medani, and Edith Rothchild for comments on the first draft of this paper.

1. Francis M. Deng, "Africa and the New World Dis-Order," *The Brookings Review* 11, no. 2 (Spring 1993), p. 34.

2. Tom Farer, "Israel's Unlawful Occupation," *Foreign Policy,* no. 82 (Spring 1991), p. 38. Also see Michael H. Hunt, *Ideology and U.S. Foreign Policy* (New Haven: Yale University Press, 1987).

3. World Bank, *Sub-Saharan Africa: From Crisis to Sustainable Growth* (Washington, D.C.: World Bank, 1989), p. 3.

4. Stephen John Stedman, *Peacemaking in Civil Wars: International Mediation in Zimbabwe, 1974–1980* (Boulder: Lynne Rienner Publishers, 1987), pp. 5–9.

5. Highlighting the intensity of civil wars, Paul Pillar's data indicate that nearly twice as many interstate wars ended with negotiations than did civil wars. See Paul R. Pillar, *Negotiating Peace: War Termination as a Bargaining Process* (Princeton: Princeton University Press, 1983), pp. 5–7.

6. Daniel Frei, "Conditions Affecting the Effectiveness of International Mediation," *Papers of the Peace Science Society* (International), 26 (1976), p. 70.

7. On these variables, see Donald Rothchild and Caroline Hartzell, "The Peace Process in the Sudan, 1971–72," in Roy Licklider, ed., *Stopping the Killing: How Civil Wars End* (New York: New York University Press, 1993), pp. 68–77.

8. I am indebted to Monila Kuchena of the University of Zimbabwe for helpful comments on the impact of these mediation initiatives, Thika, Kenya, July 21, 1993. For other examples, see I. William Zartman, "Testimony to the House Foreign Affairs Africa Subcommittee," March 31, 1993, p. 8 (typescript copy).

9. Ernst B. Haas, "Human Rights: To Act or Not to Act?" in Kenneth Oye, Donald Rothchild, and Robert Lieber, eds., *Eagle Entangled: U.S. Foreign Policy in a Complex World* (New York: Longman, 1979), p. 181.

10. Senate Resolution 94, *Congressional Record—Senate,* vol. 139, no. 46 (April 3, 1993), p. S4508; and House Concurrent Resolution 131, 103d Congress, 1st Sess. (August 3, 1993), pp. 5–6.

11. "Kenya: A Difficult Courtship," *Africa Confidential* 34, no. 20 (October 8, 1993), p. 4.

12. Sir Brian Urquhart, "Traits of Successful Conflict Resolvers," in W. Scott Thompson, James Laue, Brian Urquhart, and Chester A. Crocker, eds., *Dialogues on Conflict Resolution: Bridging Theory and Practice* (Washington, D.C.: U.S. Institute of Peace, 1993), p. 35.

13. For an extended discussion of this, see Donald Rothchild, "Conclusion: Regime

Management in West Africa," in I. William Zartman, ed., *Conflict Resolution in West Africa* (Washington, D.C.: Brookings Institution, forthcoming).

14. "The Kampala Document: Towards a Conference on Security, Stability, Development and Cooperation in Africa," in Olusegun Obasanjo and Felix G.N. Mosha, eds., *Africa: Rise to Challenge* (New York: Africa Leadership Forum, 1993), pp. 312–313.

15. Donald Rothchild, "Africa's Ethnic Conflicts and Their Implications for United States Policy," in Robert I. Rotberg, ed., *Africa in the 1990s and Beyond: U.S. Policy Opportunities and Choices* (Algonac, Mich.: Reference Publications, 1988), pp. 277–278.

16. Chester A. Crocker, *High Noon in Southern Africa* (New York: W.W. Norton, 1992), p. 262.

17. *Foreign Broadcast Information Service (FBIS)*, Sub-Saharan Africa, vol. 92, no. 238 (December 10, 1992), p. 20, and Donald Rothchild and John Ravenhill, "Retreat from Globalism: U.S. Policy in the 1990s," in Kenneth A. Oye, Robert J. Lieber, and Donald Rothchild, eds., *Eagle in a New World* (New York: HarperCollins, 1992), p. 399.

18. Herman J. Cohen, "South Africa: The Current Situation," *U.S. Department of State Dispatch* 3, no. 30 (July 27, 1992), pp. 587–588.

19. *The (Johannesburg) Citizen,* October 14, 1992, p. 6, as reprinted in *FBIS* 92, no. 201 (October 16, 1992), p. 8.

20. Bill Clinton, "A Democrat Lays Out His Plan: A New Covenant for American Security," *Harvard International Review* (Summer 1992), p. 62.

21. Marina Ottaway, *South Africa: The Struggle for a New Order* (Washington, D.C.: Brookings Institution, 1993), p. 211.

22. *FBIS* 92, no. 157 (August 13, 1992), p. 11.

23. Jeffrey Davidow, *A Peace in Southern Africa* (Boulder: Westview Press, 1984), p. 117.

24. See Donald Rothchild and Caroline Hartzell, "The Case of Angola: Four Power Intervention and Disengagement," in Ariel E. Levite, Bruce W. Jentleson, and Larry Berman, eds., *Foreign Military Intervention* (New York: Columbia University Press, 1992), pp. 163–207.

25. Telegram from Secretary of State to All African Diplomatic Posts, April 14, 1984, p. 3 (National Security Archive).

26. Memorandum for the Secretary of Defense Through the Under Secretary of Defense for Policy, September 19, 1985, p. 1 (National Security Archive).

27. Confidential interview conducted by the author, Nairobi, March 1, 1991, and Witney W. Schneidman, "Conflict Resolution in Mozambique: A Status Report," *CSIS Africa Notes,* no. 121 (February 28, 1991), p. 6.

28. "Testimony by Assistant Secretary of State for African Affairs, Mr. Herman J. Cohen, Before the House Foreign Affairs Subcommittee on Africa," October 8, 1992, p. 4 (typescript copy).

29. Ibid., p. 7.

30. *Africa Confidential* 34, no. 10 (May 14, 1993), p. 4.

31. *Africa Confidential* 30, no. 17 (August 25, 1989), p. 3.

32. Terrence Lyons, "Great Powers and Conflict Reduction in the Horn of Africa," in I. William Zartman, ed., *Cooperative Security: Reducing Third World Wars* (Syracuse, N.Y.: Syracuse University Press, forthcoming), ms. p. 16.

33. Terrence Lyons, "The Transition in Ethiopia," *CSIS Africa Notes,* no. 127 (August 27, 1991), p. 5.

34. Lyons, "Great Powers and Conflict Reduction," ms. p. 22.

35. U.S. Department of State, Bureau of Public Affairs, "The U.S. and Sudan: Peace and

Relief" (Washington, D.C.: Department of State, February 1989), pp. 1–3. Senator Edward Kennedy endorsed this initiative on the same day. See *Congressional Record—Senate,* vol. 135, no. 13 (February 8, 1989), p. S1296.

36. Colin Legum, "Horn of Africa: Super-Powers' Cautious New Initiative," *Third World Reports,* L.F/2 (February 8, 1989), p. 1.

37. For an excellent analysis of this international relief effort, see Francis M. Deng and Larry Minear, *The Challenges of Famine Relief* (Washington, D.C.: Brookings Institution, 1992), chap. 3.

38. Eddie Becker and Christopher Mitchell, *Chronology of Conflict Resolution Initiatives in Sudan* (Fairfax, Va.: George Mason University, Institute for Conflict Analysis and Resolution, 1991), pp. 111–112.

39. Author's interview with Herman J. Cohen, Washington, D.C., June 13, 1993.

40. Becker and Mitchell, *Chronology,* p. 139.

41. Author's interviews with Bona Malwal and Francis M. Deng, Washington, D.C., May 5, 1993.

42. Bona Malwal, "Breathing New Life into the American Initiative?" *Sudan Democratic Gazette,* no. 14 (July 1991), p. 4–5.

43. An exception here was the initiative taken on October 21, 1993 by Congressman Harry Johnston, the chairman of the House Africa Subcommittee of the U.S. Congress, to facilitate an accord between the two main southern factions (the SPLM/SPLA and the SPLM-United), culminating in the Washington Declaration. In this document, the two southern guerrilla factions agreed to the right of self-determination for the people of southern Sudan, the Nuba mountains, and other marginalized areas; an immediate ceasefire between these southern factions; and an agenda for peace and reconciliation. See *Sudan Democratic Gazette,* no. 42 (November 1993), p. 3.

44. Georges Nzongola-Ntalaja, "The Zairian Tragedy: A Challenge for the Clinton Administration," *Africa Demos* 3, no. 1 (February 1993), p. 9.

45. Gillian Gunn, "A Guide to the Intricacies of the Angola-Namibia Negotiations," *CSIS Africa Notes,* no. 90 (September 8, 1988), p. 12.

46. Rothchild and Hartzell, "The Case of Angola," p. 185, and Michael McFaul, "The Demise of the World Revolutionary Process: Soviet-Angolan Relations Under Gorbachev," *Journal of Southern African Studies* 16 (1990), pp. 182–183.

47. Crocker, *High Noon,* p. 397.

48. "United States: A New Man in Africa," *Africa Confidential* 34, no. 8 (April 16, 1993), p. 3.

49. Raymond W. Copson and Theodros S. Dagne, *Somalia: Operation Restore Hope* (Washington, D.C.: Congressional Research Service, January 19, 1993), p. 1.

50. See Hussein M. Adam, "Somalia: Militarism, Warlordism or Democracy?" *Review of African Political Economy,* no. 54 (1992), p. 18, and Rakiya Omaar, "Somalia: At War with Itself," *Current History* 91, no. 565 (May 1992), p. 233.

51. Ken Menkhaus and Terrence Lyons, "What Are the Lessons to Be Learned from Somalia?" *CSIS Africa Notes,* no. 144 (January 1993), p. 7.

52. *FBIS* 93, no. 058 (March 29, 1993), p. 1. On this, I have also benefited from discussions with Professor Abdi I. Samatar, University of California at Berkeley, April 24, 1993.

53. Abdullah A. Mohamoud, "Somalia: The Futility of Peace Talks," *West Africa* (June 28–July 4, 1993), p. 1112.

54. Donald Rothchild, "Conflict Management in Angola," *TransAfrica Forum* 8, no. 1 (Spring 1991), p. 97.

55. Tony Lake, "Remarks," delivered at the Brookings Africa Forum Luncheon, May 3, 1993 (Internet copy).

56. "An Exit Interview with 'Hank' Cohen," *CSIS Africa Notes*, no. 147 (April 1993), p. 5.

57. "Angola: The Toothless Watchdogs," *Africa Confidential* 34, no. 5 (March 5, 1993), p. 1.

58. Robert S. Jaster, "The 1988 Peace Accords and the Future of South-western Africa," *Adelphi Papers*, no. 253 (Autumn 1990), p. 35.

59. Andrew Meldrum, "Lessons from Angola," *Africa Report* 38, no. 1 (January–February 1993), p. 24.

60. Danson P.L. Esese, "The U.S. Economic Aid Policy in Post–Cold War Africa: A Case Study of Zaire, 1960 to the present," paper presented at the Fourth Annual East-African American Studies Colloquium, Thika, Kenya, July 19–24, 1993, p. 18.

61. Elizabeth Becker, "Showdown with the Khmer Rouge," *Washington Post*, November 8, 1992, p. C7.

62. "Angolan War Spawns Complex Web of Profiteers," *AfricaNews* 38, no. 5 (April 5–18, 1993), p. 5.

11

Inter-African Negotiation

I. WILLIAM ZARTMAN

IN INTER-AFRICAN RELATIONS, two is a conflict, three is company, and fifty-one is a crowd of free riders. African negotiations over conflict and cooperation are a highly developed exercise, with their own characteristics and patterns, strengths and limitations. In terms of outcomes, bilateral negotiations and broad multilateral negotiations tend to be ineffective in dealing with conflict; in between, mediation is frequently needed to bring negotiations among conflicting parties to fruition. In cooperation, multilateral negotiations have a high record of success, although the impact of the product has its own limitations and characteristics. In this chapter, I will present the characteristics of that process as practiced in Africa, give examples, and seek explanations for those characteristics.

In assessing these results and in analyzing the process by which they are achieved, one should remember that conflict is an inevitable—and sometimes a functional or even desirable—condition of interstate relations and that negotiation is a means of limiting it. Cooperation—although desirable and sometimes functional—is by no means inevitable, and negotiation is the means of achieving it. As a result, the playing field has different slopes according to the subject, imparting different types of difficulties to the negotiation process. Across this distinction runs another, related to the size of the teams. At one end of a spectrum stand conflicts and cooperations that are highly personalized in the head of state, with little interest and involvement by society; at the other are conflicts and cooperations that are national causes, affecting society deeply and arousing deep popular sentiments.[1] This dichotomy has its impact on negotiations, although the distinction is not as sharp as might be expected. Personalist leaders speak in the name of their societies and mobilize societal interest behind their positions; yet states and societies do not negotiate—only people do.

Bilateral Conflict Negotiations

Direct bilateral negotiations are not an effective way of ending conflict in Africa. Nor are large-scale multilateral negotiations in regional or subregional organizations, although these organizations do play an important role in setting the norms and pa-rameters for terminating conflicts—either by victory or by reconciliation. It is "tri-lateral" or mediated bilateral negotiations that are most effective.[2]

Four reasons for this suggest themselves. First, because of the engrossing na-ture of African conflict and its often functional aspect, African states or leaders in conflict are so taken up with the unilateral pursuit of the dispute that they are unable to conceive of bi- or multilateral solutions on their own; they need help. Whether the conflict is a personal dispute between heads of state or the result of a societal feeling of personal right or of neighboring hostility, it becomes an emo-tional and political cause of high importance, leaving little leeway for creative thinking on alternative solutions; this characteristic is reinforced by the small size of foreign policy establishments, by the absence of a loyal opposition and of pub-lic political debate, and by the personal engagement of the head of state in for-eign disputes.

Second, until the 1990s, African conflicts sparked a competitive race for allies, first within the continent and then outside. Bilateral conflicts generally did not remain bilateral but engaged factions within the continent initially and then Eu-ropean powers and superpowers. This characteristic both prevents bilateral set-tlements and, paradoxically, facilitates mediation. The search for allies can be turned into an invitation to mediation when the level of assistance sought finds a foreign policy opportunity in reconciliation rather than reinforcement. Since the end of the Cold War, the possibility of finding allies within the superpower com-petition has vanished, and with it, the interest in allying with conflicting parties seems to have evaporated as a dominant characteristic. Although this may not be a lasting feature, the disinterest in taking sides in a conflict is paralleled by a low-ered interest and leverage in mediating as well.

Third, there is usually little incentive for African states to reduce, let along re-solve, their conflicts and little pressure to push them to bilateral accommodation. Conflicts, as noted, are popular and useful, particularly when kept at a low, less costly level; they can then be revived at any time for purposes of national gain and national unity. Somalia's, Libya's, and Morocco's long-held irredentist claims on their neighbors are extreme cases in point, but so are the various border dis-putes, structural rivalries, and recurrent involvements in neighboring politics that make up much of African conflict.[3]

Few unmediated bilateral negotiations had any significant effect on the con-flict. A few examples illustrate the problems. The border dispute that has trou-bled relations between Morocco and Algeria since their independence was ini-tially and occasionally the subject of direct negotiations. As early as the three first years of the 1960s, the Moroccan kings met with the presidents of the Provisional Government of the Algerian Republic (GPRA) to discuss that problem, among others; when independence came to Algeria in 1962, the agreements to settle the problem between sovereign states were pushed aside since they were unwitnessed and were considered nonbinding.[4] Instead, war broke out, and the dispute was taken up by the newly created Organization for African Unity. After further mediation, King Hassan II and President Ahmed Ben Bella met at Saidia in April 1965 and renewed the GPRA's commitment. Ben Bella was overthrown by his army three months later, with the Saidia agreement cited as one of the specific grievances.[5]

Once again, the OAU provided the framework for a reconciliation between King Hassan and the new Algerian ruler, Colonel Houari Boumedienne, in 1968—leading to bilateral summits in the following two years and then a final border treaty, again in the context of the OAU. The implementation of the Rabat border agreement of 1972 was interrupted by the eruption of the Western Saharan issue, which destroyed all chances of an effective bilateral negotiation. As the war continued beyond initial expectations of duration, moving toward an apparent stalemate and division of the territory, preparations began for a bilateral summit at the end of 1978.[6] Boumedienne's death canceled these plans; Hassan expected the new president to be more flexible, but the new president, Colonel Chadli BenJedid, had to consolidate his own position before any of his purported flexibility could be shown.

It took another five years and a new stalemate more favorable to Morocco— with many intervening failed mediations—to produce a bilateral summit in February 1983. Despite high hopes and an agreement, the mutual understanding fell apart almost immediately, specifically because there was no third party present to "hold the bets" and witness the agreement. Instead, each party soon felt betrayed by the other. A second summit was held in May 1987 under the auspices of Saudi King Fahd, followed by multilateral summit meetings a year later in Algiers among the Arab heads of state and then in February 1989 in Marrakesh to inaugurate the regional Arab Maghreb Union (UMA). Whatever agreements have emerged from these meetings have shown the necessity of witnesses and active mediation. The lesson from this lengthy conflict, still unended, is not that mediated and trilateral negotiations are ipso facto assured of success, but that bilateral negotiation is ipso facto assured of failure. As in other cases, the presence of one or more third parties to "midwife" and witness an agreement is a necessary but not sufficient condition of success.

There are many other examples in the negative. Conflicts between Angola and Zaire, Somalia and Ethiopia, Sudan and Ethiopia, Mali and Burkina Faso, Senegal and Mauritania, among others, were not settled by bilateral summits; when settlement or progress toward settlement was made, it was in meetings that included other parties in addition to the principals. Even in internal wars, which, in principle, are particularly difficult to mediate, settlements, when reached, have been the result of third-party assistance, as in Rwanda in 1993, Angola in 1990, Mozambique in 1992, Liberia between 1991 and 1994, Ethiopia in 1991, Somalia in 1992 and 1993 (and thereafter), and so on.[7] Since bilateral failure is so pervasive, it is pointless to look for other necessary ingredients. Instead, it is vital to turn to mediation to find out what else is necessary to make that condition sufficient.

Mediation

Africa does not lack mediators. Whether from a continental cultural tradition or from a conscious interest in maintaining the African state system,[8] African heads of state do more than stand ready to be of assistance—they rush in in numbers, often competing to bring good and even better offices to the resolution of their colleagues' conflicts, to the point where there is a confusion of marriage counselors trying to restore domestic tranquility in the African family. At least, this profusion of mediators permits some conclusions on the characteristics of success—contextual, tactical, and personal.[9]

Mediators pursue their own interests in their activities;[10] African mediators have an overriding interest in preserving the African state system and hence maintaining acceptance of the status quo. They therefore also have a framework within which to seek to place their mediated resolutions, reinforcing their efforts and facilitating acceptance of them.[11]

African mediators tend to come from neighboring states—from the same subregion, if not from contiguous states; indeed, contiguous states often have enough problems of their own with their immediate neighbor to be disqualified or at least handicapped in mediation. There is one major exception: When the conflict is an internal dispute between a government and an insurgency in which a neighboring state serves as the insurgents' sanctuary, the neighbor can be a useful mediator if it "delivers" the agreement of the insurgents.[12] Mediators also tend to come from states of the same colonial background as the disputants when both of the conflicting parties are French- or English-speaking, illustrating the importance both of personal political ties and of communications.

Mediation is a personal affair, conducted by African heads of state with other heads of state. It does not lend itself to practice by lesser officials—a point that is crucial in understanding the stillbirth of the OAU Commission of Mediation, Arbitration and Conciliation, which mandated respected jurists and civil servants but not current or former heads of state.[13] There are three roles available to the mediator—communicator, formulator, manipulator; African heads of state operate primarily in the first two, overcoming obstacles to communications between the conflicting parties and helping them find and formulate mutually acceptable ways out of their conflict. As such, an adjunct function of the personal mediator is to reduce the aspects of risk and mistrust that impede the parties' agreement to reconciliation. Since the conflict not only bears on the issue at hand but also colors the whole tone of relations between the disputants, these parties do not trust each other's word and do not know how much risk is involved in their agreement; the mediator becomes the agent of trust and the assessor of risk.

The condition for effective mediation is the hurting stalemate, which makes it possible for the mediator to be welcomed in his or her offer of a way out.[14] Both aspects are necessary, and neither alone is sufficient: The stalemate makes the mediation possible; the mediator makes the stalemate fruitful. As a result of these characteristics, the African mediator's primary weapon is persuasion, which rein-forces the personal nature of the task. The mediators' main leverage is their abil-ity to help their compatriots out of the bind into which their conflict has led them. Unfortunately, there are not enough studies of the actual mediatory ex-changes among heads of state to permit a detailed analysis, but all available evi-dence indicates it is an exercise in pure persuasion.[15]

There are a few exceptions, none of them very clear due to the nature of the subject. King Fahd, host of the 1987 summit between King Hassan and President BenJedid, was operating as Morocco's past funding source and Algeria's potential funding source of the future, whether specific financial arrangements were men-tioned or not.[16] When the World Council of Churches moved the government of Sudan and the Southern Sudanese Liberation Movement (SSLM) toward Addis Ababa, where an agreement to end the war was eventually signed, it threatened, on occasion, to withdraw from mediation and resume humanitarian supplies to the SSLM if its efforts were rejected.[17] President Samora Machel of Mozambique, who served as one of the several mediators in the Lancaster House negotiations in 1979 leading to Zimbabwean independence, threatened to close down the Pa-triotic Front's bases in Mozambique if its leader, Robert Mugabe, did not go along with the setlement being negotiated.[18] Similarly, the Frontline States, particularly Angola, threatened the SouthWest African People's Organization (SWAPO) with loss of support and sanctuary if it did not stay in the Namibian negotiations.[19] There may be other examples. Added together, they indicate that, rarely, promises of side payments and, more frequently, threats to withdraw from mediation are used but that mediation in Africa is essentially persuasion. Most participants in African conflicts are independent enough of neighbors' support and sure enough of alternatives to be invulnerable to threats and brides.

Some cases have already been mentioned. The three successful moments of agreement between Algeria and Morocco—whatever the problems of renewed conflict new events would bring later on—were the result of mediation, either third-party or institutional. The war of 1963 was ended through the good offices of Emperor Haile Selassie and Malian President Modibo Keita; the border treaty of 1972 was prepared by the mediation of Tunisian President Habib Bourguiba and then by the context of the OAU summit of 1968 when King Hassan made his first trip to Algiers; the agreement to set aside the Saharan conflict, proceed with Maghreb unity without a Saharan participant, and resolve the dispute by a refer-endum on terms favorable to Morocco came out of the border summit of 1987 chaired by King Fahd. The recurrent Mali-Burkinabe (Voltaic) border dispute was mediated by an OAU ad hoc commission composed of French-speaking states of the region, bringing a cease-fire in July 1975, and again by a series of mediators—Libya and Algeria, who failed at the end of 1985, and then Senegal and Ivory Coast within the framework of the French-speaking West African Eco-nomic Community, who succeeded in January 1986.

Mediators also abounded in the Horn of Africa, until conflict overtook the states themselves in the 1990s and defied all attempts to bring the conflict under control. President Ibrahim Abboud of Sudan stepped into the 1963–1964 border war between Somalia and Ethiopia to being about a cease-fire and other conflict management measures. President Julius Nyerere of Tanzania attempted the same in the "bandit" war between Somalia and Kenya the following year but was hindered by his approach and his own problems with Kenya; he was succeeded by President Kenneth Kaunda of Zambia in 1967–1968, who was able to get the parties talking as a new stalemate weighed in on them. When the conflict management arrangements the disputants had agreed to failed to produce the next step, Somalia invaded Ethiopia. No one was able to mediate, although the United States did successfully press the Soviet Union to guarantee that Ethiopia would not cross the border as it threw back the Somali invaders in 1978. Eight years later, Somalia offered a new round of conflict management measures; Djibouti, the host of the Inter-Governmental Agency on Drought and Development (IGADD), and the IGADD secretariat served as mediators to bring the two heads of state together in January 1968 and finally, in April 1988, win Ethiopian agreement to the proposals.[20] Ironically, the withdrawal of Ethiopian support and control of Somali rebels left them free to overthrow their own government in 1990, just as the Ethiopian government fell to its own ethnic rebellions.

In internal conflicts—increasingly the predominant type of African conflict—the key to effective mediation seems to be the ability to guarantee fair treatment and a share in the new political system for all parties, rather than any tangible side payments. In Liberia, first the Liberian Council of Churches and then fellow members of the Economic Community of West African States tried again and again in 1990 and 1991 to mediate a cease-fire that would last between the factions, coming closest to an agreement in July 1993 when the mediation was taken over by the OAU special envoy, former Zimbabwean President Canaan Banana, who was able to add military contingents from outside the area to ECOMOG. Another three-year civil war, in Rwanda, was brought to a mediated agreement in August 1993—temporarily—under the auspices of the OAU and Tanzania, made possible by the introduction of a U.N. peacekeeping force.

However, in internal as in interstate conflicts, the necessary condition is still the mutual hurting stalemate, without which the parties have no interest in being saved from their conflict by meddling outsiders. The war in southern Sudan was successfully ended following a stalemate in 1972 by layers of mediation, beginning with the efforts of the World Council of Churches and the All-African Council of Churches, backed by the assistant secretary-general of the OAU, Mohammed Sahnoun; Emperor Haile Selassie acted as the mediator of last resort at a crucial juncture.[21] When the Addis Ababa agreement was dismantled by its author, President Jaafar Numeiri, ten years later and war broke out again, mediation became more difficult—first because of the active support of the new Marxist government of Ethiopia behind the Sudan People's Liberation Movement/Sudan People's Liberation Army (SPLM/SPLA) and then, after 1989, because the SPLM/SPLA lost its support when the Ethiopian government fell and the northern Sudanese government became intransigent when replaced by a Muslim fundamentalist military junta. The shift in fortunes blocked mediated resolution throughout the 1980s and into the 1990s. Many mediators tried to resolve the conflict, but none succeeded. The same judgment bears on the Eritrean conflict, which resisted repeated attempts at mediation throughout its thirty-year history until the Ethiopian government was finally overthrown.[22]

Elsewhere, an interesting set of mediations was conducted by the current OAU presidents as well as by the presidents of Togo and Nigeria and, later, a large number of African heads of state in the war in Chad. These occurred both during the period of General Felix Malloum, leading to the establishment of the Transitional Government of National Unity (GUNT) under Goukouni Weddei, and then after the final takeover by Hissene Habré, leading to the return of nearly all the former dissidents into the new government fold.[23]

The cases of mediation are many, but it is difficult to sort out all the reasons why some have failed. In general, failed attempts did not benefit from the conditions and tactics that caused success—effective perception of stalemate by all parties, skillful persuasion by the mediator, convincing formula for a way out that is at least minimally satisfactory to all. At best, one can conclude that the mediator can pull an agreement on a salient solution out of a propitious context—that is, accomplish a negotiation that overcommitment to the conflict prevents the parties from doing by themselves—but he or she cannot create a ripe moment and a winning solution out of thin air among peers, in Africa or anywhere else.

Multilateral Conflict Negotiation

The OAU has been the major multilateral African forum for conducting negotiations to deal with conflict,[24] although it has also been joined, on occasion, by subregional organizations, such as IGADD, ECOWAS, and CEAO. Very often, the latter type of organization was not created for conflict reduction at all but rather provided a ready forum where heads of state could meet for other reasons and work out differences in the corridors; conflict reduction became a necessary precondition for carrying out their other business. Two different functions need to be distinguished: One is the role of ad hoc multilateral committees established to deal with specific conflicts, and the other is the role of the plenary of summit meetings of the multilateral fora themselves.

There is no need to spend time on the major African committee envisaged to reduce conflict among African states—the Commission for Mediation, Arbitration and Conciliation. Indicated by the OAU Charter, it never came into existence since it conflicted with the rapidly established characteristics of inter-African relations as being the domain of heads of state. Instead, the OAU appointed ad hoc committees to deal with conflicts as they arose on the summit agenda, with membership carefully allocated to language, ideological, regional, experience, and other interest groups. Their record was not good—success in one out of three cases in some two dozen instances in the first two decades of the organization.[25] In addition, many of the successes were only temporary, with the conflict breaking out in another form later on (and requiring a new committee). On the other hand, batting .333 may not be a bad average when the circumstances are considered. Very often, conditions were not propitious, and more frequently still, the purposes of the mother organization were something other than conflict resolution—as will be discussed—and they therefore overrode the efforts of the committee. In addition, in a few more cases, conflict management—the reduction of the means of conflict rather than the settlement of basic issues—was the outcome of committee efforts. Unfortunately, it is impossible to calculate a similar batting average for private efforts at mediation to see whether OAU committees did better than individual heads of state.

Committee mediation has been a more important function of the OAU than its record might indicate, however. It did overcome one major defect of private mediation in that it provided coordination where private efforts often competed among themselves. This competition then allowed the parties to the conflict to sit by and wait for better terms to come along in the hands of other private mediators. In OAU committees, many of the members were passive, overlooking and legitimizing the activities of the few members who did the active mediation. Furthermore, OAU committees were constrained by the guidelines of the organization and its summits; they could not seek just any terms for agreement, for they were at the same time the standard-bearers of OAU principles. That dual role sometimes made it impossible to find terms of agreement to which both sides could subscribe. It is difficult to fault either the OAU committees or the private mediators in such conflicts as the Somali-Ethiopian dispute or the Western Sahara; the two contestants' positions were simply irreconcilable, and resolution had to await a change in the cost of holding out for one or both that would then soften their positions.

Thus, an OAU committee was named to mediate the Somali-Ethiopian border problem at the 1973 summit, and when it failed, another was named at the 1976 summit. As they operated under the 1964 OAU resolution affirming the sanctity of colonial boundaries, they had little leeway to meet Somalia's grievances; instead, they reaffirmed the principle. But an OAU committee extracted a promise (false, as it turned out) from Ghana not to practice subversion against the Ivory Coast, Upper Volta, and Niger in 1965, in accordance with OAU Charter principles, and another intervened to free Guineans held in Ghana on the way to the OAU summit the following year. In such cases, OAU committees, acting within charter principles, made it possible for transgressing states to return to behavioral norms without loss of face, a task for which multimembered OAU committees were even better suited than private mediators.

In these situations, risk, trust, persuasion, and stalemate are the common ingredients of success. The actual negotiations are accomplished by skillfully luring the erring parties back from the limbs on which they have crawled, while the mediator gives assurances on risk and trust and provides an atmosphere of unity and fraternity that prevents another party from crowing. Since the conflicting parties have no dispute with the mediator, it becomes difficult for them to refuse his or her assurances and reject the atmospherics.

The OAU itself, in its biennial ministerial and annual presidential meetings, is not a conflict resolution mechanism. It provides corridors and committees that operate as described and principles that provide guidelines for solutions. But a body of more than fifty members is not a mechanism for resolving disputes. If it does come to the point of decreeing a solution, either the conflict or a good deal of negotiation has already taken place, thereby making the solution acceptable; otherwise, the conflict goes on. This has been the fate of the major conflicts that have torn the OAU apart—the second Congo crisis, Biafra, the dialogue with South Africa, Sahara, Chad.

Yet in the OAU's handling of each of these conflicts, there has been some important and even skillful negotiation. A prime example that shows the possibilities of negotiation within the organization versus the political stance of its summits is the Sahara. The OAU revived the 1964–1967 committee to investigate the causes of the Saharan war as a committee of wisemen to resolve the Western Saharan issue in 1978. The committee was diligent and creative in trying to bridge the positions of Algeria and Morocco. Then, at the 1981 summit, under pressure from an impending recognition of the Sahrawi Arab Democratic Republic (SADR), Morocco agreed to a referendum and the wisemen were transformed into an implementation committee of the OAU. The committee met three times and, by painstaking negotiation with the parties, essentially established guidelines for a referendum that were still in place as the parties moved toward a vote under U.N. auspices a decade later; at the same time, the committee held back the efforts of various parties at various times to undo previous aspects of the evolving agreement. However, at the close of the third meeting ("Nairobi III" in February 1982), the OAU Council of Ministers disavowed its committee by admitting the SADR to membership; curiously, the heads of state on the committee did not have the commitment to put their decisions into effect nonetheless.

Other cases of OAU negotiations show similar characteristics. The work of the non-OAU committee on Chad meeting in Kano and Lagos in 1979, which set up the GUNT, was followed by an OAU committee on Chad and then the 1981 summit in Nairobi. Intense negotiations produced a plan for a multinational peacekeeping force and a timetable for negotiations between the Chadian factions, elections, and the withdrawal of the African troops.[26] Yet for all its coherence, the plan was unreal: Funding, mission, sanctions, and contingency plans were not provided. Some skillful negotiations bringing the conflicting parties close to agreement were undercut by the lack of political commitment within the OAU to carrying the project to fruition.

Thus, the OAU summit—as distinguished from its committees—plays a number of roles in regard to conflict negotiations. It sets principles, appoints committees, and provides a forum and corridors, but because of its own political divisions and the fear of offending other heads of state, it has been unable to take forthright positions of reconciliation in African disputes. The 1989 summit assiduously avoided the bitter dispute between Senegal and Mauritania; earlier summits were unable to follow through with their own conflict management and resolution mechanisms in the Saharan and Chadian conflicts.

Under criticism for its inability to rid Africa of its recurrent and intermittent conflicts, particularly as expressed in the articulate and visionary call for the Conference on Security, Stability, Development and Cooperation in Africa launched by former Nigerian President Olesegun Obasanjo in Kampala in May 1991,[27] the OAU voted in its 1993 summit to create a new division of the secretariat on conflict prevention, management, and resolution.[28] The Kampala Document also called for the constitution of a Council of Elders—former heads of state who could serve as mediators and peacemakers. Former Presidents Leopold Senghor of Senegal, Julius Nyerere of Tanzania, Aristide Pereira of Cape Verde, and Obasanjo volunteered their services, but the OAU did not adopt the proposal, preferring its own ad hoc elders. The organization also undertook a more proactive role in preventive as well as resolving mediation, eliciting invitations to provide good-office missions in Togo, Congo, Rwanda, and Liberia to both forestall and end violence. In so doing, the African universal organization took a major step toward formalizing its personal and ad hoc efforts to reduce conflict and facilitate negotiation among—and within—its members.

Negotiation for Cooperation

Negotiation means overcoming conflict with agreement, but many negotiations lead to agreement on new cooperation rather than simply the end of old conflict. All the regional and subregional organizations in Africa, including the OAU itself, were established through negotiation, and a major multilateral set of cooperation agreements of the postwar world—the Yaoundé series and then the Lomé series between the European Communities and African and other states—also involved repeated negotiations on the African side.[29] As in conflict negotiations, there is little that is uniquely or specifically African in these experiences, but at the same time, it is clear that African diplomats are negotiating and are developing a broad experience that, when successfully used, underscores some important universal lessons and characteristics of the process.

In African multilateral negotiations for cooperation, as in multilateral negotiations over conflict, the political purposes of the negotiating session override the technical commitments of the negotiated outcome. Indeed, cooperative negotiations can be divided into diplomatic and integrative cooperation; in the former, it is the declaration of the moment, attendance at the meeting, announcement of an intent to join or not to join that matters, whereas in the latter, it is the long-term engagement that is important. In the first case, the substance of the negotiations is needed as an occasion or a cover for the diplomatic event of the moment, but its coherence, feasibility, and reality are less important. In the second, the substance *is* the event, and parties do not leave the table before they have agreed to something that will work.

In 1968, for example, Zaire negotiated an Economic Union of Central Africa

(UEAC) to win the Central African Republic and Chad away from the Customs Union of the Central African States of former French Equatorial Africa, including the rival state of Congo. The goal was a diplomatic event in which the important matter was to see who would attend "Mobutu's party"; the substance of the economic "union" was secondary, and the negotiators did not waste time over its details. When the CAR left UEAC to return to UDEAC, the remaining members were not even contiguous. Although this is a particularly striking example, it is typical of a large number of cooperative negotiations, and it is a consideration even in those cases where integrative cooperation is also present.[30]

In the substance of cooperation, the technical expertise often comes from outside, since African states' technical resources are sometimes limited. The Mano River Union of Liberia, Sierra Leone, and Guinea was based on a 1972–1973 United Nations Development Program mission report, and the subregional economic organizations—ECOWAS, the Preferential Trade Area (PTA) of east and central Africa, and the Economic Union of the States of Central Africa (CEEAC)—were based on studies of the Economic Commission for Africa.[31] The fact that the Mano River Union as well as CEAO conflicted with provisions of ECOWAS, negotiated with the same members and others at about the same time, was an instance of political decision bypassing the technical engagements. In the case of African negotiations with the EC, the external source of expertise has particularly difficult implications for Africa. European states are able to coordinate their political and technical diplomacy into an agreed proposal for aid and other aspects of their relationship with associated African states under the Yaoundé Conventions and with the African, Caribbean, and Pacific states under the subsequent Lomé Conventions that can be presented as a take-it-or-leave-it offer.[32] Only in 1975, in the negotiation of the first Lomé Convention, did the African states develop enough solidarity among themselves, with the political clout of Nigerian leadership, and coordinate their own technical and political inputs to be able to make their own proposals as a basis for discussion and finally for agreement.[33]

At the same time, when the two inputs operate together, they play a crucial role in African negotiations for cooperation, and the fact that some states effectively integrate political and technical components of their diplomacy while others do not gives the former a clear edge in specific negotiations. A country that provides a proposed text has a clear edge over the others, and African cooperative negotiations frequently proceed on the basis of a single negotiating text. The case of the Lomé I negotiations and the examples of the external proposals for subregional economic communities are echoed on the intra-African level by a case such as the Arab Maghreb Union negotiated at Marrakech in 1989. Morocco and Algeria had minimalist and diplomatic notions of cooperation, and Libya and Mauritania were less precise in their expectations. But Tunisia came with a well-prepared draft that served as the basis of the agreement. (At an earlier time of bilateral cooperation, it was Libya that came to Jerba with a political draft for a union in 1974, which Tunisia signed but then repudiated on closer examination.) The same characteristic marked the negotiation of the OAU itself in Addis Ababa in 1963, when Ethiopia proposed its own draft, elaborated by experts on the basis of the Rio Treaty of the Organization of American States in conjunction with the Monrovia-Lagos Group of African states; in this case, the similar Ethiopia and Monrovia-Lagos texts were confronted by a very different draft for a tighter union proposed by the Casablanca Group of African States that provided an alternative that could be rejected as individual provisions were selected.[34]

Once the single negotiating text is in hand, African multilateral diplomacy generally proceeds, in a classical fashion, by amendment and consolidation. Amendment involves the addition of proposals not contained in the main draft. An example is Tunisia's detailed proposal for the Commission for Mediation, Arbitration and Conciliation added to the OAU Charter at Addis Ababa. The degree to which additional proposals are integrated into the main proposal is an indicator of the primacy of integrating over simply diplomatic cooperation involved in the negotiations. Consolidation is often more characteristic, referring to a watering down of proposals to the lowest common denominator in order to achieve the necessary consensus. Since consensus rather than coherence is required for diplomatic cooperation, consolidation by watering down is a frequent characteristic. It is also a common feature in the negotiation of OAU resolutions.

In multilateral cooperative negotiations, African state representatives behave as other negotiating parties do but with some characteristics exhibited more strongly than others. The main emphasis in this analysis has been on the distinction between diplomatic and integrative cooperation, and the history of resulting regional and subregional organizations of cooperation bear out the point. Yet such organizations do exist, even if inefficacy is often the price paid for their continued existence. More strikingly, when they die, they have to be reinvented, as the experiences of north, west, east, central, and southern Africa all show. Their creation, maintenance, and reinvention all take negotiation, whether of the diplomatic or of the integrative kind.

Conclusions

African states are becoming increasingly experienced in negotiation, and their negotiators often err through being overly accommodating rather than overly intransigent. They know better how to make a deal than how to keep one. Negotiators are more successful in dampening or managing the current rounds of conflict or in providing frameworks for the current rounds of cooperation than in devising lasting resolutions or durable integration. That, however, is no mean achievement, for it provides limits to conflict and experience in cooperation and it reinforces the nature and rules of the ongoing African system of international relations.

Such behavior may be so pervasive because it finds its roots in cultural traditions, but such explanations are more likely to be exaggerated cultural determinism. The tradition of blood money in some areas and the absence of a negotiating tradition at all in others may be just as characteristic.[35] More important has been the role negotiation has played in achieving independence.[36] All formerly colonial African states (with the possible exception of Guinea Bissau) achieved independence through some degree of negotiation, in most cases after only minimal violence, and where violent struggle was prolonged (as in Algeria, Zimbabwe, Namibia, Angola, and Mozambique), negotiation was all the more important.[37] Such experience and conditioning has been crucial to the establishment of contemporary political cultures and behaviors. In that sense, Africa can be said to have a culture of negotiation, contrasted, for example, with the culture of violence that some observers have noted growing within Latin American countries.[38]

Such a culture faces important challenges in the future. It is promising in terms of the outcome of the major conflict on sociopolitical integration in South Africa, where the experiences of neighboring states may be used to overcome the absence of a negotiating tradition within South Africa itself. In a situation that, by many counts, is prerevolutionary, the specter of a bloodbath for both sides brought a change from a conciliating to a winning mentality at the beginning of the 1990s and opened up the long process of negotiating a new constitutional regime in South Africa.[39] A negotiated solution would be a major achievement in avoiding violence and peacefully meeting African goals. Colonial training in negotiation is also absent in Ethiopia, where a negotiated solution to the problems of empire, with Somalia and with Eritrea, also poses a challenge to African practices of peaceful change. Yet limited negotiations have taken place in the conflicts on the Horn of Africa, with some results for conflict management if not for full resolution, giving partial lessons for the region.

Because the challenge is ongoing, it is more important than ever to end with the traditional call for more research. So little has been done on the actual practice of negotiation in Africa, as has been noted, and yet the field of examples is rich. The challenge of finding out "who said what to whom with what effect," so necessary to a deep understanding of negotiating behavior, is probably no greater in Africa than elsewhere and may actually be lessened by the value given to the practice. The few studies that exist have shown that the challenge can be overcome. A better understanding of the African process can expand an understanding of the methods and potential of the process itself and also reinforce the culture of negotiation in Africa.

Notes

1. On state-society relations in Africa, see Jean-François Bayard, *L'Etat en Afrique* (Paris: Fayard); Donald Rothchild and Naomi Chazan, eds., *The Precarious Balance* (Boulder: Westview Press, 1989).

2. I. William Zartman, "Conflict Prevention, Reduction and Resolution," in Francis Deng, ed., *Conflict in Africa* (Washington, D.C.: Brookings Institution, 1991).

3. For a discussion of the causes of African conflicts, see I. William Zartman, *Ripe for Resolution: Conflict and Intervention in Africa*, 2d ed. (New York: Oxford University Press,

1989), chap. 1. On the Somali and Moroccan irredenta, see ibid., chaps. 2 and 3; on Libya, see René Lemarchand, ed., *The Green and the Black* (Bloomington: Indiana University Press, 1988).

4. I. William Zartman, *International Relations in the New Africa* (Englewood Cliffs, N.J.: Prentice-Hall, 1966), p. 110; Nicole Grimaud, *La Politique exterieure de l'Algerie* (Paris: Karthala, 1984), chap. 6.

5. Zartman, *Ripe for Resolution,* p. 31.

6. Ibid., p. 52.

7. For a discussion of some cases, see I. William Zartman, ed., *Negotiating Internal Conflict* (Washington, D.C.: Brookings Institution, 1994); Manus Midlarsky, ed., *The Internationalization of Communal Strife* (London: Routledge, 1992).

8. Robert G. Armstrong et al., *Socio-political Aspects of the Palaver in Some African Countries* (Paris: UNESCO, 1979); see Sally Engle Merry, "Mediation in Non-Industrial Societies," in Kenneth Kressel and Dean Pruitt, eds., *Mediation Research* (San Francisco: Jossey Bass, 1989), but cf. Laura Nader and Harry Todd, eds., *The Disputing Process—Law in Ten Societies* (New York: Columbia University Press, 1978), where mediation appears only in non-African cases. For divergent African attitudes toward negotiation and conflict management, see the "conflict resolution" sections in Zartman, *Ripe for Resolution,* chaps. 2–5.

9. For some recent studies, both conceptual and applied, on mediation, see Kressel and Pruitt, *Mediation Research*; Saadia Touval and I. William Zartman, eds., *International Mediation in Theory and Practice* (Boulder: Westview Press, 1985); and Christopher Mitchell and Keith Webb, eds., *New Approaches to International Mediation* (Westport, Conn.: Greenwood, 1988).

10. See Touval and Zartman, eds., *International Mediation,* esp. pp. 8–10, 251–254.

11. See I. William Zartman, "Africa as a Subordinate State System," *International Organization* 21, no. 3 (1967), pp. 545–564; Yassin El-Ayouty and I. William Zartman, eds., *The OAU After Twenty Years* (New York: Praeger, 1984), esp. chaps. 2 and 7.

12. See Touval and Zartman, eds., *International Mediation,* pp. 257ff; I. William Zartman, "Negotiations and Prenegotiations in Ethnic Conflict: The Beginning, the Middle and the Ends," in Joseph Montville, ed., *Conflict and Peacemaking in Multiethnic Societies* (Lexington, Mass.: Heath, 1990), esp. pp. 520–524, 530–532.

13. C.O.C Amate, *Inside the OAU* (New York: St. Martin's, 1968), chap. 5.

14. See Zartman, *Ripe for Resolution,* chap. 6.

15. For two exceptional accounts, see John Stremlau, *The International Politics of the Nigerian Civil War* (Princeton: Princeton University Press, 1977), chaps. 6 and 7; Saadia Touval, *The Boundary Politics of Independent Africa* (Cambridge, Mass.: Harvard University Press, 1972), chap. 9.

16. Zartman, *Ripe for Resolution,* p. 68.

17. Hizkias Assefa, *Mediation of Civil Wars* (Boulder: Westview Press, 1987), pp. 128ff.

18. Jeffrey Davidow, *A Peace in Southern Africa* (Boulder: Westview Press, 1984), Stephen John Stedman, *Peacemaking in Civil War* (Boulder: Lynne Rienner, 1988). I am grateful to Robert Lloyd for bringing this case to my attention.

19. See I. William Zartman, *Ripe for Resolution,* chap. 5.

20. On the earlier rounds, see Touval, *Boundary Politics,* chap. 9; on the later rounds, see Zartman, *Ripe for Resolution,* chap. 3.

21. Assefa, *Mediation*; Dunstan Wai, *The African-Arab Conflict in the Sudan* (New York: Africana, 1981).

22. There is room for a good study on the diplomacy of the Eritrean conflict. For a good overview, see Marina Ottaway, "The Eritrean Rebellion," in I. William Zartman, ed., *Negotiating Internal Conflicts* (Washington, D.C.: Brookings Institution, 1994). The 1980–1981 period is covered in I. William Zartman, *African Insurgencies: Negotiations and Mediation* (Washington, D.C.: State Department, 1989), IRR 206, pp. 8–10.

23. On the earlier period, see Virginia Thompson and Richard Adloff, *Conflict in Chad* (Berkeley: University of California Institute of International Studies, 1981); I. William Zartman, "Conflict in Chad," in Arthur Day and Michael Doyle, eds., *Escalation and Intervention* (Boulder: Westview Press, 1986); and Dean Pittman, "The OAU and Chad," in Yassin El-Ayouty and I. William Zartman, eds., *The OAU After Twenty Years* (New York: Praeger, 1984), pp. 297–326. On the later period, see William Foltz, "Negotiations in the Chadian Rebellion," in I. William Zartman, ed., *Negotiating Internal Conflicts* (forthcoming); and Zartman, *African Insurgencies,* pp. 13–14.

24. On the OAU role in general, see Yassin El-Ayouty, ed., *The OAU After Ten Years* (New York: Praeger, 1975); Michael Wolfers, *Politics in the Organization of African Unity* (New York: Barnes and Noble, 1976); El-Ayouty and Zartman, eds., *OAU After Twenty Years*; R. A. Akindele, *The Organization of African Unity 1963–1988,* special issue, *Nigerian Journal of International Affairs,* vol. 14, no. 1 (1988); I. William Zartman, "Mediation in Regional Organizations: The OAU in Chad," in Jacob Bercovitch and Jeffrey Rubin, eds., *Mediation in International Relations* (London: Macmillan, 1991).

25. Figured from annex 6, mediation efforts, in El-Ayouty and Zartman, eds., *OAU After Twenty Years.*

26. On the Chadian peacekeeping force, see the chapters by Dean Pittman and Henry Wisemen in El-Ayouty and I. William Zartman, eds., *OAU After Twenty Years,* (New York: Praeger, 1984), and Nathan Pelkovits, "Peacekeeping: The African Experience," in Henry Wiseman, ed., *Peacekeeping: Appraisals and Proposals* (New York: Pergamon, 1983).

27. Olesegun Obasanjo et al., *The Kampala Document* (New York: African Leadership Forum, 1991).

28. Cf. I. William Zartman, "Conflict Reduction: Prevention, Management and Resolution," in Francis Deng and I. William Zartman, eds., *Conflict Resolution in Africa* (Washington, D.C.: Brookings Institution, 1991).

29. See I. William Zartman, *The Politics of Trade Negotiations Between Africa and the European Communities* (Princeton: Princeton University Press, 1971); John Ravenhill, *Collective Clientelism: The Lomé Convention and North-South Relations* (New York: Columbia University Press, 1985); Frans Alting von Geusau, ed., *The Lomé Convention and a New International Economic Order* (Leyden: Sijtof, 1977); John Ravenhill, "When Weakness Is Strength: The Lomé IV Negotiations," in I. William Zartman, ed., *Europe and Africa: The New Phase* (Boulder: Lynne Rienner Publishers, 1993).

30. Cf. I. William Zartman, *International Relations in the New Africa* (Lanham, Md.: University Press of America, reprint, 1987), esp. pp. 147ff.

31. Peter Robson, *Integration, Development and Equity* (London: Allen & Unwin, 1983).

32. Zartman, *The Politics of Trade Negotiations,* p. 225 and passim; I. William Zartman, "Lomé III: Relic of the 1970s or Model for the 1990s?" in C. Cosgrove and J. Jamar, eds., *The European Community's Development Policy: The Strategies Ahead* (Bruges: College d'Europe, de Tempel, 1986).

33. Ravenhill, *Collective Clientelism*; Joanna Moss, *The Lomé Conventions and Their Implications for the United States* (Boulder: Westview Press, 1982); I. William Zartman, "An American Point of View," in Franz Alting von Geusau, ed., *The Lomé Convention, and*

a New International Economic Order (Leyden: Sijtof, 1977) esp. pp. 141ff; John Ravenhill, "Evolving Patterns of Lomé Negotiations," in I. William Zartman, ed., *Europe and Africa: The New Phase* (Boulder: Lynne Rienner Publishers, 1991).

34. Boutros Boutros-Ghali, *The Addis Ababa Charter* (New York: Carnegie Endowment for International Peace, International Conciliation Series 546, 1964); T. O. Elias, "The Charter of the OAU," *American Journal of International Law* 59, no. 2 (1965), pp. 243–276; Lawrence Marinelli, *The New Liberia* (New York: Praeger, 1964), pp. 138–140.

35. See the discussion of various subregional attitudes toward negotiation in Zartman, *Ripe for Resolution,* pp. 49ff, 109ff, 156ff.

36. See Donald Rothchild, "Racial Stratification and Bargaining: The Kenya Experience," in I. William Zartman, ed., *The 50% Solution* (New Haven: Yale University Press, 1987). Unfortunately, similar studies—or even purely historical accounts—do not exist for most other African countries.

37. Jeffrey Davidow, *A Peace in Southern Africa: The Lancaster House Conference* (Boulder: Westview Press, 1984); Stephen Stedman, *Peace Making in a Revolutionary Civil War: Zimbabwe* (Boulder: Lynne Rienner Publishers, 1990); Zartman, *Ripe for Resolution,* chap. 5. Unfortunately, there are no similar studies of a number of other cases.

38. Daniel Garcia, "Negotiating with the Rebellion in Columbia," in I. William Zartman, ed., *Negotiating Internal Conflicts* (forthcoming).

39. See I. William Zartman, "Negotiations in South Africa," *Washington Quarterly* 11, no. 4 (1988), pp. 141–158; Zartman, "Negotiating in South Africa," in I. William Zartman, ed., *Negotiating Internal Conflicts* (forthcoming).

12

Promoting Democracy in Africa: U.S. and International Policies in Transition

LARRY DIAMOND

A Sorry History

SINCE THE FIRST STIRRINGS of Africa's independence movements, self-determination, freedom, democracy, and human rights have been important foreign policy goals for the United States in Africa.[1] Unfortunately, until the end of the Cold War, those idealistic goals often took a back seat to more "pragmatic" and even cynical calculations of U.S. national interest. America's foreign policy record in postindependence Africa is not one in which the United States can take unmitigated pride. In a recent candid review, the then U.S. deputy assistant secretary for human rights (and former ambassador to Somalia), James K. Bishop, acknowledged that during the Cold War, "independent Africa was viewed as yet another playing field on which the struggle between the Soviets and ourselves was to be waged."[2]

That overriding strategic goal—countering the expansion of Soviet military and political power—was often the driving force in U.S. relations with African regimes. In exchange for locating military communications facilities on their soil, the United States tolerated repressive traditional autocracies in Morocco and Ethiopia. While rhetorically supporting the struggles for independence in Angola and Mozambique, the United States continued military assistance to the Salazar dictatorship in order to retain much needed access to the Azores for long-distance military aircraft. While imposing an arms embargo on South Africa, the United States also established a National Aeronautics and Space Administration (NASA) tracking station on its soil.[3] No doubt, other concessions (including intelligence cooperation) were offered to the apartheid regime in exchange, and it was really not until the 1980s that Congress imposed (over the resistance of the Reagan administration) tough economic sanctions on that odious regime.

Although U.S. policy succeeded to a great extent in "containing communism" in Africa (most of all because the continent provided infertile soil for that ideology to take hold), it generally failed in its more noble professed goals—to promote development, democracy, and peaceful resolution of conflict. One finds a particularly "dismal balance sheet," Michael Clough argued, when examining the fate of the six countries—Ethiopia, Kenya, Liberia, Somalia, Sudan, and Zaire— that "received the largest share of U.S. assistance to Africa" from 1962 to 1988.[4] In all six countries, U.S. economic and military assistance went primarily to the regime of a single authoritarian leader, and in every case, the country's political and economic situation deteriorated markedly during (if not partly as a result of) this prolonged U.S. assistance. Four of the six client dictators were violently overthrown (Haile Selassie in 1974, Gaafar Mohamed Nimeiri in 1985, Samuel K. Doe in 1990, and Mohamed Siad Barre in 1991). Five of the six countries experienced bloody civil war, and with the rise of competitive party politics in Kenya, Daniel arap Moi has seemed intent on inflaming ethnic tension as a means for hanging on to power.

From the very beginning of his rise to power in the turbulence of postindependence Congolese politics, Mobutu Sese Seko (then just Colonel Mobutu) received critical military and intelligence support from the United States and the West, which subsequently intervened militarily on his behalf on several occasions. Incredibly, this assistance and collaboration continued through the 1980s, even after the independent academic community had long since come to the passionate consensus (backed up by the many frustrated international financial bureaucrats who had tried to straighten out Mobutu) that, to quote the respected American professor Crawford Young in 1985, "*Hope for reform of the present regime is impossible to sustain.*"[5] He added, "From 1961 to 1990 no other African country ranked among the top recipients of American aid as consistently as Zaire."[6] Eager for access to Zairian air bases (which the United States used in the mid-1980s to funnel covert military assistance to UNITA in Angola) and obsessed with a fear that the fall of Mobutu would bring "the consequent disintegration of Zaire into unstable segments open to radical penetration," as Secretary of State Cyrus Vance wrote in his memoirs, one U.S. administration after another deluded itself into thinking that it could somehow reform this most wily, corrupt, and megalomaniacal of all African dictators.[7]

Even as the "third wave" of global democratic change began to sweep through the world in the 1980s and as the United States launched unprecedented efforts to promote democracy worldwide, U.S. policy toward Africa was rather slow to change.[8] The failure of the United States to reject and denounce outright Samuel Doe's blatantly rigged and outrageous self-declared presidential election victory in October 1985 was a particularly sorry moment for Liberia—and for U.S. policy. Willful self-delusion and support for Liberia's "genuine progress" toward greater democracy was to continue on the part of high U.S. officials for another three years.[9]

Although U.S. policy under the Bush administration and Assistant Secretary of

State Herman Cohen gave increasingly strong moral and rhetorical support to the democratic trend beginning to take form in Africa, old habits died hard. In 1989, the administration argued against cuts in aid to the entrenched authoritarian regimes in Kenya, Somalia, and Zaire. The U.S. ambassador to Kenya, Smith Hempstone, took a principled stand on behalf of democratic change in Kenya, but the administration in Washington did not seriously distance itself from Moi's corrupt dictatorship.[10] Disturbing in all these instances was not only the persistence of the United States in politically and morally misguided policies but also its refusal to acknowledge its own mistakes and share of responsibility for the disasters that befell countries like Liberia and Somalia. The same applies to the former European colonial powers, who—again, until very recently—happily aided, invested in, and traded with many of the most corrupt and abusive regimes on the continent, with little serious concern for democratic reform. France's policy was particularly blatant, propping up francophone African dictators with huge financial subventions and military support (and when necessary, direct military intervention) in order to maintain a diffuse cultural and commercial hegemony.

Change in U.S. and International Policies Toward Africa

It is my principal premise here that the policies of the United States (and other major democracies) toward Africa began to change dramatically around 1990, moving toward a greater concern for democracy, accountability, and human rights; that these policies are continuing to change today; and that American policy in particular will increasingly be driven by this goal. What explains this historic shift?

It is by now almost trite to observe that the end of the Cold War has thoroughly transformed the context for U.S. foreign policy. In his defining statement on the Clinton administration's new Africa policy, Secretary of State Warren Christopher candidly acknowledged this when he declared, "During the long Cold War period, policies toward Africa were often determined not by how they affected Africa, but by whether they brought advantage or disadvantage to Washington or Moscow. Thankfully, we have moved beyond the point of adopting policies based on how they might affect the shipping lanes *next* to Africa rather than the people in Africa."[11] In fact, this movement began earlier in the 1980s, well before the collapse of communism, with "a slow but perceptible trend toward military disengagement from Africa" on the part of the two superpowers, facilitated by their "increased willingness and ability . . . to work together to mediate a variety of international disputes in these areas."[12] This Soviet-American cooperation was particularly crucial to one of the most important U.S. diplomatic achievements in Africa during the 1980s, the 1988 accords that brought about the withdrawal of Cuban troops from Angola and the independence of Namibia.[13]

The end of the Cold War has brought a number of closely interrelated changes in the political and strategic situation in Africa. Of course, the United States no longer needs to worry about countering the spread of Soviet military and political influence in the region. Thus, "Western strategic interest in access to Africa's ports and airfields has become much less pressing. Even during the [Persian] Gulf conflict the U.S. found little need for access rights previously negotiated with African governments."[14] Nor does the Western alliance need to worry about the spread of hostile ideological and economic systems. Socialism and communism are increasingly recognized and dismissed as failures by African intellectual and political leaders, and the only other transnational rival political model, Islamic fundamentalism, is inapplicable to large parts of sub-Saharan Africa and blatantly undemocratic anyway. Thus, the United States and other Western democracies are increasingly free to deal with Africa on the basis of enduring principles rather than narrow, short-term, and strategic self-interest.

But this is not the only salient change in context. For the last decade or so, especially since 1990, powerful forces have been gathering from the ground up in Africa, pressuring for democratic change. The global "third wave" of democracy has finally caught up with the indigenous politics and thinking of Africa, and the demonstration effects from various individual country transitions have been powerful. Two events in February 1990 were particularly crucial in unleashing a "second African liberation": (1) the toppling of President Mathieu Kerekou from effective power and initiation of a transition to democracy in Benin by a national conference Kerekou himself had called, and (2) the unbanning of the ANC and release from prison of Nelson Mandela and other key ANC leaders in South Africa. Inspired by these changes as well as the stunning (widely televised) downfall of communism in Eastern Europe and disgusted with the oppression, corruption, and economic and moral bankruptcy of one-party and military rule, countries throughout Africa were swept by a wave of regime openings and popular demands for multiparty democracy. By the end of 1991, roughly twenty-six African countries (half the total) could be "classified as either democratic or moderately or strongly committed to democratic change."[15]

Throughout the 1980s, Africa experienced an explosion of independent associations and media mobilizing against the political oppression and economic predation of authoritarian regimes. Increasingly, these went beyond isolated and severely repressed efforts of resistance, coalescing into broad national movements for democracy and human rights on the part of the churches, trade unions, student and professional associations, women's groups, producer groups, human rights and legal associations, as well as intellectuals, journalists, and various informal networks.[16] In a wide range of African countries—including Benin, Nigeria, Ghana, Niger, Mali, Cameroon, Zambia, Kenya, South Africa, Zimbabwe, and even in such relentlessly unyielding dictatorships as Mobutu's in Zaire and Banda's in Malawi—this produced broad cultural and political change that finally destroyed the legitimacy of the African one-party state.

Corresponding to these organizational and political developments from the grassroots in Africa has been a powerful intellectual shift, akin to what has happened in Latin America, embracing democracy as a virtue in itself, even by intellectuals on the political Left. These intellectuals did much to puncture the pompous claims of African dictators to their own indispensability and to convey this new African thinking to the West. They argued that "postponing democracy does not promote development" and that ethnic conflict was not the product of democracy but rather of exploitative and undemocratic political leaders "who politicize ethnicity in their quest for power" and then, having incited ethnic conflict, "use the threat of such conflict to justify political authoritarianism."[17] Moreover, these intellectuals showed that "traditional African political systems were infused with democratic values" and standards of accountability and that the postindependence dictatorships perverted culture and history in denouncing democratic participation and constitutionalism as "unAfrican."[18] It became increasingly difficult for the West to continue to accept the legitimacy of African authoritarian regimes when African intellectuals were candidly denouncing the pervasive economic and political failures of authoritarian rule and pointing to democracy as the only way out of the continent's morass. Indeed, African intellectual leaders put the West on the spot when they made statements like that of Peter Anyang' Nyong'o (secretary-general of the African Association of Political Science) in his keynote address to the Pan-African Conference in Namibia in May 1991: "Those who truly desire to put the people first must condition aid and development assistance to African countries on democracy and the observance of human rights. This is a nonnegotiable demand as far as the African people are concerned."[19]

African nongovernmental organizations engaged in development also became increasingly explicit and forceful in their identification of democratic participation as a crucial requirement for economic development in Africa. This view was formalized at Arusha in February 1990, when these NGOs issued the African Charter for Popular Participation in Development and Transformation and in a follow-up declaration in 1991. In his comments on the African Charter, the widely respected head of the Economic Commission for Africa, Adebayo Adediji argued that *"democracy, accountability, and development for transformation* [must] become internalized in every country and deep-rooted at every level of our society, . . . in contrast to *despotism, authoritarianism, and kleptocracy."*[20]

The impact of this groundswell of democratic resistance, mobilization, and intellectual rethinking on the policies of the industrialized democracies should not be underestimated. For many years, the United States in particular had been pushing a rhetorical and moral commitment to democracy and human rights. This stance had long been suspected and denounced by many African politicians, diplomats, intellectuals, and social forces as self-serving, manipulative, "neoimperialist," arrogant, and hypocritical. Now Africans themselves (and no longer just those in South Africa) were demanding political freedom and democracy in unprecedented numbers, with moving courage and forthrightness, and were calling upon the United States and the West to come to *their* assistance, not that of the regime. This much wider popular mobilization for democracy would have been hard to ignore in any circumstance, but it was especially compelling when the termination of the Cold War gave the United States the freedom to support these genuine struggles for liberty.

The foreign policy shift, however, was not just a response to demands and courageous mobilization by democrats in Africa. It was also the result of bitter disillusionment on the part of Western aid donors, who were independently coming to the inescapable conclusion that economic development could not be pursued in isolation from concern for accountable and responsive governance and that development assistance to African dictatorships had generally proved a disastrous failure. As Table 12.1 shows, official development assistance to African countries from all sources increased dramatically during the 1980s; for the thirty-two (nonoil) countries of sub-Saharan Africa (with populations over 1 million), the median increase in official development assistance during the decade exceeded 100 percent. In fact, in countries such as Mozambique, Uganda, the Ivory Coast, Chad, Malawi, and Togo, development assistance more than tripled during the 1980s. Yet this same decade saw the GNP per capita in Africa *shrink* at an average annual rate of over 1 percent per year, although GNP was growing annually in every other region of the world.[21] Increasingly, sub-Saharan Africa was becoming the locus of world poverty: Its share of the world's poor is expected to increase from 16 percent in 1985 to 30 percent by the end of the century.[22] By 1989, total external debt for sub-Saharan Africa stood at $147 billion—99 percent of its annual gross domestic product, almost four times its annual export earnings, and twice the level recorded just seven years previously.[23] Despite an annual inflow of $15 billion in international aid by 1990 (more than twice the amount received in 1980), standards of living were visibly deteriorating.[24] Moreover, it was dictatorships most of all that were being rewarded for this lack of performance; in 1990, the six largest African recipients of official development assistance were all highly authoritarian regimes (rated "not free" by Freedom House).[25] Obviously, what the democratic West was doing was failing miserably.

By the late 1980s, Western aid agencies and foreign ministries were beginning to rethink their policies and strategies fundamentally. "After years of focusing on technical economic factors," both the bilateral donors and the major multilateral institutions began to give increasing attention to the political causes of Africa's development failure and to the need for political prescriptions.[26] A particularly prominent watershed was the publication by the World Bank in 1989 of a new development strategy, outlined in *Sub-Saharan Africa: From Crisis to Sustainable Growth*, which had a tremendous impact in reorienting attention to the need for political accountability, public debate, press freedom, political participation, pluralism, decentralization, consensus building, and hence legitimacy in order to achieve real economic development.[27] The following year, at the Bretton Woods Committee meeting in Washington, "World Bank President Barber Conable listed better governance as the primary requirement for economic recovery in Africa."[28] This emphasis continued in other policy statements and strategies that

TABLE 12.1   Official Development Assistance to Sub-Saharan Africa, 1981–1990

		Official Development Assistance (ODA) (in millions of $U.S.)			Percent Increase in ODA	ODA as Percent of GNP	ODA as Percent of GNP	Annual Percent Growth in GDP
		1981	1985	1990	1981–90	1985	1990	1981–90
1[a]	Mozambique	144	300	946	556.9	9.2	65.7	2.9
2	Tanzania	703	487	1,155	64.3	7.9	48.2	2.8
3	Ethiopia	245	715	888	262.4	15.1	14.6	1.8
4	Somalia	374	353	428	14.4	14.5	45.9	2.4
6	Chad	35	182	315	800.0	—	28.6	5.9
9	Malawi	137	113	479	249.6	11.0	25.7	−0.7
11	Burundi	117	142	265	126.5	13.7	24.0	3.9
12	Zaire	394	325	823	108.9	7.5	10.9	1.8
13	Uganda	136	182	557	309.6	—	18.4	2.8
14	Madagascar	234	188	382	63.2	8.2	12.3	1.1
15	Sierra Leone	91	66	70	23.1	5.5	7.8	1.5
16	Mali	230	380	474	106.1	34.9	19.4	4.0
18	Niger	194	304	358	84.5	19.8	14.2	−1.3
19	Rwanda	153	181	287	87.6	10.7	13.4	1.0
20	Burkina Faso	212	198	315	48.6	18.4	9.9	4.3
22	Benin	82	96	261	218.3	9.5	—	2.8
25	Kenya	449	438	1,000	122.7	7.9	11.4	4.2
27	Ghana	145	203	465	220.7	4.1	7.4	3.0
28	Central African Republic	111	104	232	109.0	15.9	17.8	1.5
29	Togo	63	114	210	233.3	17.5	13.0	1.6
30	Zambia	232	328	438	88.8	15.4	14.0	0.8
31	Guinea	90	119	292	224.4	6.5	10.4	—
33	Mauritania	214	207	211	−1.4	31.2	20.0	1.4
34	Lesotho	94	94	138	46.8	16.5	24.5	3.1
40	Liberia	108	90	115	6.5	8.8	—	—
42	Sudan	632	1,128	792	25.3	15.6	9.3	2.9
45	Zimbabwe	212	237	343	161.8	4.9	5.5	2.9
46	Senegal	398	295	739	85.7	12.2	12.7	3.0
48	Ivory Coast	124	125	689	455.6	1.9	6.9	0.5
53	Cameroon	265	159	483	82.3	2.1	4.3	2.3
56	Congo	92	98	209	127.1	3.5	7.3	3.6
71	Botswana	97	96	148	52.6	13.7	5.5	11.3
	Median				107.5			2.8

[a] Numbers in left-hand column indicate ranking of countries in *1992 World Development Report,* from poorest to richest.

Source: World Bank, *World Development Report* (New York: Oxford University Press, 1986, 1987 and 1992).

drew strong connections between governance, development, and such elements of democracy as the rule of law.[29]

"Governance" now became the watchword for the Africa programs of the bank, the U.S. Agency for International Development, and other major Western donors. If this was not yet explicit conditionality on multiparty democracy and human rights, it was certainly a move in that direction.

In fact, by 1990, the United States was establishing democracy as an explicit consideration in its aid programs. In that year, AID adopted a "democracy initiative" that (1) made the promotion and strengthening of democracy worldwide one of the central aims of the organization; (2) vowed to weigh progress toward economic liberalization and democratization in deciding assistance levels for individual countries; and (3) promised to "incorporate participation and democracy" into the full range of its economic, social, and environmental programs, in part by emphasizing local decisionmaking and control.[30] Subsequently, all of AID's regional bureaus launched extensive policy reviews to develop appropriate strategies and programs for promoting democracy in each region of the developing world. In the evolution of its own programmatic and strategic thinking, the AID Africa Bureau's early emphasis on "governance" has metamorphosed into "democratic governance," encompassing not only the administrative goals (associated with the World Bank) of increasing accountability, legitimacy, predictability of rules, and institutional capacities but also the principles of political pluralism, competition, participation, and liberty that constitute liberal democracy.[31]

The British and French governments moved in a similar direction. In June 1990, two months after U.S. Assistant Secretary of State for African Affairs Herman Cohen announced that democratization would join economic reform and human rights as a condition for U.S. assistance, British Foreign Secretary Douglas Hurd declared that Britain's assistance would favor "countries tending toward pluralism, public accountability, respect for the rule of law, human rights, and market principles."[32] This important speech was a landmark in the evolution of British policy toward Africa. In her subsequent elaboration, Britain's Minister of Overseas Development Lynda Chalker reiterated that the country's bilateral aid program would be shaped around an emphasis on "good government," defined not only as "sound economic and social policies" and technically competent administration but also as openness, accountability, pluralism, press freedom, human rights, the rule of law, extensive participation . . . and therefore democracy. She indicated that (like USAID) Britain would also give increasing attention in its aid program to supporting democratic institutions (including legislatures), NGOs, financial accountability, press freedom, and human rights monitoring, and she identified a number of specific projects in this regard.[33]

About the same time as Douglas Hurd's June 1990 speech at the Franco-African summit at La Baule, France, President François Mitterrand announced a dramatic turn in France's traditionally hegemonic and commercially driven relations with its former African colonies. Henceforth, Mitterrand warned, France would link its aid to institutional progress toward democracy, "as evidenced by free elections held under universal suffrage, freedom of the press, independence of the judiciary, multipartyism, and the abolition of censorship."[34] Indeed, by then, France had already pulled the plug on Mathieu Kerekou's political life-support system in Benin, suspending aid to his notoriously corrupt and repressive regime and thereby compelling him to hold the national conference that stripped him of power.

> Progressively clearer messages conveyed France's new "line" to Francophone Africa: severe political conditionalities on aid, with higher levels of French budgetary and other subventions to countries introducing basic political reforms. More ominously, France renounced automatic future honoring of long-standing "mutual defence" treaties *under whose very loose interpretation* French force of arms had been committed to sustain regimes threatened by insurrection. In this domain too the French position was that such support, *if at all forthcoming*, would be determined by the country's human rights record, and whether it was moving towards democratic reforms.[35]

Given France's tremendous leverage with its former African colonies, "fiscally sustaining one-third of the African states to the point of annually balancing the budgets of many," this pressure could not but have dramatic consequences.[36] In Benin, Mali, Niger, and Madagascar, it has helped to produce real, if still fragile, transitions to democracy; in Senegal, more progress toward a truly competitive democracy; in Chad, the Congo, and elsewhere, varying (and often ambiguous) degrees of political liberalization; and in the Ivory Coast, Gabon, and Cameroon, multiparty competition albeit without free and fair elections and real political freedom.

In anglophone Africa, the most decisive sign of a real change in policy on the part of the United States, Britain, and the democratic West more generally came in Kenya. As early as May 8, 1990, U.S. Ambassador Smith Hempstone had warned that "there is a strong tide flowing in our Congress, which controls the purse strings, to concentrate our economic assistance on those of the world's nations that nourish democratic institutions, defend human rights, and practice multiparty politics."[37] For a time, Western aid continued to flow to Kenya's one-party regime, but international anger and pressure mounted with the country's deepening descent into brazen corruption, political assassination and imprisonment, torture, other flagrant abuses of human rights, and "a growing culture of sycophancy and fear."[38] In 1991, the Scandinavian countries joined the United States in warning of an aid cutoff if human rights conditions were not improved. In September 1991, Denmark froze all new aid to Kenya. Finally, at the November 1991 Paris meeting of the Consultative Group for Kenya, the country's international aid donors "established explicit political conditions for assistance, making Kenya a precedent for the rest of Africa."[39] New aid was suspended for six months, pending "the early implementation of political reform"—including "greater pluralism, the importance of the rule of law and respect for human rights, notably basic freedoms of expression and assembly, and . . . firm action to deal with issues of corruption."[40] Private diplomatic messages reinforced this historic pressure for democratic reform. One week later, a special conference of Kenya's ruling party voted to repeal the ban on opposition parties; the vote was rubber-stamped by the parliament the following week, paving the way for multiparty parliamentary and presidential elections. In January 1992, President Moi conceded bitterly that the change to multiparty politics was a result of Western pressure.[41] A similar decision by international donors in May 1992 to freeze $74 million in aid to Malawi (following the first mass protest demonstrations in twenty-eight years) also compelled the ironfisted regime of Hastings Banda in Malawi to open up. After releasing hundreds of political prisoners and legalizing opposition political movements, the regime was dealt a severe blow in June 1993 when 63 percent of the voters opted for multiparty democracy in a national referendum. These international pressures have not yet produced real democracy in Kenya (given the rigging, violence, and intimidation surrounding the December 29, 1992, elections) or even multiparty elections in Malawi to date. But they have helped to generate real political openings and eroded the ability of these authoritarian regimes to perpetuate themselves in power, free of political opposition and scrutiny.

With the change of administrations in Washington, the commitment to democracy in U.S. policy toward Africa (and globally, as well) appeared to intensify. In his most important foreign policy statement during the 1992 presidential campaign, Bill Clinton had criticized "Mr. Bush's ambivalence about supporting democracy, his eagerness to defend potentates and dictators." Vowing to make the promotion of democracy a central theme of his administration's foreign policy and foreign aid program, he called for the United States to "encourage and nurture the stirrings for democratic reform that are surfacing all across Africa, from the birth of an independent Namibia, to the pressure for democratic reforms in Kenya."[42]

In an extensive delineation of the new administration's Africa policy, Secretary of State Warren Christopher outlined, on May 21, 1993, a "new substantial American relationship with Africa" centered around three themes: the promotion of democracy and human rights, the achievement of sustainable development, and the peaceful resolution of conflict. On the first goal, he declared:

> The Clinton Administration will provide strong and visible support for the movement toward freedom in Africa—the movement toward democracies and toward free markets. . . .
>
> At the heart of our new relationship will be an enduring commitment to democracy and human rights—and that includes women's rights. President Clinton has made it clear that promoting democracy and human rights is a pillar of American foreign policy. And that pillar stands just as tall in Africa as it does in every part of the world. . . .
>
> We cannot hold Africa to a lesser standard for human rights than we apply to other parts of the world. I want to make clear that the United States will take human rights into account as we determine how to allocate our scarce resources for foreign assistance.[43]

Several signs of change were soon apparent. Among them was a dramatic shift in priorities for distributing the more than $1 billion in U.S. development assistance for Africa. "Topping the provisional list for 1993 is . . . South Africa, followed by Ethiopia and Mozambique. Zaire, Liberia, and Sudan get nothing."[44] The new administrator of AID, Brian Atwood, accentuated the new administration's policy on aid in his confirmation statement to the Senate on April 29: "We cannot be everywhere. In particular, we can no longer afford to be in countries where corruption, authoritarianism or incompetence makes development doubtful. What is important is achieving results. If money cannot be productively used in a particular situation, it should not be spent." Pledging to help forge a new, bipartisan national consensus on foreign aid policy, he listed as the first element of that consensus the goal of "helping the developing world respond to the growing demand for democracy, social justice and human rights."[45]

In May 1993, Deputy Treasury Secretary Laurence Summers announced the United States would forgive at least half the official debt of about eighteen low-income African countries, provided they adhere to economic liberalization policies.[46] After many years of active U.S. support for Jonas Savimbi's UNITA (despite extensive evidence of *its* violations of human rights and the insincerity of its professed commitments to democracy), the Clinton administration granted diplomatic recognition to the government of Angola on May 19, acknowledging the ruling party's victory in a presidential election whose legitimate result UNITA violently rejected. Precisely to demonstrate his commitment to democracy in Africa, "President Clinton chose to invite the first President of a democratic Namibia, Sam Nujoma, as the first African head of state to be received at his White House."[47] Significantly, Nigerian President Ibrahim Babangida failed to obtain an invitation to visit the Clinton White House, despite his intense interest in doing so, specifically because of his abusive rule and the growing doubts about his commitment to honoring his own democratic transition program.

The new policy was also evident in the forcefulness of the U.S. response to President Babangida's annulment of the results of the June 12, 1993, presidential election in Nigeria, which was supposed to have been the final step on the way to the military's complete withdrawal from power on August 27 (and that was won by a southerner for the first time in the country's thirty-three-year history). On the eve of the election, the United States had already declared that a postponement (which a shadowy pro-Babangida group was seeking in court) would be "unacceptable," and this had resulted in the expulsion from Nigeria of the head of the U.S. Information Service (USIS) in Lagos, Michael O'Brien. Now, the United States immediately declared the Nigerian military's June 23 annulment and cancellation of the transition "an outrageous decision" and suspended its modest $22.8 million aid program, while also imposing other diplomatic sanctions. The depth of U.S. prodemocracy sentiment was accentuated by a letter to Secretary Christopher from the Congressional Black Caucus urging even tougher action and declaring that the military's annulment of the Nigerian election "must not be allowed to stand." Britain also moved quickly to denounce the military's action, impose sanctions, especially directed at the military, and freeze its outstanding aid package (£14.5 million).[48]

This international drama surrounding the military's effort to abort its own transition to democracy in Nigeria was instructive in several respects, not all of them positive. First, it underscored that the United States and Britain are now prepared to act even when action may be seen to conflict with significant economic interests. (Nigeria has long been one of the largest and most reliable suppliers of oil to the United States, and both British and American oil companies have huge investments in Nigeria.) Second, it suggested that timely and forceful international pressure for democracy can have some impact. Although the clear victor in the Nigerian presidential election (Moshood Abiola) was not inaugurated, the Nigerian military was forced to back down from its initial outright cancellation of the transition, and Babangida was ousted from power at the end of August in favor of a (superficially) civilian-led transitional government.

Ultimately, however, the deepening political stalemate in Nigeria may raise questions about the ability of Western democracies to affect the political destiny of a relatively resourceful African country, even one so deep in debt and economic misery as Nigeria. International prodemocratic sensitivities did not keep the Nigerian military from overthrowing the civilian interim government in mid-November 1993 and liquidating all the democratic structures that had painstakingly been constructed and elected in the preceding years. Yet concern to win back the favor of the United States and Britain—and ultimately of the international financial community—may well have been a factor in inducing the new military regime, led by General Sani Abacha, to appoint a federal cabinet composed almost entirely of civilian politicians and to act with restraint in its initial dealings with the press and interest groups. The regime was no doubt further chastened in its first few months by its failure to regain sufficient legitimacy in American eyes even to enable its foreign minister to visit Washington. Yet the Nigerian drama also showed that the Western democracies have yet to stand with one voice for democracy in Africa when the economic stakes are large. While effectively denouncing U.S. and British intervention in Nigeria's affairs, Babangida singled out France and Germany (along with Ireland and Russia) for "appreciation . . . of the patience and understanding" (read lack of criticism) they displayed in the crisis.[49]

In fact, recent developments have called into question the depth and seriousness of France's commitment to democratization in Africa. At the November 1991 francophone conference in Paris, President Mitterrand diluted the message he had given a year earlier at La Baule, saying that each African country "will, I am sure, be able completely independently to decide on the appropriate procedures and pace once the direction has been set."[50] This seemed to signal that "France would not dictate methods of political change. Six days after Mitterrand's speech, troops loyal to [Togolese dictator] Eyadema launched a coup in Lomé" in an effort to derail a democratic transition.[51]

French policy conditionality, it would seem, has yet to break free of France's commercial interests in Africa and perhaps as well of the corrupting influence of money in French politics. Although international pressure forced President Paul Biya of Cameroon to hold a multiparty presidential election, it failed in Cameroon (as it failed in the Ivory Coast and Kenya) to produce a free and fair election. Despite the widespread evidence of electoral fraud—which may very well have made the difference in Biya's narrow official defeat of opposition candidate John Fru Ndi in the October 1992 election—France endorsed the election results and proceeded two months later to grant Cameroon roughly $110 million in new loans (while the United States suspended $14 million in aid following the election).[52] This barely enabled Cameroon to reschedule its debts to the IMF and World Bank (failing that, all international aid would have been halted).[53] The following May, "Mr. Biya was welcomed in Paris by both Mr. Mitterrand and the new French prime Minister Edouard Balladur. In Rwanda soldiers loyal to President Juvenal Habyarimana have been responsible for atrocities against Rwanda's Tutsi minority. Yet Mr. Mitterrand continues to help the regime."[54]

Unfortunately, France's ambivalence in its commitment to promoting democracy in Africa is deeply rooted in its own democratic political system. There is a strong symbiosis between France's powerful—many would say hegemonic (or even "neocolonial")—influence in its former African colonies and the participation of African rulers in French political life via circuits of information and the financing of electoral campaigns. In recent years, this symbiosis has been challenged but not entirely disrupted by democratic pressures from Africa, from African diaspora communities resident in France, and from reformist elements within French politics and society.[55] Money is the crucial force that perpetuates it. Three decades after independence, France's former African colonies remain heavily dependent on its budget subsidies, technical assistance, and military support, while employing a common currency (the CFA franc) controlled by the French treasury. And within France, "corruption has so permeated the [political] affairs of the Fifth Republic" that it has "even included the specter of African Heads of State making clandestine financial contributions to the electoral campaigns of French presidential candidates."[56] Close personal ties between top French and African political leaders cement this compromise of democracy. Charles Pasqua, minister of interior in France's new right-of-center government, "is a personal friend of both President Biya and President Omar Bongo, and is on good terms with President Eyadema" of Togo.[57] The three would rate on any current list of African authoritarian leaders resisting the democratic winds of change.

U.S. Programs to Promote Democracy in Africa

Although diplomacy and aid conditionality have become increasingly important instruments for U.S. efforts to promote democracy in Africa, a more subtle but perhaps profound impact has been achieved through the work of various political assistance programs. These programs have been aimed not only at strengthening the formal institutions of democracy in Africa—free and fair elections, independent legislatures and judiciaries, effective local governments, instruments of public accountability, and efficient administration—but have also sought to develop the constituent elements of a democratic civil society. Many of the grants have gone directly to independent organizations and media working to build the culture and practices of a free society. Spending only a tiny fraction of the more than $1 billion that the United States devotes annually to economic, humanitarian, and security assistance for Africa, these political assistance programs have contributed significantly to the successful democratic transitions in Namibia, Benin, and Zambia and to democracy-building efforts across the continent.

Since its formation in 1983, the National Endowment for Democracy (NED) has funded a wide range of efforts to promote democracy in Africa. Funded mainly by an annual appropriation from the U.S. Congress ($35 million in fiscal year [FY] 1994) but governed by an independent, bipartisan board of directors, NED makes grants directly and through its four core institutes: the National Democratic Institute of International Affairs (NDI), the International Republican Institute (IRI), the Free Trade Union Institute (FTUI), and the Center for International Private Enterprise (CIPE). The former two are affiliated with the Democratic and Republican parties in the United States, the latter two with the American Federation of Labor and Congress of Industrial Organizations (AFL-CIO) and the U.S. Chamber of Congress, respectively.

During 1992, NED grants supported human rights education, research, and advocacy in Nigeria, Liberia, Burkina Faso, Ethiopia, Sudan, and Zaire. NED-supported human rights organizations in Nigeria—especially the Civil Liberties Organisation, the Constitutional Rights Project, and the Committee for the Defense of Human Rights—have been at the forefront of efforts to mobilize democratic consciousness, expose authoritarian abuses, campaign for a rule of law, and resist the efforts of the military dictatorship in Nigeria to perpetuate itself in power. In Kenya, NED has given financial support to the League of Kenya Women Voters and to the *Nairobi Law Monthly,* whose editor, Gitobu Imanyara, was one of three people awarded NED's biennial democracy award by President Clinton in April 1993. During 1992, NED also supported research, discussion, and civic education programs aimed at consolidating democracy in Botswana, Senegal, Namibia, and Zambia; programs to facilitate discussion and debate of policy issues (including televised presidential debates) in Ghana and Mali; and training of election monitors and observers in Cameroon and Burkina Faso. In a number of African countries—including Ethiopia, Liberia, Malawi, and Sierra Leone—and among Sudanese exiles in England, NED has given vital support to independent publications that are attempting to raise democratic awareness and expose the abuses of authoritarian rule.[58]

NED is also administering roughly $2 million in funds from AID to advance the democratic transition in South Africa. These have been heavily invested in programs to train civic, political, and church leaders for the work of democracy in a new South Africa, to support grassroots civic education and community action efforts, to strengthen black community organizations in civil society, to prepare for nonracial elections, and thereby to develop the infrastructure of a free and pluralistic society.[59]

In addition to the funds channeled through NED, USAID invested tens of millions of dollars in helping to prepare South Africa for its first nonracial elections in April 1994. Slightly more than a quarter of its FY 1994 South African aid budget of $80 million was devoted to that task, as was a total of roughly $35 million since FY 1992. This includes a projected $16 million in support for voter education, $2.7 million on "election support for political parties," $5.5 million for election monitoring, $1.5 million for electoral administration, and $8 million for various activities in support of conflict resolution—all sums without precedent in American political assistance efforts in Africa.[60] Millions of dollars more in support for voter education and electoral monitoring and administration came from European aid agencies and private international business contributions.

NED funding also supports a number of regional efforts at democratic development across Africa. One of the most developed of these is Groupe d'Etudes et de Recherches sur la Démocratie et le Développement Économique et Social (GERDDES), founded in May 1990 and based in Cotonou, Benin. A pan-African civil society organization seeking to build the culture of democracy, to promote its institutional consolidation, and "to put democracy at the service of development," GERDDES-Africa "counts over two thousand members spread across more than 20 African countries, from Zaire in the South to Senegal in the west and Chad in the north."[61] In its first two years, GERDDES-Africa has participated in several national conferences that led to the creation of new constitutions; trained more than 1,000 election observers; sponsored educational seminars and lectures; conducted a number of studies on the process of democratization; and initiated a regular newsletter, *Democracy and Development.*[62]

Many of the regionwide programs of NED in Africa, as well as a number of individual country grants, are administered by NED's four core institutes. In November 1991, NDI cosponsored with GERDDES a regional training seminar on election monitoring (one of several it has organized in Africa) attended by more than 100 representatives from political parties and civic organizations in 15 African countries. Assistance in election monitoring has been one of the most important achievements of both NDI and IRI in Africa. International election monitoring and assistance efforts supported by NDI contributed significantly to the success of the democratic transitions in Namibia, Benin, and Zambia. The joint effort of NDI and the Carter Center of Emory University is credited with playing a particularly instrumental role in the Zambian effort, which trained and placed more than 3,500 Zambians at polling places throughout the country while mobilizing and supporting a wide range of indigenous civic organizations.[63] Strengthening such domestic capacities is a major goal of these international assistance efforts.

Increasingly, election monitoring in Africa involves a wide range of international organizations, including the Commonwealth, the OAU, and the U.N., and is making what are very likely to be lasting improvements in the ability of African countries to conduct free, fair, and widely credible elections.[64] A decade of experience in a wide range of countries has generated and refined techniques, such as the preparation of a parallel vote tabulation (an independent check by election monitors on the accuracy of official vote tallies), that virtually assure the success of election monitoring when sufficient resources and political will are present.[65] Even when the will to administer a free and fair election is lacking, an independent election monitoring effort can play a critical role in documenting fraud and denying the winners so elected domestic and international legitimacy. Such was the effect of NDI's international observer delegation to the October 1992 Cameroonian elections. "In its final report, NDI found serious fault with the electoral process and noted that widespread irregularities called into question the validity of the outcome. The report concluded that 'Cameroon's election system seemed designed to fail.'"[66]

In addition to election monitoring and support for electoral reform and administration (including legal and technical advice to African governments), NDI is engaged in a variety of training and support efforts to strengthen Namibia's national legislature; to train the political parties in Zambia and Niger in campaign, fund-raising, media, and organizing techniques; and to conduct voter education programs in South Africa and Namibia.[67] IRI has been conducting similar election monitoring and party training programs in Africa. Along with NDI, it organized party training seminars and election monitoring efforts in Angola, and it also participated with Commonwealth observers in the Kenyan election monitoring effort. During 1992, it also sponsored youth-oriented civic education in Nigeria and a series of workshops in Zimbabwe to encourage public dialogue among opposition groups and public education about policy issues.[68]

Throughout Africa, FTUI has been working to train organizers for independent trade unions, educate them about their rights as well as the workings of democracy, and assist them in developing their organizational structures and in communicating better with their members. This has involved not only a very substantial investment in working with South Africa's black trade unions (a critical bulwark of the prodemocracy movement there) but also programs in such varied countries as Benin, Burkina Faso, Congo, Ethiopia, and Angola. CIPE's projects have aimed to enhance the understanding of and commitment to liberalizing economic reforms and to strengthen indigenous chambers of commerce and other entrepreneurial organizations in such countries as Kenya, Botswana, Tanzania, Mauritius, Zimbabwe, Namibia, Ghana, Mozambique, and South Africa.[69]

More and more in recent years, AID has been developing into a major instrument of U.S. efforts to promote democracy in Africa. Its Bureau for Africa is now funding a four-year, $12.5-million program of electoral assistance activities, which has provided much of the funding for related efforts by NDI and IRI as well as the African-American Institute (AAI) and the International Foundation for Electoral Systems (IFES). With support from AID, AAI helped organize international observer delegations for the November 1992 and February 1993 presidential elections in Madagascar, which had the stunning democratic outcome (as in Benin and Zambia) of dealing the incumbent a resounding defeat (as happened in Benin and Zambia).[70] AID has funded not only electoral assistance but also many of the institutions and activities in building civil society that are necessary for democratic consolidation. "Under its Democracy and Human Rights Fund for Africa, [AID's] Africa Bureau is providing financial and technical support to indigenous institutions in 35 countries for small, short-term projects, such as election assistance, newsletters and newspapers on human rights, civic education, women's rights, legal libraries, judicial training, and professional workshops and seminars."[71] In Mali, for example, it is now supporting civic education projects and providing assistance to lawyers' associations and the judicial system. As Guinea prepared for legislative elections in late 1993 and presidential elections in early 1994, AID "earmarked assistance for civic education, political party building, pollwatcher training, and observer missions."[72] Moreover, shortly after the Rwandan government and the rebel Rwandan Patriotic Front (RPF) signed a peace accord in August 1993, AID implemented a multifaceted democratic governance initiative, in conjunction with several international development NGOs, to assist the development of the free press, the national assembly, and private associations involved in civic education.[73]

Another leg of the American democracy promotion effort is provided by the U.S. Information Agency (USIA) and its U.S. Information Service missions abroad. Much of the traditional work of USIA over the past forty years—educational and cultural exchanges, training of journalists, provision of independent news and information—has involved nurturing democratic cultures and societies. Increasingly in recent years, however, democracy building has been a central focus of USIA's mission. In Africa and throughout the developing and post-Communist worlds, USIA administers a wide range of activities to explain and advance the concept of democracy; to make available information and counsel on the various institutional and policy options for those trying to develop and consolidate democracy; and to facilitate the forging of contacts and ties with American institutions for those democratic goals. An important example of this effort has occurred in Nigeria, where USIA has been administering some $2 million in funding for exchanges to help develop Nigerian programs in journalism training, political science, public opinion polling, economic policy analysis, civic organization, and so on. In addition to its now-famous Fulbright scholarly exchanges, USIA takes a number of foreign professionals to the United States each year for month-long visits; sponsors lecture tours by American media and policy experts (with a growing emphasis on and demand for speakers on democracy); funds academic and other institutional linkages; and provides books on the theory and practice of democracy and free markets, also facilitating their translation and republication in other languages.

Drawing on their own funding, as well as funding from USAID and roughly $4 million (in FY 1994) in a human rights fund for Africa (administered by the State Department),[74] USIS missions have taken a number of initiatives to respond to democratic openings, demands, and needs in Africa. In South Africa, USIS has supported projects to address issues of community violence, land reform, market

economic reform, and integration of the military and to support public administration training for the historically disadvantaged groups. In Ethiopia, Uganda,
Tanzania, Zambia, Zimbabwe, Namibia, and Ghana, USIS sponsors training and
exchange programs to strengthen indigenous bar associations and law schools
and thereby improve the training of African judges and lawyers and the overall
administration of justice. Just as African lawyers visit the United States, a number
of American lawyers spend time in Africa (typically two to four weeks) to help
develop training and judicial administration programs on a pro bono basis. At
this writing, similar programs are being planned to aid in the development of
local government and business managerial expertise. USIA also has a growing
journalism training program that seeks to enhance the skills of African journalists and editors in covering the political process, economic and financial reporting, and management of the media.[75]

Although many of its activities also serve the long-standing goal of promoting
appreciation of American institutions and values, USIA is increasingly sensitive
to the need to foster an understanding of democracy as a generic idea. Toward
this end, USIA published, in October 1991, an impressive and highly readable
thirty-two-page pamphlet entitled *What Is Democracy,* that has already been
translated into thirty other languages, with over 200,000 copies distributed. Prior
to the historic 1993 referendum on multiparty democracy in Malawi, USIS translated that pamphlet into the principal indigenous language and disseminated it
widely (while also supporting a surge of voter education via the radio).

These various governmental and nongovernmental programs amount to a
substantial and growing American investment in Africa's "second liberation."
And the United States is not alone in these endeavors. The four German party
foundations—the Konrad Adenauer, Friedrich Ebert, Friedrich Naumann, and
Hans Seidel Stiftungen (which are, like NED, publicly funded but autonomous)—have been engaged in these activities much longer than NED, and they
have budgets much larger than NED's.[76] Even if U.S. spending through AID and
USIA is factored in, Germany is probably spending as much or more (as a proportion of its GNP) than the United States on democracy promotion.[77] The
Friedrich Ebert Stiftung alone had, as of the beginning of 1992, thirty-one
projects and programs in some twenty-five African countries disbursing roughly
$20 million in funds for such democratic goals as promoting civil society, devel-
oping democratic local government, and the "promotion of a social dialogue and
democratic consensus."[78]

Democracy assistance efforts are spreading, too. Britain recently established
the Westminster Foundation for Democracy, modeled after NED, and Africa is
one of its principal regional foci. Canada has a parallel organization, the International Center for Human Rights and Democratic Development, which again
has an active Africa program. The Scandinavian overseas development organizations have increasingly supported civil society groups that build democracy. And
the pressure on Japan to establish some kind of democracy promotion program
of its own is growing internationally. This momentum will likely increase apace

with democratic reform inside Japan, which is in the process of transforming its current system, wherein one party is dominant.

Finally, it should be noted that these various democracy promotion organizations are moving toward closer coordination and exchange of information, ideas, and strategies. An important step in this regard was NED's hosting of an international meeting of nongovernmental democracy promotion organizations from the United States, Canada, Britain, and Germany (with the director of Japan's Institute for International Affairs participating as an observer) at Airlie House in February 1993. "The meeting was the first of its kind to bring together these institutions, which, though varied in structures, constituencies, and mandates, share the goal of helping to strengthen democratic government around the world."[79]

How Effective?

The various political assistance efforts for democracy have yet to receive a comprehensive and searching evaluation, though individual projects are evaluated in compliance with U.S. law. Plainly, when millions of dollars are expended on a crash basis in advance of a crucial target date—such as the April 1994 elections in South Africa—there are bound to be leakages, losses, and sheer waste. By the same token, democratic assistance in the high-risk circumstances of Africa's ethnically divided and historically autocratic polities will inevitably suffer seemingly disastrous washouts—such as the brutal military coup in Burundi only months after a USIS-AAI-sponsored conference there on "Democratization in Africa: The Role of the Military" or the implosion of the democratic transition in Nigeria in mid-1993 and the resulting national political crisis, which threw a number of democracy-building exchange programs into temporary suspension. Yet even where democratic aspirations seem to have been set back by a questionable election or the continued heavy-handed manipulation of executive power—as has happened in Cameroon, Kenya, and even Ghana—external assistance may enable civic organizations and independent media to resist political domination, raise public consciousness, and monitor the performance of government much more effectively than in the past. This may lay the groundwork for more profound and enduring democratic gains in future elections or for political breakthroughs, and it may, in combination with closer international scrutiny, impose more potent limits on the ability of incumbent governments to abuse human rights with impunity.

In the typical small, poor African country, modest grants—$10,000 to $50,000—can make a real difference in the development of a fledgling civic organization or the training of democratic lawyers and journalists, and these dollars can also be dispersed more quickly and to a wider range of needy and promising organizations and projects. But ironically, such small grants are often more challenging to monitor, both because newly emergent and small-scale NGOs often still have informal procedures and lack administrative and accounting expertise and because the cost of independently auditing them tends to be prohibitive relative to the size of the grant itself. NED, which was criticized in a 1991 report of the General Accounting Office for inadequate monitoring of its grant recipients, has since strengthened its auditing and review procedures in ways designed to strike a balance between accountability and cost-effectiveness, auditing small grantees periodically. For newly developing democracies, there are other decided advantages to receiving assistance from leaner and less organizationally complex sources. In contrast to AID, which has extremely cumbersome bureaucratic procedures for awarding as well as monitoring grants, USIA and especially NED and its affiliates are able to move much more quickly (and often creatively) to respond to rapidly emerging needs and opportunities for democratic assistance.[80]

Although we still await a comprehensive and dispassionate scholarly assessment of these assistance programs, it is clear to many observers, myself included, that, at a minimum, particular organizations and civil society sectors (probably most dramatically, the human rights movement in Africa) have been strengthened and helped to survive by financial and technical assistance from abroad. No less significant is the moral encouragement they have drawn from the simple knowledge that they are not anonymous and isolated against the forces of a tyrannical state or abusive ruling elite—that they have powerful and alert friends abroad. Weighed against the hundreds of millions of dollars that various Western aid agencies pour into economic development (not to mention military!) assistance for Africa annually, the relatively tiny investments in Africa's civil societies and emergent democratic elites have probably been, *on balance,* well spent. As one scholar of global democratic assistance efforts concluded, "If a fraction of projects have succeeded in their aims, political aid has been a highly cost-effective instrument."[81]

Toward a Democratic Partnership

The increasing inclination of the United States and other major bilateral and multilateral donors to condition aid to Africa on democracy, human rights, accountability, and good governance is likely to continue into the indefinite future and to become more persistent and refined. So are diplomatic pressure in this direction and direct political assistance for democratic institutions and movements. Americans, as well as Europeans and other citizens of well-established democracies, have an important stake in the successful democratization of Africa. And it is not just a moral stake: Democracy is absolutely vital to a more just, peaceful, and stable world order, based on a global rule of law. As I have argued elsewhere:

> Democratic countries do not go to war with one another or sponsor terrorism against other democracies. They do not build weapons of mass destruction to threaten one another. Democratic countries are more reliable, open, and enduring trading partners, and offer more stable climates for investment. Because they must answer to their own citizens, democracies are more environmentally responsible.

They are more likely to honor international treaties and value legal obligations since their openness makes it much more difficult to breach them in secret. Precisely because they respect civil liberties, rights of property, and the rule of law within their own borders, democracies are the only reliable foundation on which to build a new world order of security and prosperity.[82]

The end of the Cold War has not erased the global threats to America's vital economic and security interests. International terrorism, the proliferation of nuclear, chemical, biological, and missile weapons technology, drug trafficking, smuggling, financial fraud, ethnic "cleansing," territorial aggression, and the rising numbers of refugees and immigrants fleeing oppression and injustice—all these threaten the economic and security interests of the United States and its allies. Moreover, because these threats are more diffuse in a multipolar world, they are, in some ways, more difficult to control. Collective security, anchored in the covenants and institutions of the United Nations and other multilateral organizations, has become an essential strategy for managing these diffuse threats. But progress toward democracy is also indispensable.

The linkage between democracy and collective security is abundantly apparent on the African continent. Grave threats to international order, regional security, and human life do not emanate from the small but growing number of democracies in Africa—in particular, Botswana, Gambia, Namibia, and Benin. They emanate from countries where dictatorship has utterly destroyed the fabric of social order and human decency and restraint—Somalia, Liberia, and Zaire. They come from dictatorships such as that in Sudan, which sponsor international terrorism and promulgate religious intolerance, human rights violations, and starvation as warfare on a staggering scale. They erupt in ethnic genocide in a country such as Burundi, where democracy has never taken root and was brutally erased by the military once again in November 1993. They come from military dictatorships such as that in Nigeria, which has become a major locus of the international drug trade and a mecca for international financial swindlers and which faces the specter of national disintegration precisely because of the refusal of these massively corrupt and power-hungry officers to surrender power. Many experts are urging the United Nations to develop an "early warning" system for identifying possible outbreaks of civil war or humanitarian crisis. Those who have studied the evolution of such conflicts already know that common root causes include the monopoly of power and resources by a single ruling group, the absence of dialogue and dissent, and the systematic repression of individual and group rights—in other words, the absence of democracy, with its provisions for power sharing and protections for minorities.

Western publics are also becoming increasingly outraged by various forms of political corruption in their own countries, and they are mobilizing against it. Italy and Japan are being shaken to their political roots by movements for reform. Momentum for reform of campaign finance and political lobbying laws is growing in the United States. And the obscene ties that bind French democrats and African dictators and their clients are also being subjected to closer scrutiny and escalating pressure for political reform within France itself.

Thus, there are powerful reasons of self-interest for the United States and other Western democracies to encourage, foster, and support the democratic trend in Africa and to oppose forthrightly the persistence of authoritarian rule. Failure to do so will only sink the continent deeper and deeper into the hopeless quagmire of famines, civil wars, ethnic slaughters, and other humanitarian crises from which the world cannot simply walk away.

These imperatives are increasingly appreciated not only by policymakers but also by sophisticated publics in the United States and the European democracies. They know that their electorates will not support foreign aid programs if they do not show results. Conditionality, then, can only be expected to intensify.

Moreover, international pressure for democracy is becoming increasingly embedded in global institutions and legal frameworks. This goes well beyond the growing concern of the World Bank and international donor groups about issues of governance and political freedom and pluralism. International organizations like the U.N., the Conference on Security and Cooperation in Europe (CSCE), and the Organization of American States (OAS) are becoming more and more explicitly involved in efforts to promote free elections, human rights, and other institutional aspects of democracy.[83] International law is moving toward affirming a basic right of all peoples to democratic governance, and pressure is growing on international institutions and member governments to guarantee this right and enforce it when it is violated.[84]

Transnational efforts are also developing outside of governmental institutions, in civil society. Following explicitly on the highly effective model of Amnesty International, volunteers from a dozen countries in the north and the south came together in 1993 to form Transparency International (TI), a nonprofit, nongovernmental organization with the explicit purpose of fighting corruption in international business transactions. Through the work of private citizens in countries around the world, it will seek to forge a coalition of governments, businesses, development agencies, and NGOS that will voluntarily agree to rigorous standards of conduct formulated by TI. It will also "educate the public on issues of corruption" through meetings, studies, and an annual report; serve as an information clearinghouse; "provide assistance and expertise" to international businesses and governments to help them implement the standard of conduct; and "research compliance with the standard and in appropriate cases . . . investigate serious contraventions."[85] Although TI will begin with a limited focus on "bribery that significantly affects international business transactions," its capacity to provide an independent and global structure for the pursuit of accountability adds a vital new dimension to international democracy-building efforts.

None of this should be taken as a new form of imperialism or the harbinger of new conflict between Africa and the West. Rather, this increasing global concern for democracy opens new opportunities for partnership in the search for development, social justice, and the peaceful resolution of conflict in Africa. If democracy can be shown to work better in the pursuit of these goals, it will be far easier to make the political case for more aid and more generous debt relief and to attack the deep structural issues of poverty and inequality that Africans rightly wish to place on the global political agenda. There will be little moral and political room for them to do so effectively, however, until they get their own houses in order: No African regime that demands "international justice" on north-south issues is going to be taken seriously when it denies justice to its own people at home. In the meantime, aid will continue to flow, but it is increasingly going to be available only (or primarily) to those regimes that move seriously to institutionalize democracy and human rights.

There are going to be setbacks and very grave crises ahead. Many of the new democracies (or putative democracies) in Africa manifest deeply worrying signs of shallowness, corruption, and instability. A number of authoritarian ruling cliques—like those of the military in Nigeria, of Biya in Cameroon, and of Moi in Kenya—seem just as willing as Mobutu has been in Zaire to plunge their countries into chaos rather than to yield to domestic and international pressures for fundamental democratic change. The rapidly accelerating decay of the state—to the point of virtual irrelevance for the lives of many Africans—makes Liberian- or Somali-style chaos a growing possibility for more than a few African countries. However, Africa's fate is by no means sealed in anarchy or tyranny. If popular forces within these countries and democratic governments abroad mobilize resources effectively and hold fast to their principles, viable democracies can gradually be constructed. In any case, long-standing personal autocracies will not survive indefinitely. The day of the dictator in Africa is slowly but inexorably drawing to a close.

Notes

1. Since "democracy" is a term open to many interpretations and appropriations—including those of African one-party dictatorships that have styled themselves "people's democracies," "guided democracies," "one-party democracies," and so on—a definition is necessary at the outset. Throughout this chapter, "democracy" denotes a system of government based on extensive competition for power through regular, free, fair, and essentially peaceful elections; a highly inclusive political regime, such that no adult social group is formally or effectively excluded from rights of participation and citizenship; and extensive civil liberties—freedoms of speech, press, assembly, movement, organization, conscience, and due process of law—sufficient to guarantee that political competition and participation are meaningful. Although this generic definition does not prescribe any particular constitutional structure and is therefore not, in my view, ethnocentric, it does seem to require, as a matter of practicality if not principle, a multiparty system. Experience with numerous one-party regimes, particularly in the postcolonial period, strongly suggests that the features of democracy mentioned here cannot develop in circumstances where political party competition and opposition are prohibited. On the conceptual issues, see Larry Diamond, Juan J. Linz, and Seymour Martin Lipset, eds., *Democracy in Developing Countries: Africa* (Boulder: Lynne Rienner Publishers, 1988), pp. xvi–xvii; Larry

Diamond, "The Globalization of Democracy," in Robert O. Slater, Barry M. Schutz, and Steven R. Dorr, "Global Transformation and the Third World (Boulder: Lynne Rienner Publishers, 1993), pp. 39–40; and Philippe C. Schmitter and Terry Lynn Karl, "What Democracy Is . . . and Is Not," *Journal of Democracy* 2, no. 3 (Summer 1991), pp. 75–88. On the empirical and normative requirement for multiparty competition in Africa, see Claude Ake, "Rethinking African Democracy," *Journal of Democracy* 2, no. 1 (Winter 1991), pp. 32–44, and Peter Anyang' Nyong'o, "Africa: The Failure of One-Party Rule," *Journal of Democracy* 3, no. 1 (January 1992), pp. 90–96.

2. Ambassador James K. Bishop, "Text of Remarks in Cleveland, Ohio, October 23, 1992" (State Department, Bureau of Human Rights), p. 1.

3. Ibid., p. 2.

4. Michael Clough, *Free at Last? U.S. Policy Toward Africa and the End of the Cold War* (New York: Council on Foreign Relations, 1992), p. 77.

5. Quoted in ibid., p. 85. Emphasis in the original.

6. Ibid., p. 80.

7. Michael G. Schatzberg, *Mobutu or Chaos: The United States and Zaire, 1960–1990* (Lanham, Md.: University Press of America, and Philadelphia: Foreign Policy Research Institute, 1991), pp. 61–87.

8. The "third wave" is Samuel Huntington's term for the rapid, "snowballing" increase in the number of democracies in the world, beginning with the transitions to democracy in 1974–1975 in Portugal, Spain, and Greece and continuing through the numerous African transitions of the early 1990s. The first "long wave" of democratization ended in the early 1920s, and the second wave ran from the end of World War II to the early 1960s, each followed by a "reverse wave" of democratic breakdowns. Samuel P. Huntington, "Democracy's Third Wave," *Journal of Democracy* 2, no. 2 (Spring 1991), pp. 12–34, and his *The Third Wave: Democratization in the Late Twentieth Century* (Norman: University of Oklahoma Press, 1991).

9. Clough, *"Free at Last?"* pp. 94–95.

10. Ibid., pp. 99–100. Assistant Secretary Cohen's refusal to meet with human rights activists or to publicly criticize the Moi regime during his 1990 visit to Kenya was particularly regrettable.

11. "The United States and Africa: A New Relationship," Remarks by Secretary of State Warren Christopher at the 23rd African-American Institute Conference, Reston, Va., May 21, 1993, p. 2.

12. John Harbeson and Donald Rothchild, "Africa in Post-Cold War International Politics: Changing Agendas," in Harbeson and Rothchild, eds., *Africa in World Politics,* 1st ed. (Boulder: Westview Press, 1991), p. 8.

13. Donald Rothchild, "Regional Peacemaking in Africa: The Role of the Great Powers as Facilitators," in John Harbeson and Donald Rothchild, eds., *Africa in World Politics,* 1st ed. (Boulder: Westview Press, 1991), pp. 292–296.

14. Bishop, "Remarks," p. 7.

15. Richard Joseph, "Africa: The Rebirth of Political Freedom," *Journal of Democracy* 2, no. 4 (Fall 1991), p. 15.

16. For a summary of recent evidence, see Larry Diamond, "Civil Society and the Development of Democracy: Some International Perspectives and Lessons," paper presented to the workshop on "Civil Society and Democracy," Goree Institute, Dakar, Senegal, March 15–17, 1993; Naomi Chazan, "Africa's Democratic Challenge: Strengthening the State and Civil Society," *World Policy Journal* 9, no. 2 (Spring 1992), pp. 279–308; Peter

Lewis, "Political Transition and the Dilemma of Civil Society in Africa," *Journal of International Affairs* 27, no. 1 (Summer 1992), pp. 31–54; and Michael Bratton and Nicholas van de Walle, "Toward Governance in Africa: Popular Demands and State Responses," in Goran Hyden and Michael Bratton, eds., *Governance and Politics in Africa* (Boulder: Lynne Rienner Publishers, 1992), pp. 27–56.

17. Ake, "Rethinking African Democracy," pp. 34 and 35.

18. Ibid., p. 34; see also Anyang' Nyong'o, "Africa: The Failure of One-Party Rule," p. 91; and George B.N. Ayittey, *Indigenous African Institutions* (Ardsley-on-Hudson, N.Y.: Transnational Publishers, 1991).

19. Anyang' Nyong'o, "Africa: The Failure of One-Party Rule," p. 96.

20. Quoted in Robert Charlick, "The Concept of Governance and Its Implications for AID's Development Assistance Program in Africa," an internal AID document, Associates in Rural Development, Washington, D.C., June 1992, p. 1 (emphases in original).

21. World Bank, *World Development Report 1992* (Washington, D.C.: World Bank, 1992), p. 196, table A.2.

22. Ake, "Rethinking African Democracy," p. 35.

23. The United Nations Development Programme and the World Bank, *African Development Indicators* (Washington, D.C.: World Bank, 1992), tables 6–21, 2–1, and 2–14.

24. Samuel DeCalo, "The Process, Prospects, and Constraints of Democratization in Africa," *African Affairs* 91, no. 362 (January 1992), p. 14.

25. The countries, in descending order of aid, were Tanzania, Kenya, Mozambique, Ethiopia, Zaire, and Sudan. See Table 12.1, and Freedom House, *Freedom in the World: Political Rights and Civil Liberties, 1990–91* (New York: Freedom House, 1991), pp. 454–455. All but one (Senegal) of the top six recipients of U.S. economic and military assistance during fiscal year 1990 were also highly authoritarian; see the Department of State internal document *Country Reports on Human Rights Practices for 1991*, pp. 1658–1659.

26. Charlick, "The Concept of Governance," p. 2.

27. World Bank, *Sub-Saharan Africa: From Crisis to Sustainable Growth* (Washington, D.C.: World Bank, 1989).

28. Ake, "Rethinking African Democracy," p. 36.

29. See, for example, World Bank, *Managing Development: The Governance Decision* (Washington, D.C.: World Bank, 1991).

30. The U.S. Agency for International Development, "The Democracy Initiative," an internal AID document, December 1990, p. 3.

31. Charlick, "The Concept of Governance," pp. 6–8.

32. Quoted in Ake, "Rethinking African Democracy," p. 39.

33. "Good Government and the Aid Programme," Address of Mrs. Lynda Chalker to ODI/Chatham House (1991).

34. Summarized in Pearl T. Robinson, "The National Conference Phenomenon in Francophone Africa," paper presented to the UCLA African Studies Conference, Los Angeles, Calif., February 1993, p. 11.

35. Decalo, "Democratization in Africa," pp. 19–20; emphases in the original.

36. Ibid., p. 19.

37. Quoted in Ake, "Rethinking African Politics," p. 39.

38. The quote is from Joel D. Barkan, "Kenya: Lessons from a Flawed Election," *Journal of Democracy* 4, no. 3 (July 1993), p. 89. For documentation, see the U.S. State Department's Annual *Country Reports on Human Rights Practices,* the annual and periodic special

reports of Amnesty International and Africa Watch, and Gibson Kamau Kuria, "Confronting Dictatorship in Kenya," *Journal of Democracy* 2, no. 4 (Fall 1991), pp. 115–126.

39. Barkan, "Kenya: Lessons from a Flawed Election," p. 91.

40. Quoted in ibid., from the World Bank, Press Release of the Meeting of the Consultative Group for Kenya, Paris, November 26, 1991.

41. Githu Muigai, "Kenya's Opposition and the Crisis of Governance," *Issue* ("A Journal of Opinion" of the U.S. African Studies Association) 21, no. 1-2 (1993), p. 29.

42. "American Foreign Policy and the Democratic Ideal," Remarks by Governor Bill Clinton, Pabst Theatre, Milwaukee, Wisc., October 1, 1992, pp. 5 and 6.

43. Christopher, "The United States and Africa: A New Relationship," pp. 2 and 5.

44. *The Economist*, May 29, 1993, p. 46.

45. *Frontlines* an in-house newsletter, U.S. Agency for International Development, Washington, D.C., June 1993, pp. 3–4.

46. *West Africa*, May 31–June 6, 1993, p. 902.

47. Christopher, "The United States and Africa: A New Relationship," p. 5.

48. *Newswatch* (Lagos), July 5, 1993, pp. 14–15.

49. "Laying the Foundation of a Viable Democracy and the Path of Honour," Address by the president and commander-in-chief of the armed forces of the Federal Republic of Nigeria, General Ibrahim Badamasi Babangida, to the nation on Saturday, June 26, 1993, in *Newswatch* (Lagos), July 5, 1993, pp. 17–18.

50. Opening speech of François Mitterrand, President of France, at the Fourth Conference of the Heads of State and Government of the Francophone Countries, Paris, November 19, 1991; English translation, French Embassy and Press Service, Washington, D.C., p. 2.

51. John R. Heilbrunn, "The Social Origins of National Conferences: A Comparison of Benin and Togo," *Journal of Modern African Studies* 31, no. 2 (June 1993), pp. 277–301.

52. *Africa Report* (March-April 1993), p. 62. Worse still, reports the defeated opposition candidate Fru Ndi, "The French government's ministry to Cameroon openly accused the U.S. government" of supporting his party, the Social Democratic Front (SDF) in charges that were repeated by the government-controlled press.

53. *West Africa*, July 11, 1993, p. 1146.

54. *The Economist*, May 29, 1993, p. 46.

55. Robinson, "The National Conference Phenomenon in Francophone Africa," p. 6.

56. Ibid., pp. 8–9. Only an appreciation of this complex web of reciprocal interests, Robinson suggested, can adequately explain former French prime minister and once and future presidential candidate Jacques Chirac's statement, made at the time of the Benin national conference, that multipartyism was a "political error" and a "luxury" for developing countries.

57. *The Economist*, May 29, 1993, p. 46.

58. National Endowment for Democracy, *1992 Annual Report* (October 1, 1991–September 30, 1992) (Washington, D.C.: NED, 1992), pp. 32–41.

59. Ibid., pp. 37–38.

60. (Cape Town) *Cape Times*, February 15, 1994, p. 6.

61. Honoré Koffi Guie, "Organizing Africa's Democrats," *Journal of Democracy* 4, no. 2 (April 1993), p. 120.

62. Ibid.

63. Larry Garber and Eric Bjornlund, "Election Monitoring in Africa," in Festus Eribo,

Oyeleye Oyediran, Mulatu Wubneh, and Leo Zonn, eds., *Window on Africa: Democratization and Media Exposure* (Greenville, N.C.: East Carolina University, Center for International Programs, March 1993), pp. 28–50; Eric Bjornlund, Michael Bratton, and Clark Gibson, "Observing Multiparty Elections in Africa: Lessons from Zambia," *African Affairs* 91 (1992), pp. 405–431.

64. Garber and Bjornlund, "Election Monitoring in Africa," and Larry Garber, "The OAU and Elections," *Journal of Democracy* 4, no. 3 (July 1993), pp. 55–59.

65. Larry Garber and Glenn Cowan, "The Virtues of Parallel Vote Tabulations," *Journal of Democracy* 4, no. 2 (April 1993), pp. 94–107.

66. National Democratic Institute of International Affairs, "1992: A Year in Review" (Annual Report), (Washington, D.C.: NDIIA, 1993), p. 8. The thoroughness and effectiveness of NDI's election monitoring experience and its early warning of serious flaws in Kenya's preparations for the December 1992 elections may help to explain why the Kenyan government hindered its efforts to work with Kenyan civic organizations to develop a nonpartisan election monitoring program and ultimately excluded NDI from the international observing process.

67. Ibid., pp. 8–12.

68. National Endowment for Democracy, *1992 Annual Report,* pp. 36–39.

69. Ibid.

70. *African Voices* 2, no. 1 (Spring 1993), p. 2. *African Voices* is "a newsletter on democracy and governance in Africa" of the USAID Bureau for Africa.

71. *African Voices* 1, no. 1 (Summer 1992), p. 2.

72. *African Voices* 2, no. 1 (Spring 1993), p. 5.

73. *African Voices* 2, no. 3 (Fall-Winter 1993), p. 5.

74. These global human rights funds are sometimes referred to as "116E accounts" after the relevant section of the legislation that designates their transfer from AID to the State Department for management. Grants from this fund are typically more innovative and groundbreaking because they can be awarded by local U.S. embassies in amounts of $25,000 or less without approval from Washington.

75. Interview with Robert LaGamma, director, Office of African Affairs, U.S. Information Agency, Washington, D.C., November 8, 1993.

76. In 1988, the German government spent a total of $170 million on the four party foundations. Even if we factor out their overseas spending on more traditional types of economic and social development, they probably still spent about $85 million on supporting democratic political institutions, trade unions, media, and associations abroad. Michael Pinto-Duschinsky, "Foreign Political Aid: The German Political Foundations and their U.S. Counterparts," *International Affairs* 67, no. 1 (1991), pp. 33–63. My estimate of $85 million is derived from applying the percentages on the first four types of foreign activities he listed in table 4 to the total funding amounts he gave in table 1.

77. In 1992, I estimated, "All told, America spends no more than $200 million annual in political assistance to democratic forces and institutions, and perhaps $400 million if one includes as an estimate of USIA's effort 20 percent of its roughly $1 billion budget;" Larry Diamond, "Promoting Democracy," *Foreign Policy* 87 (Summer 1992), p. 46. This has no doubt increased, at least somewhat, under the Clinton administration, which recommended an increase in the NED budget for fiscal year 1994 from $30 to $50 million (cut back by Congress to $35 million) and that seems to be sharply increasing democracy-related spending by AID and USIA.

78. "The Activities of the Friedrich Ebert Foundation, by Region," document pre-

sented at the summit meeting of democracy promotion organizations sponsored by the National Endowment for Democracy, Airlie House, Warrenton, Va., February 4–6, 1993.

79. *Journal of Democracy* 4, no. 2 (April 1993), p. 141.

80. In some instances, the response can be quite rapid—within one to two months. Not only USIS missions but also private U.S. foundations such as the Ford Foundation are often able to disperse smaller grants (e.g., less than $25,000 or $50,000) from the field office, without the more extensive bureaucratic procedures that require approval from a U.S.-based headquarters, with all the delays that implies, especially for the continent with the worst communications linkages to the developed world.

81. Pinto-Duschinsky, "Foreign Political Aid," p. 60.

82. Diamond, "Promoting Democracy," pp. 30–31.

83. See the articles in the symposium on "International Organizations and Democracy," *Journal of Democracy* 4, no. 3 (July 1993), pp. 3–69.

84. Thomas M. Franck, "The Emerging Right to Democratic Governance," *American Journal of International Law* 86 (1992), pp. 46–91; Morton H. Halperin and Kristin Lomasney, "Toward a Global 'Guarantee Clause,'" *Journal of Democracy* 4, no. 3 (July 1993), pp. 60–69; and Morton H. Halperin, "Guaranteeing Democracy," *Foreign Policy* 91 (Summer 1993), pp. 105–122.

85. Transparency International, "Statement of Decisions," Latimer House, United Kingdom, July 25, 1992; see also *African Voices* 1, no. 2 (Fall-Winter 1992), p. 3.

13

Political and Military Security

HERMAN J. COHEN

A SOLEMN SIGNING ceremony at the United Nations headquarters in New York on December 22, 1988, inaugurated a profound change in African thinking about political and military security. On that day, the governments of Angola, Cuba, and South Africa signed three protocols opening the way for the implementation of U.N. Resolution 435 and the independence of Namibia.[1] The prospect that Namibia—Africa's last colony—would be independent by March 1990 was of enormous significance by itself. But in addition, the New York accords brought Africa across some important thresholds.

• A Cuban agreement to remove all its troops from Angola marked the end of Cuban "internationalism" in support of African Marxist regimes. Cuban troops and military trainers were removed from Mozambique and Ethiopia as well.

• Unofficial but real cooperation between the United States and the Soviet Union in bringing about the New York accords marked the beginning of the end of the Cold War in Africa.[2]

• In Namibia, the transition from South African rule to independence was made under the supervision of a substantial United Nations presence, marking the return of the U.N. to political-military intervention in Africa for the first time since the peacekeeping operation in the Congo from 1960 to 1963.

• The fact that the U.N. Security Council required that Namibia reach independence only after a pluralistic election sent a signal that the African one-party state was losing its legitimacy in the international community.

• In South Africa, the departure of Cuban troops from both Angola and the continent of Africa, as well as the end of U.S.-Soviet competition in southern Africa, undercut the right-wing rationale that apartheid was the only barrier to an "international Communist" takeover of that troubled country. Only a year after the New York accords, a new generation of white political leaders had come to power and had begun the process of dismantling apartheid.

The four-year period following the New York accords of December 1988 (1989–1993) was marked by a proliferation of efforts to end conflict and liberalize politics throughout Africa. The results have been mixed. At the end of 1993, Africa had fewer conflicts, a greater degree of political openness, and a larger number of elected governments than at the beginning of 1989. But for every two steps forward toward pluralism and national reconciliation, there has been one step backward toward unstable government and fragile postconflict structures.

Africa's Civil Wars Begin to Wind Down

Among the many impediments to African development since the great wave of independence between 1959 and 1974, civil conflict has been the most devastating. Wars and insurgencies in Angola, Mozambique, Ethiopia, Sudan, Liberia, the Western Sahara, Rwanda, Uganda, Somalia, and Chad destroyed economies and threw millions of refugees onto the health and welfare systems of neighboring countries. Billions of dollars in disaster relief assistance furnished by international relief agencies and donor governments were vital to saving lives and keeping the affected nations afloat, but development necessarily took a back seat to this emergency activity.

Informal Soviet-U.S. cooperation in bringing about the 1988 accords became more structured after the Bush administration came to office in Washington in January 1989. As part of a worldwide effort to work together to solve regional problems, the U.S. and Soviet governments began a pattern of formal consultations on Africa.[3] It was no coincidence, therefore, that the wars in Ethiopia and Angola received priority attention from the two superpowers as they began to address Africa's "regional problems." The Gorbachev government in the USSR was particularly anxious to be relieved of its arms supply commitments amounting to approximately $1 billion per year to each of those self-styled Marxist regimes.[4]

Ethiopia

Despite U.S. and Italian efforts to mediate a peaceful solution between mid-1989 and early 1991, Ethiopia's thirty-year war ended the last week of May 1991 with a military victory by the two biggest insurgent groups, the Tigrayan People's Liberation Front (TPLF) and the Eritrean People's Liberation Front. In the final moments of the war, American diplomats took advantage of their long-standing ties to the TPLF and EPLF leadership, as well as the U.S. role as official mediator, to broker a peace package that led to: (1) an all-parties conference of national reconciliation in July 1991; (2) a self-determination referendum in Eritrea in May 1993;

(3) a commitment by all insurgent leaders to pluralistic democracy; and (4) a decision to maintain a common market between Ethiopia and Eritrea after the latter's independence.[5]

At the end of 1993, Ethiopia and Eritrea were still at peace, with the TPLF and EPLF insurgent leadership well ensconced in power in their respective countries. Although both governments had yet to cross thresholds to democracy, they had taken steps toward political and economic liberalization, thereby lowering the humanitarian burden of the international community that has responded with substantial development assistance. Nevertheless, the relatively positive situation in these countries contrasted dramatically with neighboring Sudan and Somalia, where civil conflict intensified between 1989 and 1993 (as I will discuss). As a result, the Horn remained Africa's most insecure subregion at the end of 1993.

Angola

If the Soviet-U.S. partnership had leverage anywhere in Africa in 1989, it was in Angola where the two superpowers were important arms suppliers to their respective clients, the Angolan government and the UNITA rebel movement. Under the triple mediation of the Portuguese, Soviet, and American governments, the Angolan warring parties negotiated a peace accord that was signed in Lisbon on May 31, 1991. The accord called for the encampment and disarmament of all fighters, the formation of a new national army made up equally of troops from both sides, and the holding of free and fair elections in a time frame between sixteen and twenty-four months after the signing. The entire process was to be monitored by United Nations peacekeeping forces.[6]

Angolan presidential and parliamentary elections were held on September 26, 1992, despite the fact that the disarmament, encampment, and formation of a new national army called for by the Lisbon agreements were far from completed. U.N. and other international observers declared the elections to be free and fair. The results gave the ruling MPLA party a large majority in parliament and incumbent President dos Santos a 49 percent plurality, requiring a runoff in the presidential race.

Within days after the election, Jonas Savimbi, the president of UNITA, declared the election results to be fraudulent despite the near unanimous views of all the observers to the contrary. In addition, the U.N. monitoring force of four hundred soldiers had been too small to prevent cheating in disarmament and encampment by both sides immediately preceding the elections. It was inevitable, therefore, that hostilities would resume, and by the end of October 1992, Angola was again in flames.[7] Between the resumption of fighting in October 1992 and mid-1993, the military advantage was with UNITA, which had infiltrated troops into many areas in the central highlands from which it had previously been excluded. By dint of heavy arms purchases through the sale of oil futures, the Angolan government was able to bring the fighting to a stalemate by September 1993.[8] In the interim, the American government formally recognized the Angolan government, thereby enhancing the latter's legitimacy.

As of the end of 1993, negotiations were under way in Lusaka, Zambia, through the mediation of the United Nations. Preliminary to the negotiations, UNITA informed mediator Blondin Beye that it agreed to withdraw from territories conquered after the September 1992 elections and to abide by the Lisbon peace agreement of May 1991.[9] However, what UNITA wanted in exchange was expected to be substantial. This included significant power sharing in the central government, a highly decentralized federal system with UNITA governors in several provinces, and an important share of Angola's abundant oil and mineral revenues.[10] While negotiations were going on, hundreds of thousands of Angolans were either dying or under severe stress from lack of food, medicine, and shelter due to the fighting. Having ended their arms supply relationships with their former Angolan clients, the American and Russian governments found their leverage significantly reduced.

Mozambique

Unlike the government in its lusophone sister Angola, the newly independent government of Mozambique did not become a Cold War pawn in 1975 and beyond. The anti-Portuguese guerrilla movement, Front for the Liberation of Mozambique, was never contested by other groups at independence, whereas Angola had three competing movements. The Popular Movement for the Liberation of Angola was installed in power by a Cuban expeditionary force in 1975, but the Marxist FRELIMO in Mozambique was universally recognized as the legitimate ruling party, even by the United States.[11] Nevertheless, Mozambique suffered a civil war that many observers characterized as the worst in sub-Saharan Africa in terms of refugees and civilian casualties.

Mozambique's problem came from its involvement in the independence struggle of neighboring Southern Rhodesia (later to become Zimbabwe) and, after 1980, in the anti-apartheid struggle in neighboring South Africa. Because the FRELIMO government provided safe havens for anti-Rhodesian freedom fighters, the white Rhodesian intelligence service organized, financed, and trained an anti-FRELIMO guerrilla movement in Mozambique. Called the National Renewal Movement of Mozambique, the guerrilla group combined Rhodesian aid and anti-FRELIMO grievances among ethnic groups in central Mozambique to develop a particularly vicious and formidable insurgency. After Rhodesia became independent Zimbabwe in 1980, South African military intelligence became RENAMO's godfather.[12] Ironically, because the Mozambican civil war had no Cold War component and because the RENAMO rebel movement was befriended only by white Rhodesia and later by white South Africa, it was more difficult to negotiate a settlement there than in Angola where the Soviet and American superpowers could pressure their respective clients. The FRELIMO government insisted that it could not legitimize a movement such as RENAMO by negotiating with it.

After the signing of the Angolan peace accords of May 31, 1991, U.S. President Bush met with Mozambican President Chissano the following month in Washington. At that meeting, Bush prevailed upon Chissano to agree to negotiate with RENAMO without any preconditions.[13] Most of the second half of 1991 was lost in the search for a mutually acceptable mediator, which later turned out to be a Roman Catholic lay order in Rome called Sant Egidio. Both the Italian and American governments provided extensive technical assistance to this mediation effort. The negotiations concluded with a peace accord signed in Rome at the end of October 1992, just as the Angolan peace was falling apart. With the failed experience of Angola as a lesson, the U.N. Security Council approved a large peacekeeping operation in Mozambique of 8,000 personnel with a determination to delay the required democratic election until all military dispositions had been completed, including the encampment and disarmament of all fighters, the organization of a new national army, and the establishment of RENAMO as a political party. As of the end of 1993, Mozambique was continuing the process of implementing the agreements. Travel in the interior was safe, and many of the million refugees outside of Mozambique, especially those in neighboring Malawi, were wending their way home in an act of spontaneous repatriation. Although fragile, the peace in Mozambique appeared sustainable given the heavy international support mechanism that has been established.[14]

Liberia

When Master Sergeant Samuel K. Doe and a small band of noncommissioned officers overthrew the Liberian government in 1980, there was euphoria among the nation's tribal populations, who rejoiced at the idea that the "apartheid" rule of the minority Americo-Liberian group was coming to an end. By 1985, however, that good feeling had succumbed to disillusionment because Doe's government had become an exclusive territory of the Krahn and Mandingo tribes and was characterized by increasing corruption and oppression. After Doe rigged the presidential election of 1985, it was only a matter of time before challenges to his rule would emerge. He managed to head off several amateurish coup attempts between 1985 and 1988, but he came up against an insurgent movement in Nimba County in 1989 that proved to be his undoing.

Led by a Libyan-trained Americo-Liberian adventurer named Charles Taylor, a small band of guerrillas began to attack government installations and personnel in Nimba County during Christmas 1989. The Liberian army played right into Taylor's hands by burning down villages and killing innocent civilians wherever the insurgents made an appearance. This had the effect of adding ardent, revenge-seeking young male recruits to Taylor's operation among the Mano and Gio populations. There were, in fact, so many recruits that the Libyan government had to mount an airlift through Burkina Faso to keep the insurgents supplied with munitions.[15]

By April 1990, the insurgents were at the gates of Monrovia, having driven the Liberian army out of 90 percent of Liberian territory. Final victory eluded Taylor, however, for two reasons. First, he lost a significant portion of his fighters when one of his lieutenants, named Prince Johnson, broke away to establish a rival guerrilla operation. Second, Doe was able to defend the presidential palace with his specially trained presidential commandos. With no escape possible in their surrounded redoubt, Doe's men fought as if their lives depended on it, which they did. While the siege of Monrovia was going on, the city itself was rapidly starving because international agencies could not bring in relief supplies. In the rest of Liberia, approximately 600,000 people, one-fourth of the population, had fled across borders to take refuge in neighboring Liberia, Sierre Leone, and Guinea.

Between April and August 1993, several significant events took place.

• The American government decided to abstain from playing a role in the search for a solution to the Liberian conflict despite its special historical relationship with Liberia.[16]

• The U.S. Navy stationed a 2,500-man amphibious force off the coast of Liberia to help evacuate American citizens, but it did not use this force to stop the fighting in Monrovia.

• Under Nigerian leadership, the governments of the Economic Community of West African States assumed a major role in the Liberian conflict, first as mediators and then as a military intervention force (ECOMOG), which arrived in Monrovia in June 1990.

• President Doe was assassinated by Prince Johnson after he walked into a trap, despite the presence of ECOMOG troops.

For three years, until mid-1993, the ECOWAS military force known as ECOMOG jousted with Charles Taylor's army, eventually wearing Taylor down to the point where he accepted a peace agreement that called for disarmament, the encampment of forces, the establishment of an interim government, and the holding of democratic elections under international supervision. As of the end of 1993, slow progress was being made in the organization of an interim government, and the first U.N. peace keeping troops from Tanzania and Zimbabwe were starting to arrive. The ECOWAS military intervention had become something of a role model for the concept of Africans engaging in conflict management at the regional and subregional level.

Insecurity in the Horn: Sudan and Somalia

In stark contrast to the forward movement in the resolution of the four conflicts just described, the conflicts in Sudan and Somalia appeared to be intractable as 1993 came to a close.

Sudan

A military coup overthrew the democratically elected government of Sadik El Mahdi in June 1991. Within a year, it became apparent that the military regime was essentially a cover for the radical National Islamic Front (NIF), a fundamentalist political movement led by Hassan Turabi. That severely dimmed the prospects for a negotiated settlement of the three-decade-old war between the Sudanese government and rebel southern Sudanese insurgents in the southern third of the country, led by Colonel John Garang. The southern rebel movement was and continues to be called the Sudan People's Liberation Movement. The most important grievance of the largely Christian-animist southern black population was the Khartoum government's policy of imposing Islamic Sharia law and Arab culture on the entire country. With the NIF in power, it was not likely that Khartoum would make concessions in this area.

By mid-1991, the three southern provinces had already suffered tremendous devastation in the destruction of livestock and infrastructure, along with the deaths of tens of thousands of innocent civilians and the departure of hundreds of thousands of refugees to neighboring countries. The situation was made even worse in July 1991 when the SPLM split over policies and personalities. A breakaway group led by Colonel Riak Machar denounced Garang for alleged arbitrary and oppressive rule over the movement. Machar also called for a change of the movement's war aims. While Garang continued to seek to overthrow the regime in Khartoum, Machar decided that the movement should fight to split the three southern provinces away from Sudan and form a new state. The two groups engaged in combat, and the Machar group gave intelligence support to the Sudanese army in an effort to eliminate Garang. Machar had hoped that, in return for his help against Garang, the Khartoum government would accept the right of the southern people to decide their own future in a referendum. At a tripartite negotiating meeting in Abuja, Nigeria, in July 1992, however, Machar found that the Sudanese government would not consider self-determination for the south as an option but was willing to consider exempting the south from the application of Sharia law.

Trilateral fighting continued in the south until October 1993, when Garang and Machar went to Washington, D.C., for negotiations conducted by Chairman Harry Johnston of the House Africa Sub-Committee. These negotiations led to a cease-fire between the two rebel factions, which was holding as 1993 came to a close. There was no sign, however, of any movement toward resumed negotiations between the south and the north. During their visit to Washington, Riak Machar continued to call for southern secession, while John Garang said that he would try to negotiate a very loose confederation, failing which he, too, would opt for secession. Meanwhile, the war continued under conditions that relief workers were calling the most devastating in human terms of all the conflicts in Africa.[17]

Somalia

December 1993 marked the first anniversary of the U.N. military intervention to restore order after the collapse of the Somali central government in January 1991 created a catastrophic situation of anarchy and massive starvation. The first phase of the intervention was called UNITAF and was under American military command from December 1992 to May 1993. This phase effectively restored security to the point where international and Somali relief agencies could reestablish humanitarian relief networks, thereby allowing food and medicine to flow to those in need. The intervention also permitted Somali farmers in the southern river valleys to plant crops during March 1993, thus assuring sufficient production for Somalia's basic food needs during the second half of 1993.

As previously ordered by the U.N. Security Council,[18] the American command handed control of the peace enforcement operation to a U.N. command in May 1993. The mission of the U.N. operation, known as UNOSOM II, was to help the Somali people begin to reestablish government, civic society, and economic activity. Unfortunately, the accomplishment of this mission was delayed indefinitely because of violent disputes between armed Somali clan militias, the absence of any political consensus among the Somali clans, and the hostility of some of the clans to the United Nations presence. In particular, clan leader Mohamed Farah Aideed, who played a major role in the military defeat of former dictator Siad Barre in January 1991, attacked U.N. military personnel patrolling his home base in the southern half of the Somali capital of Mogadishu. The deaths of sixteen American soldiers in September 1993 sent shock waves through public opinion in the United States, prompting President Clinton to order the total pullout of U.S. forces no later than March 31, 1994.[19]

As of early 1994, efforts by mediators from the neighboring countries of Ethiopia and Eritrea to forge a political consensus among the Somali clan and military leaders appeared to be accomplishing nothing. Warlord Aideed continued to threaten the United Nations, and as the departure of American forces loomed closer, the total collapse of the U.N. peace enforcement operation was feared. If that happened, Somalia could return to its earlier situation of total anarchy and mass starvation. More and more troop contributors to UNOSOM II were expressing the view that the lives of their military should not be at risk if the Somalis themselves could not end their squabbling. The disillusionment of the international community with the Somali operation was also causing major rethinking about the U.N.'s role in the resolution of civil wars, with a growing reluctance in the Security Council to consider every new civil war a "threat to international peace and security."[20]

The first African casualty of this loss of zeal in the Security Council was Burundi, whose fledgling democracy suffered a botched coup in October 1993 in which tens of thousands of people were killed in ethnic fighting. When the restored democratic government and the loyal elements of the army requested U.N. monitors to help restore confidence within the population, the Security Council refused to become involved. The refusal aroused the Organization of African Unity to seek urgent funding to send two hundred African monitors.[21] The OAU's quest was successful, and at the end of 1993, preparations were made to bring the two hundred civilian and military personnel to Burundi as that nation slowly pulled itself back together after yet another tragedy in its long history of ethnic conflict.[22]

African Conflict Management: An Idea Whose Time Is Coming

In July 1993, the Organization of African Unity held its thirty-first annual heads of state conference in Cairo, Egypt. At their 1992 meeting in Dakar, Senegal, the heads of state ordered that a study be done to determine the feasibility of establishing a conflict management mechanism within the OAU secretariat. In Cairo, OAU Secretary-General Salim Salim presented a plan to establish a conflict management department that would concentrate on early warning of potential conflict within or between member states, followed by intensive mediating efforts to prevent violence from breaking out. The idea that the OAU, as a multilateral assembly of sovereign African governments, would involve itself in the internal affairs of a member state constituted a major breakthrough in doctrine for that organization.

The OAU heads of state had little choice but to overcome their collective, deeply felt aversion to involvement in the internal affairs of member states. The noninterference doctrine had begun to make the organization look increasingly redundant after the intensive American mediation efforts in Ethiopia, Angola, and Mozambique, as well as the mediating work of the Italians, Portuguese, Soviets, and the U.N. secretary-general in a variety of African internal conflict situations. The Nigerian-led peace enforcement operation in Liberia known as ECOMOG, which began in August 1990, and the U.S.-led humanitarian operation in Somalia, which began in December 1992, were signals that the OAU had better start to become involved in conflict management if it wanted to avoid becoming completely irrelevant.

The OAU heads of state approved Salim's proposal with the policy guidance that placed an emphasis on conflict prevention.[23] They expressed the view that should violence break out on a large scale, the OAU would lack the resources to replicate the actions of ECOMOG in Liberia. Large-scale peacekeeping activities could only be undertaken by the United Nations Security Council, with Africans supplying peacekeeping troops as required. The first real test for the OAU came in Burundi in November 1993, even before the new conflict management mechanism could get off the ground. With the Security Council reluctant to take on peacekeeping responsibilities for yet another civil conflict, the OAU had to jump into the breach quickly, which it did rather rapidly (as discussed earlier). Given that the Burundi operation was handled with a modicum of success, the new OAU conflict management mechanism is likely to require significant international support in order to get started.[24]

Political Security: Africa's Avalanche of "Democratic" Elections

At the end of 1993, it was difficult to identify more than a handful of sub-Saharan African countries that had not experienced some type of opening toward political pluralism in the previous three years. The laggards are described as follows.

• The Sudan actually reversed course after a military coup overthrew a multiparty democracy in June 1989. Since then, independent newspapers, labor unions, student groups, and political parties have been effectively suppressed, and there has been no sign of any movement back toward democratic government.

• Equatorial Guinea has gone through a sham of a democratization process to which nobody has given any credence. Opposition parties were legalized, but leaders were arrested and mistreated as soon as they appeared. The situation was so bad that foreign observers refused to visit despite the government's invitation.

• Zaire began a political liberalization process in April 1990 with a proliferation of new privately owned newspapers, new political parties, and new powers of freedom of speech for all. A transitional government put in place by a national conference of political, economic, and civic leaders in mid-1992 was designed to stabilize the catastrophic economic situation and prepare for presidential and parliamentary elections. Unfortunately, President Mobutu has refused to honor his own commitment to allow the transitional government to govern, creating a political impasse that has led to a total collapse of the country's economy. As Zaire continued to disintegrate at the end of 1993, Mobutu and his lieutenants from the Ngbandi ethnic group were essentially running a Mafia-type operation in the city of Kinshasa. They continued to divert the government's hard-currency earnings into their private channels under the protection of a well-compensated presidential militia.[25]

• Togo has gone through an aborted democratization process similar to Zaire's. This is not surprising since Presidents Eyadema of Togo and Mobutu of Zaire are close friends. Togo was opened to a liberalized press and multipartyism in 1991, but it succumbed to military terrorism in 1993 with 50,000 oppositionists going into exile out of abject fear of the security forces. Eyadema won the 1993 presidential election by default as the result of an opposition boycott. Among international observers, however, only the French were willing to give the elections any credence.

• Nigeria went through a long and elaborate process between 1991 and 1993 designed to move the country from military to civilian rule through democratic procedures. The presidential election of June 1993 was supposed to be the jewel in the crown of democracy after legislatures and governors had already been elected in the federal states. Before the votes could be counted, however, President Babangida canceled the entire election, allegedly because of fraud among the candidates. A transition government lasted until November 1993, at which point General Sani Abacha seized power in the name of the military. As of mid-1994, there was little evidence that the Nigerian military had any intention of returning the country to civilian rule.[26]

In the rest of Africa, openings toward democracy varied from tiny to wide. Here is a summary of where the various countries stood with respect to political liberalization at the end of 1993.

- Well-established democracies: Botswana, Senegal, the Gambia, Mauritius.
- Successful but still young transitions to multiparty democracy: Zambia, Mali, Madagascar, Niger, Benin, Lesotho, Cape Verde, Sao Tome, Seychelles, Central African Republic, Namibia, Zimbabwe.
- Recent flawed elections considered representative nevertheless: Ghana, Kenya, Ivory Coast, Gabon, Burkina Faso.
- Free and fair elections undercut by wars, coups, and violence: Angola, Burundi, Djibouti, the Congo, Comoros.
- Political liberalization evolving, but elections still pending: Ethiopia, Uganda, Tanzania, Mozambique, Liberia, Rwanda, Malawi, South Africa, Eritrea, Guinea, Guinea Bissau.
- Politics liberalizing, but authoritarian rule still in place: Chad, Swaziland, Mauritania, Cameroon.
- Military rule continues undiluted: Zaire, Nigeria, Sierre Leone, Sudan, Togo.[27]

There appears to be widespread public support in Africa for political and economic change. The fundamental reason is clear. Thirty years of the African one-party state implementing the "command economy" advocated by Western European social democrats in the 1950s and 1960s have, for the most part, failed to deliver development. In most cases, per capita income and social services have declined as a result of these failed economic policies.[28]

Africa's development partners in the industrialized world began to advocate and then demand economic liberalization toward market systems in the early 1980s. It was not until the early 1990s that political liberalization entered north-south relations in Africa. The north did not have to push too hard, however: There was considerable demand for more open political systems among Africans themselves. If thirty years of expenditure on development programs did nothing else in Africa, it produced large numbers of educated people who are now demanding more representative forms of government. As a result, there are no longer any African governments that insist on maintaining the one-party state. Democratization is absolutely "politically correct" throughout Africa.

Africa's great political problem for the 1990s is not how to get rid of the one-party form of government but how to marry democratization with African culture and values. As can be seen from the breakdown shown earlier, African governments are defining and implementing political pluralism in different ways. In a number of cases, free and fair multiparty elections have not necessarily guaranteed political stability or effective government. Indeed, with experience, a number of the political groups holding power in one-party states have learned to manipulate the "democratic process" in order to validate their tenure.

In Kenya, for example, one million potential new young voters were not able to vote in the December 1992 multiparty elections because they could not obtain adult identification cards in time to apply for voter registration cards. These young voters were generally expected to vote with the opposition.[29] Nevertheless, the election resulted in a new Kenyan parliament in which the opposition had grown from 0 percent in the previous one-party legislature to 45 percent. President Moi was reelected with only 38 percent of the vote, indicating that he would probably have lost if the opposition could have agreed on one candidate instead of fielding three. The Kenyan political scene was therefore changed in favor of more openness and more participation despite preelectoral manipulation. It is now very difficult for the Kenyan government to suppress freedom of the press and free speech, as it had done before the elections. But Kenya is not really more stable as a result. Official corruption in international business dealings continues, and the ethnic violence fomented by the ruling Kenya African National Union (KANU) party before the elections has continued. A multiparty election is clearly only the first step in building both a truly representative, accountable government and a responsible, competent opposition.

The Congo had one of Africa's most successful transitions from a one-party, Marxist form of government to multiparty democracy. The elections that resulted, however, produced a total impasse in government because none of the ethnic-based parties was able to achieve a majority in the national assembly. Because of long-standing hatreds and mistrust caused by the original one-party system, party alliances have been shifting constantly, making it virtually impossible for the government to govern. Congolese politics have moved from official channels back to the streets, where sporadic violence flares up as the politicians find it impossible to come to terms.[30]

A number of transitional experiences have been positive. Namibia has found equilibrium since its independence in March 1990. The opposition is truly "loyal" in the Western parliamentary tradition, and the government is able to govern in the interests of the general good. Multiparty elections in Lesotho in 1993 gave a similar result to that in Namibia. It will require several more years of experience, however, before these excellent beginnings can be said to have been consolidated.

Cape Verde voted to depose the Marxist-Leninist government it had between 1975 and 1990 in favor of a newly formed pluralistic party. The former ruling party continues to exist in opposition, and the former president continues to be a respected personality.

The Zambian elections in 1992 ended twenty-eight years of Kenneth Kaunda's one-man, one-party rule. The elections were totally free and fair and peaceful. Since then, the government has remained faithful to democracy and openness, but it is facing great difficulties in coping simultaneously with political and economic reform.

The elections in Benin in 1990 were marked by forgiveness and amnesty on the part of the winners toward the former one-party, Marxist rulers who lost. The government has continued to be relatively stable despite severe economic difficulties.

Elections in Ghana in 1993 resulted in the confirmation in power of the original military rulers, who had taken over in a coup d'état fifteen years earlier. The opposition losers claimed that the election must have been fraudulent by definition because the former one-party rulers had no claim to legitimacy. International observers saw a flawed election but insisted the imperfections were neutral in character, benefiting neither side. The ruling group's economic management for the previous ten years had been effective and "clean" enough to make it unsurprising that they had won, despite the authoritarian nature of their regime.[31]

Africa's Political Liberalization: Lessons Learned, 1985–1993

Political and economic reforms implemented in Africa from 1985 through mid-1994 have been inherently destabilizing. Both types of reform were designed to redistribute power and wealth from minorities to majorities and thereby set the stage for investment and growth. This type of change is designed to make all categories of citizens winners in the medium and long term, but in the short term, there is a significant number of losers. The latter are concentrated in the politically active and sensitive urban areas, making it all the more difficult to achieve meaningful change. Nevertheless, Africa appears to have no other options at this stage of its political-economic evolution, which means that private-sector, independent activity must be expanded and supported in order to keep the urban elites fully engaged in the process of change.

Experiences of the 1985–1993 period indicate the main elements of successful political and economic liberalization in Africa.

• Participation, Decentralization, and Civil Society: When all ethnic groups and geographic regions are represented in the political and governmental structures, people feel they are participating in the decisionmaking process and identify with the system in place. Various forms of proportional representation, as in Namibia, and significant decentralization of power to provinces and local districts, as is proposed in South Africa, appear to help fulfill these requirements in Africa. In addition, the development and strengthening of the intermediation groups—generally known by the term *civil society*—appears to be essential for successful communications between democratic governments and the population.

• Fairness: Under the military authoritarian rule of Moussa Traore, Mali had one of the most effective structural adjustment programs in Africa.

Nevertheless, there were street riots in Bamako in 1991 that led to the military shooting civilians, a military coup, a national conference, and the establishment of a multiparty political system. The riots that brought about the change were caused essentially by the fact that the president, his family, and his government ministers were continuing to enrich themselves while most people were forced to tighten their belts under structural adjustment. If corruption and the illicit amassing of wealth by government officials continues in newly elected regimes, the legitimacy of government is destroyed.

• Governance: To the extent that governments perform their functions transparently and in an accountable manner, African populations will have confidence in their ability to influence policy. In Cameroon, for example, because oil revenues have never been published in any official budget nor in any central bank report, it is not surprising that so many Cameroonians do not trust the government. Here again, no amount of democracy in the form of free and fair elections can offset the absence of credible governance. Indeed, despite their continued "semiauthoritarian" regimes, the comparatively better governance in Ghana and Uganda make these two countries relatively attractive to aid donors and potential investors.

• Amnesty and Reconciliation: Change always creates losers as well as winners in the economic and political arenas, but when change creates fear for the loss of life and property, resistance will be strong and often violent. Although the gridlocked situations in Zaire, Togo, and Cameroon stem from complex origins, the revanchist and punitive outlooks of many oppositionists in those countries make it that much more difficult for groups in power to accept the risks of transition. Fortunately, in South Africa, the Pan-Africanist Congress's slogan "one settler—one bullet" does not represent the mainstream of majority black opinion. The best examples of the politics of reconciliation during political transition have taken place in Cape Verde, Benin, Mozambique, Namibia, and Burundi.

The overall outlook for change in Africa as of mid-1994 could be described as a rising curve of political and economic liberalization. The degree of success will be uneven, depending on local circumstances. Success will reflect a combination of pluralism, governance, fairness, national reconciliation, and the growth of democratic institutions required to make the new political and economic systems function the way they should. To the extent that these factors rate highly, the chances that structural adjustment will succeed in the economic area are enhanced. And succeed it must because economic issues have probably been the most significant factor in the popular demand for greater political liberalization throughout Africa. Consequently, foreign assistance donors are likely to increasingly concentrate their attention on the successful performers.[32]

Notes

1. U.N. Security Council Resolution 435, adopted at its 2087th meeting on September 29, 1978.

2. Chester A. Crocker, *High Noon in Southern Africa* (New York: Norton, 1992). Chapter 16 gives a good analysis of the growing cooperation between the United States and the USSR in solving African security problems.

3. When I became assistant secretary of state for Africa in April 1989, I was instructed to work closely with my Soviet counterparts to seek solutions to security problems in Africa.

4. This was made clear to me during my first formal consultation with Soviet Vice Minister Adamishin in June 1989. Adamishin indicated the Soviets had no hope of ever being repaid for their arms shipments to Angola and Ethiopia.

5. U.S. Embassy in London, unclassified telegram no. 9785, dated May 28, 1991. The British press of May 28 and 29 provides full stories of the decisions made by the Ethiopian victors, who were gathered in London for a final negotiating conference with the defeated Mengistu government.

6. Alan Riding, "Angola and Rebels Sign Pact Ending 16-Year War," *New York Times,* June 1, 1991, sec. 1, p. 1.

7. Tom Kuntz, "Angola: From the Brink of Peace to the Brink of War," *New York Times,* November 15, 1992, sec. 4, p. 3.

8. My contacts in the U.S. intelligence community informed me that the main sales of arms to the Angolan government came from Israel, Bulgaria, and Czechoslovakia.

9. The accords signed in Lisbon on May 31, 1991, are officially called the "Bicesse" accords because they were negotiated in the Lisbon suburb of Bicesse in a school for hotel employees located there.

10. "Angola: Le Gouvernement dément être parvenu à un accord avec UNITA," *Le Monde,* December 7, 1993, p. 6.

11. In 1988, South Carolina Public Television ran a documentary on Angola that featured an interview with Admiral Rosa Couthino, the last Portuguese military governor of Angola prior to independence in 1974. In that interview, Admiral Couthino said that he had personally gone to Havana to request Cuban troops in order to guarantee that the MPLA would take power.

12. Robert Gersony, *Summary of Mozambican Refugee Accounts of Principally Conflict-Related Experience in Mozambique,* report submitted to the Bureau for Refugee Programs, Department of State, April 1988.

13. I was then serving as senior director for African affairs on the National Security Council staff and was present for the Bush-Chissano meeting. Until that point, Chissano had insisted that he would engage in talks with RENAMO only after they accepted the existing constitution, the existing FRELIMO government, and an amnesty for all rebel fighters who surrendered.

14. Alan Cowell, "Mozambique Leader and Rebels Sign Peace Pact," *New York Times,* August 27, 1993, sec. A, p. 10.

15. During June 1991, President Blaise Compaore told me that he had agreed to act as a conduit for arms to the Liberian insurgents because of his friendship with Charles Taylor and because he wanted to help rid Liberia of an oppressive, corrupt government.

16. In April 1990, a command decision was made in the National Security Council that the United States would confine itself to the protection and evacuation of U.S. citizens.

My proposal to travel to Monrovia to suggest that President Doe resign and go into exile was refused.

17. Ward Johnson, "Sudanese Government Wars with Populace," *New York Times,* April 3, 1993, sec. 1, p. 22; and Donatella Lorch, "Sudan Is Described as Trying to Placate the West," *New York Times,* March 26, 1993, sec. A, p. 3; Committee on Foreign Affairs, House of Representatives, "Recent Developments In Sudan," Hearing before the Subcommittee on Africa, March 10, 1993.

18. United Nations Security Council Resolution 794, December 3, 1992.

19. Eric Schmitt, "U.S. Mission in Somalia: Seeking a New Rationale," *New York Times,* August 27, 1993, sec. A, p. 10.

20. Paul Lewis, "Reluctant Warriors: U.N. Member States Retreat from Peacekeeping Role," *New York Times,* December 12, 1993, sec. A, p. 22.

21. The Organization of African Unity contacted the Global Coalition for Africa, where I was employed as senior adviser, in October 1993, requesting assistance in raising funds for the two hundred monitors. Calls to the governments of Belgium, France, the United States, and Sweden received positive responses within twenty-four hours.

22. During July 1993, free and fair democratic elections in Burundi ended several centuries of minority rule when the majority Hutu ethnic group won power through the victory of the Front for Burundi Democracy (FRODEBU) political party. The transfer of power was peaceful thanks to the statesmanship of President Buyoya, a member of the Tutsi minority ethnic group who had taken power in a military coup in 1987. The attempted coup in October by a rump Tutsi element in the army touched off ethnic killings reminiscent of ethnic massacres that had taken place periodically in Burundi as far back as anyone could remember. In previous pogroms, the Tutsi rulers massacred in order to remain in power. In 1993, the Hutus took their revenge in villages throughout the country.

23. Heads of State and Government of the Organization of African Unity (OAU), *Declaration AHG/DECL.3 (XXIX) Rev. 1,* June 30, 1993. Text available from the executive secretariat of the OAU to the United Nations, 346 East 50th St., New York, N.Y., 10022.

24. Salim Ahmed Salim, secretary-general of the Organization of African Unity, statement at the inaugural ministerial meeting of the Central Organ of the Mechanism for the Prevention, Management and Resolution of Conflict, Africa Hall, Addis Ababa, November 17, 1993. Executive secretariat of the OAU to the United Nations, Press Release NY/OAU/BUR/47/93, 346 East 50th Street, New York, N.Y., 10022.

25. House of Representatives, Africa Sub-Committee Hearings on "The Crisis In Zaire," October 26, 1993.

26. Kenneth B. Noble, "In Nigeria's Mess, A Frustration for All of Africa," *New York Times,* August 22, 1993, sec. 4, p. 3, and Jean-Paul Garfield, "Le President Manque," *Jeune Afrique,* no. 1709 (October 7, 1993), p. 30.

27. Rolph van der Hoeven and Fred van der Kraaij, eds., *Structural Adjustment and Beyond—Longterm Development in Sub-Saharan Africa, Appendix 3,* (London: James Currey Publishers, May, 1994). Van der Kraaij provides an excellent, detailed survey of the state of political liberalization in Africa, country by country in the context of economic reform.

28. Ismail Serageldin, *Development Partners: Aid and Cooperation in the 1990s:* (Stockholm: Swedish International Development Authority, July, 1993). Pages 83–95 provide an in-depth discussion of what went wrong in Africa's development process between 1960 and 1985. Serageldin is a World Bank vice president.

29. Kenneth B. Noble, "Kenya's Multiparty Vote Faces Critics' Wrath," *New York Times,* December 27, 1992, sec. 1, p. 11.

30. Zyad Limam, "Lissouba peut-il s'en sortir?" *Jeune Afrique,* no. 1682 (April 1, 1993), p. 16.

31. Reuters, "Clean Sweep Confirmed in Ghana's Elections," January 4, 1993.

32. Serageldin, *Development Partners,* pp. 119–125; Organization for Economic Co-Operation and Development, "DAC Orientations on Participatory Development and Good Governance," Paris, 1993, OECD document no. OCDE/GD(93)191.

14

Reconciling Sovereignty with Responsibility: A Basis for International Humanitarian Action

FRANCIS M. DENG

OVER THE PAST SEVERAL years, the intensification of internal conflicts around the world has resulted in unprecedented humanitarian tragedies, and in some cases, it has led to partial and even total collapse of states. This has brought pressures for global humanitarian action, sometimes involving forced intervention, as well as an urgent quest for peacemaking and peacekeeping the world over. The response of the international community to this mounting toll of post–Cold War tragedies emanating mostly from internal conflicts has inevitably begun to erode traditional concepts of sovereignty in order to ensure international access to the affected masses within state borders. This has, in turn, generated a reaction from vulnerable states, designed to reassert the traditional principles of sovereignty and territorial integrity. The resulting tug-of-war is acquiring a cross-cultural dimension that is confronting the international community with severe dilemmas, for both positions represent legitimate concerns.

The guiding principle for reconciling these positions is to assume that under normal circumstances, governments are concerned about the welfare of their people, will provide them with adequate protection and assistance, and if unable to do so, will invite or welcome foreign assistance and international cooperation to supplement their own efforts. The conflict arises only in the exceptional cases when the state has collapsed or the government is unwilling to invite or permit international involvement, while the level of human suffering dictates otherwise. This is often the case in civil conflicts characterized by racial, ethnic, or religious crises of national identity in which the conflicting parties perceive the affected population as part of "the enemy." It is essentially to fill the vacuum of moral responsibility created by such cleavages that international intervention becomes a moral imperative.

The paradox of the compelling circumstances that necessitate such intervention is that the crisis has gone beyond prevention and has become an emergency situation in which masses of people have fallen victim of the humanitarian tragedy. Since it is now more costly to provide the needed humanitarian relief than it would have been at an earlier stage, the obvious policy implication is that the international community must develop normative and operational principles for a doctrine of preventive intervention. Such an approach would require addressing the root causes of conflict, establishing mechanisms for an appropriate institutional level of response, and formulating strategies for timely intervention.

The Magnitude of the Crisis

The events in the former Yugoslavia and the unfolding conditions in the former Soviet Union demonstrate that the crisis is truly global. As U.N. Secretary-General Boutros Boutros-Ghali observed in his *Agenda for Peace*: "Poverty, disease, famine, oppression and despair abound, joining to produce 17 million refugees, 20 million displaced persons and massive migrations of peoples within and beyond national borders. These are both sources and consequences of conflict that require the ceaseless attention and the highest priority in the efforts of the United Nations."[1]

Although the global dimension of the crisis needs to be stressed, it is fair to say that some regions are more affected than others. Africa is perhaps the most devastated by internal conflicts and their catastrophic consequences. Of an estimated 25 million internally displaced persons worldwide, about 15 million are African, as are 6 million of the 17 million refugees in the world. African leaders, diplomats, scholars, and intellectuals have recognized the plight of their countries and their people and are demonstrating a responsiveness commensurate to the challenge, recently culminating in a series of interrelated initiatives. Among them are the Africa Leadership Forum's Conference on Security, Stability, Development and Cooperation in Africa (CSSDCA), embodied in the Kampala Document before the OAU; the International Peace Academy (IPA) Consultations on Africa's Internal Conflicts, first launched at Arusha in March 1992; and the Secretary-General's Proposals for an OAU Mechanism for Conflict Prevention and Resolution, which was first endorsed by the Council of Ministers and the Assembly of Heads of State and Government in Dakar, Senegal in June 1992.[2]

Secretary-General Salim A. Salim introduced the item to the Council of Ministers at Dakar with these moving words:

> Conflicts have cast a dark shadow over the prospects for a united, secure and prosperous Africa which we seek to create. . . . Conflicts have caused immense suffering to our people and, in the worst case, death. Men, women and children have been uprooted, dispossessed, deprived of their means of livelihood and thrown into exile

as refugees as a result of conflicts. This dehumanization of a large segment of our population is unacceptable and cannot be allowed to continue. Conflicts have engendered hate and division among our people and undermined the prospects of the long-term stability and unity of our countries and Africa as a whole. Since much energy, time and resources have been devoted to meeting the exigencies of conflicts, our countries have been unable to harness the energies of our people and target them to development.[3]

In the consultation organized by the OAU and the IPA in Addis Ababa (May 18–21, 1993), the president of the International Peace Academy, Olara Otunnu, spotlighted the magnitude of the crisis when he said: "There is a 'curse' stalking the African continent. Entire societies are being decimated by internecine wars. Indeed, some states have simply collapsed in the wake of these conflicts, and more countries could potentially be exposed to the same fate. What can be done to stem this tide of self-destruction? This is one of the most important and urgent challenges facing Africa."[4]

The regional focus is important not only for appreciating the context of conflict but also for devising an appropriate response at that level before pursuing further measures at the international level. To respond at either level the issue of sovereignty must be addressed.

The Issue of Sovereignty

Protecting and assisting the masses of the people affected by internecine internal conflicts entails reconciling the possibility of international intervention with traditional concepts of national sovereignty. During the extensive consultations conducted in connection with the U.N. study on internally displaced persons, representatives of several governments commented that national sovereignty carries with it responsibilities that if not met put a government at risk of forfeiting its legitimacy. One spokesperson for a major power even said, "To put it bluntly, if governments do not live up to those responsibilities" (among which he specified the protection of minority rights), "then the international community should intervene, if necessary by force." Similar views were expressed by representatives of African countries who were voicing a global humanitarian concern.

Such pronouncements have almost become truisms that are rapidly making narrow concepts of legality obsolete. When the international community does decide to act—as it did when Iraq invaded Kuwait, when Somalia descended into chaos and starvation, and (albeit less decisively) when the former Yugoslavia disintegrated—controversy about issues of legality becomes futile or of limited value as a brake to guard against precipitous change.

One observer has recently summarized the new sense of urgency regarding the need for an international response, the ambivalence of the pressures for the needed change, and the pull of traditional legal doctrines:

In the post–Cold War world . . . a new standard of intolerance for human misery and human atrocities has taken hold. . . . Something quite significant has occurred to raise the consciousness of nations to the plight of peoples within sovereign borders. There is a new commitment—expressed in both moral and legal terms—to alleviate the suffering of oppressed or devastated people. To argue today that norms of sovereignty, non-use of force, and the sanctity of internal affairs are paramount to the collective human rights of people, whose lives and well-being are at risk, is to avoid the hard questions of international law and to ignore the march of history.[5]

The conclusions of a 1992 international conference on human rights protection for internally displaced persons—attended by human rights specialists, experts from humanitarian organizations, international lawyers, U.N. and regional organization officials, and government representatives—underscored the extent of changes in perspectives on the confrontation between the universal standards of human rights and the parochialism of traditional ideas of sovereignty. The report on the conference states that the "steady erosion" of the concept of absolute sovereignty is making it easier for international organizations, governments, and nongovernmental organizations to intervene when governments refuse to meet the needs of their populations and when substantial numbers of people are at risk. The concept of sovereignty, it continues, is becoming understood more in terms of conferring responsibilities on governments to assist and protect persons residing in their territories—so much so that if governments fail to meet their obligations, they risk undermining their legitimacy.[6] The scrutiny of world public opinion as represented by the media makes it difficult for governments to ignore these obligations or defend their failure to act. The report noted that "participants considered it essential for the international community to continue to 'chip away' and 'pierce' narrow definitions of sovereignty so that sovereignty would not be a barrier to humanitarian intervention."[7]

But to intervene is not an easy choice. Former U.N. Secretary-General Javier Perez de Cuellar highlighted the dilemmas when he said in 1991: "We are clearly witnessing what is probably an irresistible shift in public attitudes towards the belief that the defense of the oppressed in the name of morality should prevail over frontiers and legal documents." But he also added, "Does [intervention] not call into question one of the cardinal principles of international law, one diametrically opposed to it, namely, the obligation of non-interference in the internal affairs of states?"[8] In his 1991 annual report, he wrote of the new balance that must be struck between sovereignty and the protection of human rights:

> It is now increasingly felt that the principle of non-interference with the essential domestic jurisdiction of States cannot be regarded as a protective barrier behind which human rights could be massively or systematically violated with impunity. . . . The case for not impinging on the sovereignty, territorial integrity and political independence of States is by itself indubitably strong. But it would only be weakened if it were to carry the implication that sovereignty, even in this day and age, includes the right of mass slaughter or of launching systematic campaigns of decimation or forced exodus of civilian populations in the name of controlling civil

strife or insurrection. With the heightened international interest in universalizing a regime of human rights, there is a marked and most welcome shift in public attitudes. To try to resist it would be politically as unwise as it is morally indefensible. It should be perceived as not so much a new departure as a more focused awareness of one of the requirements of peace.[9]

Preferring to avoid confronting the issue of sovereignty, he called for "a higher degree of cooperation and a combination of common sense and compassion," arguing that "we need not impale ourselves on the horns of a dilemma between respect for sovereignty and the protection of human rights. . . . What is involved is not the right of intervention but the collective obligation of States to bring relief and redress in human rights emergencies."[10]

In *Agenda for Peace*, current Secretary-General Boutros Boutros-Ghali wrote that respect for sovereignty and integrity is "crucial to any common international progress," but he went on to say that "the time of absolute and exclusive sovereignty . . . has passed," that "its theory was never matched by reality," and that it is necessary for leaders of states "to find a balance between the needs of good internal governance and the requirements of an ever more interdependent world."[11] As one commentator noted, "The clear meaning was that governments could best avoid intervention by meeting their obligations not only to other states, but also to their own citizens. If they failed, they might invite intervention."[12]

However, the motives for external intervention are not always sure to be altruistic. Self-interest therefore dictates an appropriate and timely action in self-protection. This was the point made by the secretary-general of the Organization of African Unity, Salim Salim, in his bold proposals for an OAU mechanism for conflict prevention and resolution. "If the OAU, first through the secretary-general and then the Bureau of the Summit, is to play the lead role in any African conflict," he said, "it should be enabled to intervene swiftly, otherwise it cannot be ensured that whoever (apart from African regional organizations) acts will do so in accordance with African interests."[13] Criticizing the tendency to respond only to worst-case scenarios, Salim emphasized the need for preemptive intervention: "The basis for 'intervention' may be clearer when there is a total breakdown of law and order . . . and where, with the attendant human suffering, a spill-over effect is experienced within the neighbouring countries. . . . However, pre-emptive involvement should also be permitted even in situations where tensions evolve to such a pitch that it becomes apparent that a conflict is in the making."[14]

The secretary-general went as far as to suggest that the OAU should take the lead in transcending the traditional view of sovereignty, building on the African values of kinship solidarity and the notion that "every African is his brother's keeper."[15] Considering that "our borders are at best artificial," Salim argued, "we in Africa need to use our own cultural and social relationships to interpret the principle of non-interference in such a way that we are enabled to apply it to our advantage in conflict prevention and resolution."[16]

In traditional Africa, third-party intervention for mediation and conciliation is always expected, regardless of the will of the parties directly involved in a conflict. Even in domestic disputes, relatives and elders intercede without being invited. Indeed, "saving face," which is critical to conflict resolution in Africa, requires that such intervention be unsolicited. But of course, African concepts and practices under the modern conditions of the nation-state must still balance consideration for state sovereignty with the compelling humanitarian need to protect and assist the dispossessed.

The normative frameworks proposed by the OAU secretary-general and the U.N. secretary-general's *Agenda for Peace* are predicated on respect for the sovereignty and integrity of the state as crucial to the existing international system. However, the logic of the transcendent importance of human rights as a legitimate area of concern for the international community—especially where order has broken down or where the state is incapable or unwilling to act responsibly to protect the masses of citizens—would tend to make international inaction quite indefensible. Even in less extreme cases of acute internal conflicts, the perspectives of the pivotal actors on such issues as the national or public interest are bound to be sharply divided both internally and in their relationship to the outside world. After all, internal conflicts often entail a contest of the national arena of power and therefore sovereignty. Every political intervention from outside has its internal recipients, hosts, and beneficiaries. Under those circumstances, there can hardly be said to be indivisible national sovereignty behind which the nation stands united.

Furthermore, it is not always easy to determine the degree to which a government of a country devastated by civil war is truly in control when, as often happens, sizable portions of the territory are controlled by rebel or opposing forces. Frequently, though a government may remain in effective control of the capital and the main garrisons, much of the countryside in the war zone will have practically collapsed. How would a partial but significant collapse such as this be factored into the determination of the degree to which civil order in the country has broken down? No government can present a clear face to the outside world and keep others from stepping in to offer protection and assistance in the name of sovereignty if it allows hundreds of thousands (and maybe millions) to starve to death when food can be made available to them; to be exposed to deadly elements when they could be provided with shelter; to be indiscriminately tortured, brutalized, and murdered by opposing forces, contesting the very sovereignty that is supposed to ensure their security; or to otherwise allow them to suffer in a vacuum of moral leadership and responsibility. Under such circumstances, the international community is called upon to step in and fill the vacuum created by such neglect. If the lack of protection and assistance is the result of the country's incapacity, the governments would, in all likelihood, invite or welcome such international intervention. But where the neglect is a willful part of a policy emanating from internal conflict, preventive and corrective interventions become necessary.

It is most significant that the Security Council, in its continued examination of the secretary-general's *Agenda for Peace,* welcomed the observations contained in the report concerning the question of humanitarian assistance and its relationship to peacemaking, peacekeeping, and peace building.[17] In particular, the council established that under certain circumstances, "there may be a close relationship between acute needs for humanitarian assistance and threats to international peace and security."[18] Indeed, the council "[noted] with concern the incidents of humanitarian crises, including mass displacements of population becoming or aggravating threats to international peace and security."[19] It further expressed the belief "that humanitarian assistance should help establish the basis for enhanced stability through rehabilitation and development" and "noted the importance of adequate planning in the provision of humanitarian assistance in order to improve prospects for rapid improvement of the humanitarian situation."[20]

Absolute sovereignty is clearly no longer defensible; it never was. The critical question now is under what circumstances the international community is justified in overriding sovereignty to protect the dispossessed population within state borders. The common assumption in international law is that such action is justified when there is a threat to international peace. The position now supported by the Security Council is that massive violations of human rights and displacement within a country's borders may constitute such a threat.[21] Others contend that a direct threat to international peace is too high a threshold because it would preclude action on too many humanitarian crises. Indeed, they argue, the time has come to recognize humanitarian concern as a ground for intervention. Insistence on a threat to international peace as the basis for intervention under Chapter VII of the U.N. Charter has become more a legal fiction than the principle justifying international action, nearly always under conditions of extreme humanitarian tragedies.

To avoid costly emergency relief operations, the international community must develop a response to conflict situations before they deteriorate into humanitarian tragedies. This calls for placing an emphasis on peacemaking through preventive diplomacy, which would require an understanding of the sources of conflicts and a willingness to address them at their roots.

Addressing the Causes of Conflict

In most countries torn apart by war, the sources and causes of conflict are generally recognized as inherent in the traumatic experience of state-formation and nation-building, complicated by colonial intervention and repressive postcolonial policies. The starting point, as far as Africa is concerned, is the colonial nation-state, which brought together diverse groups that were paradoxically kept separate and unintegrated. Regional ethnic groups were broken up and affiliated with others within the artificial borders of the new state, and colonial masters imposed a superstructure of law and order to maintain relative peace and tranquility.

The independence movement was a collective struggle for self-determination that reinforced the notion of unity within the artificial framework of the newly established nation-state. Initially, independence came as a collective gain that did not delineate who was to get what from the legacy of the centralized power and wealth. But because colonial institutions had divested the local communities and ethnic groups of much of their indigenous autonomy and sustainable livelihood, replacing them with a degree of centralized authority and dependency on the welfare state system, the struggle for control became unavoidable once control of these institutions passed on to the nationals at independence. The outcome was often conflict—over power, wealth, and development—that led to gross violations of human rights, denial of civil liberties, disruption of economic and social life, and the consequential frustration of efforts for development.

As the Cold War raged, however, these conflicts were not seen as domestic struggles for power and resources but as extensions of the superpower ideological confrontation. Rather than help resolve them peacefully, the superpowers often worsened the conflict by providing military and economic assistance to their own allies.

Although the end of the Cold War has removed this aggravating external factor, it has also removed the moderating role of the superpowers, both as third parties and as mutually neutralizing allies. As Liberia, Ethiopia, Somalia, Mozambique, and Sudan illustrate, the results have been unmitigated brutalities and devastations.

It can credibly be argued that the gist of these internal conflicts is that the ethnic pieces that were put together by the colonial glue, reinforced by the old world order, are now pulling apart and that ethnic groups are reasserting their autonomy or independence.

Old identities, undermined and rendered dormant by the structures and values of the nation-state system, are reemerging and redefining the standards of participation, distribution, and legitimacy. In fact, it may be even more accurate to say that the process has been going on in a variety of ways and within the context of the constraints imposed by the nation-state system.

The larger the gap in the participation and distribution patterns based on racial, ethnic, or religious identity, the more likely the breakdown of civil order and the conversion of political confrontation into violent conflict. When the conflict turns violent, the issues at stake become transformed into a fundamental contest for state power. The objectives may vary in degree from a demand for autonomy to a major restructuring of the national framework, either to be captured by the demand-making group or to be more equitably reshaped. When the conflict escalates into a contest for the "soul" of the nation, it turns into an intractable zero-sum confrontation. The critical issue then is whether the underlying sense of injustice, real or perceived, can be remedied in a timely manner, avoiding the zero-sum level of violence. As the report of the Arusha Consultation put it, "The general conviction was that, despite their apparently diverse causes, complex nature and manifold forms, internal conflicts in Africa were basically the result of denial of basic democratic rights and freedoms, broadly conceived; and that they tended to be triggered-off by acts of injustice, real or imagined, precisely in situations where recourse to democratic redress seemed hopeless."[22]

The report summarized the challenge of conflicts as symbolizing a quest for justice:

> The most comprehensive set of "preventive measures" in this regard was thought to be the development and maintenance of a democratic state in which, among other things, civil society was vibrant, there was effective justice and the rule of law, there was equitable access to political power and economic resources by all citizens and groups, the various regions of the country were treated fairly and equitably in all matters of public concern, and there was sufficient economic growth and development to ensure reasonably decent livelihood or at least realistic hope for social progress.[23]

Viewing the crisis from the global perspective, it is also pertinent to recall the words of U.N. Secretary-General Boutros-Ghali, who observed in *An Agenda for Peace*: "One requirement for solutions to these problems lies in commitment to human rights with a special sensitivity to those of minorities, whether ethnic, religious, social or linguistic."[24] On the need to strike a balance between the unity of larger entities and respect for the sovereignty, autonomy, and diversity of various identities, the secretary-general noted:

> The healthy globalization of contemporary life requires in the first instance solid identities and fundamental freedoms. The sovereignty, territorial integrity and independence of states within the established international system, and the principle of self-determination for peoples, both of great value and importance, must not be permitted to work against each other in the period ahead. Respect for democratic principles at all levels of social existence is crucial: in communities, within states and within the community of states. Our constant duty should be to maintain the integrity of each while finding a balanced design for all.[25]

Where discrimination or disparity is based on race, ethnicity, region, or religion, it is easy to see how it can be combatted by appropriate constitutional provisions and laws protecting basic human rights and fundamental freedoms. Where discrimination or disparity arises from conflicting perspectives on national identity, especially one based on religion, the cleavages become more difficult to bridge. In some instances, religion, ethnicity, and culture become so intertwined that they are not easy to disentangle. Such is the case in the Sudan, where Islam has gained momentum and is aspiring to offer regionwide and, indeed, global ideological leadership. Islam in the Sudan has been closely associated with Arabism, which also gives the movement a composite ethnic, cultural, and religious identity, even though the Islamists themselves espouse the nonracial ideals of the faith. The composite identity of Islam and Arabism poses the threat of subordination to non-Muslims who also perceive themselves as non-Arabs. It is consequently resisted, especially in the south.

What makes the role of religion particularly formidable is that there are legitimate arguments on both sides of the religiously based conflict. On the one hand, the Islamists, representing the Arabized Muslim majority, want to fashion the nation on the basis of their faith, which they believe does not allow the separation of religion from the state. The non-Muslims, on the other hand, reject this, seeing it as a means of inevitably relegating them to a lower status as citizens; they insist on secularism as a more mutual basis for a pluralistic process of nation-building. The dilemma is whether an Islamic framework should be used to encompass a religiously mixed society, imposing a minority status on the non-Muslims, or whether secularism should be the national framework, thereby imposing on the Muslim majority the wishes of the non-Muslim minority. The crisis of national identity that this dualism poses is that there is not yet a consensus on a framework that unquestionably establishes the unity of the nation; during most of the colonial period, the country was governed as two separate parts in one, and since independence, it has intermittently been at war with itself over the composite factors of religion, ethnicity, race, and culture.

The report of the Arusha Consultation states: "Two sociological factors were considered pivotal in the internal conflict equations in Africa. One was religious fundamentalism, the other, ethnicity. Both needed to be carefully monitored."[26] Monitoring them is, indeed, both critical and urgent since they are at the core of the challenge of nation-building in countries that are religiously, ethnically, and culturally mixed, especially where these forms of identity correlate and deepen internal divisions.

Operational Strategies of Intervention

Although addressing the issue of sovereignty and the root causes of conflict are critical prerequisites to intervention, formulating credible operational principles is the most pivotal factor in the equation. These principles relate to institutional mechanisms and strategies for action, both preventive and corrective.

Ideally, from an institutional or organizational perspective, problems should be addressed and solved within the immediate framework, with wider involvement necessitated only by the failure of the internal efforts. This means that conflict prevention, management, or resolution progressively moves from the domestic domain to the regional and, ultimately, the global levels of concern and action.

As already noted, those conflicts in which the state is an effective arbiter do not present particular difficulties since they are manageable within the national framework. The problem arises when the state itself is a party to the conflict. Under those conditions, external involvement becomes necessary. In the African context, it is generally agreed that the next best level of involvement should be the OAU, but there are constraints on the role of the OAU. One has to do with limited resources, both material and human. But perhaps even more debilitating is the question of political will since in the intimate context of the region, governments feel they are subject to conflicts arising from the problematic conditions of state-formation and nation-building and are therefore prone to resist any form of external scrutiny. And since the judge of today may well be the accused of tomorrow, there is a temptation to avoid confronting such problems. The result is evasiveness and benign neglect.

Beyond the OAU, the United Nations is the next logical organization, for it represents the international community in its global context. But the U.N. also suffers from the constraints that affect the OAU, though to a lesser degree. It, too, must deal with the problem of resources and the reciprocal protectiveness of vulnerable governments.

As recent events have demonstrated, the role of the major Western powers acting unilaterally, multilaterally, or within the framework of the United Nations—though often susceptible to accusations of strategic motivation—has become increasingly pivotal. The problem in this regard is more one of their unwillingness to become involved or their lack of adequate preparedness for such involvement.

Perhaps the most important aspect of the involvement of Western industrial democracies in foreign conflicts is the fact that these nations are often moved to act by the gravity of the humanitarian tragedies involved. This makes their involvement both an asset in terms of arresting the tragedy and a limitation in terms of preventing the tragedy at an earlier stage. Even with respect to humanitarian intervention, lack of preparedness for an appropriate and timely response is generally acknowledged as a major limitation.[27]

In fact, the established policies that drive the international system inadvertently reinforce violent disintegration. Nevertheless, some argue that there is a strong presumption that the interests of these countries are powerfully engaged and that they will eventually be driven to uphold and promote those interests through humanitarian intervention in crisis situations. Industrial democracies, it is argued, cannot operate without defending standards of human rights and political procedures that are being egregiously violated. Indeed, they themselves cannot prosper in an irreversibly international economy if large, contiguous populations descend into endemic violence and economic depression.

Given these compelling reasons and the lack of preparedness for any well-planned response, the United States and Western European countries are particularly prone to crisis-induced reactions that are relatively easy to execute and that are more symbolic than effective in addressing the substantive issues involved.

There will always be elements in a country who will welcome intervention, especially among the disadvantaged groups to whom it promises tangible benefits. But since intervention is, of course, a major intrusion from the outside, resistance on the grounds of national sovereignty or pride is also a predictable certainty. For that reason, the justification for intervention must be reliably persuasive, if not beyond reproach: "The difference between an intervention that succeeds and one that is destroyed by immune reaction would depend on the degree of spontaneous acceptance or rejection by the local population."[28]

To avoid or minimize this "immune reaction," such an intervention would have to be broadly international in character. The principles used and the objectives toward which the intervention is targeted must transcend political and cultural boundaries or traditions and concomitant nationalist sentiments. In other words, it must enjoy an effective degree of global legitimacy. "The rationale that could conceivably carry such a burden presumably involves human rights so fundamental that they are not derived from any particular political or economic ideology."[29]

The strategy for preventive or corrective involvement in conflict should comprise gathering and analyzing information and otherwise monitoring situations with the view to establishing an early warning system through which the international community could be alerted to act.

The quest for a system of response to conflict and attendant humanitarian tragedies was outlined by the U.N. secretary-general when, referring to the surging demands on the Security Council as a central instrument for the prevention and resolution of conflicts, he wrote that the aims of the United Nations must be:

> To seek to identify at the earliest possible stage situations that could produce conflict, and to try through diplomacy to remove the sources of danger before violence results;
>
> Where conflict erupts, to engage in peacemaking aimed at resolving the issues that have led to conflict;
>
> Through peace-keeping, to work to preserve peace, however fragile, where fighting has been halted and to assist in implementing agreements achieved by the peacemakers;
>
> To stand ready to assist in peace-building in its differing contexts: rebuilding the institutions and infrastructures of nations torn by civil war and strife; and building bonds of peaceful mutual benefit among nations formerly at war;
>
> And in the largest sense, to address the deepest causes of conflict: economic despair, social injustice and political oppression. It is possible to discern an increasingly common moral perception that spans the world's nations and peoples, and which is finding expression in international laws, many owing their genesis to the work of this Organization.[30]

What is envisaged is a three-phase strategy that would involve monitoring developments to draw early attention to impending crises, interceding in time to avert the crisis through diplomatic initiatives, and mobilizing international action when necessary.[31] The first step would be to detect and identify the problem through various mechanisms for information collection, evaluation, and reporting. If a sufficient basis for concern were established, the appropriate mechanism should be invoked to take preventive diplomatic measures and avert the crisis. Initially, such initiatives might be taken within the framework of regional arrangements, for example, the Conference on Security and Cooperation in Europe, the Organization of American States, or the Organization of African Unity. In the U.N., such preventive initiatives would naturally fall on the secretary-general acting personally or through special representatives. If diplomatic initiatives did not succeed and depending on the level of human suffering involved, the secretary-general might decide to mobilize international response, ranging from further diplomatic measures to forced humanitarian intervention not only to provide emergency relief but also to facilitate the search for an enduring solution to the causes of the conflict. A strategy aimed at this broader objective would require a close understanding of the causal link between the conditions and developments leading to the outbreak of the crisis.

Conclusion

In balancing national sovereignty and the need for international action to provide protection and assistance to victims of internal conflicts, certain principles are becoming increasingly obvious policy guidelines. First, sovereignty carries with it responsibilities for the well-being of the population. It is from this precept that the legitimacy of a government derives, whatever the political system or the prevailing ideology. The relationship between the controlling authority and the populace should ideally ensure the highest standards of human dignity, but at a minimum, it should guarantee food, shelter, physical security, basic health services, and other essentials.

Second, in many countries in which armed conflicts and communal violence cause massive internal displacement, the country is so divided on fundamental issues that legitimacy—and, indeed, sovereignty—are sharply contested. This is why there is always a strong faction inviting or at least welcoming external intervention. Under those circumstances, the validity of sovereignty must be judged, using reasonable standards to assess how much of the population is represented, marginalized, or excluded.

Third, living up to the responsibilities of sovereignty implies that there is a transcendent authority capable of holding the supposed sovereign accountable. Some form of an international system has always existed to ensure that states conform to accepted norms or face the consequences, whether in the form of unilateral, multilateral, or collective action. Equality among sovereign entities has always been a convenient fiction; it has never been backed by realities because some powers have always been more dominant than others and therefore have been explicitly or implicitly charged with responsibility for enforcing the agreed upon norms of behavior.

Fourth, such a role imposes on the dominant authority or power certain leadership responsibilities that transcend parochialism or exclusive national interests and serve the broader interests of the community or the human family.

When these principles are translated into practical action in countries torn apart by internal conflicts, a number of implications emerge. For example, sovereignty cannot be an amoral function of authority and control; respect for fundamental human rights must be among its most basic values. Similarly, the enjoyment of human rights must encompass equitable and effective participation in the political, economic, social, and cultural life of the country, at least as a widely accepted national aspiration. This system of sharing must guarantee that all individuals and groups belong to the nation an on equal footing with the rest of the people, however identified; they must also be sufficiently represented and not discriminated against on the basis of the prevailing views of identity.

To ensure that these normative goals are met or at least genuinely pursued, the international community as represented by the United Nations is the ideal authority. The imperatives of the power structures and processes may, however, require that authority be exercised by other powers capable of acting on behalf of the international community. Bilateral and multilateral action may therefore be justified under certain circumstances.

Any type of less collective action should be closely circumscribed to avoid its exploitation for less lofty objectives of a more exclusively national character—objectives that may erode the transcendent moral authority of global leadership for the good of all humankind.

Although the world is far from a universal government, the foundations, the pillars, and perhaps even the structures of global governance are taking shape with the emergence of a post–Cold War international order in which the internally dispossessed are bound to benefit. Unmasking sovereignty to reveal the gross violations of human rights is no longer an aspiration; it is a process that has already started. Governments and other human rights violators are being increasingly scrutinized for such violations. What is now required is to make them fully accountable and to provide international protection and assistance for the victims of human rights violations and unremedied humanitarian tragedies within their domestic jurisdiction. In other words, what is called for is not something entirely new; rather, it is an intensification and improvement of what has already been unfolding.

Notes

1. Boutros Boutros-Ghali, *An Agenda for Peace: Preventive Diplomacy, Peacemaking and Peacekeeping* (New York: United Nations, 1992), p. 7.

2. The main documents in these three areas of African initiative are: *The Kampala Document Toward a Conference on Security, Stability, Development and Cooperation in Africa* (Kampala, Uganda: Africa Leadership Forum and Secretariat of the Organization of African Unity and the United Nations Economic Commission for Africa, 1991); International Peace Academy, *Africa's Internal Conflicts: The Search for a Response,* Report of an Arusha, Tanzania, High-level Consultation, March 23–25, 1992, prepared by Dent Ocaya-Lakidi; OAU, Council of Ministers, Fifty-sixth Ordinary Session, June 22–27, 1992, *Report of the Secretary-General on Conflicts in Africa: Proposals for an OAU Mechanism for Conflict Pre-*

vention and Resolution CM/1710 (L.VI) (Addis Ababa: Organization of African Unity, June 1992); OAU, Council of Ministers, Fifty-seventh Ordinary Session, February 15–19, 1993, *Interim Report of the Secretary-General on the Mechanism for Conflict Prevention, Management and Resolution* CM/1747 (L.VI) (Addis Ababa: Organization of African Unity, February 1993); OAU, Council of Ministers, Fifty-seventh Ordinary Session, February 15–19, 1993, *Report of the Secretary-General* CM/Plen/Rpt (L.VII) (Addis Ababa: Organization of African Unity, February 1993). Also pertinent to the issues involved is U.N. Secretary-General Boutros Boutros-Ghali's report, *An Agenda for Peace,* originally published as document A/47/277 S/24111, June 17, 1992.

   3. OAU, *Resolving Conflicts in Africa,* p. 3.

   4. Ocaya-Lakidi, *Africa's Internal Conflicts,* p. 2.

   5. David J. Scheffer, "Toward a Modern Doctrine of Humanitarian Intervention," *University of Toledo Law Review* 23 (Winter 1992), p. 259.

   6. Refugee Policy Group, *Human Rights Protection for Internally Displaced Persons: An International Conference* (Washington, D.C.: June 1991), p. 7.

   7. Ibid.

   8. U.N. press release SG/SM/4560, April 24, 1991. Cited in Gene M. Lyons and Michael Mastanduno, *Beyond Westphalia: International Intervention, State Sovereignty and the Future of International Society* (Hanover, N.H.: Dartmouth College, 1992), p. 2. Portions of the statement also cited in Scheffer, "Toward a Modern Doctrine of Humanitarian Intervention," p. 262.

   9. J. Perez de Cuellar, *Report of the Secretary-General on the Work of the Organization* (New York: United Nations, 1991), pp. 12, 13.

   10. Ibid., p. 13.

   11. Boutros-Ghali, *An Agenda For Peace,* p. 5.

   12. Scheffer, "Toward a Modern Doctrine of Humanitarian Intervention," pp. 262–263.

   13. OAU, Council of Ministers, *Report of the Secretary-General on Conflicts in Africa.*

   14. Ibid.

   15. Ibid.

   16. Ibid.

   17. Note by the president of the Security Council, S/25344, February 26, 1993.

   18. Ibid., p. 1.

   19. Ibid., p. 2.

   20. Ibid.

   21. Note by the president of the Security Council, S/25344.

   22. Ocaya-Lakidi, *Africa's Internal Conflicts,* pp. 9–10.

   23. Ibid., pp. 18–19.

   24. Boutros-Ghali, *An Agenda for Peace,* p. 9.

   25. Ibid., pp. 9–10.

   26. Ocaya-Lakidi, *Africa's Internal Conflicts,* p. 78.

   27. John Steinbruner, "Civil Violence as an International Security Problem," memorandum dated November 23, 1992, addressed to the Brookings Institution Foreign Policy Studies Program staff. See also Chester A. Crocker, "The Global Law and Order Deficit: Is the West Ready to Police the World's Bad Neighbors?" *Washington Post,* December 20, 1992, p. C1.

   28. Steinbruner, "Civil Violence as an International Security Problem."

   29. Ibid.

30. Boutros-Ghali, *An Agenda for Peace,* pp. 7–8.

31. For a more elaborate discussion of these phases as applied to the crisis of the internally displaced, see the U.N. study in document E/CN.4/1993/35 and the revised version of that study in my book, *Protecting the Dispossessed: A Challenge for the International Community* (Washington, D.C.: Brookings Institution, 1993). The study was considered by the Commission on Human Rights at its forty-ninth session, its findings and recommendations endorsed, and the mandate of the special representative of the secretary-general extended for two years to continue to work on the various aspects of the problem as presented in the study.

About the Book and Editors

African states have been on the periphery of world politics since independence, and they will likely continue to be marginalized as Cold War tensions disappear and economic and political ties to the industrialized world weaken. This book explores Africa's changing position, addressing the region's colonial heritage as well as the historical, economic, and cultural factors that have shaped the continent's standing in world affairs. The contributors also analyze some of the most intense conflicts and examine the evolution of relations with other regions and powers.

The second edition of *Africa in World Politics* has been fully revised and updated to explore trends in the region and the world. The focus on Russia's role in contemporary Africa has been significantly reduced, and francophone Africa and regional organizations have been given increased coverage. In addition, important new issues such as democratization, conflict resolution, territorial concerns, and humanitarian intervention are covered in depth. The result is a thought-provoking and up-to-date text written by leading scholars in their fields.

John W. Harbeson is professor of political science in the Graduate School and at City College of the City University of New York and the author of *The Ethiopian Transformation* (Westview Press, 1988).

Donald Rothchild is professor of political science at the University of California–Davis and the coeditor (with Naomi Chazan) of *The Precarious Balance: State and Society in Africa* (Westview Press, 1988).

About the Contributors

Thomas M. Callaghy is professor and chair of the Department of Political Science at the University of Pennsylvania. His most recent book is *Hemmed In: Responses to Africa's Economic Decline,* coedited with John Ravenhill. His current work focuses on the relationship between economic and political change in Africa.

Herman J. Cohen was assistant secretary of state for Africa during the four years of the Bush administration (1989–1993), completing a thirty-eight year career in the U.S. Foreign Service. In September 1993, he joined the Global Coalition for Africa, a north-south forum promoting policy consensus on African development issues.

Francis M. Deng is a senior fellow in the Foreign Policy Studies program at the Brookings Institution as well as the special representative of the United Nations secretary-general on the issue of internally displaced persons. He served as Sudan's minister of state for foreign affairs; as its ambassador to Canada, the United States, and Scandinavia; and as a human rights officer in the United Nations Secretariat.

Larry Diamond is a senior research fellow at the Hoover Institution and coeditor of the *Journal of Democracy.* He is the author and editor of numerous works on democracy, democratization, and democracy promotion globally and in Africa. Among his recent edited works are *The Global Resurgency of Democracy* and *Capitalism, Socialism, and Democracy Revisited* (both edited with Marc F. Plattner), *Political Culture and Democracy in Developing Countries,* and *Transition Without End: Nigerian Politics, Governance, and Civil Society, 1986–93* (edited with Anthony Kirk-Greene and Oyeleye Oyediran).

John W. Harbeson is professor of political science in the Graduate School and at City College of the City University of New York. He is currently in Nairobi, Kenya, serving in the Office for East and Southern Africa of the U.S. Agency for International Development. His books include *The Ethiopian Transformation: The Quest for the Post-Imperial State,* and he is coeditor of *Civil Society and the State in Africa* and the first edition of *Africa in World Politics.*

Jeffrey Herbst is an associate professor of politics and international affairs at Princeton University. He is the author of *State Politics in Zimbabwe* and *The Politics of Reform in Ghana.* During 1992–1993, he was a Fulbright visiting professor at the University of Cape Town and the University of the Western Cape.

Carol Lancaster is deputy administrator of USAID. Her previous government service includes the Africa chair in the Department of State's Policy Planning Staff (1977–1980), the post of deputy assistant secretary for economic affairs in the State Department's Bureau of African Affairs (1980–1981), and staff positions in the Office of Management and Budget, the House of Representatives, and the Senate. More recently, she has been an assistant professor in the School of Foreign Service at Georgetown University (1981–1993).

Guy Martin is associate professor of political science at Clark Atlanta University in Atlanta, Georgia. He previously taught at the International Relations Institute of Cameroon, Yaoundé (1976–1984), the University of Nairobi's Diplomacy Training Program (1984–1990), and the American University's School of International Service, Washington, D.C. (1991–1992). He has published widely on African politics, development, and international relations and is currently editing a volume on the political parties of sub-Saharan Africa, to be published in 1994.

Ali A. Mazrui is director of the Institute of Global Cultural Studies and Albert Schweitzer Professor in the Humanities at the State University of New York at Binghamton. He is also a senior scholar at Cornell University and Albert Luthuli Professor-at-Large at the University of Jos in Nigeria. Mazrui's books include *Cultural Forces in World Politics* and *Africa Since 1935* (editorial coauthor), vol. 8 of the UNESCO General History of Africa. Mazrui is a former president of the African Studies Association of the United States, and he is also the author and narrator of the BBC-PBS television series *The Africans: A Triple Heritage.*

John Ravenhill is associate director of the Research School of Pacific Studies, Australian National University, where he is also a senior fellow in the Department of International Relations. His books include *Collective Clientelism: The Lomé Conventions and North-South Relations, Africa in Economic Crisis* (editor), *Politics and Society in Contemporary Africa* (coauthor), *Pacific Economic Relations* (coauthor), and *Hemmed In: Responses to Africa's Economic Decline* (coauthor). He is the editor of the Cambridge University Press series *Cambridge Asia-Pacific Studies.*

Donald Rothchild is professor of political science at the University of California–Davis. He has been a member of the faculty at universities in Uganda, Kenya, Zambia, and Ghana. His books include *Racial Bargaining in Independent Kenya, Scarcity, Choice and Public Policy in Middle Africa* (coauthor) and *Politics and Society in Contemporary Africa* (coauthor). Among his edited works are *Ghana: The Political Economy of Recovery, State Versus Ethnic Claims* (coeditor), *The Precarious Balance: State and Society in Africa* (coeditor), and *Eagle in a New World* (coeditor).

Crawford Young is Rupert Emerson and John Bascom Professor of Political Science at the University of Wisconsin–Madison, where he has taught since 1963. He has served as visiting professor at universities in Uganda, Zaire, and Senegal. His major books include *The Rise and Decline of the Zairian State* (with Thomas Turner), *Ideology and Development in Africa, The Politics of Cultural Pluralism,* and *Politics in the Congo.* He was president of the African Studies Association

(ASA) in 1982–1983 and was given the Distinguished Africanist Award by ASA in 1990.

I. *William Zartman,* Jacob Blaustein Professor of International Organization and Conflict Resolution and director of African Studies at SAIS John Hopkins, is the author of a number of works on Africa and its relations, including *Ripe for Resolution: Conflict and Intervention in Africa* and *International Relations in the New Africa.*

Index

AAI. *See* African-American Institute

Abacha, Sani, 62, 261, 287

Abboud, Ibrahim, 239

Abdallahi, 133–134

Abduh, Muhammad, 79

Abiola, Moshood, 261

Abuja peace process, 222. *See also* Sudanese civil war

Accord de Nonagression et d'Assistance en Matière de Défense (ANAD), 178, 187(n44)

Accra All-African Peoples' Conference, 26

ACP Group (African, Caribbean, and Pacific Group). *See* Lomé Conventions

Adamishin, 292(n5)

ADB. *See* African Development Bank

Adedji, Adebayo, 53, 54, 57–58, 254

Adjustment in Africa: Reforms, Results, and the Road Ahead (World Bank), 58

AEF. *See* Fédération de l'Afrique Equatoriale Française

al-Afghani, Jamal al Din, 79

AFL-CIO. *See* American Federation of Labor/Congress of Industrial Organizations

Africa Leadership Forum, 213, 243, 296

Africa Make or Break: Action for Recovery (Oxfam), 57

African/African-American Summit, 184(n14)

African Alternative Framework to Structural Adjustment Programmes for Socio-Economic Recovery and Transformation (AAF-SAP) (ECA), 26, 55, 57

African-American Institute (AAI), 265

African, Caribbean, and Pacific (ACP) Group. *See* Lomé Conventions

African Center for Monetary Studies, 189

African Charter for Popular Participation in Development and Transformation, 254

African Development Bank (ADB), 102, 153, 189

African Governance Program, 179

African National Congress (ANC), 156, 253
 conflict management participation, 211, 214, 215
 and southern Africa, 148–149, 154, 156, 162(n13)

African nationalism, 26, 33–34, 35, 69, 84. *See also* Decolonization process

African unity, 26–27, 33–34, 191

Africa's Adjustment and Growth in the 1980s (World Bank), 55

Afrique Equatoriale Française. *See* Fédération de l'Afrique Equatoriale Française

Afrique Occidentale Française. *See* Fédération de l'Afrique Occidentale Française

Afro-Arab relations, 71–76, 92–93
 African centrality in Arab world, 74–76
 and culture, 75
 and race, 72, 73–74
 See also Islam

Agenda for Peace (Boutros-Ghali), 296, 299, 300, 301, 303

Ahimsa, 87

AID. *See* U.S. Agency for International Development

Aideed, Muhammad Farah, 91, 139, 140,
    225, 285
AIDS, 156, 157
Algeria
    conflict management participation, 238
    decolonization process, 28, 88
    French postcolonial influence, 31, 107
    Islam in, 76
    and Morocco, 235–236, 238
    and regional cooperation, 244
    and Western Sahara conflict, 107, 242
Ali, Muhammed, 132
All-African Council of Churches, 239
All-African Peoples' Conference (Accra).
    See Accra All-African Peoples'
    Conference
American Federation of Labor/Congress of
    Industrial Organizations (AFL-CIO),
    263
Amhara kingdom, 132
Amin Dada, Idi, 34
AMU. *See* Arab Maghreb Union
ANAD. *See* Accord de Nonagression et
    d'Assistance en Matière de Défense
ANC. *See* African National Congress
"Anger of the Al-Hababy Sandstorm, The"
    (Ibrahim), 74
Angola, 102, 150, 171, 236
    decolonization process, 28, 36, 86, 250
    and South Africa, 113, 155
    U.S. political assistance programs, 265
    U.S. recognition, 260, 280
    See also Angolan civil war; Angolan civil
    war conflict management
Angolan civil war, 89, 92, 105
    and arms sales, 213, 251, 279, 292(nn 4,
    8)
    and Cold War, 6, 281
    and decolonization process, 36
    and democratization, 12, 13
    South African role, 216, 222–223, 228, 281
    See also Angolan civil war conflict
    management
Angolan civil war conflict management,
    211, 216–218, 236, 278–279
    Bicesse accords, 210, 218, 226, 227, 228,
    281, 292(n9)
    failure of, 212, 226, 227, 228

and international disengagement, 45
    Portuguese role, 113, 210, 212, 217–218,
    227, 228
    UN role, 210, 278, 280, 281
    U.S. role, 102, 113, 216, 217, 218, 222–224,
    226
    and U.S.-Soviet cooperation, 252, 278,
    279, 280
Anyaoku, Eleazar Emeka, 70
AOF. *See* Fédération de l'Afrique
    Occidentale Française
Arab-Israeli conflict, 75, 136
Arab League, 74
Arab Maghreb Union (AMU), 189, 236,
    244–245
Arafat, Yassir, 75
Arusha Consultations on Africa's Internal
    Conflicts (IPA), 296, 303, 304
Arusha Declaration (1967), 34
ASEAN. *See* Association of South East
    Asian Nations
Asia, 24. *See also* Newly industrialized
    countries; *individual countries*
Assimilation doctrine, 164
Association doctrine, 164–165
Association of South East Asian Nations
    (ASEAN), 191
Atwood, J. Brian, 63, 259–260
Australia, 116
Azanian People's Organization, 215
Al-Azhar University, 79

Babangida, Ibrahim Badamasi, 58, 61, 260,
    261, 287
Baker, James, 218, 220–221
Balandier, Georges, 34
Balladur, Edouard, 169, 175, 181–182, 262
Banana, Canaan, 239
Banda, Hastings, 211, 253, 259
Banda, Kamuzu, 13
Barre, Mohamed Siad, 127, 142, 199,
    205(n20)
    military defeat of, 130, 139, 251, 285
Barroso, Durao, 217
Bashir, Omer al, 221
Basutoland, 35
Bayart, Jean-François, 184(n17)
Bechuanaland, 35

Bedie, Konan, 182

Belgian Congo, 90, 278. *See also* Zaire

Belgium, 28, 82, 100, 112

Ben Bella, Ahmed, 236

Benin, 92, 109, 111, 181, 195. *See also* Benin, democratization in

Benin, democratization in, 179, 253, 270
  and French policies, 257–258
  reconciliation, 290, 291
  and U.S. political assistance programs, 263, 265–266

BenJedid, Chadli, 236, 238

Berlin Conference (1884–1885), 28, 69

Beye, Blondin, 281

Biafra conflict, 195, 242

Bicesse accords, 210, 218, 226, 227, 228, 292(n9)

Bilal, 80

Bishop, James K., 250

Biya, Paul, 59, 180, 182, 261, 262, 272

Black nationalism, 73–74. *See also* African nationalism

Bonaparte, Napoleon, 132

Bongo, Omar, 107, 111, 182, 262

Bosnian conflict, 12

Botchwey, Kwesi, 48, 56, 58

Botswana, 23, 150, 151
  boundaries, 159, 160
  democratization, 263, 265, 270
  and regional cooperation, 122(n41), 204(n4)

Boumedienne, Houari, 236

Bourguiba, Habib, 238

Boutros-Ghali, Boutros, 75, 91, 296, 299, 300, 301, 303, 306

Bowman, Larry, 147

Braudel, Fernand, 164

Brazzaville group, 191

Bretton Woods Agreement, 6

Brezhnev, Leonid, 7

Bulgaria, 292(n8)

Bunche, Ralph, 89, 93

Burkina Faso, 174, 177, 178, 236
  democratization, 179, 263, 265
  and France, 107, 110

Burundi
  Belgian postcolonial influence, 28
  civil war, 89–90, 211, 285, 286, 293(nn 21, 22)
  and democratization, 13, 18, 268, 270, 291
  French military presence, 176
  precolonial identity, 23
  and regional cooperation, 199, 202, 204(n4)
  and United Nations, 285, 286
  and Zaire, 92

Bush administration
  and Cold War, 8
  and conflict management, 279, 281–282
  and democratization, 251–252
  Somalia intervention, 139, 140, 210, 215, 224–225, 284–285, 297
  and Sudan, 220–221
  See also United States; U.S. *headings*

Buthelezi, Mangosuthu, 214

Buyoya, 293(n22)

Caisse Française de Développement (CFD), 169, 173

Callaghy, Thomas, 15

Cambodia, 228

Camdessus, Michel, 50–51, 109

Cameroon, 63, 92, 109, 172, 174
  foreign economic aid, 104, 120(n9), 173, 175, 180, 262
  See also Cameroon, democratization in

Cameroon, democratization in, 179, 253, 272, 291
  and French policies, 180, 182, 258, 261–262, 275(n52)
  and U.S. political assistance programs, 263, 265, 268

Camp David Accords, 75

Canada, 8, 82, 267

Cape Verde, 289, 291

Carrington, Lord Peter, 216

Carter, Jimmy, 181, 215, 219–220, 221

Carter Center, 179, 219–220, 264

Cartier, Raymond, 185(n25)

Casablanca Group, 245

CDU. *See* Christian Democratic Union

CEAO. *See* Communauté Économique de l'Afrique de l'Ouest

Cellule Africaine de l'Elysée, 169

Center for International Private Enterprise
(CIPE), 263, 265
Central African Republic (CAR), 179, 244
French postcolonial influence, 32, 109,
110, 176, 181
Central American Common Market, 191
CEPGL. *See* Communauté Économique
des Pays de Grands Lacs
Ceuta, 113
CFA. *See* Communauté Financière
Africaine
CFA franc zone, 27, 32, 121(n28)
and democratization, 262
devaluation, 64, 109, 174–175, 182–183,
190
economic problems in, 33, 108–109,
121(n27)
Equatorial Guinea membership, 28, 112
CFAO. *See* Compagnie Française de
l'Afrique Occidentale
CFD. *See* Caisse Française de
Développement
Chad, 255, 258
conflict management, 240, 242, 243
French military presence, 107, 109, 110,
176, 181
Libya conflict, 33, 34, 107, 110
and regional cooperation, 200, 244
Chalker, Lynda, 257
Chiluba, Frederick, 51–52, 61–62, 64
China, 222, 228
Chirac, Jacques, 107, 168, 275(n56)
Chissano, Joaquin A., 219, 281–282,
292(n13)
Christian Aid, 57
Christian Democratic Union (CDU)
(Germany), 104, 105
Christian evangelism, 35
Christianity, 69–70, 76, 284
Coptic, 71, 73, 76, 130, 132
Christian Social Union (CSU) (Germany),
104, 105
Christopher, Warren, 252, 259
CIPE. *See* Center for International Private
Enterprise
Civil Liberties Organisation (Nigeria), 263
Civil society, 290

Civil wars. *See* Regional/internal conflicts;
specific countries and conflicts
Clinton administration, 63, 214–215, 224,
228
and democratization, 59, 252, 259–261,
276(n77)
See also United States; U.S. *headings*
Clough, Michael, 251
CODESA. *See* Convention for a
Democratic South Africa
Cohen, Herman, 217, 219, 220, 221–222,
251–252, 257
Cold War, 4–6
and colonialism, 35
and democratization, 250–251
détente, 6–7, 136
and French postcolonial influence, 170–
171
globalist posture, 102, 120(n12)
and Horn of Africa, 130, 136, 138
1980s, 7–10
nonalignment, 5, 70, 85–86, 87–88, 170–
171
and OAU, 191
Reagan administration renewal of, 7, 102
and regional/internal conflicts, 6, 281,
302
See also Cold War, end of
Cold War, end of, 3, 9
and conflict management, 235
and democratization, 10, 59, 209, 252,
255, 270
and foreign economic aid, 119–120(n9)
and Horn of Africa, 127–128, 142
and human rights, 220
and international consensus, 8, 14, 18–
19, 128, 252
and international disengagement, 8, 42,
45, 95–96
and regional/internal conflicts, 127–128,
302
and U.S.-Soviet cooperation, 252, 278,
279, 292(n3)
Colonialism, 23
and African nationalism, 33–34
and African unity, 26–27
and Christianity, 76
and Cold War, 35

and economies, 27
and Horn of Africa, 128, 130–133
linguistic dominance, 69, 83
and nation-state system, 23, 25, 26,
   38(n12), 301–302
recolonization, 89–92
and regional economic cooperation, 27,
   190–191
and regional/internal conflicts, 35–37
See also Decolonization process;
   European postcolonial influence;
   French postcolonial influence
Committee for the Defense of Human
   Rights (Nigeria), 263
Common African and Malagasy
   Organization. *See* Organisation
   Commune Africaine et Malgache
Common Agricultural Policy (EU),
   122(n43)
Commonwealth, 29–30, 70
   and democratization, 264, 265
   and South Africa, 39(n21), 102, 103
Commonwealth Group, 215
Commonwealth Institute, 103
Communauté Économique de l'Afrique de
   l'Ouest (CEAO), 178, 195, 202,
   204(n4), 205(n12), 240, 244
Communauté Économique des Pays de
   Grands Lacs (CEPGL), 202, 204(n4)
Communauté Financière Africaine (CFA),
   27
Comoros, 181
Compagnie Française de l'Afrique
   Occidentale (CFAO), 172
Compaore, Blaise, 292(n15)
Comprehensive Anti-Apartheid Act (1986),
   214
Conable, Barber, 59, 255
Condominium, 134
Conference on Security and Cooperation
   in Europe (CSCE), 271, 307
Conference on Security, Stability,
   Development and Cooperation in
   Africa (CSSDCA) (Kampala), 213, 243,
   296
Conflict management, 234–243, 245–246
   ANAD, 178, 187(n44)
   bilateral negotiations, 234–236

Burundi, 285, 286, 293(nn 21, 22)
civil wars vs. interstate wars, 211
ECOMOG, 110, 177–178, 198, 210, 211,
   224, 239, 283
Eritrean-Ethiopian conflict, 34, 215, 219–
   220, 240, 246, 279–280
and international disengagement, 45,
   283, 285, 286, 292–293(n16)
mediation, 237–240
need for, 210–211
1980s, 8
and third-party status, 211–212
See also Humanitarian intervention;
   International military involvement;
   OAU conflict management; Regional/
   internal conflicts; UN conflict
   management; U.S. role in conflict
   management; *specific countries and
   conflicts*
Conflict Management Group, 215
Congo, 172, 174, 244
   conflict management, 210, 242
   democratization, 179, 258, 265, 289
   French postcolonial influence, 109, 175,
      180–181, 188(n51), 258
Congo (Brazzaville), 32, 92
Congressional Black Caucus, 260
Conseil de l'Entente, 109, 170
Constitutional Rights Project (Nigeria),
   263
Consultative Group for Kenya, 258
Convention for a Democratic South Africa
   (CODESA), 214, 215
Copts, 71, 73, 76, 130
Cot, Jean-Pierre, 107, 168, 169
Council of Elders, 243
Couthino, Rosa, 292(n11)
Crocker, Chester A., 214, 223, 226
CSCE. *See* Conference on Security and
   Cooperation in Europe
CSSDCA. *See* Conference on Security,
   Stability, Development and
   Cooperation in Africa
CSU. *See* Christian Social Union
Cuba, 10, 222, 226, 281, 292(n11)
   Angola withdrawal, 102, 216, 223, 252,
      278

Cultural receptivity, 69–70, 71, 77–78, 92–93

Customs Union of the Central African States. *See* Union Douanière Economique de l'Afrique Centrale

Customs Union of the Central African States, 244

Czechoslovakia, 292(n8)

de Brazza, Savorgnan, 164

Debt crisis, 45–47
    as cause of economic weakness, 7, 57–58
    relief, 7, 65, 102, 180
    and structural adjustment conditionality, 7, 8, 9, 46
    and structural adjustment programs, 45–46, 53, 65
    See also Foreign economic aid

Deby, Idriss, 110

Decolonization process
    and African unity, 33–35
    and democratization, 3, 4, 17, 60
    foreign assets seizures, 34
    and fragmentation, 25–26, 38(n5), 70
    and French postcolonial influence, 166, 167, 183–184(nn 10, 11)
    and nation-state system, 23–24, 25, 26–27, 38(n12), 301–302
    and negotiation, 246
    Nehru's armed liberation approach, 86, 88–89
    and nonviolence, 85
    and regional economic cooperation, 191
    and regional/internal conflicts, 24–25, 36, 281
    reversal of, 89–92
    struggles against colonial influence, 33–35
    U.S. policies, 250
    See also Colonialism; European postcolonial influence; French postcolonial influence

de Gaulle, Charles, 32, 84, 105, 166, 168

de Klerk, F. W., 214

Democracy and Development (GERDDES), 264

Democratic party (United States), 263

Democratic Unionist party (Sudan), 220

Democratization, 178–179, 250–272
    and civil society, 290
    and Cold War, 250–251
    and decolonization process, 3, 4, 17, 60
    definition of, 272(n1)
    and end of Cold War, 209, 252, 255, 270
    French policies, 111–112, 179–182, 252, 262, 270–271, 275(n56)
    future prospects, 269–272
    and governance, 13, 291
    and international security, 11–12, 269–270
    and modernization theory, 16
    and nation-state system, 128–129
    and reconciliation, 291
    and regional cooperation, 264
    and regional/internal conflicts, 12, 13, 209
    and structural adjustment programs, 10, 15–16, 59–62, 128, 290–291
    "third wave" of, 10–11, 251, 253–255, 273(n8), 288–290
    U.S. policies, 250–252, 255, 274(n25)
    U.S. political assistance programs, 262–269, 276(nn 66, 74, 76–77), 277(n80)
    UN role, 264, 271, 278
    See also Democratization conditionality; South African democratic transition

Democratization conditionality, 11–13, 14–18, 58–62, 255–262
    African belief in, 254
    British policies, 257, 260–261
    Clinton administration policies, 259–261, 262
    criticisms of, 14–15, 16–18
    and economic reform, 47
    and end of Cold War, 59
    and European Union, 96
    French policies, 180–182, 188(n51), 257–258, 261–262
    and Horn of Africa political identity, 137–139
    Kenya, 11, 61, 258–259
    vs. structural adjustment conditionality, 11–12
    USAID policies, 256, 257
    See also Democratization

Democratization, obstacles to, 61, 179, 268,
    272, 286–287
  and economic reform, 59–60
  global economy, 3
  regional/internal conflicts, 12, 13
  Western support for authoritarian
    governments, 180–182, 188(n51), 250–
    252, 261–262, 274(n25), 287
Deng, Francis M., 209
Denmark, 100, 258
Development. *See* Economic reform;
    Structural adjustment conditionality;
    Structural adjustment programs
Development Gap, 57
Dhlakama, Afonso, 219
Dinkas, 73
Diop, Cheikh Anta, 39(n28)
Diouf, Abdou, 78, 178
Diouf, Elizabeth, 78
Djibouti, 12, 13, 91, 137, 199
  French postcolonial influence, 32, 109,
    110, 176
  political identity, 127, 130, 137, 141–142
  See also Horn of Africa
Doe, Samuel K., 198, 251, 282, 283
Dominican Republic, 113
dos Santos, José Eduardo, 217, 227, 280
Dubois, W. E. B., 33

East African Common Services
    Organization, 191
East African Community, 199, 201
*East Asian Miracle, The: Economic Growth
    and Public Policy* (World Bank), 57
Eastern Europe, 9, 10, 253
East and Southern Africa Economic
    Community, 152
EC-ACP Lomé Conventions. *See* Lomé
    Conventions
ECCAS. *See* Economic Community of
    Central African States
ECOMOG. *See* Economic Community of
    West Africa's Monitoring Group
Economic Commission for Africa (ECA),
    26, 54–56, 57, 198, 244
Economic Commission for Latin America,
    191

Economic Community of Central African
    States (ECCAS), 189, 190, 191,
    194(table), 200
  establishment process, 192, 200, 244
Economic Community of West African
    States (ECOWAS), 26, 189, 191
  conflict management participation, 110,
    177–178, 198, 210, 211, 224, 239, 240, 283
  effectiveness of, 190, 196–198
  establishment process, 192, 194–196,
    205(nn 11, 12), 244
  membership, 194(table)
Economic Community of West Africa's
    Monitoring Group (ECOMOG), 110,
    177–178, 198, 210, 211, 224, 239, 283
Economic integration. *See* Regional
    economic cooperation
Economic liberalization. *See* Economic
    reform; Structural adjustment
    conditionality; Structural adjustment
    programs
Economic reform, 48–54
  and Cold War, 5
  and expatriate advisors, 51–52
  failure of, 52–54
  and foreign investment, 44
  future prospects, 63–66
  importance of, 52–53
  neoorthodox beliefs, 138
  1970s, 6
  1980s, 7–8
  obstacles to, 60
  social and political impact of, 52, 60, 62
  See also Structural adjustment
    conditionality; Structural adjustment
    programs
Economic Union of Central Africa
    (UEAC), 243–244
Economic weakness
  and colonialism, 27
  debt crisis, 7, 45–47, 53, 57–58
  and democratization, 287
  and foreign investment, 95–96, 106
  and fragmentation, 25
  and global economy, 7, 9
  and international disengagement, 42–43
  See also Economic reform; Foreign
    economic aid; Foreign investment;

specific countries; Structural
adjustment conditionality
ECOWAS. *See* Economic Community of
West African States
EDF. *See* European Development Fund
EEC. *See* European Economic Community
Egypt, 23, 29, 72, 75, 76, 88
and colonialism, 132, 133–134
and Sudan, 36, 133–134
See also Horn of Africa
Elf-Aquitaine, 180, 181, 188(n51)
Elf-Congo, 181
English language, 81
Enhanced Structural Adjustment Facility,
49, 63–64, 101–102
Environmental Defense Fund, 57
EPLF. *See* Eritrean People's Liberation
Front
EPRDF. *See* Ethiopian People's
Revolutionary Democratic Front
Equatorial Guinea, 28, 112, 287
Eritrea, 28, 140–141, 143, 285. *See also*
Eritrean-Ethiopian conflict; Horn of
Africa
Eritrean-Ethiopian conflict, 127
conflict management, 34, 215, 219–220,
240, 246, 279–280
and decolonization process, 25, 27, 36
Eritrean independence, 140–141
and nation-state system, 45
and Selassie regime, 136
See also Horn of Africa
Eritrean People's Liberation Front (EPLF),
141, 200, 215, 219, 279
Estado Novo, 29
Ethiopia
conflict management, 8, 210, 226, 236,
239, 241, 246
conflict management participation, 143,
215, 285
conflict with Somalia, 129–130, 236, 239,
241, 246
democratization, 13, 18, 179, 250, 265
foreign economic aid, 101, 104, 259,
274(n25)
imperialism of, 145(n17)
inaccessibility in, 131, 132
internal conflict, 127, 129–130

Islam in, 76–77
languages, 142, 145(n22)
and Mahdist revolution, 133
political identity, 127, 129–130, 131–132,
134–136, 142–143, 145(n22)
precolonial identity, 23, 131–132
and recolonization, 91
and regional cooperation, 199, 245
socialism, 7
and Sudan, 236
and United States, 36, 136, 212–213, 251,
259
U.S. political assistance programs, 263,
265, 267
See also Eritrean-Ethiopian conflict;
Horn of Africa
Ethiopian People's Revolutionary
Democratic Front (EPRDF), 130, 141,
142–143, 220
Eurafrique, 165, 167
European Community (EC), 32, 201, 213.
See also European Economic
Community; European Union; Lomé
Conventions
European Development Fund (EDF), 99,
173
European Economic Community (EEC),
82, 116, 191, 206(n27). *See also*
European Community; European
Union
European postcolonial influence, 28–30
cultural, 32, 34–35, 39(n28)
linguistic, 32, 35, 39(n28), 81–84
resistance to, 33–35
See also French postcolonial influence
European Union (EU), 95–101
Common Agricultural Policy, 122(n43)
economic aid from, 99(table), 99–102,
100(table), 104, 119–120(nn 9, 11)
Maastricht Treaty, 118(n1)
and South Africa, 105, 114–116, 122(n39),
122(nn 39, 41, 42)
trade relations with Africa, 95, 96–99,
97(table), 98(table), 119(nn 5–8)
See also European Community;
European Economic Community;
Lomé Conventions; *specific countries*
Export-Import Bank, 213

Eyadéma, Gnassingbe, 111, 182, 197, 261, 262, 287

FAC. *See* Fonds d'Aide et de Coopération
Fahd (King of Saudi Arabia), 236, 238
Fanon, Franz, 35
FAR. *See Force d'Action Rapide*
FAS. *See* Francophone sub-Saharan Africa; French postcolonial influence
Fashoda crisis, 133
al-Fayturi, Muhammad Miftah, 74
Fédération de l'Afrique Equatoriale Française (AEF), 25, 31
Fédération de l'Afrique Occidentale Française (AOF), 25, 31, 38(n5), 166
FNLA. *See* National Front for the Liberation of Angola
Foccart, Jacques, 33, 106, 169
Fonds d'Aide et de Coopération (FAC), 173
Force d'Action Rapide (FAR), 109, 176
Ford Foundation, 277(n80)
Foreign economic aid
  Belgium, 112
  and end of Cold War, 119–120(n9)
  European Union, 99(table), 99–102, 100(table), 104, 119–120(nn 9, 11)
  France, 9, 32, 40(n31), 99, 106, 121(n21), 173–174
  future prospects, 63
  and human rights, 213
  increase in (1980s), 255, 256(table)
  and international disengagement, 8–9, 96, 119(n4)
  1970s, 6–7
  Portugal, 113
  post-apartheid South Africa, 153, 259
  U.S. policies, 250–252, 254–255, 274(n25)
  See also Debt crisis; Democratization conditionality; Structural adjustment conditionality
Foreign investment, 7, 131, 174
  and economic weakness, 95–96, 106
  France, 106, 174
  international disengagement, 43–45
  South Africa, 101, 103, 105
  and structural adjustment programs, 11, 50–51

France
  disengagement, 8–9, 33, 40(n35)
  economy, 15, 167–168
  and Horn of Africa, 132, 133
  and South Africa, 108, 114, 121(n24), 171
  support for authoritarian governments, 180–182, 188(n51), 261–262, 287
  trade relations with Africa, 97, 98, 171–173, 185(n25)
  See also European Union; French economic aid; French postcolonial influence
France-Afrique, 165, 166, 167
France Against Itself (Luthy), 30–31
Franco, Francisco, 37
Franco-African summits, 32, 106–107, 170, 171, 174, 180, 185(n21)
Francophone sub-Saharan Africa (FSSA), 163, 178–179, 183(n1). *See also* French postcolonial influence
Francophonie, 32, 39(n28), 163–164
Franc zone. *See* CFA franc zone
Freedom House, 255
Free Trade Union Institute (FTUI), 263, 265
Frei, Daniel, 211
FRELIMO. *See* Mozambique Liberation Front
French economic aid, 32, 40(n31), 99, 106
  and CFA franc zone, 175
  and democratization conditionality, 180–182, 188(n51), 257–258
  disengagement, 8–9, 63
  and export promotion, 121(n21)
  multilateralization, 173–174
  and structural adjustment conditionality, 111, 120(n9), 174
French Equatorial Africa Federation. *See* Fédération de l'Afrique Equatoriale Française
French postcolonial influence, 24, 28, 30–33, 105–112, 163–183
  and Cold War, 170–171
  and colonial policies, 164–166
  cultural, 32, 39(n28), 163–164
  and death of Houphouet-Boigny, 182, 190

and decolonization process, 166, 167,
183–184(nn 10, 11)
and democratization, 111–112, 179–182,
252, 262, 270–271, 275(n56)
former Spanish colonies, 28
Franco-African summits, 32, 106–107,
170, 171, 174, 180, 185(n21)
institutional framework, 106–107, 169–
171, 185(nn 21, 23)
intelligence services, 32–33
investment, 106, 174
linguistic dominance, 32, 39(n28), 81–84,
93, 105
and Lomé Conventions, 165–166
Maghreb, 31, 32, 170
military presence, 32, 109–111, 175–178,
181
and Nigeria, 91–92, 195
policy continuity, 167–169
political status, 31–32, 107–108
postcolonial federation attempts, 25,
38(n5)
and regional economic cooperation, 195
trade relations, 97, 98, 171–173, 185(n25)
and United States, 184(n14)
See also CFA franc zone; European
postcolonial influence; Francophone
sub-Saharan Africa; French economic
aid
French Revolution, 164
French West African Federation. *See*
Fédération de l'Afrique Occidentale
Française
Frente Popular para la Liberación de
Saguia el Hamra y Rio de Oro, 37
Friedrich Ebert Stiftung, 267
Friedrich Naumann Stiftung, 267
FRODEBU. *See* Front for Burundi
Democracy
*From Crisis to Sustainable Growth. See Sub-
Saharan Africa: From Crisis to
Sustainable Growth*
Front for Burundi Democracy
(FRODEBU), 293(n22)
Front for the Liberation of Mozambique,
281
Fru Ndi, John, 262, 275(n52)

FSSA. *See* Francophone sub-Saharan
Africa
FTUI. *See* Free Trade Union Institute
Functionalism/neofunctionalism, 200–201
Fund for Cooperation, Compensation, and
Development (ECOWAS), 196

Gabon, 25, 107, 112, 174, 182
democratization, 179, 258
foreign economic aid, 173, 175, 180
French military presence, 32, 109, 110,
176, 181
trade relations, 171, 172
Gambia, 270
Gandhi, Mohandas, 85, 86–89, 93
Garang, John, 221, 284
Gbadolite summit, 217
General Agreement on Tariffs and Trade
(GATT), 117, 123(n46)
Generalized System of Preferences (GSP),
117
GERDDES. *See* Groupe d'Etudes et de
Recherches sur la Démocratie et le
Développement Économique et Social
German language, 82
Germany, 6, 103–105
and democratization, 15, 261, 267,
276(n76)
economic aid, 63, 64, 104
and South Africa, 103, 105, 114
trade relations with Africa, 97–98, 103–
104
See also European Union
Ghana, 26, 45, 63, 104, 109
conflict management, 212, 241
democratization, 60, 179, 253, 267, 290,
291
and regional cooperation, 191, 197
U.S. political assistance programs, 263,
265, 267, 268
See also Ghanaian economic reform
Ghanaian economic reform, 48, 52, 54, 55,
58, 60
and democratization, 61
and expatriate advisors, 52
and foreign economic aid, 49
Gilpin, Robert, 64–65

Giscard d'Estaing, Valéry, 32, 108, 110, 168, 182
Gleneagles agreement, 102
Global Coalition for Africa, 293(n21)
Global economy, 3, 6, 9
  African marginalization in, 14, 41–45, 47, 50
  commodity prices, 96, 118
  and end of slave trade, 41–42
  increased interdependence of, 7, 8, 14
  openness of, 64–65
  and structural adjustment conditionality, 8, 50
  See also Economic reform; Foreign investment; International disengagement; Structural adjustment conditionality; Trade relations
Goa, 86, 89
Gorbachev, Mikhail, 8, 279
Gowan, Yakubu, 195
GPRA. *See* Provisional Government of the Algerian Republic
Gran, Ahmed, 132
Great Britain, 70, 102
  and colonialism, 24, 35, 37(n2)
  conflict management participation, 210, 216
  and decolonization process, 25, 36
  and democratization conditionality, 257, 260–261
  economic aid, 64, 100, 101–102, 120(nn 9, 11)
  and English language, 82
  foreign investment, 44, 101
  and Horn of Africa, 132, 133–134, 135
  political assistance programs, 267
  postcolonial influence, 28, 29–30
  and South Africa, 101, 102–103, 114, 121(n24)
  trade relations with Africa, 97–98, 120(nn 9, 11)
  See also European Union
Groupe d'Etudes et de Recherches sur la Démocratie et le Développement Économique et Social (GERDDES), 264
GSP. *See* Generalized System of Preferences

Guinea, 171, 241
  decolonization process, 28, 166, 167, 183–184(n10)
  democratization, 179, 266
  French postcolonial influence, 31, 32, 110
  and regional cooperation, 191, 202, 204(n4), 244
Guinea-Bissau, 28, 86, 113, 246
Gulf War, 25, 253
GUNT. *See* Transitional Government of National Unity

Habré, Hissene, 33, 110, 240
Habyarimana, Juvenal, 262
Hallstein Doctrine, 103
Hans Seidel Stiftung, 105, 267
Harare Declaration, 102
Harmand, Jules, 165
Hassan II (King of Morocco), 113, 236, 238
Hassan, Muhammed Abdille, 137
Hassel, Stephane, 111
Hausa, 71, 73
Hawkins, Anthony, 153
Hempstone, Smith, 252, 258
Hofmeier, Rolf, 103–104
Holmes, Oliver Wendell, 138
Hong Kong. *See* Newly industrialized countries
Honwana, Fernando, 216
Horn of Africa
  conflict management, 8, 238–239, 246
  and decolonization process, 36–37
  defined, 129–131
  See also Horn of Africa political identity; *specific countries*
Horn of Africa political identity, 127–144, 145(n3), 146(n24)
  and colonialism, 128, 130–133
  Djibouti, 127, 130, 137, 141–142
  "domestic" politics, 138–143
  and economic/political conditionality, 137–138
  Eritrea, 140–141
  Ethiopia, 127, 129–130, 131–132, 134–136, 142–143, 145(n22)
  and fundamentalist Islam, 127, 129, 143–144
  and inaccessibility, 130–131

"international" politics, 143–144
and regional/internal conflicts, 127–128, 129–130
Somalia, 129, 130, 136–137, 139–140
Sudan, 133–134, 140
Houphouet-Boigny, Felix, 31–32, 86, 107, 166, 177
death of, 182, 190
Humanitarian intervention, 295–308
need for, 296–297
operational strategies, 304–307
Somalia, 139, 140, 210, 215, 224–225, 284–285, 297
and sovereignty, 297–301
See also Conflict management
Human rights, 11, 213, 220
global funds, 266, 276(n74)
and humanitarian intervention, 298, 303
See also Democratization; Humanitarian intervention
Huntington, Samuel, 15–16, 17, 273(n8)
Hurd, Douglas, 257
Hyden, Goran, 56

Ibrahim, Salah A., 74
IDA. *See* International Development Association
IFES. *See* International Foundation for Electoral Systems
IFIs (International financial institutions). *See* Structural adjustment conditionality
Ifni, 28
IGADD. *See* Inter-Governmental Agency on Drought and Development
Imanyara, Gitobu, 263
IMF. *See* International Monetary Fund
Imperial Conference (1926), 29
Independence. *See* Decolonization process
India, 85–89, 93
Indigenous religions, 77
Inflation, 7
Informal economy, 66
Inkatha Freedom Party (South Africa), 211, 214
Institute for International Affairs (Japan), 268

Inter-Governmental Agency on Drought and Development (IGADD), 239, 240
International Center for Human Rights and Democratic Development, 267
International Development Association (IDA), 99, 102
International disengagement, 33, 40(n35), 42
and conflict management, 45, 283, 285, 286, 292–293(n16)
economic aid, 8–9, 96, 119(n4)
and end of Cold War, 8, 42, 45, 95–96
foreign investment, 43–45
1970s, 6–7
International financial institutions (IFIs). *See* Foreign economic aid; Structural adjustment conditionality
International Foundation for Electoral Systems (IFES), 265
International military involvement
French military presence, 32, 109–111, 175–178, 181
Great Britain, 30
Somalia, 6, 30, 110, 139, 140, 181, 210, 215, 224–225
International Monetary Fund (IMF), 49, 63–64, 101–102, 109, 175. *See also* Foreign economic aid; Structural adjustment conditionality
International Peace Academy (IPA), 296, 297, 303
International relations theory, 13, 18, 128, 145(n3)
International Republican Institute (IRI), 263, 264, 265
IPA. *See* International Peace Academy
Iraq, 37(n2)
IRI. *See* International Republican Institute
Islam, 34–35, 69–70, 76–80, 131
African centrality in, 79–80, 93
and Arab identity, 71, 72–73, 303–304
fundamentalism, 76, 127, 129, 143, 284
and religious tolerance, 77–79
See also Afro-Arab relations
Israel, 292(n8)
Issayas Afewerki, 141, 143

Italy, 15, 28, 100, 270
    conflict management participation, 210,
        212, 219, 279
    and Horn of Africa, 132, 133, 135, 137
Ivory Coast, 25, 31, 109, 172, 174, 195
    conflict management, 241
    conflict management participation, 177,
        238
    and democratization, 179, 258, 261
    economic advantages of, 63
    foreign economic aid, 173, 175, 180, 255
    French military presence, 32, 109, 176,
        181
    French political support, 107, 182

Japan, 6, 24, 57, 82–83
    and democratization, 15, 267–268, 270
    disengagement, 8, 44–45, 119(n4)
Johannes IV (Emperor of Ethiopia), 132,
    135, 136
Johnson, Prince, 282–283
Johnston, Harry, 232(n43), 284

Kaba, Soriba, 59
Kampala Forum. *See* Conference on
    Security, Stability, Development and
    Cooperation in Africa
KANU. *See* Kenya African National Union
Kaunda, Kenneth, 51, 61, 85, 211, 239, 289
Keita, Modibo, 31, 38(n5), 238
Kenya, 30, 35, 73, 127, 171, 212
    conflict management participation, 143
    economic advantages of, 63
    foreign economic aid, 62, 101, 104, 213,
        274(n25)
    foreign investment, 44, 45
    human rights, 213
    and regional cooperation, 199, 201
    and Somalia, 239
    and United States, 251, 252
    See also Horn of Africa; Kenya,
        democratization in
Kenya, democratization in, 18, 253, 289
    foreign economic aid conditionality, 11,
        61, 258–259
    obstacles to, 61, 179, 251, 252, 261, 268,
        272

U.S. political assistance programs, 263,
    265, 276(n66)
Kenya African National Union (KANU),
    289
Kerekou, Matheiu, 253, 257
Khmer Rouge, 228
Killick, Tony, 56
King, Martin Luther, Jr., 85, 89, 93
Kissinger, Henry, 136
Koffigoh, 111
Konrad Adenauer Stiftung, 267
Kulthum, Umm, 75
Kuwait, 25

Lagos Plan of Action (1980), 26, 189, 198–
    199, 200. *See also* Economic
    Community of Central African States;
    Economic Community of West
    African States; Preferential Trade Area
    of East and Southern Africa
Lagos Treaty (1975), 177, 195. *See also*
    Economic Community of West
    African States
Lancaster House negotiations, 216, 238
Languages
    and Afro-Arab relations, 71
    colonial dominance, 69, 81–84
    Ethiopia, 145(n22)
    Swahili, 73
Latin America, 10, 24, 46, 113, 254
    regional cooperation in, 191, 245, 271,
        307
Latin American Free Trade Area, 191
Lawson, Nigel, 102
League of Kenya Women Voters, 263
League of Nations, 37(n2), 135
Le Floch-Prigent, Loik, 180, 181
Lesotho, 23, 155, 159–160, 289
    and regional cooperation, 122(n41), 199,
        204(n4)
Liberia, 90, 171, 292(n15)
    and democratization, 251, 252, 259, 263,
        270
    and regional cooperation, 202, 204(n4),
        244
    and United States, 252, 259, 263
    See also Liberian civil war conflict
        management

Liberian civil war conflict management, 236, 282–283
  ECOMOG role, 110, 177–178, 198, 210, 211, 224, 239, 283
  implementation stage, 226
  international disengagement, 45
  OAU role, 34
Liberian Council of Churches, 239
Libya, 28, 238, 244
  Chad conflict, 33, 34, 107, 110, 235
  and Liberian civil war, 282, 292(n15)
Lissouba, Pascal, 180, 181, 188(n51)
Loi-cadre, 25, 166
Lomé Conventions, 116–118, 119(n2)
  Eurafrican monetary zone, 175
  European Development Fund, 99, 173
  and French postcolonial influence, 165–166
  German policies, 104
  and international disengagement, 9, 96, 98, 117–118
  Latin American membership, 113
  negotiations, 243, 244
  Nigerian role, 195
  sensitive products, 118, 122(n43)
  and South Africa, 115–116, 122(n42)
  STABEX, 116, 122(n45)
Luthuli, Albert, 85, 86, 89, 93
Lyautey, 164
Lyons, Terence, 225

Maastricht Treaty on European Union, 118(n1)
MacArthur, Douglas, 82
Machar, Riak, 284
Machel, Samora, 216, 218, 238
Madagascar, 23, 171, 174
  democratization, 258, 265–266
  French postcolonial influence, 32, 109, 181, 258
Maghreb, 87–88, 116
  French postcolonial influence, 31, 32, 170
  See also specific countries
Mahdi, Ali, 225
al-Mahdi, Sadiq, 221, 283
Mahdi, Seyyid Muhammad el, 91
al-Mahdi al-Majdhub, Muhammad, 73–74
Mahdiyya movement (Sudan), 91, 133

Major, John, 102, 103
Malawi, 101, 151, 199, 255
  democratization, 13, 253, 259, 263, 267
Malaysia, 25
Mali, 174, 178, 191, 236
  democratization, 179, 253, 258, 263, 266
  foreign economic aid, 104, 173
  French postcolonial influence, 31, 32, 33, 109–110, 258
  structural adjustment programs, 290–291
Mali Federation, 166
Malloum, Felix, 240
Manchester Pan-African Congress, 26
Mandela, Nelson, 75, 253
  and southern Africa, 148–149, 152–153, 157, 214
Mano River Union, 178, 202, 204(n4), 244
Marabouts, 78
Marchés Tropicaux, 110
Marten, David, 181
Martin, Guy, 32, 105, 106
Massemba-Debat, Alphonse, 32
Mauritania, 112, 171, 179, 236, 242
  French postcolonial influence, 32, 109, 110
  and regional cooperation, 197, 244
Mauritius, 13, 18, 25, 118, 265
M' Ba, Leon, 166
Mbembe, Achille, 62
M'Bow, Moukhtar, 70
McNamara, Robert, 6
Media, 11, 197
Meles Zenawi, 136, 141, 143
Melilla, 113
Menelik II (Emperor of Ethiopia), 130, 132, 133, 135, 137, 141, 142
Mengistu Haile Mariam, 127, 129, 136, 142, 220
Menkhaus, Ken, 225
Menon, Krishna, 86
Messmer, Pierre, 183–184(n10)
Meyer, Roelf, 215
Middle East, 24, 37n2, 72
Mitterrand, François, 32, 33, 107, 108
  and democratization conditionality, 257, 261, 262
  and French military presence, 109, 110

and policy continuity, 106, 168–169, 184(n17)

Mitterrand, Jean-Christophe, 33, 106, 170

MMD. *See* Movement for Multi-party Democracy

MNR. *See* Resistência Nacional Mozambiquano

Mobutu Sese Seko, 34, 84, 112, 222, 251
  conflict management participation, 211, 217
  French support for, 110, 182
  resistance to democratization, 59, 253, 272, 287

Modernization theory, 5, 16

Moi, Daniel arap
  conflict management participation, 143, 211, 212, 218
  resistance to democratization, 11, 59, 61, 62, 258–259, 272
  U.S. support for, 251, 252

Monrovia group, 191

Monrovia-Lagos Group, 245

Monsengwo, Laurent, 222

Moose, George, 184(n14)

Morocco, 23, 28, 76, 171, 244, 250
  and Algeria, 235–236, 238
  European postcolonial influence, 31, 107, 113
  See also Western Sahara conflict

Movement for Multi-party Democracy (MMD) (Zambia), 61, 62

Mozambiqan civil war conflict management, 211–212, 236
  U.S. role, 210, 218–219, 226, 281–282, 292(n13)
  UN role, 227–228

Mozambique, 7, 105, 113, 150, 171
  civil war, 90, 224
  conflict management participation, 216, 238
  decolonization process, 28, 36, 86, 250
  and democratization, 12, 13, 265, 291
  foreign economic aid, 102, 104, 255, 259, 274(n25)
  and regional cooperation, 199
  and South Africa, 148, 155, 218
  and United States, 259, 265

See also Mozambiqan civil war conflict management

Mozambique Liberation Front (FRELIMO), 218, 281

Mozambique National Resistance Movement. *See* Resistência Nacional Mozambiquano

MPLA. *See* Popular Movement for the Liberation of Angola

Mugabe, Robert, 211, 216, 218, 238

Muhammad Abdul Wahab, Al-Ustadh, 75

Muzorewa, Abel, 216

NAFTA. *See* North American Free Trade Area

Nairobi Law Monthly, 263

NAM. *See* Non-Aligned Movement

Namibia, 103, 121(n24), 228
  decolonization process, 34, 90
  democratization, 263, 265, 267, 270, 289, 290, 291
  U.S. political assistance programs, 263, 265, 267
  See also Namibian conflict management

Namibian conflict management, 211, 212
  UN role, 210, 227, 278
  U.S. role, 102, 222–224, 226, 252

Nasser, Gamal Abdel, 88

National Democratic Institute of International Affairs (NDI), 263, 264, 265, 276(n66)

National Endowment for Democracy (NED), 263–265, 268, 269

National Front for the Liberation of Angola (FNLA), 222

National Islamic Front (NIF), 284

Nationalism. *See* Decolonization process

National Party (Zambia), 62

National Renewal Movement of Mozambique, 281

National Union for the Total Independence of Angola. *See* Uniao Nacional para a Independência Total de Angola

Nation-state system
  and African unity, 26–27
  and decolonization process, 23–24, 25, 26–27, 38(n12), 301–302

and democratization, 128–129
and economic reform, 48
Horn of Africa, 128, 130, 137–138, 145(n3)
OAU support for, 26, 27
and regional/internal conflicts, 27, 45,
301–302
See also Horn of Africa political identity
NATO. *See* North Atlantic Treaty
Organization
NDI. *See* National Democratic Institute of
International Affairs
NED. *See* National Endowment for
Democracy
Négritude, 35
Nehru, Jawaharlal, 85–86, 87–89, 93
Neocolonialism. *See* Structural adjustment
conditionality
Neoorthodox economics. *See* Structural
adjustment programs
Neorealist international relations theory.
See Realist/neorealist international
relations theory
Netherlands, 100
New international economic order
(NIEO), 7
Newly industrialized countries (NIC), 6,
15, 56, 57
New neocolonialism. *See* Structural
adjustment conditionality
New York accords, 278–279. *See also*
Angolan civil war conflict
management; Namibian conflict
management
NGOs. *See* Nongovernmental
organizations
Nguema, Macias, 28, 112
NIEO. *See* New international economic
order
NIF. *See* National Islamic Front
Niger, 104, 171, 172, 195, 241
democratization, 179, 253, 258, 265, 266
287
and France, 109, 181, 258
Nigeria, 26, 30, 76, 112
civil war, 34, 195, 211
conflict management participation, 110,
210, 222, 240, 283
economy, 53, 58, 63, 101

foreign arms sales to, 62
foreign investment, 44, 101
and France, 91–92, 171
indigenization decrees, 34, 205(n11)
and regional economic cooperation, 195,
196, 197, 203, 205(nn 11, 12)
regional hegemony, 91–92, 110
trade relations with European Union,
97–98, 171
See also Nigeria, democratization in
Nigeria, democratization in, 60, 253
obstacles to, 18, 61, 179, 260–261, 270, 272
and U.S. political assistance programs,
263, 268
Nimeiri, Gaafar Mohamed, 251
el-Nimeiry, Jaafar, 79, 93
Nixon, Richard, 6
Nkomati pact, 218
Nkrumah, Kwame, 26, 27, 85, 191
Non-Aligned Movement (NAM), 171. *See
also* Nonalignment
Nonalignment, 5, 70, 85–86, 87–88, 89, 93,
170–171
Nongovernmental organizations (NGOs),
11, 254, 268–269
Nonviolence, 85, 86
North Africa. *See* Maghreb
North American Free Trade Area
(NAFTA), 190
North Atlantic Treaty Organization
(NATO), 88
Nouvel Observateur, Le, 110
Nuers, 73
Nujoma, Sam, 260
Numeiri, Jaafar, 239
Nyerere, Julius, 33–34, 239, 243
Nyong'o, Peter Anyang', 254

Oakley, Robert, 225
OAS. *See* Organization of American States
OAU. *See* Organization of African Unity
OAU conflict management, 34, 210, 224,
240–243
Burundi, 285, 286, 293(n21)
Commission for Mediation, Arbitration
and Conciliation, 237, 240
and humanitarian intervention, 305, 307
Kampala Forum, 213, 243

Morocco-Algeria conflict, 235–236, 238
Salim proposal, 286, 296–297, 299, 300
Sudan, 211, 222
Obasanjo, Olesegun, 243
Obote, Milton, 78–79, 85–86, 102
O'Brien, Michael, 260
OCAM. *See* Organisation Commune
Africaine et Malgache
Occidental Petroleum Corporation (OXY),
181
Ogaden war (1977), 6
OIC. *See* Organization of the Islamic
Conference
Oil, 7, 53, 96, 112, 150
Okello, John, 26
OPEC. *See* Organization of Petroleum
Exporting Countries
Operation Lifeline Sudan, 221
Organisation Commune Africaine et
Malgache (OCAM), 170
Organization of African Unity (OAU)
and colonialism, 33
and democratization, 264
Lagos Plan of Action (1980), 26, 189,
198–199, 200
and nation-state system, 26, 27
negotiations for, 245
and Organization of the Islamic
Conference, 70, 79
and regional economic cooperation, 191,
197, 203
See also OAU conflict management
Organization of American States (OAS),
245, 271, 307
Organization of Petroleum Exporting
Countries (OPEC), 96
Organization of the Islamic Conference
(OIC), 70, 79–80
Oromo Liberation Front, 141, 220
Oromo people, 132
Ottoman Empire, 132
Otunnu, Olara, 297
Overseas Private Investment Corporation,
213
Oxfam, 46, 57
OXY. *See* Occidental Petroleum
Corporation

Oye, Kenneth, 65

Pakistan, 24
Palestine Liberation Organization (PLO),
74
Palestinians, 74–75
Pan-Africanist Congress (South Africa),
215, 291
Pan-African unity. *See* African unity
Papua New Guinea, 24
Paris Club, 46
Parti colonial, 165
Pasqua, Charles, 262
Patriotic Front, 216, 238
Penne, Guy, 106
Pereira, Aristide, 243
Perez de Cuellar, Javier, 298–299
Philippines, 24
Pillar, Paul R., 230(n5)
PLO. *See* Palestine Liberation Organization
Policy dialogue, 66
Polisario Front, 107
Pompidou, Georges, 106, 168, 170
Popular Movement for the Liberation of
Angola (MPLA), 216, 217, 222, 223,
280, 281, 292(n11)
Portugal, 27, 28–29, 34, 35–36
conflict management participation, 210,
212, 217–218, 227, 228, 280
economic aid, 113
and European Union, 112
and Goa, 86, 89
and Horn of Africa, 131–132
and Latin America, 24
and South Africa, 113–114
trade relations with Africa, 97
and United States, 250
Post-apartheid South Africa, 160–161
and boundaries, 159–160
and European Union, 114–116, 122(nn 39,
42)
foreign economic aid, 153, 259
foreign investment, 44
investment in southern Africa, 154
nonalignment, 89
and southern Africa, 92, 147, 148–149,
152–160, 155(table), 163(n13), 190
trade relations, 114–116, 122(nn 39, 42)

See also South Africa; South African
  democratic transition
Post-neocolonialism, 44
Preferential Trade Area of East and
  Southern Africa (PTA), 152, 189, 191
  effectiveness of, 199–200
  establishment process, 192, 198–199, 244
  membership, 194(table)
Príncipe, 200
Provisional Government of the Algerian
  Republic (GPRA), 235, 236
PTA. *See* Preferential Trade Area of East
  and Southern Africa

Rabat border agreement (1972), 236
Racism, 34–35, 86–87. *See also* Colonialism;
  South African struggle against
  apartheid
Ramaphosa, Cyril, 215
Ravenhill, John, 40(n35)
Rawlings, Jerry, 48, 52, 60, 61, 197
Reagan administration
  and conflict management, 102, 218–219
  renewal of Cold War, 7, 8, 102
  and South Africa, 214, 250
  See also United States; U.S. *headings*
Realist/neorealist international relations
  theory, 13, 18, 128, 129
Refugees, 156, 157, 283
Regional cooperation, 26, 243–245, 264. *See
  also* Conflict management; Regional
  economic cooperation; *specific
  organizations*
Regional economic cooperation, 189–204,
  204(n4)
  and colonialism, 27, 190–191
  and decolonization process, 191
  disputes, 202
  effectiveness of, 190, 196–198, 199–200
  establishment process, 191–192, 194–196,
    198–199, 205(nn 11, 12, 20)
  future of, 203–204
  and industrialization, 192–193, 205(n6)
  and OAU, 191, 197, 203
  rationales for, 192–194, 205(n8)
  southern Africa, 152–153, 162(n13), 190
  theories, 200–203

See also CFA franc zone; *specific
  organizations*
Regional/internal conflicts
  and Cold War, 6, 281, 302
  and colonialism, 35–37
  and decolonization process, 24–25, 36,
    281
  and democratization, 209, 270
  and end of Cold War, 127–128, 302
  and humanitarian intervention, 140
  and injustice, 302–303
  international disengagement, 6, 7
  and nation-state system, 27, 45, 301–302
  and recolonization, 89–90
  and religion, 303–304
  See also Conflict management;
    Humanitarian intervention; U.S. role
    in conflict management; *specific
    countries and conflicts*
Religion, 69–70, 303–304. *See also*
  Christianity; Islam
RENAMO. *See* Resistência Nacional
  Mozambiquano
Republican party (United States), 263
Resistência Nacional Mozambiquano
  (MNR; RENAMO), 36, 105, 113
  and conflict management, 218, 219, 282,
    292(n13)
  and South Africa, 155, 281
Rhodesia, 213, 216, 281. *See also* Zimbabwe
Rio Treaty, 245
Robinson, 275(n56)
Rocard, Michel, 111
Rostow, W. W., 5
Roussin, Michel, 169–170
RPF. *See* Rwandese Patriotic Front
Rubenson, Sven, 132
Ruggie, John Gerard, 64
Russia, 8, 62, 228. *See also* Soviet successor
  states
Rwanda, 23, 28, 92, 262
  conflict management, 210, 211, 224, 226,
    236, 266
  and democratization, 13, 262, 266
  French military presence, 110, 176, 181
  and regional cooperation, 199, 202,
    204(n4)

Rwandese Patriotic Front (RPF), 211, 266

Sadat, Anwar, 76
SADC. *See* Southern African Development
  Community; Southern African
  Development Conference
SADCC. *See* Southern African
  Development Coordination
  Conference
SADR. *See* Sahrawi Arab Democratic
  Republic
Sahnoun, Mohammed, 239
Sahrawi Arab Democratic Republic
  (SADR), 242
Salazar, Antonio de Oliveira, 250
Salim, Salim Ahmed, 70, 286, 296–297, 299
Sankara, Thomas, 107
Sant Egidio, 219
São Tomé, 200
Sassou Nguesso, Denis, 180
Satyagraha, 85–87, 89, 93
Saudi Arabia, 75
Savimbi, Jonas, 212, 217, 218, 227, 228, 260,
  280
Sayyid. *See* Hassan, Muhammed Abdille
Scandinavian countries, 82, 258, 267. *See
  also* European Union; *specific countries*
Schweitzer, Albert, 87
SCOA. *See* Société Commerciale de l'Ouest
  Africain
SDF. *See* Social Democratic Front
Sekou Toure, Ahmed, 38(n5), 80, 166
Selassie, Haile (Emperor of Ethiopia), 135–
  136, 141, 142, 145(n17)
  conflict management participation, 211,
    238, 239
  U.S. support for, 212–213, 251
Senegal, 31, 39(n28), 63, 112, 172, 174
  conflict management participation, 177–
    178, 224, 238
  democratization, 179, 258, 263
  foreign economic aid, 120(n9), 173, 175,
    274(n25)
  French postcolonial influence, 32, 109,
    176, 258
  and Mauritania, 236, 242
  and regional cooperation, 191, 195, 197
  religion in, 77–78

Senghor, Leopold Sedar, 31, 32, 38(n5), 165,
  243
Seychelles, 13, 18
Shevardnadze, Eduard, 218
Sierra Leone, 202, 204(n4), 244, 263
Singapore. *See* Newly industrialized
  countries
Sklar, Richard L., 62
Slave trade, 41–42
Smith, Adam, 138
Social Democratic Front (SDF)
  (Cameroon), 275(n52)
Socialism, 7
Société Commerciale de l'Ouest Africain
  (SCOA), 172
Somalia, 89
  and democratization, 12, 13, 251, 252, 270
  economic/political conditionality, 139
  and Ethiopia, 129–130, 236, 239, 241, 246
  and Kenya, 239
  political identity, 130, 136–137, 139–140,
    224
  and recolonization, 91
  and regional cooperation, 199, 205(n20)
  and Republic of Somaliland, 90, 127, 137
  See also Horn of Africa
Somali conflict management, 34, 45, 235,
  236, 284–285
  Ethiopian role, 143, 215
  and political identity, 143
  UN/U.S. military intervention, 139, 140,
    210, 215, 224–225, 284–285, 297
Somaliland, Republic of, 90, 127, 137. *See
  also* Horn of Africa
Somali National Army, 139
Somali Youth League, 137, 139
South Africa
  and Angola, 113
  and Angolan civil war, 216, 222–223, 228,
    281
  and decolonization process, 35–36
  and European Union, 105, 122(n41)
  and European Union (EU), 105, 114–116,
    122(n39), 122(nn 39, 41, 42)
  foreign investment, 101, 103, 105
  investment in southern Africa, 154
  Islam in, 76
  and Mozambique, 218

and Namibia, 121(n24)
and South African Customs Union, 122(n41), 204(n4)
trade relations, 115(table), 115, 122(n41), 149–152, 151(table), 171
See also Post-apartheid South Africa; South African democratic transition; South African struggle against apartheid
South African Customs Union, 122(n41), 204(n4)
South African Defense Force, 157
South African democratic transition, 13, 290
  and conflict management participation, 156–157
  negotiating process, 211, 213, 214–215, 245
  and New York accords, 278–279
  and reconciliation, 291
  and U.S. political assistance programs, 263–264, 265, 266–267, 268
  See also Post-apartheid South Africa; South African struggle against apartheid
South African struggle against apartheid, 242, 246, 253
  ANC-Inkatha Freedom Party conflict management, 211
  and Angolan civil war, 278
  Commonwealth policies, 39(n21), 102, 103
  European policies, 102–103, 105, 108, 112, 113–114, 115, 121(n24)
  NGO role, 11
  and OAU, 34
  and *satyagraha*, 86–87, 89
  and southern African regional cooperation, 148
  southern African roles, 156, 281
  UN role, 157
  U.S. policies, 103, 210, 213, 214–215, 250
  See also South African democratic transition
South Asia, 43
Southern Africa, 147–161
  boundaries, 159–160
  and decolonization process, 35–36

migration, 158–159
and post-apartheid South Africa, 92, 147, 148–149, 152–160, 155(table), 163(n13), 190
refugees, 156, 157
as region, 147–149
regional economic cooperation, 152–153, 162(n13), 190
regional/internal conflicts, 8, 25
South African destabilization of, 147–148, 155
trade relations, 149(table), 149–152, 150(table), 151(table)
See also specific countries
Southern African Development Community (SADC), 148, 152, 153. *See also* Southern African Development Coordination Conference
Southern African Development Conference (SADC), 189, 204(n4)
Southern African Development Coordination Conference (SADCC), 113. *See also* Southern African Development Community
Southern African Development Coordination Council, 26
Southern Rhodesia, 35. *See also* Zimbabwe
Southern Sudanese Liberation Movement (SSLM), 238
South Korea. *See* Newly industrialized countries
SouthWest African People's Organization (SWAPO), 238
Soviet successor states, 8, 9, 113, 295. *See also* Russia
Soviet Union, 5, 7, 8, 279, 292(n4)
  and Angolan civil war, 216, 222, 223, 279, 292(n4)
  conflict management participation, 8, 217, 218, 223, 252, 278, 279, 280, 292(n3)
  See also Cold War; Russia; Soviet successor states
Spain, 24, 28, 37, 112–113, 114
Special Facility for Africa, 101, 104
SPLA. *See* Sudan People's Liberation Movement/Sudan People's Liberation Army

SPLM. *See* Sudan People's Liberation Movement/Sudan People's Liberation Army
SSA (Sub-Saharan Africa). *See* French postcolonial influence; *specific countries and topics*
SSLM. *See* Southern Sudanese Liberation Movement
STABEX, 116, 122(n45)
Stages of Economic Growth, The: A Non-Communist Manifesto (Rostow), 5
Stedman, Stephen, 211
Strange, Susan, 65
Strauss, Franz-Josef, 105
Structural adjustment conditionality, 49–52
  criticisms of, 14–15, 16–18
  and debt crisis, 7, 8, 9, 46
  and European Union, 96, 100, 104
  French policies, 111, 120(n9), 174
  and grassroots participation, 9–10
  and Horn of Africa political identity, 137–139
  vs. political conditionality, 11–12
  See also Economic reform; Structural adjustment programs
Structural Adjustment Facility, 49
Structural adjustment programs, 9
  and African integration with global economy, 11, 45, 46–47
  African opposition to, 10, 26, 51, 54–56, 57, 60
  and debt crisis, 45–46, 53, 65
  and democratization, 10, 15–16, 59–62, 128, 290–291
  failure of, 52–54, 56–57
  and foreign investment, 11, 50–51
  future prospects, 291
  and international disengagement, 44
  and modernization theory, 16
  and policy dialogue, 66
  social and political impact of, 60, 62
  Western criticisms of, 54–56, 57
  See also Economic reform; Structural adjustment conditionality
Sub-Saharan Africa (SSA). *See* French postcolonial influence; *specific countries and topics*

Sub-Saharan Africa: From Crisis to Sustainable Growth (World Bank), 55, 58–59, 255
Sudan, 29, 213, 236
  Arabization, 72–73
  and colonialism, 132, 133, 134
  conflict management participation, 210, 211, 239
  decolonization process, 26, 91, 133–134
  and democratization, 12, 13, 251, 259, 263, 270, 287
  foreign economic aid, 101, 104, 274(n25)
  Islam in, 79, 93, 144, 284, 303–304
  Mahdist revolution, 91, 133
  political identity, 133–134, 140
  and United States, 213, 259, 263
  See also Horn of Africa; Sudanese civil war
Sudanese civil war, 45, 127, 129
  conflict management, 210, 220–222, 232(n43), 238, 239–240, 283–284
  and decolonization process, 25, 36–37
  and Islam, 284, 303–304
Sudan People's Liberation Movement/ Sudan People's Liberation Army (SPLM/SPLA), 220, 221, 222, 232(n43), 239, 284
Suez war (1956), 88
Summers, Laurence, 260
Swahili language, 73
SWAPO. *See* SouthWest African People's Organization
Swaziland, 23, 35, 159–160
  and regional cooperation, 122(n41), 199, 204(n4)
Sweden, 63
Syncretism, 77
SYSMIN, 104, 116–117

Taha, Mahmoud Muhammad, 79, 93
Taiwan. *See* Newly industrialized countries
Tanganyika, 26, 30. *See also* Tanzania
Tanzania, 13, 26, 34, 73, 150
  conflict management participation, 211, 224, 239
  foreign economic aid, 104, 274(n25)
  and regional cooperation, 199, 201

U.S. political assistance programs, 265, 267

Taylor, Charles, 282–283, 292(n15)

Teclehaimanot of Gojjam, 133, 135

Teodros (Emperor of Ethiopia), 132, 135, 136, 142

Thatcher, Margaret, 102, 103

TI. *See* Transparency International

Tigrayan People's Liberation Front (TPLF), 279

Togo, 171, 240
  and democratization, 179, 261, 287, 291
  foreign economic aid, 101, 104, 255
  French postcolonial influence, 109, 110, 111, 181, 182, 261
  and regional cooperation, 195, 197

Tovias, 123(n46)

Toynbee, Arnold, 132

TPLF. *See* Tigrayan People's Liberation Front

Trade and Development Bank (PTA), 198

Trade relations
  European Union, 95, 96–99, 97(table), 98(table), 119(nn 5–8)
  France, 97, 98, 171–173, 185(n25)
  Germany, 97–98, 103–104
  Great Britain, 120(nn 9, 11)
  international disengagement, 42, 47
  and regional economic cooperation, 193
  South Africa, 114–116, 115(table), 122(nn 39, 41, 42), 149–152, 151(table), 171
  southern Africa, 149(table), 149–152, 150(table), 151(table)
  United States, 99
  See also Global economy; Lomé Conventions; Regional economic cooperation

Transitional Government of National Unity (GUNT) (Chad), 240, 242

Transparency International (TI), 271

Traore, Moussa, 33, 290

Treaty of Rome, 116, 191

Treaty of Ucciali, 135

Tshisekedi wa Mulumba, Etienne, 222

Tunisia, 23, 31, 76, 238, 244–245

Turabi, Hassan, 284

Tutu, Desmond, 85, 89, 93

UDEAC. *See* Union Douanière Economique de l'Afrique Centrale

UEAC. *See* Economic Union of Central Africa

Uganda, 30, 34, 46, 73, 122(n45), 214
  civil war, 211, 212, 213–214
  democratization, 13, 267, 291
  foreign economic aid, 102, 255
  religion in, 78–79

Umkhonto we Sizwe, 156

UNDP. *See* UN Development Program

União Nacional para a Independência Total de Angola (UNITA), 36, 105, 113, 155, 213, 216
  and conflict management, 217, 222, 223, 227, 228, 280–281
  U.S. support for, 251, 260
  See also Angolan civil war

Union Douanière Economique de l'Afrique Centrale (UDEAC), 112, 202, 204(n4), 244

Union du Maghreb Arabe, 26

Union Monétaire Ouest Africaine, 189

Union Panafricaine pour la Démocratie et le Progrès Social (UPADS), 180

UNITA. *See* União Nacional para a Independência Total de Angola

United Arab Emirates, 25

United Kingdom. *See* Great Britain

United Nations
  African influence in, 10, 25, 70–71
  African membership in, 5
  and debt crisis, 46
  and democratization, 264, 271, 278
  economic aid, 99
  Economic Commission for Africa, 26, 54–56
  and Horn of Africa, 137
  and humanitarian intervention, 300, 301, 306, 307
  and recolonization, 90
  and structural adjustment conditionality, 10
  See also UN *headings*

UN Charter, 5

UN conflict management
  Angolan civil war, 210, 278, 280, 281
  disengagement, 285, 286

early warning system proposals, 270, 306, 307

Eritrean-Ethiopian conflict, 36, 145(n14)

and humanitarian intervention, 305

Mozambique, 227–228

Namibia, 210, 227, 278

Somalia, 90, 139, 140, 210, 215, 224–225, 225, 284–285

South Africa, 102, 114, 121(n24), 157, 215

Sudan, 211

UN Development Program (UNDP), 244

UN Operations in Mozambique (UNOMOZ), 219

UN Operations in Somalia (UNOSOM), 139, 140, 285

United States, 46, 70

and Angolan civil war, 213, 251

and Arab-Israeli conflict, 75

and CFA franc zone, 109

and colonialism, 24

and democratization, 15, 250–252

democratization in, 15, 270

and end of Cold War, 8, 59

and English language, 81

and Eritrean-Ethiopian conflict, 36

erosion of economic hegemony, 6, 7

and Ethiopia, 36, 136, 212–213, 251, 259

and French economic aid, 121(n21)

and French postcolonial influence, 184(n14)

occupation of Japan, 82–83

racial lineage system in, 72

and recolonization, 90

and Somalia, 139, 251, 252

and South Africa, 103, 121(n24), 210, 213, 214–215, 250

support for authoritarian governments, 250–252, 254–255, 274(n25)

trade relations with Africa, 99

See also Cold War; Democratization conditionality; Foreign economic aid; Structural adjustment conditionality; U.S. *headings*; Western powers

U.S. Agency for International Development (USAID), 63, 215, 256, 257

and U.S. political assistance programs, 263, 264, 265–266, 269, 276(n74)

U.S. Chamber of Congress, 263

U.S. Information Agency (USIA), 266–267, 269, 277(n80)

U.S. political assistance programs, 262–268, 276(nn 66, 76)

budget for, 276(n77)

effectiveness of, 268–269, 277(n80)

National Endowment for Democracy, 263, 264–265, 268, 276(n66)

USAID role, 263, 264, 265–266, 269, 276(n74)

USIA role, 266–267, 269, 277(n80)

U.S. role in conflict management, 209–210, 212–230

Angolan civil war, 102, 113, 216, 217, 218, 222–224, 226, 280

direct mediation, 219–224, 232(n43)

disengagement, 283, 292–293(n16)

effectiveness of, 225–226

and end of Cold War, 252

and implementation failure, 228

implementation stage, 226–228

indirect mediatory activity, 215–219

military-diplomatic intervention, 224–225

pressure on internal actors, 212–215

and regional cooperation, 177–178

See also specific countries and conflicts

UNOMOZ. *See* UN Operations in Mozambique

UNOSOM. *See* UN Operations in Somalia

UPADS. *See* Union Panafricaine pour la Démocratie et le Progrès Social

Upper Volta, 241

Uruguay Round. *See* General Agreement on Tariffs and Trade

USAID. *See* U.S. Agency for International Development

USIA. *See* U.S. Information Agency

Uti possidetis, 27, 38(n12)

Vance, Cyrus, 215, 251

Waltz, Kenneth, 145(n3)

Washington Concepts Paper, 218

Washington Declaration, 232(n43)

Weddei, Goukouni, 240

West Africa, 197

West African Clearing House (ECOWAS), 196
West African Economic Community, 238
West African Rice Development Association, 189
Western powers
    African identification with, 5–6
    and humanitarian intervention, 305
    and modernization theory, 5
    See also specific countries and topics
Western Sahara, 28
Western Sahara conflict, 40(n45)
    conflict management, 34, 235, 238, 241, 242, 243
    and decolonization process, 25, 37
    and French postcolonial influence, 107
West Indies, 25
Westminster Foundation for Democracy, 267
What Is Democracy (USIA), 267
Wilsonian international relations theory, 13, 18
Wolof, 71, 73
World Bank, 99
    and CFA franc zone, 109, 175
    1970s leadership of, 6, 7
    reports, 55–56, 57, 58, 66, 255
    Special Facility for Africa, 101, 104
    See also Foreign economic aid; Structural adjustment conditionality
World Council of Churches, 238, 239
World War II, 28, 30, 82, 135, 137

Yaoundé Conventions, 243, 244
Yeltsin, Boris, 62
Young, Crawford, 251
Yugoslavia, 295, 297

Zaire, 45, 77, 92, 171, 174, 224, 236
    Belgian postcolonial influence, 28, 34, 112

conflict management, 34, 210, 211, 222, 227
conflict management participation, 211, 217
decolonization process, 26, 28, 90, 278
foreign economic aid, 101, 104, 173, 180, 274(n25)
French military presence, 110, 176, 181
French support for Mobutu regime, 110, 182
languages, 73, 81, 84
and regional cooperation, 200, 202, 204(n4), 243–244
and United States, 251, 252, 259, 263
See also Zaire, resistance to democratization in
Zaire, resistance to democratization in, 179, 259, 270, 272, 287
    and popular pressure, 253
    and reconciliation, 291
    and U.S. political assistance programs, 263
    and Western support for authoritarianism, 251, 252
Zambia, 18, 34, 150, 199, 224, 239
    democratization, 61–62, 253, 263, 264, 265–266, 267, 289
    economic reform, 49, 51, 52, 64, 65
    trade relations, 151, 171
Zanzibar, 26. *See also* Tanzania
Zenawi, Meles, 225
Zimbabwe, 7, 44, 63, 150, 151, 155
    conflict management, 210, 211, 212, 216, 226, 238
    decolonization process, 34, 35, 281
    democratization, 13, 253, 265, 267
    and France, 171, 176
    and regional cooperation, 199
    and Spain, 112
    U.S. political assistance programs, 265, 267
    See also Rhodesia

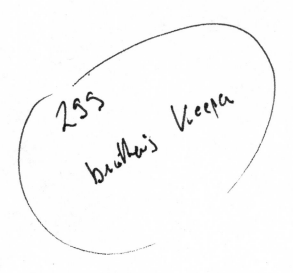

255

brothers keeper